BONDS OF PLURALISM: THE FORM AND
SUBSTANCE OF URBAN SOCIAL NETWORKS

WILEY SERIES IN URBAN RESEARCH

TERRY N. CLARK, Editor

Resources for Social Change: Race in the United States
by James S. Coleman

City Classification Handbook: Methods and Applications
Brian J. L. Berry, Editor

Bonds of Pluralism: The Form and
Substance of Urban Social Networks
by Edward O. Laumann

BONDS OF PLURALISM: THE FORM AND SUBSTANCE OF URBAN SOCIAL NETWORKS

EDWARD O. LAUMANN

University of Michigan

A WILEY-INTERSCIENCE PUBLICATION

John Wiley & Sons
NEW YORK • LONDON • SYDNEY • TORONTO

Library of Congress Cataloging in Publication Data:

Laumann, Edward O.
   Bonds of pluralism.

   (Wiley series in urban research)
   Bibliography: p.
   1. Detroit metropolitan area—Social conditions.
2. Social structure. 3. Sociology, Urban. I. Title.
[DNLM: 1. Social conditions. 2. Urban population.
3. Urbanization. HT 151 L375b 1973]

HN80.D6L38   309.1'774'3404   72-6445
ISBN 0-471-51845-X

Printed in the United States of America

10-9 8 7 6 5 4 3 2 1

To Talcott Parsons and George C. Homans

The Wiley Series in Urban Research

Cities, especially American cities, are attracting more public attention and scholarly concern than at perhaps any other time in history. Traditional structures have been seriously questioned and sweeping changes proposed; simultaneously, efforts are being made to penetrate the fundamental processes by which cities operate. This effort calls for marshaling knowledge from a number of substantive areas. Sociologists, political scientists, economists, geographers, planners, historians, anthropologists, and others have turned to urban questions; interdisciplinary projects involving scholars and activists are groping with fundamental issues.

The Wiley Series in Urban Research has been created to encourage the publication of works bearing on urban questions. It seeks to publish studies from different fields that help to illuminate urban processes. It is addressed to scholars as well as to planners, administrators, and others concerned with a more analytical understanding of things urban.

TERRY N. CLARK

Preface

The Detroit Area Study (DAS), a continuing facility for graduate training and faculty research, was established in 1951 at the University of Michigan. It is a basic unit in the graduate training program of the university's Department of Sociology. In addition, the Survey Research Center of the Institute for Social Research, through an administrative relationship, provides DAS with professional aid in all phases of survey research.

The three main objectives of the Detroit Area Study are (1) to train students in methods of survey and related types of field research in the social sciences, (2) to serve as a major resource for basic research by the social scientists at the University of Michigan, and (3) to make social science data available to greater Detroit and to other communities with similar interests and problems.

Each year faculty members are asked to propose a research topic that will provide the central focus for that year's DAS. In 1965 I proposed to do a broadly conceived study of the impact of an individual's ethnic, religious, and socioeconomic characteristics on his attitudes, values, and patterns of social participation. But I obviously could not conduct a study of the size and scope of the 1965–1966 DAS alone. Many of my colleagues and students played an active and critical role in the work of this study, both intellectually and practically. Although these others cannot be held directly accountable for the final product reported in this book, I am very anxious to acknowledge my many intellectual debts accumulated over the past six years and to express my appreciation to all those who have contributed in so many important ways to this study.

If I were to single out the one person who has played the most significant role in this collective endeavor, it would be Howard Schuman, Director of the DAS, who as close friend and colleague did much to encourage me to undertake the venture and later to shape the most fundamental aspects of study design, content, and execution. We were ably assisted in the early phases of the study by the three DAS teaching fellows, James Norr, Stephen J. Cutler, and Robert Zehner, who assumed major responsibility for coordinating questionnaire construction and the field operations. Once the data were in hand I benefited from the ideas and practical assistance of my research assistants, Stephen Cutler, Jane Hood, Michael Harrison, Gerald Hikel, and Moshe Hartman, who assumed responsibility for supervising the computer processing of the data and aided in the data analysis.

I have literally deluged certain of my colleagues with working papers and drafts of the manuscript. I am especially indebted to the following people for intellectual and socioemotional support far beyond the normal range of collegial duty: Paul Siegel, Otis Dudley Duncan, Leon Mayhew, Guy E. Swanson, David Segal, Gudmund Iverson, Beverly Duncan, James C. Lingoes, Thomas Smith, William Gamson, and Robert W. Hodge, all at least at one time of the University of Michigan, and Norman Bradburn and Morris Janowitz of the University of Chicago. Paul Siegel was particularly helpful in working through some key methodological issues with me and served as an uncompromising, insightful critic of my various efforts. In a number of cases I fear that I have not satisfactorily met all of his and others' criticisms.

I also gratefully acknowledge the support of those organizations that provided the crucial financial assistance to make this study possible. The University of Michigan's Horace H. Rackham School of Graduate Studies gave me a grant for costs of data collection in the first phase of the study and provided a faculty research fellowship that enabled me to work full time on the project in the summer of 1967. The National Institute of Mental Health grant (MH-13464-01) and the National Science Foundation grant (GS-1929) provided funds for many phases of the data analysis, permitting a much more extensive analysis than was originally anticipated. Finally, a Ford Foundation Faculty Research Fellowship (700-376) in 1970–1971 provided support for my sabbatical year at the Zentralarchiv für empirische Sozialforschung of the University of Cologne, West Germany, during which time I completed most of the book. I am particularly indebted to Professor Erwin K. Scheuch of the University of Cologne and members of the Zentralarchiv, most notably Drs. Franz U. Pappi and Hans-Dieter Klingemann, for their many kindnesses in providing an intellectually stimulating and comfortable environment for writing.

I would like to take this opportunity to thank these students in the 1965–1966 DAS for their crucial help in the basic data-gathering phase of the study: James Ajemian, Joyce Avedesian, Jim Boudouris, Jessica Cohler, Rosita Daskol, Judy Edelman, Dave Ermann, David Featherman, Stanley Fukawa, Randall Goon, Joyce Ketlar Herrst, Dale Helland, Ellen Ho,

James House, Carolyn Jenne, Roy Kass, Susan Laumann, Jeylan Mortimer, Joanne Muller, Neil Paterson, Dan Perlman, Gary Shenk, James Schrag, Elaine Selo, Carla Shagass, Nancy Silverman, Miriam Sonn, Alden Speare, Sue Ann Spearing, Don Spencer, Walter Swap, G. W. Stevenson, and Stanley Weiss.

Last but by no means least I thank my secretaries, Sharon McEndarfer and Jane Hikel, at the Center for Research in Social Organization, for their expert typing of the many drafts and revisions. I also acknowledge the help of Albert J. Reiss, Jr., then Director of the Center, as well as the use of Center facilities, which made my tasks very much easier.

EDWARD O. LAUMANN

Ann Arbor, Michigan
August 1972

Contents

FIGURES AND TABLES

CHAPTER I.   **THE FORM AND SUBSTANCE OF URBAN SOCIAL STRUCTURE: AN OVERVIEW**   1

The Form of Urban Social Structure,   2
The Substance of Urban Social Structure,   8
Methodological Considerations,   12
    Analytic Techniques,   12
    The Source of the Data,   17
Summary Overview of Contents,   18

PART I.   **FORM: NETWORKS**

CHAPTER II.   **FRIENDS OF URBAN MEN: ACCURACY OF DESCRIPTION, MUTUAL CHOICE, AND ATTITUDE AGREEMENT**   27

The Problem of Reporting Friends' Characteristics,   27
Source of the Data,   28
Accuracy in Report of Friends' Characteristics,   29
The Reciprocation of Friendship Choices,   32
Friendship and Attitude Similarity,   34
A Model of Interpersonal Orientations and Shared Attitudes: The Case of Party Preference,   36
Summary,   38

CHAPTER III.   **THE SOCIAL STRUCTURE OF ASCRIPTIVE MEMBERSHIP GROUPS**   42

The Multidimensional Nature of Group Attraction and Repulsion,   42

The Social Structure of Ethnic Groups,   43
The Social Structure of Religious Groups,   51
The Social Structure of Ethnoreligious
Groups,   58
Summary and Conclusions,   67

CHAPTER IV.   **THE SOCIAL STRUCTURE OF OCCUPATIONS: THE
ROLE OF ACHIEVEMENT-BASED CRITERIA IN FRIEND-
SHIP CHOICE**   **73**

Achievement-Oriented Criteria of Friendship
Choice,   73
The Social Structure of Occupational Groups,   75
Summary,   81

CHAPTER V.   **THE HOMOGENEITY OF FRIENDSHIP NETWORKS**   **83**

Microstructural Analysis of Friendship
Networks,   83
Friendship and Homogeneity,   85
Measuring Homogeneity and the Plan of
Analysis,   86
Homogeneity and Social Position,   89
Homogeneity and Other Features of Friendship
Networks,   92
Homogeneity and Attitudes,   98
Ethnoreligious and Occupational Homogeneity
Considered Simultaneously,   105
Conclusions,   108

CHAPTER VI.   **INTERLOCKING AND RADIAL FRIENDSHIP NETS: A
FORMAL FEATURE WITH IMPORTANT
CONSEQUENCES**   **111**

The Structure and Function of Intimate Face-to-
Face Groups,   111
Interlocking and Radial Networks: Some
Expectations,   113
An Aside on Method: Multiple Classification
Analysis,   119
Form of Network and Social Position,   120

Form of Network and Other Features of Intimate
Interaction,   123
Form of Network and Attitudes,   126
Discussion,   128

PART II.   SUBSTANCE: ATTITUDES AND VALUES

CHAPTER VII.   VOLUNTARY ASSOCIATION MEMBERSHIP AND
THE THEORY OF MASS SOCIETY   133

        STEPHEN J. CUTLER

Social Participation and the Theory of Mass
Society,   133
Hypotheses and Measurement,   139
    Voluntary Association Membership,   140
    Powerlessness,   141
    Dogmatism,   141
    Tolerance of Ideological Nonconformity,   142
    Involvement in Voluntary Associations,   143
    Friendship Networks in Voluntary
    Associations,   143
    Nonintegrative Effects of Association
    Membership,   144
Analysis of the Data,   145
Findings,   145
Discussion,   153

CHAPTER VIII.   A REEXAMINATION OF THE STATUS
INCONSISTENCY HYPOTHESIS   160

        EDWARD O. LAUMANN AND DAVID R. SEGAL

Introduction,   160
The Status Inconsistency Model,   160
Criticisms of the Model,   162
Questions for Investigation,   163
Status Dimensions,   163
The Analytic Model,   165
Findings,   168
    Status Inconsistency and Ethnoreligious Group
    Differences,   168

The Impact of Status Concern,   176
Summary and Conclusions,   180

CHAPTER IX.   THE PERSISTENCE OF ETHNORELIGIOUS DIFFER-
ENCES IN THE WORLDLY SUCCESS OF THIRD- AND
LATER-GENERATION AMERICANS   186

The Differential Worldly Success of Minority
Groups,   186
Some Preliminary Considerations,   188
The Analytic Model,   189
Findings,   189
Discussion,   195

CHAPTER X.   URBAN SOCIAL STRUCTURE: SOME CONCLUSIONS
AND PROSPECTS   199

APPENDIX A.   SOCIAL DISTANCE AS A METRIC: A SYSTEMATIC
INTRODUCTION TO SMALLEST SPACE ANALYSIS   213

DAVID D. MCFARLAND AND DANIEL J. BROWN

Introduction,   213
A Short History of Social Distance,   214
Metrics, Physical Distance, and Social
Distance,   217
   Properties of Metrics,   217
   Properties of Physical and Social Distance,   222
Two Concepts of Social Distance,   226
The Concept of a Proximity Measure,   228
Proximity Measures and Metrics,   230
Conditional Proximities,   232
Relative Distance,   234
The Friendship Example,   236
The Problem of Group Size,   238
The Dimensional Representation of
Proximities,   240
Computational Procedures,   241
Differences Among Iterative Programs,   242
   The Initial Breakthrough,   243
   Applicable Metrics,   244
   The Solutions,   247

Trial Dimensionality and Initial
Configurations, 248
Local Optima, 248
Objectives of Iterative Procedures,   251

APPENDIX B.   **SAMPLING DESIGN FOR THE 1965–1966 DETROIT**
AREA STUDY   **254**

   HOWARD SCHUMAN

   Introduction,   254
   Description of Geographic Area,   254
   Theoretical Population,   255
   Sample Size and Sampling Fraction,   255
   Selection of the Sample,   256
    Correcting the City Directory,   256
    Apartment Supplement to the City Directory
    Sample,   257
    Area Sample,   257
   Special Weighting,   258
   Noninterviews,   258

APPENDIX C.   **THE STUDY INSTRUMENTS**   **262**

   I. Interview Schedule,   262
   II. Self-Administered Questionnaire,   296

BIBLIOGRAPHY   **299**

AUTHOR INDEX   **327**

SUBJECT INDEX   **331**

Figures and Tables

FIGURE 1.1. A hypothetical model for the structural-functional analysis of characteristics of the individual, structure of friendship networks, and functions of different network structures, 13

TABLE 2.1. Summary indicators of the accuracy of report of friends' social attributes by the main respondent ($N = 118$), 30

TABLE 2.2. Perceived party preference of friend by actual party preference of friend, for Republican and Democratic main respondents: percent distribution, 31

TABLE 2.3. The percent distribution of reciprocated and nonreciprocated choices of main respondent and telephone respondent, 33

TABLE 2.4. Comparison of the percentages of agreement according to the random pair model and the actually observed agreement between friends, 36

FIGURE 2.1. Diagram of *ABX* model, 37

TABLE 2.5. The main respondent's accuracy of perception of his friend's attitude toward political parties by reciprocated—nonreciprocated friendship pair: percent distribution, 38

TABLE 3.1. Percent distributions of respondents and friends by their ethnic origins and self-selection, ratios of self-selection and indexes of dissimilarity, 44

TABLE 3.2. Socioeconomic characteristics of the 22 ethnic groups: percent foreign born, mean rating of social standing, mean occupational status, mean family income, and mean school years completed, 46

TABLE 3.3. Indexes of dissimilarity of friendship choices for 22 ethnic groups, 48

FIGURE 3.1. Graphic portrayal of proximities of ethnic groups, according to the indexes of dissimilarity data. Coefficient of alienation = .187, 50

TABLE 3.4. Percent distributions of respondents and friends by their religious preferences and self-selection, ratios of self-selection and indexes of dissimilarity, 54

TABLE 3.5. Socioeconomic and socioreligious characteristics of 15 religious groups, 55

TABLE 3.6. Indexes of dissimilarity of friendship choices for the 15 ethno-religious groups, 56

FIGURE 3.2. Graphic portrayal of proximity of religious groups, according to

the indexes of dissimilarity of friendship choices. Coefficient of
alienation = .180, **57**

TABLE 3.7.   Socioeconomic and socioreligious characteristics of 27 ethnoreligious groups, **60**

TABLE 3.8.   Indexes of dissimilarity of friendship choices for 27 ethnoreligious
groups, **62**

FIGURE 3.3*a*.   Cross section of the three-dimensional solution in terms of the
first and third axes for all groups, **64**

FIGURE 3.3*b*.   Cross section of the three-dimensional solution in terms of the
second and third axes for Protestant groups only, **65**

FIGURE 3.3*c*.   Cross section of the three-dimensional solution in terms of the
second and third axes for Catholic and Jewish groups, **66**

FIGURE 3.3*d*.   Graphic portrayal of the three-dimensional solution, based on the
indexes of dissimilarity of friendship choices among 27 ethnoreligious groups. Coefficient of alienation = .132, **68**

TABLE 4.1.   Percent distributions of respondents and friends by their occupational categories and self-selection, ratios of self-selection and
indexes of dissimilarity, **76**

TABLE 4.2.   Selected socioeconomic characteristics of men in 16 occupational
categories, **77**

TABLE 4.3.   Indexes of dissimilarity of friendship choices for 16 occupational
groups, **78**

FIGURE 4.1.   Graphic representation of the two-space solution for indexes of
dissimilarity of friendship choices among occupational groups.
Coefficient of alienation = .122, **80**

TABLE 5.1.   Product-moment correlations of ethnoreligious and occupational
homogeneity measures and selected demographic characteristics of
the respondents: for the total sample, three educational levels,
and Protestants and Catholics, **90**

TABLE 5.2.   Product-moment correlations of ethnoreligious and occupational
homogeneity measures and selected characteristics of the associational networks: for the total sample, three educational levels,
and Protestants and Catholics, **94**

TABLE 5.3.   Product-moment correlations of ethnoreligious and occupational
homogeneity measures and selected attitudes: for the total sample,
three educational levels, and Protestants and Catholics, **100**

TABLE 5.4.   Occupational homogeneity by strength of party preference: percent
distributions, total sample, **104**

FIGURE 6.1.   Types of friendship networks, **113**

FIGURE 6.2.   A hypothetical model for the structural-functional analysis of interlocking and radial networks, **117**

TABLE 6.1.   Types of friendship networks. (Answers to Q25, "Of your three
best friends, how many of them are good friends with one
another?".), **119**

TABLE 6.2.   Correlation ratios (etas) of selected demographic and social characteristics of respondents and their involvement in an interlocking or radial network, 121

TABLE 6.3.   Correlation ratios (etas) of selected features of friendship networks and their interlocking or radial character, 123

TABLE 6.4.   Tolerance for political extremists and type of friendship network, 127

TABLE 7.1.   Distribution of number of voluntary association memberships, 140

TABLE 7.2.   Matrix of product-moment correlations of selected socioeconomic items and dependent variable indices, 146

TABLE 7.3.   Summary of gross and net effects of voluntary association membership variables on the dependent variables, 147

FIGURE 8.1.   Hypothetical regression of economic liberalism on education, under varying conditions of ethnoreligious effects, 167

TABLE 8.1.   Tests for differences among various regression parameters for the 15 ethnoreligious groups for selected political and social attitudes and measures of social participation, regressed on educational attainment, 170

FIGURE 8.2.   Regression lines of political party preference by educational attainment, for the 15 ethnoreligious groups, 173

TABLE 8.2.   Groups deviating significantly from the common slope, $\bar{b}$, according to the Tukey test for men with high status concern, 178

APPENDIX 8.A.   Means and standard deviations on selected socioeconomic characteristics, political and social attitudes and measures of social participation for the 15 ethnoreligious groups, 182

TABLE 9.1.   Summary of tests for common slope, identity of regression lines, and specific group departures from the common slope, for the total sample, second generation, and third and later generations, 190

TABLE 9.2.   Regression parameters for fathers' and sons' educational attainment, for 14 ethnoreligious groups three or more generations in the United States, 192

TABLE 9.3.   Regression parameters for fathers' and sons' occupational prestige, for 14 ethnoreligious groups three or more generations in the United States, 193

TABLE 9.4.   Occupational percent distributions of the ethnoreligious status groups, grouped by approximately equal means on the Duncan Index of Socioeconomic Status, 194

TABLE 9.5.   Indexes of dissimilarity of the occupational distributions of ethnoreligious groups, grouped by approximately equal means on the Duncan Index of Socioeconomic Status, 195

FIGURE A.1.   Configurations of points that give different visual impressions can, when analyzed in terms of different metrics, yield identical interpoint distances, 222

TABLE A.1.   Properties of a proximity measure, 229

FIGURE A.2. Partial order of distances under conditional monotonicity, 233

FIGURE A.3. A three-dimensional pyramid-shaped figure, drawn only approximately to scale, to illustrate the discussion in the text of conditional proximity and relative distance concepts, 236

FIGURE A.4. Isosimilarity contours for a given radius, R, for three different Minkowski metrics, 245

FIGURE A.5. Rotation of a rigid object changes the city block distances between its vertices, 246

BONDS OF PLURALISM: THE FORM AND
SUBSTANCE OF URBAN SOCIAL NETWORKS

CHAPTER 1

The Form and Substance
of Urban Social Structure:
An Overview

Americans increasingly find themselves living in large sprawling cities or their satellite towns. In 1968 64.3 percent lived in metropolitan areas in contrast to 59.0 percent a mere eighteen years before, an increase of 9 percent (U. S. Bureau of the Census, 1969: 42). While the pace of urbanization appears to be leveling off, the 1960s was a period of intensified awareness at the private and governmental levels of the many problems and (let us be fair) advantages and opportunities attendant on urban living both for the individual and his intimates and for larger social aggregates. To the casual nonparticipant observer, city life is one of incessant bustle, staggering variety, constant conflict and change, and impersonality in interpersonal relations. But if one looks more closely, he can detect behind the booming confusion remarkably orderly processes of social intercourse. It is to the analysis of this orderliness that this book is addressed.

In this introductory chapter I attempt to sketch a broad overview of the theoretical and methodological rationale underlying the empirical research reported in the following chapters. Although the data used to test various derivative propositions from this rationale are drawn exclusively from a sample survey conducted by the Detroit Area Study in the spring and summer of 1966, I am hopeful that this orienting framework will prove more generally useful in the comparative study of urban social systems in the United States and in other countries.

This framework synthesizes the perspectives of three disparate and rather independently developed theoretical and research traditions. The first, the "stratification tradition," was begun with Max Weber's elaboration of the work of Karl Marx. Weber's focal concerns were the analysis of society in terms of the interrelations and divergent interests of economic class and status groupings. In this book I am especially concerned with describing the systematic ways in which class and status groups in a

1

metropolis differ in the characteristic *content* or substance of their group interests, attitudes, and behavior. The second, the "sociometric tradition," was inspired by the sociological formalism of Georg Simmel (1950, 1964; see especially Caplow, 1968) and has recently received the attention of sociologists and social psychologists interested in small group structure and functioning, especially as it relates to social influence and control (for example, Festinger, 1950; Homans, 1951, 1961; Moreno, 1953; Blau, 1964). The third, the "network" approach, has been of special interest to anthropologists such as, Radcliffe-Brown (1952), Nadel (1957), and Max Gluckman (1955, 1962) who are concerned with the general problem of describing social organizations. It has also been of interest to urban anthropologists studying the transition from tribalism and rural communities to more modern forms of social organization in urban settings (see Mitchell, 1969a, 1969b; Barnes, 1954, 1969; Wolfe, 1970; Wellman and Whitaker, 1971). Note that one common concern of these latter two traditions is the identification of the consequences of certain "formal" properties of social structures for the functioning of the system, such as their homogeneity of composition, density of interaction, and interconnectedness of the "net."[1]

THE FORM OF URBAN SOCIAL STRUCTURES

Probably the most popular concepts in the sociological lexicon and in vulgarized sociological writing are *structure* and various correlative descriptive terms about structure, such as hierarchy, dominance, structural differentiation, structural change, power or class structure, and urban social structure. (The term "system" is often used mistakenly as a synonym for structure. See Buckley, 1967, for an excellent discussion of the term.) Despite the many nuances of the term "structure," differing with various authors, the root meaning seems to refer to a persisting order or pattern of relationships among some units of sociological analysis, be they individual actors, classes of actors, or even behavioral patterns (see Nadel, 1957: 1–19). The crucial problem, of course, is what we mean by "pattern" or "order."

The apparent consensus in the use of the term masks the unfortunate fact that there is little agreement on the concepts and the methodology in terms of which one will measure or, perhaps more modestly, describe given "social structures." Admittedly there does appear to be some agreement on how to describe structures that can be conceived to be constructed on a single dimension (that is, are unidimensional), such as the age, income, or educational structure of a given community. (Indeed, one suspects that the popularity of analyzing "economic class" and "power" structures stems in large part from their *apparent* unidimensional structure that enormously simplifies the problems of analysis.) Taking the age structure as an example, we can unambiguously arrange persons (units of analysis) along a continuum so that each is related to the others in terms of being younger, older, or the same age. In this case we have adopted an arbitrary yardstick, number of years, and imposed it on the community—even though we know that the difference between boys of five and ten years old is "socially speaking" of much greater "magnitude" than the difference between men of 50 and 55.

The difficulties escalate enormously when one wishes to describe a "structure" whose units differ simultaneously along several dimensions. For example, how can the structure of ethnoreligious groups in an urban community be described when the groups differ in terms of average socioeconomic achievement *and* socioreligious behavior patterns? Unless an adequate way of describing the structure of this system can be developed, one can hardly turn to the more fascinating problem of describing structural *change* in the system. It is this consideration, I believe, that justifies my preoccupation in this book with structure rather than with structural change, although the latter is a more fashionable topic. In other words, I assume that adequate descriptions of structure are logically prior to discussions of social change.

For the purposes of this book, the unit of structural analysis will be the individual actor (or a set of actors) in a particular kind of *social position* in a social system (see Parsons, 1951). At this stage of theoretical development it is impossible to relate a given individual's set of unique social positions in society (with respect to his manifold role relations with specific other family members, neighbors, work partners in a particular firm, and so on) to another individual's set of unique positions. We are forced for analytic purposes to categorize social positions into aggregates that hopefully share a sufficiently common core of performance requirements so that the positions may be treated as more or less equivalent. Consequently, since we will be discussing a complex urban social system, the individual's set of social positions will be characterized categorically, that is, in terms of his group memberships and social attributes, such as religious affiliation (including his denomination), ethnic origin, occupation, and the like. In short, a person's social position locates him with respect to others in the community within some socially defined and differentiated domain.

The *social structure* of a community will be defined as a persisting pattern of social relationships among social positions (see Laumann, 1966). A *social relationship* is any linkage between incumbents of different social positions that involves mutual but not necessarily symmetric orientations of a positive, neutral, or negative character (see Homans, 1951; Parsons, 1951; Blau, 1964). For example, one individual may love another who reciprocates with hatred, but in any case they are mutually oriented to each other and take each other into account in their own behavior.

While our study will be particularly addressed to social structures based upon mutual positive orientations and attractions, namely friendship relations, the procedures proposed to describe structure do not require that the structures be of this type. One could as easily describe the social structure of enemies. Depending on the social relationship considered (kinship, friendship, work or political partnership, animosity, neighborliness, and so on), the pattern or structure of relationships is likely to differ as a function of the different social forces that determine the formation of these several relationships. (Incidentally, the units of analysis could just as well be collectivities or aggregate categories so that one could speak, for example, of the industrial structure of a community in terms of buying and selling relations among firms. Or one could describe industrial structure by determining which firms "control" others through membership on the board of directors or by holding certain proportions of voting stock.)

To this point, we have been discussing the pattern or structure of relations among individual actors—what we might term the *microstructure* when we refer to an individual actor as the focal point of the structure and his pattern of social relations. By the expedient of aggregating into appropriate categories individual actors who share similar social positions, we can determine the characteristic pattern of relationships among these *categories* of social positions and thus be in a position to describe the *macrostructure* of a large community or society. This macrostructure can be described by measuring the differential likelihood of specific relationships being formed among social positions (see Laumann, 1966: 1–5). This method is adopted in the chapters to follow on the structure of ethnoreligious groups and occupational categories. In a point more elaborately treated in Appendix A, we are especially interested in seeing if we can identify the underlying dimensionality of these structures so that we can describe how the pattern of social relationships is *structurally differentiated* along specifiable dimensions or facets (see Guttman, 1959). Note that this usage of the term "structural differentiation" is not completely equivalent to Parsons' (1966) usage in that it does not necessarily correspond to functional differentiation.

The reader may have noticed by now that my treatment of the question of describing social structure rests on a fairly explicit physical analogy. In Appendix A McFarland and Brown note a number of pitfalls in taking this analogy too literally. Certainly the reader must be warned against assuming that we shall be able to make such statements as the following:

in Structure Z, Group A is *twice* as far from Group B as from Group C. He-can, however, assert that, assuming a reasonably good smallest space solution (to be discussed below), Group B is, relatively speaking, farther from Group A than Group C. In short, he can make statements at the level of rank order of groups.

In order for us to interpret the underlying dimensionality of the macro-structures in which we shall be especially interested, we must accept a crucial postulate or assumption:

> Similarities in status, attitudes, beliefs, and behavior facilitate the formation of intimate (or consensual) relationships among incumbents of social positions.

The corollary to this postulate is:

> The more dissimilar two positions are in status, attitudes, beliefs, and behavior of their incumbents, the less likely the formation of intimate (or consensual) relationships and, consequently, the "farther away" they are from one another in the structure.

This postulate asserts the *distance-generating* mechanism among social positions and groups. There is ample theoretical and empirical justification for accepting such a postulate as a reasonable starting point for analysis (see Homans, 1951, 1961; Newcomb, 1961; Laumann, 1966; and, indeed, nearly the entire corpus of sociometric literature).

Marx formulated the crucial significance of a man's position in relation to the means of production (especially with respect to ownership) in determining the most important features of his daily behavior and attitudes as well as his potential, if not self-conscious, membership in a particular class; that is, *Klasse an sich* or *für sich* (see Bendix and Lipset, 1966). Since then, social scientists have been concerned with demonstrations of the myriad implications of man's socioeconomic position for his other objective and subjective experiences and characteristics. Some fifty years after Marx, Weber (1966) stressed the sometimes independent significance of status groups (typically communities of an amorphous kind that share a common social estimate of honor or respect) for such matters.[2]

Given that social positions represent different constellations of specific tasks and activities in the social division of labor, the problem arises as to how individuals are allocated or assigned to different positions (see Davis and Moore, 1945; Wrong, 1959; Laumann, Siegel, and Hodge, 1970: 1–2, 63–65, 121–23; Parsons, 1970). Two fundamental mechanisms by which this allocation process is accomplished have been identified (see Linton, 1936; Parsons, 1951, 1970; Mayhew, 1968; Schneider, 1969: 51–63). On the one hand, individuals may be assigned to specific positions by *ascription,* that is, by virtue of possessing some quality or characteristic such as age, sex, or birth in a particular family or racial group. For example, in a society operating under the rule of primogeniture, the first-born son of the king will be "assigned" the position "king" upon his father's death. He enters the position by virtue of birth and not by having done anything to "earn" or "merit" the position. Membership in a particular status group is usually a matter of ascription—that is, of being born into it. On the other hand, individuals may be assigned to specific social positions on the basis of their "relevant" performances, merit, or *achievement,* that is, by virtue of having performed certain tasks according to a standard of performance that is presumably relevant to the performance of the tasks incumbent in that social position. For example, admission into a particular college in the position of student may be contingent on the student's having previously demonstrated certain proficiencies presumably relevant to performance of academic tasks. Entry into most occupational roles in modern societies tends to emphasize criteria for admission that are achievement based rather than ascription based.

To be sure, actual societies typically operate with mixtures of ascriptive and achievement-oriented criteria for allocating people to given positions, although it is usually the case that they emphasize one or the other type of criteria in particular domains of social life. Thus, for example, Catholic priests have always been men (an ascriptive criterion for admission) although entry into the priesthood is predominantly determined by meeting certain performance standards of training and interest. In the analysis to follow, we shall assume that membership in ethnoreligious groups is predominantly a matter of ascription by birth (even though it occasionally happens that adults decide to change their religious affiliation—see Warren, 1970a, 1970b), while entry into occupational roles is predominantly on the grounds of achievement or merit.

With these considerations in mind in conjunction with some techniques to be discussed below, we shall attempt to describe the macrostructure of ethnoreligious groups, regarded as predominantly ascriptive membership groups, and occupational categories, regarded as entered predominantly on the basis of achievement-oriented criteria, in the Detroit metropolitan area. With these results in hand, we shall then turn to a microstructural analysis of friendship relations. Especially relevant at this point will be certain perspectives derived from what we have called the *social network approach,* which has enjoyed a long and important history in anthropological and sociological theory and research. Beginning in the early 1950s, a number of British social anthropologists interested in studying urban communities in modernizing and "developed" societies have considerably sharpened its analytic and empirical focus. Since Mitchell (1969b) and Barnes (1969) have recently provided useful overviews and systematizations of the approach, especially from the point of view of the anthropologists, I shall note only briefly here some features of special interest to us.

As noted before, the notion of a social network is taken to mean ". . . a specific set of linkages among a defined set of persons, with the additional property that the characteristics of these linkages as a whole may be used to interpret the social behavior of the persons involved" (Mitchell, 1969b: 2). Mitchell (1969b: 14) argues that a network is most conveniently anchored on an individual rather than a group although the approach by no means precludes anchoring it on a group. From one point of view, our macrostructural analysis of friendship relations can be regarded as anchoring the analysis of networks on groups or categories of persons sharing similar social positions. Despite the admittedly difficult problems of establishing meaningful boundaries for groups or defining "similar" social positions, I think we must move in this direction if we are to analyze the structure of communities involving millions of inhabitants. To proceed with the analysis of specific linkages among all such inhabitants—that is, the total network (Barnes, 1969: 55–57)—would lead to astronomical numbers of actual and potential linkages ($= n(n - 1)/2$) well beyond the analytic resources of our largest and fastest computers, not to mention our current theoretical resources.

We shall, however, also study certain features of the *personal network* (Mitchell, 1969b: 13) or *primary zone,* to use Barnes' terminology (1969: 58–64). In the present case, we shall take the individual actor as the focal anchorage point and consider his links with three other persons identified as his friends as well as their interrelations. Two features of these partial networks—partial in the sense that they include only three others of the possibly many friends and acquaintances of ego (the focal actor) and do not include others who might be linked to ego through a common friend [that is, his *second-order zone* (Barnes, 1969: 59–60)] —will be of special interest to us. First we shall consider the homogeneity of the network—that is, how "similar" in social positions are these three others to ego and what are the "consequences" of various forms of homogeneity (or heterogeneity) for ego's orientation to the world? Second, we shall consider the *connectedness* (see Bott, 1957; Harary, Norman, and Cartwright, 1965) of the four-person network—that is, to what extent do the three friends have friendship relations *with one another* and what implications for attitudes and behavior can be shown for different degrees of interconnectedness of the primary zone?

In an important sense, one can consider memberships in voluntary associations as involving people automatically in networks of secondary and higher order—that is, indirect links are created between ego and any other member of the organization in the sense that they are connected by a mediating chain of others who are known either to ego personally or to one another. He is unlikely to be linked directly (know personally or, alternatively, have in his primary zone) every other member of the organization in question, but he is likely to have a much shorter path from himself to any other member of the organization than to a randomly chosen member of the larger urban community. In network terms, voluntary associations bound sets of persons among whom relationships are relatively dense or interconnected compared to the interconnections of a random sample of persons from the entire urban area (see Mitchell, 1969b: 17–18). Since direct links or relatively short chains between persons presumably facilitate communication of social opinions and provide the basis for influencing social behavior toward a common norm and since, according to the distance-generating postulate stated above, links tend to form between "similar" social positions, we have the underlying rationale for expecting members of such groups to be more similar in social behavior than randomly paired individuals are.

From one perspective, the considerable corpus of sociological literature that has focused on developing the "theory of mass society" (see Kornhauser, 1959), in which voluntary associations are seen as crucial links in mediating relations between the individual and the society's political elite, can be seen to be a specification of a particular theory of networks as it relates to the functioning of the political system. Consequently, we shall examine below the basic assumptions of this theory and test some derivative hypotheses on data drawn from the Detroit metropolitan area. Of particular relevance to our present discussion is an effort to examine the implications of joint membership in a voluntary association of ego and members of his primary zone. In the terms of network theory, such a coincidence involves a *multistranded* relationship between ego and other —that of friendship and of common associational membership.[3] We would expect that people in multistranded relationships would interact with one another in different contexts and are therefore less likely to be able to withdraw completely from one another as people in a single-stranded relationship are able to do and are consequently subject to greater social control (see Mitchell, 1969b: 23; Nadel, 1957: 71).

THE SUBSTANCE OF URBAN SOCIAL STRUCTURE

Overlaying our analysis of certain formal features of urban social networks is a concern for "content" somewhat more specifically linked to the American urban situation. Broadly speaking, we are interested in what general value orientations or attitudes, behavior, and styles of life characterize various social positions in the ascription- and achievement-based social structures. Such concerns derive quite naturally from perhaps the central tradition in sociology beginning with Marx's interest in the differentiation of work, political and economic experiences, and orientations according to an individual's economic class position and Weber's subsequent stressing of the potentially independent role of status groups in structuring differences in styles of life.[4] Obviously we could not begin to describe the manifold ways in which incumbents of varying social positions differ from one another. Since there is now no general theory regarding the patterning of value orientations to guide our choice, our selection of topics must necessarily be ad hoc, and to an extent opportunistic, deriving from our reading of some of the central concerns animating research on American urban communities. We have selected for special attention attitudes and behavior derived from four important institutional areas:

1. Economic and work attitudes including conceptions of the meaning of work and success, the utility of planning one's daily life, occupational preferences especially as they relate to a major axis of occupational differentiation, bureaucratic and entrepreneurial occupations, and certain aspects of economic ideology;

2. Political attitudes relating to party preference, civil liberties and dogmatism;

3. Orientations toward major ascription- and achievement-based social categories and groups including subjective identifications with social classes and ethnoreligious groups, status concern, and patterns of material style of life;

4. Family and religious value orientations and behavior.[5]

While the principal thrust of the analysis in the first part of the book is on social structure and personal networks, we shall have occasion to consider some of the attitude domains listed above as they relate to various features of American social structure that emerge out of the data analysis. In particular, we shall consider two important problems in describing American urban social structure. The first relates to the evaluation of alternative descriptive models of American religious and ethnoreligious social structure—specifically, the adequacy of the so-called Triple Melting Pot Model versus the Cultural Pluralism Model (see Herberg, 1955; Gordon, 1964). Herberg and others have contended, with not altogether convincing empirical justification, that the American religious social structure is structurally differentiated primarily into three broad religious categories—Protestant, Catholic, and Jew—and that the differences in religious belief and ethnic composition within these three categories are either minor or slowly disappearing in the wake of the complete assimilation of the ethnic communities into the host society. In particular, ethnic differences have come to the point where they are residual and unimportant. Indeed, according to this view, even the differences in religious belief and practice and other value orientations among these three communities are alleged not to be terribly important anymore —their primary existence seems to be founded on the structuring of intimate associations such that people tend to confine their choice of marriage partners and intimate friends within their respective subcommunities. On the other hand, the cultural pluralism model suggests that certain important differences in value orientations persist among the three broad categories and, in fact, in certain important respects these subcommunities are even further differentiated internally.

The second problem relates to the identification of the multidimensional nature of the occupational structure (in my sense of the term—that is, as it relates to intimate interaction).[6] While there is no question that the first axis along which the occupational structure is differentiated is the relative social standing (prestige, socioeconomic status) of occupations (see Reiss, 1961; Blau and Duncan, 1967; Laumann, 1966; Hodge and Siegel, forthcoming), it is considerably more problemmatic to identify the other dimensions of its differentiation. One possible dimension that has been suggested is one that distinguishes occupations found in bureaucratic contexts (large-scale work organizations, whether industrial or governmental, having many employees and in which authority relations among co-workers is highly formalized and well defined) from those that involve individuals in essentially self-directed work activities often emphasizing individual risk-taking and responsibility (for example, self-employed entrepreneurship) or very small autonomous work groups emphasizing considerable individual autonomy and responsibility in the execution of work tasks. This bureaucratic-entrepreneurial dimension certainly could be expected to cut across the prestige dimension for a major part of its range since one can identify working, middle and upper middle class occupations that differ in terms of their bureaucratic-entrepreneurial work context. On the basis of Miller and Swanson's (1958) work which noted important differences between their so-called entrepreneurial and bureaucratic families in terms of the different personality defense mechanisms and orientations inculcated in their children (see also McClelland, 1961; Kohn, 1969), we certainly have good reason to expect that the adult occupational structure of intimate association might reflect these values and behavioral differences as well. In an earlier study of the occupational structure (Laumann and Guttman, 1966), we presented some evidence that this was actually the case.

The second half of the book deals with a more systematic analysis of the attitude and value orientation domains mentioned above as they relate to several rather more controversial hypotheses about American society. Deriving originally from Max Weber's (1930) famous hypothesis concerning the role of the Protestant Ethic in the rise of modern capitalism, the first controversy relates to the contemporary relevance of differences in religious beliefs and values between Protestants and Catholics in explaining alleged differences between these groups with respect to their attitudes toward work and economic activity and consequent differences in worldly success [see Lenski's seminal contribution, *The Religious Factor* (1963)].

Also related to this theme of identifying important differences in attitudes and behavior among ascription- and achievement-based social positions, the second controversy concerns the hypothesis of status inconsistency (see Lenski, 1954, 1956) as an explanatory factor in people's adherence to certain political and economic beliefs and in the nature of their social participation. Merely to illustrate this proposition here, the status-inconsistency hypothesis holds that significant discrepancies in achieved and ascribed social status induces certain compensatory changes in political orientations such that status discrepant individuals are likely to be more liberal (in the sense of favoring change from the status quo) than status congruent individuals. Somewhat in the sense of a rival hypothesis, one could argue that what differences do in fact prevail between members of different ascriptive groups in their political and economic beliefs and patterns of social participation can more usefully be seen to reflect the *persistence of subcultural differences* among the ethnoreligious groups composing American society than the operation of a "status inconsistency effect" per se. We shall consider some evidence suggesting that ethnoreligious group subcultural differences apparently persist in some form even among third- and later-generation members of these groups. More interestingly, these differences are not merely trivial matters of ethnic food preferences but, rather, involve differences in educational achievements, occupational preferences and consequent worldly success, social participation patterns, traditionalism in family life, and political and economic attitudes.

Up to this point in our discussion of the "controversies" we have tended to emphasize the significance of ascriptive social positions in "determining" value orientations, interaction patterns, and the like. Nevertheless, we are simultaneously concerned with the crucial impact of differences in achieved positions (most notably educational attainment and occupation) in the determination of these same attitudes and behavior patterns. But in addition to these conventional sociological concerns that attempt, putting it crudely, to identify the implications of "class" and "status" group memberships on individual behavior (even if, as is often the case, the investigator focuses on either ascriptive or achieved status characteristics to the relative neglect of the other rather than trying to assess their simultaneous impact), we attempt to go one step further by interpolating social networks as mediating between ego's social position(s) and his actual attitudes and behavior. The following schematic diagram (see Figure 1.1) summarizes our model of the hypothesized interrelationships among various features of ego's personality and social position(s), structural characteristics of his non-kin based "primary environment" (see Scheuch, 1965) and attitudes toward politics, ethnic identity, and work that might be presumed to be especially responsive to his experiences in his current social environment.

We might informally characterize the model as a "path diagram" (see Duncan, 1966b), since it follows the logic and conventions of path analysis. That is, causal direction between two variables are indicated by single-headed arrows, double-headed arrows indicate that the model makes no assumptions about the causal ordering between variables so connected, and the variables are arranged along a dimension of temporal and causal priority from left to right.[7] Strictly speaking, it is not a path diagram because a number of the variables and their interrelationships violate some of the basic assumptions underlying linear regression analysis. Consequently, we could not estimate the path coefficients for the model from the data we will be considering. Nevertheless, we believe the model will provide a useful accounting scheme for integrating the complex set of findings to be discussed in the chapters to follow. This figure, then, schematizes our synthesis of the several traditions mentioned above. Although we can test this model with data specific only to the Detroit metropolitan area, we fully expect that it will prove applicable to other urban settings in the United States and in other countries.

METHODOLOGICAL CONSIDERATIONS

Analytic Techniques

Given the many complex theoretical objectives set for our empirical analysis, it is hardly surprising that to achieve these goals we must turn to a number of only recently developed techniques that have been designed for multivariate and multidimensional analysis of data. Indeed, one of

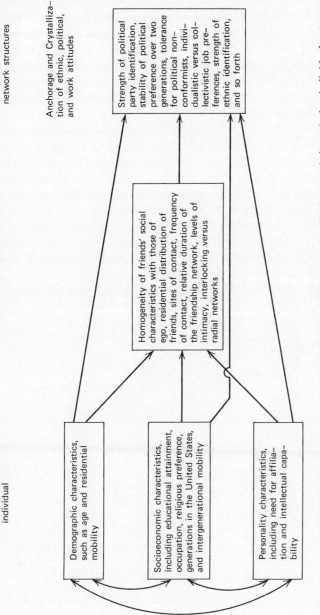

Characteristic of the individual

Demographic characteristics, such as age and residential mobility

Socioeconomic characteristics, including educational attainment, occupation, religious preference, generations in the United States, and intergenerational mobility

Personality characteristics, including need for affiliation and intellectual capability

Structure of friendship network

Homogeneity of friends' social characteristics with those of ego, residential distribution of friends, sites of contact, frequency of contact, relative duration of the friendship network, levels of intimacy, interlocking versus radial networks

Functions of different network structures

Anchorage and Crystallization of ethnic, political, and work attitudes

Strength of political party identification, stability of political preference over two generations, tolerance for political non-conformists, individualistic versus collectivistic job preferences, strength of ethnic identification, and so forth

Figure 1.1 A hypothetical model for the structural-functional analysis of characteristics of the individual, structure of friendship networks, and functions of different network structures.

these techniques, smallest space analysis, is of such recent vintage that there are few general treatments of its objectives and assumptions in the literature except of a highly technical character (see Guttman, 1968). Since it plays such a major role in our analysis, we devote a lengthy appendix (by David McFarland and Daniel Brown) to a systematic exposition of the underlying mathematical rationale for a family of analytic techniques of which smallest space analysis is but one important member. Here we sketch only in the most elementary terms the basic objectives of the technique; see Appendix A for a fuller explanation.

Before turning to a more formal presentation of the smallest space technique, let us see if we can provide an "intuitive feel" for the purpose of the analysis by considering several familiar examples. Suppose, first, that we have four cities, A, B, C, and D, and a matrix (1.1) representing the distances between each of them. Suppose, further, that we would like to draw a picture representing in a Euclidean space—familiar from our high school geometry—their relative distances and locations. Taking any arbitrary unit of physical measurement (for example, one-quarter inch equals one mile), we can perfectly portray in this particular example the *interrelationships* of the four cities by a single, straight line (see Figure 1.2)—the "picture" is *uni*dimensional because all four cities lie on the line.

Matrix 1.1

	A	B	C	D
A	—	10	30	40
B		—	20	30
C			—	10
D				—

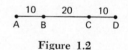

Figure 1.2

Now suppose that the distances among the four cities are as in Matrix 1.2:

Matrix 1.2

	A	B	C	D
A	—	20	40	17.29
B		—	30	25
C			—	28.26
D				—

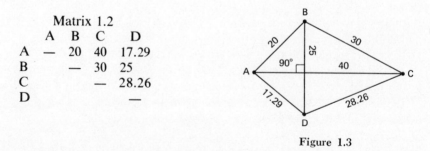

Figure 1.3

There is simply no way we can represent the interrelationships among these four cities by a single dimension, but we could draw a *two*-dimensional picture (Figure 1.3) that perfectly represents the information in Matrix 1.2. It takes the form of two pairs of triangles, ABC and ADC, and ABD and BCD, each pair of which have a common side, AC or BD respectively. The reader may verify for himself that given AC intersects BD at right angles, the lengths of the three sides of any one of these paired triangles and the length of the common side of the other paired triangles, the lengths of the two "unknown" sides are determined according to the Pythagorean theorem.

Finally, let us suppose that we were given a mileage chart indicating the air distance by the most direct route (a straight line) between every city in the United States over 50,000 inhabitants (the list of cities arranged in alphabetical order). If we were to draw the familiar map of the United States, this two-dimensional picture would more or less adequately represent the *relative* locations of these cities indicated in the mileage chart. The map permits us to visualize simultaneously all the interrelationships among the cities with respect to physical location—it facilitates the identification of all the cities that are in close proximity to one another and those that are separated by considerable distances. Thus, the map greatly simplifies our task of seeing the underlying "order" or "structure" implicit in the mileage chart—it is in this sense that the map or picture is worth a "thousand words."

More generally, any symmetric matrix of size n (that is, the number of rows equals the number of columns and the name of each row has a corresponding column) that can meaningfully be said to contain numbers representing relative distances or proximities between the various points can be represented "perfectly" in $n - 1$ *dimensions*—that is, without error or distortion.[8] Naturally we would like to have the fewest number of dimensions (that is, the smallest space) that reasonably represents the information in the matrix because our ability to "visualize" spaces in excess of three dimensions is severely limited. Consequently, if we are prepared to "overlook" certain minor discrepancies between the distances in the matrix and those in the picture, we can sometimes succeed in getting an adequate picture of the matrix that is intuitively comprehensible and faithful to its underlying order or structure despite the fact that it does not completely and accurately reflect the "true" proximities. If the smallest space obtainable does not too severely distort the proximities contained in the matrix, it can still facilitate our perceiving the underlying structure of the matrix. Smallest space analysis provides criteria by which we can evaluate the degree to which we are distorting the original data matrix of proximities in order to "force it" to fit a particular dimensional space.

Perhaps one can better understand this point if one thinks of a mileage chart giving the shortest distance by road between every American city over 50,000 people. Cities such as Denver are very high above sea level;

some others are below sea level. The distance by road between two cities reflects variations in height (mountains, and the like), curvature of the earth, and directness of route. Consequently, a more accurate picture of the relative proximities of the cities would be a three-dimensional map rather than a two-dimensional one. Most of us are prepared to live with the distortions inherent in a two-dimensional map representation because the distortions are not too severe for most purposes and the two-dimensional map is more convenient to work with. However, if one wants to consider distances among cities all over the earth, then a sphere or globe (a three-dimensional representation) is obviously much better suited to this objective.

The basic objective of smallest space analysis, then, is to determine the smallest Euclidean space in which one may adequately *portray graphically* the interrelationships of a set of points whose proximity is a function of the degree to which two points are found together relative to n other points. The purpose is to provide a graphic portrayal of a data matrix which will be simple yet faithful to the data matrix in the sense of monotonicity. For example, suppose that we are interested in describing the interrelationships among n religious groups and we have obtained data regarding the relative likelihood of members of any pair of these groups having friendship relations with one another or the degree to which they have similar profiles of friendship choices among the $n - 1$ other groups. Our interest in the resulting data matrix is focused on estimating the similarity of friendship choices between two religious groups, A and B, as compared to the similarity of choices between groups A and C. Religious group B will be considered "closer" to religious group A than is religious group C, whenever the index of dissimilarity (see Chapter 3 below) is equal to or less than the index between A and C, or:

$$\text{distance (A,B)} \leq \text{distance (A,C), whenever } I_{AB} \leq I_{AC}. \qquad (1.1)$$

The purpose of the computer's numerical calculations is to express the distance between religious groups in an actual Euclidean space. In fitting an m-dimensional Euclidean space to condition (1.1) above, m numerical coordinates are calculated for each religious group. Let x_{Ai} be the ith coordinate for religious group A. Then the Euclidean distance (in m-space) between any two religious groups A and B is given by the usual Euclidean formula:

$$\text{distance (A,B)} = \sqrt{\sum_{i=1}^{m} (x_{Ai} - x_{Bi})^2}. \qquad (1.2)$$

From any given set of x_{Ai}, distances can be calculated by formula (1.2) and then examined to see how well they satisfy the crucial monotonicity condition (1.1). For given m, the Guttman-Lingoes computer routine finds the x_{Ai} that will best fit condition (1.1), the goodness of fit being expressed by a *coefficient of alienation* (the smaller the coefficient, the better the fit).[9]

One further multivariate technique figuring prominently in the analysis below deserves brief mention here because it may be unfamiliar to the reader, namely, multiple classification analysis (see Hill, 1959; Morgan et al., 1962; see also Chapter 7). In many situations we will want to examine the relationship of a given dependent variable, for example, a political attitude or preference, to a number of independent (predictor) variables, for example, various indicators of ego's socioeconomic and ascriptive status positions, considered simultaneously. In particular, we will want to know the "net" effect of a given independent variable on the dependent variable excluding the effects of the other independent variables that may be correlated with the independent variable under examination. For example, we might want to know the effect of membership in a particular ethnoreligious group on political party preference. But we already know that socioeconomic status also has an effect on party preference and that ethnoreligious groups differ in their average socioeconomic status. Thus Anglo-American Baptists may disproportionately favor the Democratic party, but they are also disproportionately likely to be of low socioeconomic status, which is also associated with Democratic party preference. We would ideally like to know the effect of ethnoreligious group membership on the dependent variable once the correlated effect of socioeconomic status has been statistically "removed." While operating in principle similar to multiple regression techniques (see Fennessey, 1968), multiple classification analysis is the analysis of variance with unequal cell entries (reflecting the correlations among the independent variables being considered). Its advantage over multiple regression techniques is that the predictor variables may be in a form as weak as the nominal level of measurement.

Needless to say, the more familiar statistical techniques of linear regression analysis, simple cross-tabulations and percent distributions, and even the "humble" chi-square test will be employed when appropriate.

The Source of Data

During the spring and summer of 1966, interviewers from the University of Michigan Detroit Area Study conducted interviews (see Appendix C for complete interview schedule) averaging 85 minutes in length with a probability sample of 1013 native-born white men between the ages of 21 and 64 in the greater metropolitan area of Detroit. The restrictions in the definition of the population universe were dictated by our central concern to study the role of ethnoreligious group membership in differentiating a large metropolis in terms of patterns of intimate associations and a wide range of value orientations. Given limited resources that fixed an upper bound to our sample size and a desire to have reasonable numbers of second-, third-, and later-generation Americans from the range of ethnic groups in Detroit to sustain detailed analysis, we were able to determine from information in the 1960 U. S. Census that the inclusion of the foreign born, women, and blacks would hopelessly restrict the number of cases in cells of focal concern. As always, the sample design reflects an uncomfortable and often regrettable compromise among the range of study objectives which, in our case, was rather broad to begin with.

A multi-stage probability sample was drawn of dwelling units of that part of the Detroit SMSA (Standard Metropolitan Statistical Area) that was tracted in 1950 plus some small additions made to take into account recent suburban population growth. Within each dwelling unit having one or more eligible respondents, one person was selected at random for interview. A total of 985 actual interviews was obtained, of which 28 have been double weighted, yielding a final set of 1013 cases for use in analysis. These 1013 cases represent 80 percent of the eligible households sampled. Refusals to grant interviews accounted for 13.9 percent of the eligible households ($N = 1271$); another 6.4 percent was lost because no one had been found home after six calls (5.5 percent) or for other reasons. (For further details concerning the sampling design and sample completion rates, see Appendix B.)

SUMMARY OVERVIEW OF CONTENTS

Most chapters have been written to be relatively self-contained, developing their own rationale and exposition of the techniques of analysis but referring to relevant analyses elsewhere in the book when appropriate. The reader can thus turn directly to those chapters that especially interest him. Despite the relative self-containment of individual chapters, redundancy in content has been kept, I hope, to a bare minimum. In addition, there is a cumulative quality in that each chapter builds on the themes and results of earlier ones.

The empirical analysis falls into two major parts: the first pays special attention to the analysis of macrostructure and primary social networks; the second devotes more of its attention to analysis of patterns of value orientations and attitudes in terms of ego's achieved and ascribed social positions. But both parts overlap considerably in terms of shared thematic content and techniques of analysis.

Since so much of the analysis is devoted to the examination of friendship networks, it would appear quite essential that we evaluate the adequacy of our information about the characteristics of ego's friends. How accurate, for example, is ego in reporting his friends' ages, occupations, and education? Are there any systematic distortions or biases in this information? To what extent do friends mutually choose one another, given our questions on friendship choice? On a more substantive issue, is there greater attitude similarity between mutually chosen friends than between friends, only one of whom named the other as one of his three closest friends, or even between "randomly paired" individuals? Chapter 2 describes a "substudy" in which a sample of friends nominated by the main sample were interviewed by phone for information about themselves that had been reported by the main sample respondents. The results of comparing ego's report and friend's self-report suggest that we can place considerable confidence in our information about friends.

The next two chapters are devoted to smallest space analyses of the macrostructure of intimate associations among groups based on ascriptive and achieved criteria of membership, respectively.[10] I try to identify the basic dimensions along which these groups are apparently differentiated from one another. In both cases, simple unidimensional rankings of groups along some sort of "prestige" axis of relative social standing or socioeconomic status are clearly inadequate representations of the data. That is, efforts to collapse these structures into one-dimensional schemes would seriously distort their underlying structures and result in misleading conclusions. In Chapter 3 we learn that while one can make some "sense" of the social structure of ethnic and religious groups, considered separately, a much more parsimonious multidimensional interpretation is possible when one combines ethnic and religious criteria to consider the structure of ethnoreligious groups. An interpretation of the three-space solution for ethnoreligious groups suggests that the tripartite division of Protestant-Catholic-Jew (first axis), socioeconomic status (second axis), and "ethnic-religious" differences (third axis) are the basic dimensions in terms of which this structure is differentiated. Regarding the social structure of occupations in Chapter 4, we find that at least a two-dimensional solution is necessary to represent the data matrix adequately. The first axis is clearly the relative prestige or socioeconomic standing of the occupational categories and the second corresponds more or less adequately to the bureaucratic-entrepreneurial distinction discussed above.

Turning to microstructural analysis in Chapter 5, I measure the homogeneity in the composition of the primary zone (how similar or dissimilar are friends' ascribed and achieved social positions to those of ego's?) in terms of the distances among groups determined in the smallest space solutions of Chapters 3 and 4. Here I am concerned with describing the distribution of differential degrees of homogeneity in the primary zone by various attributes of ego's social positions and the relationships of homogeneity to certain attitude characteristics. For example, do men in homogeneous networks manifest greater clarity and consistency in their attitudes than those in heterogeneous networks?

In Chapter 6 I turn to the intriguing problem of analyzing the implications of differential "connectedness" in the primary zone. I am able to report remarkably consistent differences in social characteristics, attitudes and behavior of men implicated in interlocking (highly connected or closely knit) versus radial (loosely knit) networks that nicely parallels the classic distinctions drawn between social relations in *Gemeinschaft-* and *Gesellschaft-*type societies and adds support to a number of findings concerning American class and ethnoreligious groups reported in a variety of studies.

In a change of emphasis toward a more sociopsychological point of view in which we shall be especially interested in describing the relationships between ego's various social positions and his value orientations and behavior, Part Two includes three chapters that review the evidence for several theories more specifically related to the American urban context. In Chapter 7 Stephen Cutler presents some data relevant to a classic theory in political sociology, the theory of mass society. From our point of view this theory can be seen to be a specialized structural-functional theory relating certain aspects of a society's pattern of network formation —in this case, social participation in voluntary associations—with certain features of its political institutions and certain psychological orientations of its citizens. Since most of the findings do not support certain derivative hypotheses from the theory, Cutler suggests some lines along which the theory might be refined to improve its "fit" with the empirical world.

In Chapter 8, David Segal and I review the evidence for status inconsistency (discrepancy in the relative standing of ego's positions in the ascription- and achievement-based hierarchies) being an explanatory factor in adherence to certain political attitudes and patterns of social participation. We find that a rigorous specification of this hypothesis does not adequately account for the pattern of our results but that an investigation of subcultural differences among ethnoreligious groups would prove more satisfactory.

Chapter 9 pursues this theme of ethnoreligious group differentiation by exploring the persistence of ethnoreligious differences in the worldly success of third- and later-generation Americans. I adduce evidence that the groups do differ significantly in their "ability" to transmit educational and occupational achievements from fathers to sons with corresponding consequences for their overall group "success". What is more surprising is that there is evidence that this differential ability persists among third- and later-generation members of these groups, suggesting that subcultural differences are still operative among groups that "should" be completely assimilated to the host society.

Given the great diversity of findings, the concluding chapter attempts to juxtapose, highlight, and organize these findings in terms of the orienting framework developed in this chapter, especially with regard to what they say about certain features of American urban social organization, and indicates some lines along which future work might profitably go.

NOTES

1. Or as J. Clyde Mitchell puts it in his excellent overview of the concept and use of social networks:

The image of "network of social relations" to represent a complex set of interrelationships in a social system has had a long history. This use of "network," however, is purely metaphorical and is different from the notion of a social network as a specific set of linkages among a defined set of persons with the additional property that the characteristics of these linkages as a whole may be used to interpret the social behavior of the persons involved. . . . (1969b: 1–2).

2. Seymour M. Lipset (1968b: 125–26, 129–30, 132–33) summarizes these distinctions very nicely in the following comments:

Marxist sociology starts from the premise that the primary function of social organization is the satisfaction of basic human needs—food, clothing, and shelter. Hence, the productive system is the nucleus around which other elements of society are organized. Contemporary sociology has reversed this emphasis by stressing the distribution system, the stratification components of which are status and prestige. To Marx, however, distribution is a dependent function of production. . . .

While Marx placed almost exclusive emphasis on economic factors as determinants of social class, Weber suggested that economic interests should be seen as a special case of the larger category of "values," which included many things that are neither economic nor interests in the ordinary sense of the term. For Weber, the Marxist mode, although a source of fruitful hypotheses, was too simple to handle the complexity of stratification. He therefore sought to differentiate among the various sources of hierarchical differentiation and potential cleavage. The two most important sets of hierarchies for Weber were class and status. . . .

There is, of course, as Weber pointed out, a strong correlation between status and class positions. . . . The economic and class orders are essentially universalisitic and achievement-oriented. Those who get, are. He who secures more money is more important than he who has less. The status order, on the other hand, tends to be particularistic and ascriptive. It involves the assumption that high status reflects aspects of the system that are unachievable. . . .

3. As Mitchell (1969b: 22) observes:

. . . Here content refers to the *normative* content in which interaction takes place such as kinship, friendship, common religious beliefs, economic obligations, etc. It is to normative content that I refer when I use the word "content."

. . . Network links which contain only one focus of interaction are called "uniplex," or more simply, "single-stranded" relationships. Those which contain more than one content, on the other hand, following Gluckman, are called multiplex, or more simply, multi-stranded relationships.

4. As Weber (1966: 26) puts it:

In content, status honor is normally expressed by the fact that above all else a specific *style of life* can be expected from all those who wish to belong to the circle. Linked with this expectation are restrictions on "social" intercourse (that is, intercourse which is not subservient to economic or any other business's "functional" purposes). These restrictions may confine normal marriages to within the status circle and may lead to complete endogamous closure. . . .

The decisive role of a "style of life" in status "honor" means that status groups are the specific bearers of all "conventions." In whatever way it may be manifest, all "stylization" of life either originates in status groups or is at least conserved by them.

5. The selection of these four institutional areas was not completely arbitrary since we attempted to "sample" attitude and value domains from the four institutional subsectors at the societal level of analysis as discussed by Parsons (1951, 1961, 1966, 1970) in his "action frame of reference." The first area listed corresponds to the adaptive subsystem (A) or economy; the second to the goal-attainment (G) or polity; the third to the integrative (I) or stratification subsystem; and the fourth to the pattern-maintenance (L) subsystem, of which the family and religion are two crucially important components, in the AGIL paradigm.

6. Of course, we can conceive of other "kinds" of occupational structure that could be defined, for example in terms of their functional (situs) differentiation or industrial groupings and the like. These structures would in all likelihood manifest rather different forms. In short, the "form" of the structure—its dimensionality— is a function of its principle of formation—for example, on the basis of patterns of intimate interaction across occupational groups, father-son mobility (see Blau and Duncan, 1967), or job exchange patterns (intragenerational mobility from jobs in one occupational–industrial category to those in another). One suspects that these various "kinds" of occupational structure would be rather similar to one another but by no means identical since the social forces determining, say, patterns of intimate interaction are likely to be in some important respects different from those determining intergenerational occupational mobility.

7. Perhaps it is worth noting here that the diagram postulates that characteristics of individuals will have both *direct* effects on the characteristics of their attitudes (indicated by arrows drawn directly from the first set of boxes to the last) as well as *indirect* effects mediated through the kinds of friendship networks in which they are implicated. That is, we are not assuming here that all the effects of an indi-

vidual's social and personal attributes must "go through" the structure of his friendship network in order to have an impact on his attitudes.

8. If these numbers in fact represent *physical* distances, then one can *always* graphically portray the points, regardless of their number, in at most three dimensions. Under special circumstances, one can sometimes "get away" with only one (as in Figure 1.2) or two (as in Figure 1.3) dimensions. Unfortunately, the data we will be considering are *not* physical distances and normally will not meet all the restrictive conditions imposed on physical distances (see Appendix A) and, consequently, the dimensionality of its spatial representation will not necessarily be limited to only three dimensions.

9. The coefficient of alienation (whose range is between .00 and 1.00) is described in detail in Lingoes (1966) and in Guttman (1968), who notes that a coefficient of .15 or less indicates an acceptable fit between the original data matrix and the smallest space solution. This is, however, in the nature of a rule of thumb based on experience with this kind of analysis rather than a rule that rests on a rigorous mathematical proof of its adequacy. Briefly, one may describe the computation of the coefficient in the following way: The normalized *phi* is defined as the ratio of the sum of the squared differences between the distances as calculated from the coordinate system and the same distances permuted to maintain the rank-order of the original coefficients (otherwise known as the rank-images) over twice the sum of the squared distances (calculated from the coordinates), or:

$$\phi = \frac{\sum\limits_{i=1}^{n} \sum\limits_{j=1}^{n} (d_{ij} - d_{ij}^*)^2}{2 \sum\limits_{i=1}^{n} \sum\limits_{j=1}^{n} d_{ij}^2}, \text{ where } i \neq j. \tag{1.3}$$

The coefficient of alienation, then, is equal to:

$$\sqrt{1 - (1 - \phi)^2}. \tag{1.4}$$

See Appendix A for a further discussion of this and related coefficients.

10. As already noted, Appendix A by David McFarland and Daniel Brown presents a sophisticated introduction and overview of a whole family of data-reduction techniques that have been recently developed to facilitate the multi-dimensional analysis of the underlying structure of certain kinds of data matrices. While there must necessarily be exposition of mathematical rationales that involve some familiarity with mathematics, the more technical treatments and proofs have been put into footnotes for the more knowledgeable reader. The explicit aim throughout has been to write an overview that should prove comprehensible and useful to the average reader with more limited background in mathematics. The reader should have at least a nodding acquaintance with the contents of this appendix before turning to the empirical chapters employing smallest space techniques.

PART ONE

Form: Networks

CHAPTER 2

Friends of Urban Men:
Accuracy of Description,
Mutual Choice,
and Attitude Agreement

THE PROBLEM OF REPORTING FRIENDS' CHARACTERISTICS

This chapter is addressed to two broad tasks: the first is methodological and the second is substantive. For methodological purposes, we wish to examine the accuracy with which respondents report the social attributes of their friends. This is especially important in view of the fact that much of the analysis which follows will rely heavily upon the respondent's report of his friends' characteristics. Many studies (for example, Wilson, 1959; Herriott, 1963; McClosky and Dahlgren, 1960; Katz and Lazarsfeld, 1955; Berelson et al., 1954; Stark and Glock, 1968; Bell, 1963; Campbell and Alexander, 1965) have found the characteristics of an individual's friends to be of considerable importance in helping to explain certain features of his behavior and attitudes. Unfortunately, they often have not been in a position to assess the degree of accuracy of the respondent's perception of their friends' attributes, thus running the risk of an unknown degree of contamination of their explanatory variable from their dependent variable. We are in a position not only to ascertain the accuracy of report of a number of important attributes of friends for a cross-section of urban white men, but also to determine whether some attributes of friends are reported more accurately than others.[1] Some social attributes, such as occupation, are highly visible and likely to be known quite accurately by the respondent; while others, such as his friend's ethnic origin, specific religious denominational preference or membership, or political party preference, may be considerably less visible

---

This chapter is an extended version of a previously published article (Laumann, 1969a), reprinted with the permission of *Sociometry* and The American Sociological Association.

to the respondent. For some friendship pairs, political, ethnic or religious attitudes play a very important role, being frequently discussed and mutually reinforced. For others, they may be specifically denied as relevant to the friendship as in the assertion: "We don't talk politics or religion: that's a private matter." Finally, we shall examine whether there is evidence of systematic distortion or bias in the reporting of friends' attributes. For example, it is easy to imagine the respondents tending to distort occupational or educational information about their friends toward a higher status or more "favorable" report, perhaps in an effort to impress the interviewer with the "quality" of their associates or even to inflate their own self-esteem. Moreover, if the respondent is in fact uncertain about a given attribute of his friend, he might be expected to "estimate" it from knowledge of his own attribute.

From a substantive point of view, we shall be able to make some estimate of the degree to which there is mutual choice or reciprocity in friendship choices for the adult male population. Presumably a mutually chosen pair of friends should differ in predictable ways from a unilaterally chosen pair in terms of their frequency of contact, level of intimacy, and agreement on selected attitudes (see Winslow, 1937; Williams, 1959).

SOURCE OF THE DATA

A randomly drawn subsample of the main sample (drawn at the rate of one in four) was asked at the conclusion of the interview to furnish the full name, street address, and telephone number of a randomly selected friend from the first two of the three closest friends described at length by the respondent during the interview. (See Q127, Appendix C.) He was told that this friend would be called by an interviewer from the Detroit Area Study for a six- or seven-minute interview conducted over the telephone. Only 3.5 percent of the subsample ($N = 200$) failed to give this information either because they did not wish to violate their friends' privacy by revealing their names and addresses or because they did not name any friends in the interview. An additional 11 percent provided incomplete or incorrect information on their friends so that the telephone interviewer was unable to locate them by phone. Only 6.5 percent of the friends refused to grant an interview over the phone; another 8 percent were not contacted after three or more phone calls.[2] The friends were phoned between two to four months after the main respondent's interview.

The noninterviewed were disproportionately likely to be of lower occupational status (primarily in unskilled and semiskilled occupations) and educational attainment (especially likely to have only completed grade school or less), Protestant, and young (20 to 29 years of age).[3] (See Laumann, 1969a, Table 2, for detailed comparisons of the socioeconomic characteristics of interviewed ($N = 118$) and noninterviewed ($N = 82$) friends.) Such systematic discrepancies suggest that we will tend to overestimate the accuracy of report of friends' characteristics since the estimates are based on a sample somewhat biased in favor of the better educated and higher status men.

ACCURACY IN REPORT OF FRIENDS' CHARACTERISTICS

Table 2.1 summarizes a number of indicators of the accuracy of report of friends' social attributes by the main respondent. For those attributes capable of being measured by unidimensional scales, we have reported the product-moment correlations of the main respondent's report of the friend's attribute and the friend's report on the attribute.[4] Obviously age is reported with exceptional accuracy, while occupational status (as coded in the two-digit Index of Socio-Economic Status)[5] and educational attainment (a seven-category code ranging from "0–8 grades" to "17 years or more") are reported with reasonably high accuracy. Indeed, the correlations approximate those normally desired for two coders' reliability in coding the same open-ended material. Only political party preference (a seven-category code ranging from "strong Republican" party preference through "independent" [inclined toward neither party] to "strong Democratic" party preference) has a relatively low accuracy of .513.

As Robinson (1957: 19) has cogently argued, however, the product-moment correlation can easily mislead the investigator by overestimating the degree of agreement between two judges or reports because: ". . . . it measures the degree to which the paired values of the two variables are proportional (when expressed as deviations from their means) rather than identical." Thus, one could obtain, for example in the case of age, a Pearsonian coefficient near unity indicating "perfect agreement" despite the fact the main respondents consistently *overestimated* their friends' actual ages by five years. He argues that the intraclass correlation is a better measure of agreement (accuracy) than the Pearsonian correlation because it penalizes the Pearsonian for differences in the origin or level (differences in the means) and in the scale or unit (differences in the standard deviations) between the two variables under examination. When the means and standard deviations are equal, the Pearsonian and intraclass correlations are also equal; when either one or both are different, the intraclass correlation will be lower. Column 2 of Table 2.1 reports the

Table 2.1. Summary indicators of the accuracy of report of friends' social attributes by the main respondent (N = 118)

Social Attributes	(1) Product-Moment Correlation	(2) Intraclass Correlation	(3) Percent Main and Friend Identical Report	(4) Means of Main Respondent's Reports	(5) Means of Friend's Reports	(6) Significance of Difference Between Means	(7) Percent of Main Respondents Who "Don't Know" Friend's Attribute
Age	.984	.980	31.4[a]	41.8	40.9	NS	0.0
Occupation[b]	.890	.886	69.5	53.1	50.9	NS	1.7
Education	.839	.815	47.5	12.0	12.1	NS	2.5
Political party preference	.513	.495	53.4[e]	—	—	—	14.4
Religious preference	.980[d]	.980[d]	68.6[e]	—	—	—	3.4
Ethnic origin (subjective identification)	—	—	57.6[f]	—	—	—	15.2

[a] Another 54.2 percent were within two years of the friend's reported age.

[b] The current occupation of the respondent was first coded into the six-digit detailed occupation-industry code of the U.S. Bureau of the Census and then recoded by computer to the two-digit code of Duncan's Index of Socioeconomic Status (Duncan, 1961).

[c] An additional 17.8 percent were cases in which the main respondent reported an "independent" for party preference and the friend reported a specific party preference. Only 14.4 percent of the cases reported different (incorrect) party identifications.

[d] In order to calculate this correlation, we treated religious preference as a dichotomous variable, Protestant or Catholic, and deleted Jews and persons of no religious preference from the analysis.

[e] An additional 14.4 percent were cases in which the main respondent reported "Protestant, denomination unspecified," while the friend reported the specific Protestant denomination. Only 4.2 percent were incorrect (for example, the main respondent reporting Protestant, while the friend reported Catholic). Since Protestants could report one of a number of specific denominational affiliations, we determined the actual agreement between the main respondent and his friend on the friend's specific denominational membership. In a sense, this procedure requires considerably greater precision of report (and, consequently, greater opportunity for error) than simply treating the broad religious preference as Protestant or Catholic as was done in calculating the product-moment and intraclass correlations. Columns 1 and 2 for the row on religious preference are, consequently, not comparable to Column 3.

[f] Another 17.8 percent were cases in which the main respondent reported an ethnic origin from a given country, but the friend reported an origin from a neighboring country (for example, the main respondent reported Yugoslav, but the friend reported Serbian). Only 9.3 percent were definitely wrong about the country of origin (for example, reported German but actually Italian).

intraclass correlations. In every case, we see that they are nearly identical with their corresponding Pearsonian correlation, reflecting the fact that there are essentially no differences between the means and standard deviations of the main respondents' estimates of their friends' attributes and their friends' reports on their own attributes.

With regard to the categorical information of religious preference and ethnic origin, we found only 4.2 percent of the main respondents were completely wrong in reporting their friends' religious preference and 9.3 percent were definitely incorrect in reporting their friends' ethnic origin. It is in the cases of party preference and ethnic origin that the main respondents are least knowledgeable ("don't know" responses, 14.4 and 15.2 percent, respectively) and most inaccurate (incorrect reports, 14.4 and 9.3 percent, respectively).

With regard to systematic biases in reporting friends' attributes, we found no evidence of such distortions in the cases of age, occupation, educational attainment, and religious preference (see Columns 2, 4, 5, and 6 and footnotes e and f in Table 2.1). There is some evidence that main respondents tend to report that they "don't know" the ethnic origin of friends when the friends are third generation or more Americans of northwest European origin (including English, Welsh, Scotch, Irish, and German)—in short, such friends' ethnic identity is essentially "majority American," their original country of origin is of exceptionally low visibility and often there is a mixture of "nationalities" in the background of the friend adding to the difficulty of knowing the "correct" identity.

There is, however, evidence of systematic distortion in the case of party preference. Disregarding those of "independent" party preference because there are too few cases to sustain analysis, Table 2.2 clearly shows that Democratic main respondents are especially likely to perceive their friends

Table 2.2. Perceived party preference of friend by actual party preference of friend, for Republican and Democratic main respondents: percent distributions

Actual Party Preference of Friend	Republican Main Respondents			Democratic Main Respondents		
	Perceived Party Preference of Friend			Perceived Party Preference of Friend		
	Republican	Democrat	Total	Republican	Democrat	Total
Republican	81%	19%	100% (21)	29%	71%	100% (14)
Democrat	0	100	100% (6)	13	87	100% (23)
	$p = .0007$, Fisher's Exact Test, $N = 27$			$p = .2384$, Fisher's Exact Test, $N = 37$		

as being Democrats when in fact they are Republicans. This is a clear instance of the main respondents' projecting their own political attitudes onto their friends. Republican main respondents, on the other hand, are much more accurate in reporting their friend's party preference, but even they perceived 19 percent of their *Republican* friends as having a Democratic party preference.

Given the moderate associations of Republican party preference with higher educational attainment and occupational status (product-moment correlations of .291 and .425, respectively), it is quite plausible to argue that the greater inaccuracy of Democratic respondents might be attributed to their relatively lower educational attainment on the grounds that the more educated (and presumably more sophisticated) would be more likely to be accurate in reporting their friends' characteristics. While insufficient numbers preclude our explicitly testing this hypothesis with the data in hand, we can note that our efforts to show a general relationship for the whole sample between accuracy of report and educational attainment were unsuccessful in uncovering significant relationships (although they were usually in the predicted direction).

THE RECIPROCATION OF FRIENDSHIP CHOICES

Implicit in the notion of friendship is the assumption that it is a symmetric relation in which both ego and alter should choose each other as friends—what the sociometric literature refers to as reciprocated choice. Most sociometric studies are able to evaluate the extent to which there is reciprocation because they typically study populations which are in some sense conceptually closed, such as a high school (see Alexander and Campbell, 1964; Alexander, 1966), a house shared by college students (see Newcomb, 1961), a governmental agency (see Weiss and Jacobson, 1955), a small rural community (see Duncan and Artis, 1951; Lundberg and Steel, 1938; Loomis and Davidson, 1939), the medical profession in several moderate-sized communities (see Coleman et al., 1966), an Air Force unit (see Zeleny, 1947), or even the elite of a community power structure (see Hunter, 1953). In such populations it is expedient or at least feasible to gather the relevant sociometric data on the entire population, thus facilitating the identification of reciprocated choices.

When, however, one utilizes data on friends nominated by respondents in a cross-sectional sample of a large population universe, such as the Detroit metropolitan area, the determination of the degree of reciprocal choice is indeed highly problematic. In view of the more or less explicit assumption in the sociometric literature that the relationship between mutually chosen friends is probably of greater intimacy and saliency and, consequently, more likely to lead to greater similarity of attitudes toward the world, some assessment of the degree of reciprocity of choice in such a cross-sectional sample and of its significance for attitude similarity would seem to be imperative.

In an effort to determine reciprocity of choice, we asked the friend in the course of the telephone interview to think of his three closest friends and to tell us their ages, occupations, employment status (self-employed or employee), and kin relationship (whether they were related to the friend and, if so, in what way).[6] The characteristics of these three friends were then compared to the characteristics of the main respondent for a "match." When all four characteristics *exactly* matched the main respondent's characteristics, the coder was instructed to code this as "highly likely to be the same person." If only the age reported was "off" by three years of the main respondent's and all other characteristics were identical, the coder coded the case as "probably the same person." Table 2.3 presents the results of this procedure. Over 20 percent of the friends were highly likely to have reported the main respondent as one of their three closest friends, while another 22.9 percent probably reported the main respondent as one of their friends.

In order to put this estimate of 43.2 percent reciprocated choices in some perspective, we referred to two recent studies having some relevance to this problem: First, in the Coleman et al. (1966: 77) study of the diffusion of a medical innovation among doctors in four moderate-sized communities, they asked their respondents to name three doctor friends whom they saw most often socially. Thirty-seven percent of the 430 friendship designations were reciprocated. Secondly, in a sample of 1410 senior males in 30 high schools who were asked to name up to five students of the same sex that they "go around with most often" (Alexander, 1966: 46), 59.8 percent of these choices were reciprocated. Since the only demographic characteristic of our respondents that is significantly correlated with reciprocation of choice is age (.274, $p < .001$, the older the respondent, the less likely the reciprocation of choice) and since the

Table 2.3.   The percent distribution of reciprocated and nonreciprocated choices of main respondent and telephone respondent.

Highly likely to be the same person	20.3% ⎱ 43.2
Probably the same person	22.9 ⎰
Definitely not the same person	54.2
Insufficient information to make any judgment	2.5
Total ($N = 118$)	99.9%

second study permitted a higher likelihood of reciprocation (five friends reported rather than three), it would appear our estimate is at least a reasonable one and not excessively low or high.

As already noted above, such attributes as occupational status, educational attainment, religious preference (Protestant or Catholic), and party preference are unrelated to reciprocity of friendship choice. It would be reasonable to expect, however, that reciprocation be related to higher frequency of contact of the two friends, closer proximity of the friend (that is, residence in the same neighborhood), and a higher self-reported assessment of the closeness of the friendship.[7] And indeed this is precisely what we do find—all of these hypothesized relationships are significant at the .05 level or better (one-tailed test), with product-moment correlations of .202, .152, and .148, respectively.

FRIENDSHIP AND ATTITUDE SIMILARITY

But, we may ask, is there any difference in attitude similarity between those friendship pairs that are reciprocated and those that are not? Or more generally, are friendship pairs more likely to agree on attitudes than randomly paired persons? From a substantive and methodological point of view, one can readily see that these are difficult questions to answer adequately. The most critical difficulty arises from the fact that any given actor will have myriad specific attitudes toward many objects in his "life space." The saliency of given attitudes, their centrality to the person's general orientation to the world, the degree to which they are organized into a "belief system" of some consistency or coherence,[8] and the degree to which the person is affectively committed to a given orientation, among other considerations, will affect the importance and relevance of a given attitude to a friend relationship. Indeed Newcomb (1961: 16 ff.) provides an excellent discussion of the interrelations among orientations between persons (A and B) and attitudes toward objects, X, in his ABX theory of balance. Given these considerations, the simple hypothesis that agreement among friends (whether identified by reciprocated choice or simple unilateral nomination) on specified attitudes toward the world will be higher than "agreement" between randomly paired individuals is almost certainly incorrect without further specification. Only if one can assume that the attitudes in question are salient and affectively important to both parties and of common relevance,[9] can one expect that processes of mutual influence, perhaps as conceptualized in "balance theory" (see Newcomb, 1961; Heider, 1958; Festinger, 1957), will be operative.

The investigator employing a survey technique and a general population sample is faced with the difficulty of identifying attitudes that are likely to be broadly distributed, of general saliency in the population, capable of arousing significant affective commitments, and, consequently, that are likely to be the "stuff out of which friendships are made or broken." Political values and attitudes would seem to be the best candidates for possessing such characteristics. Accordingly, we selected six questions from the main interview schedule to ask the friends in the telephone interview: three were intended to tap educational values and three were drawn from the political domain.

For the purposes of testing our hypothesis that friends should have higher agreement on attitudes than randomly paired individuals, let us consider the subsample of main respondents and of friends as two *independent* samples from the same population of white males residing in the Detroit area.[10] The probability of agreement between randomly assigned pairs is equal to the sum across the set of alternative answers of the probability of choosing alternative A_i in sample 1 times the probability of choosing alternative A_i in sample 2:

$$\Sigma Pr(A_{1i}A_{2i}). \qquad (2.1)$$

Table 2.4 presents the percentages of agreement on the six attitude items as estimated according to the "random pair model" and the actually observed percentages of agreement between friends. Although the random pair model tends consistently to underestimate the actual degree of agreement for the six attitude items, discrepancies for the first five items are all quite small and can easily be accounted for in terms of the fact that the pairings are not random with respect to selected attributes (for example, education) which are also related to the attitudes in question. Consequently, one need not take into account the additional fact that the pairs are in fact friends. Only in the case of party preference does there appear to be substantial evidence that the friendship nexus itself may be enhancing attitude similarity. Of course, disproportionate agreement on political preferences may result from two quite different processes. Men may actively befriend others who agree with them politically. Political agreement may, on the other hand, be the resultant of a long-term process of mutual influence in a friendship relationship formed for quite different reasons, such as common interests in recreation or common residence. We, unfortunately, do not have the relevant information to examine the adequacy of these two rival models. On the basis of the results reported in Table 2.4, however, such further elaborations appear to be unnecessary for five of the six attitudes considered.

We still must attempt to answer the question posed above, to wit: is there any difference in attitude similarity between those friendship pairs

Table 2.4.   Comparison of the percentages of agreement according to the random pair model and the actually observed agreement between friends

Attitude Item	(1) Actual Agreement between Friends	(2) Expected Agreement (Random Model)	(3) Discrepancy (1–2)
Q1. Least education required for boy[a]	39.0%	32.8%	+6.2%
Q2. Least education required for girl[b]	43.2	43.7	−0.5
Q3. Main goals of education[c]	46.6	43.3	+3.3
Q4. Fire a high school teacher who is admitted Communist[d]	47.5	46.4	+1.1
Q5. Fire a high school teacher who is admitted KKK member[e]	38.1	33.3	+4.8
Q6. Political party preference[f]	49.6	37.6	+12.0

[a] What is the least amount of schooling that you think a young man needs these days to get along well in the world? (Q43, Appendix C.)

[b] What is the least amount of schooling that you think a girl needs these days to get along well in the world? (Q44, Appendix C.)

[c] What is the more important goal of higher education? (a) To learn about new ideas and broaden one's mind *or* (b) to get the training and degree necessary for a first rate job. (S26, Appendix C.)

[d] Suppose there is a man who admits he is a Communist. Suppose he is a teacher in a high school. Should he be fired or not? (Q47c, Appendix C.)

[e] Suppose there is a man who admits he is a Ku Klux Klansman. Suppose he is a teacher in a high school. Should he be fired or not? (Q47k, Appendix C.)

[f] Generally speaking do you think of yourself as a Republican or a Democrat? If Republican or Democrat: Would you call yourself a strong (Republican/Democrat)? If independent or other: Do you think of yourself as closer to the Republican or Democratic party? (Q80, Appendix C.)

which are reciprocated and those which are not? There is some very slender evidence that reciprocated pairs tend to have higher agreement on attitudes than unreciprocated pairs. In the questions regarding the more important goal of higher education (Q3) and the firing of a high school teacher who is an admitted Communist (Q4), reciprocated pairs had higher agreement than unreciprocated pairs (correlations of .115, $p \approx .115$, one-tailed, and .148, $p \approx .05$, one-tailed). But there was no apparent patterning for the other questions.

A MODEL OF INTERPERSONAL ORIENTATIONS AND SHARED ATTITUDES: THE CASE OF PARTY PREFERENCE

In Newcomb's development of his ABX theory of interpersonal orientations mentioned earlier, he makes the following important observations:

The key principle of individual system stability is one that involves relationships among all three categories of the ABX system. This principle postulates a psychological force upon A, varying in strength with intensity of positive A-to-B attraction . . . toward maintaining a constant relationship between A-to-X attitude and perceived B-to-X attitude. This constant relationship is one of *minimal perceived discrepancy*—in other words, of maximal similarity —in attitude. In propositional form, the stronger A's attraction toward B the greater the strength of the force upon A to maintain minimal discrepancy between his own and B's attitude, as he perceived the latter, toward the same X; and, if positive attraction remains constant, the greater the perceived discrepancy in attitude the stronger the force to reduce it. We shall refer to this force as *strain*. . . .

Modes of maintaining system stability. We have defined a system as a set of entities so related that a change in any one of them induces forces toward change in any of the others in ways that maximize the stability of certain relationships among them. . . . We must therefore consider the alternative ways in which changes in single orientations (in individual systems), . . . may so induce other within-system changes as to maintain minimal states of strain and imbalance.

. . . any of the following changes can contribute to reducing the newly aroused strain: (1) a change in A's attitude toward X, such as to reduce the perceived discrepancy with B; (2) a discrepancy-reducing change in his perception of B's attitude; (3) a reduction in the importance assigned by A to his attitude toward X; (4) a reduction in the strength of A's positive attraction toward B; or (5) a reduction in the degree of perceived common relevance that A attributes to X for himself and B. . . . (Newcomb, 1961: 13, 17)

For analysis, I shall treat the main respondent as A, the friend as B, and party preference as X. A diagrammatic representation of the ABX model is shown in Figure 2.1.

Given that A is already strongly attracted to B, then the theory predicts that A's perception of B's attitude toward X will be systematically distorted to minimize the discrepancy with A's attitude toward X. This argument leads us specifically to the prediction that A's who are in reciprocated friendship networks (and thus presumably have a strong mutual attrac-

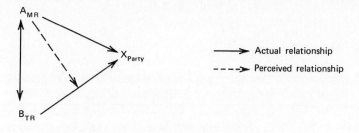

Figure 2.1   Diagram of *ABX* model.

Table 2.5. The main respondent's accuracy of perception of his friend's attitude toward the political parties by reciprocated-nonreciprocated friendship pair: percent distributions

	Perception of Party Preference					
Friendship Pair	Accurate	Inaccurate[a]	Total	Accurate	Inaccurate[a]	Total
Reciprocated[b]	45%	55%	100% (20)	51%	49%	100% (43)
Nonreciprocated	72	28	100% (57)	72	28	100% (57)
	$\chi^2 = 4.73, p < .05$, 1 d.f., $N = 77$			$\chi^2 = 3.86, p < .05$, 1 d.f., $N = 100$		

[a] "Inaccurate" perception includes those who reported their friends as being "independents" or preferring the party other than the one actually reported by the friend.

[b] In the first panel, only pairs which were "highly likely to be the same person" are treated as reciprocated choices, while the second panel also includes those who are "probably the same person". See pages 32 and 34 above for further discussion of these distinctions.

tion) will be *less accurate* in their description of B's party preference than A's who are in unreciprocated friendship networks. This prediction runs counter to the more "commonsense" notion that the more intimate the relationship, the more knowledgeable each member of the pair is of the other's salient beliefs and characteristics.

We already know from Table 2.1 that A's accuracy of perception of B's actual party preference is considerably poorer than his accuracy regarding B's other attributes, including age, occupation, religious preference, and educational attainment. Table 2.5 presents evidence that supports the prediction derived from the ABX theory: main respondents in reciprocated networks are more inaccurate than those in nonreciprocated networks. There is some evidence of a similar pattern of distortion with regard to the perception of the ethnic origin of friends ($\chi^2 = 2.22$, 1 d.f., $p \approx .15$)—main respondents in reciprocated networks are more inaccurate in reporting their friend's ethnic origins than those in nonreciprocated networks. There is no evidence of such systematic distortions in A's perception of B's other characteristics.

SUMMARY

In this chapter, we have addressed ourselves to two principal tasks. After briefly indicating some of the sampling biases that might impose qualifications on the generality of our results, we discussed the important, but often neglected, methodological questions concerning the degree of accuracy with which respondents report their friends' socioeconomic and other characteristics and the extent to which these reports are subject to systematic distortions or biases. Our evidence suggests that while certain attributes of friends are reported with quite satisfactory accuracy and minimum systematic distortion, these tend to be relatively "objective" or public facts about the friend, such as his age and occupation. As soon as one considers less visible and public attributes, such as political attitudes, there is evidence of considerable distortion in the direction of assimilating the friend's attributes toward those of the nominator (ego).

Secondly, we have addressed ourselves to the substantive questions of estimating the degree of mutual choice of friends in an adult urban population, friends being named unconstrained by any criteria of selection,[11] and of assessing the degree of attitude similarly between friends and the relevance of reciprocated choice in enhancing attitude similarity. While approximately 43 percent of the friends reciprocated the main respondents' choices, there is only slender evidence to support the notion that reciprocated pairs have greater agreement on attitudes than nonreciprocated pairs. Indeed there is little evidence that attitude agreements between friends are higher than chance expectations for most of the attitudes measured. Of course, as noted in our discussion of these findings, the results do not necessarily refute the hypothesis that friends, under certain conditions, will have greater attitude similarity than randomly paired individuals.

On the basis of the evidence presented in this chapter, I think we can reasonably conclude that we can rely upon our respondents' reports of their friends' characteristics, except perhaps for their political party preferences. Since much of the analysis in the chapters to follow is premised upon information supplied about friends, we can have considerable confidence in the results not being hopelessly distorted by systematically biased information.

NOTES

1. In this regard it would be profitable to consider the more social psychologically oriented literature on the "perception of others," including Taft, 1955; Lundy, 1956; McDavid and Harari, 1968: 127–50.

2. Another 4.5 percent were lost because friends lived outside of the calling area, which included all of southeastern Michigan (including Wayne, Macomb, and Washtenaw counties), Windsor, Canada, and its surroundings in Ontario, and northern Ohio and Indiana, and 7.5 percent were lost due to other miscellaneous reasons. See Laumann, 1969a, Table 1, for further details.

3. As Stephan and McCarthy (1958) have noted, nearly all large-scale surveys of the noninstitutional adult population consistently *underenumerate* certain categories of the population, especially those groups which have high rates of geographical mobility and reside in "group quarters" (for example, boarding houses) as opposed to "family dwelling units." Such groups are characterized by their relative youth, high male composition, and lowly socioeconomic status (unskilled and semiskilled workers of poor educational attainments). In fact, a closer examination of the noninterviewed telephone respondents (on the basis of main respondent reports) reveals that they are concentrated in a group of young, recent migrants from the South (accounting for our underenumeration of Protestants) who are employed as unskilled or semiskilled auto workers and who live in group quarters (where the telephone listing is not likely to be in their names).

Thus, the sampling biases on age, occupation, education, and the like, appear to have arisen, among other things, from missing a certain group of persons who are, unfortunately, especially likely to be missed in such surveys, particularly when the procedure of interviewing is based on the telephone contact. What we have to ask is whether this underenumerated group is so different from the rest of the population on matters of the study's concern and of sufficient numerical importance that our results are hopelessly distorted. I do not think so. Judging from the experiences of other large-scale surveys regarding coverage (see Stephan and McCarthy, 1958: 150–51, 235–72, 298), I would regard the biases of this sample as being of the same order of magnitude of these other studies. The sample, in short, is probably reasonably representative of the vast bulk of the adult white male "settled" population of the Detroit metropolitan area.

4. For a very interesting treatment of the problem of measurement error, see Siegel and Hodge, 1968.

5. See footnote b, Table 2.1.

6. It should be emphasized, first, that the telephone respondent was not informed that his name had been given to us by one of our main respondents and, second, that he was phoned at least two months *after* the main respondent had been interviewed in order to minimize the possibility of recalling that the main respondent may have mentioned that we would be calling him for an interview. We had asked the main respondents not to mention to their friends that we would be calling them for interviews, but we do not know whether we enjoyed complete cooperation with this request.

7. This information on frequency of contact, proximity to the main respondent, and assessment of the closeness of the friendship was reported for each friend by the main respondent.

8. Philip Converse (1964) provides an exceptionally lucid and stimulating discussion concerning the nature of belief systems in mass publics. He (1964: 207) defines a belief system as "a configuration of ideas and attitudes in which the elements are bound together by some form of constraint or functional interdependence." The burden of his argument is to show that these belief systems vary considerably in the degree to which their idea elements are constrained to co-vary and the extent to which these constraints are operative in different subpopulations. He presents evidence to show that the belief systems of the political elite, for example, are considerably more coherent and organized than among the mass public where idea elements, which from the standpoint of the elite's understanding of "what goes with what" *should* or *should not* belong together, are almost randomly combined.

9. Newcomb (1961: 13), defined the concept as follows: *"Common relevance* refers to joint dependence of A and B (as perceived by A, in the case of individual systems) upon the object, X. If A considers an object of high common relevance to himself and B, then he perceives that their relationship to it as that of 'common fate': the object is seen as having common consequence for both of them."

10. We, of course, know that the second sample is in fact dependent on the first. In choosing friends, there is quite clear evidence that individuals are choosing individuals who are similar to themselves in such characteristics as age, occupation, education, and religious preferences. Indeed these characteristics of reported friends and main respondents are correlated .501, .431, .316, and .485, respectively—in brief, friends are not being randomly selected from the population residing in Detroit (see Laumann, 1966: 63–87).

11. By "unconstrained," we mean that the respondents could name as friends whomever they pleased, including kin, work partners, neighbors, school friends whom they still regarded as their closest friends, and so on. Specifically asking people to name friends who must share common residence in a housing development or common membership in the same work organization or occupation, of course, serves to constrain the character of the friends mentioned. For many purposes, this latter strategy is a reasonable one to take, but it did not seem appropriate for our study.

CHAPTER 3

The Social Structure of Ascriptive Membership Groups

THE MULTIDIMENSIONAL NATURE OF GROUP ATTRACTION AND REPULSION

Almost from the beginning of empirically oriented sociological studies of American society there has been a profound interest in studying the role of ethnic groups in the economic, political, and social life of American cities and the transmutation and assimilation of these groups into the "host" society. Since 1925, Bogardus and his students, employing the classic Bogardus Social Distance Scale (1933), have charted the subjective orientations of the population toward the manifold variety of groups who have migrated to these shores. Despite some serious methodological defects in the samples employed (for example, they were typically drawn from college student populations rather than general samples of the population) and in the methods used to measure ethnic "prejudice," one finding to emerge consistently has been the differential ranking of ethnic groups along some hierarchial dimension of social desirability and willingness to accept members of a given ethnic group into such intimate social relationships as marriage, friendship, and common residence—a ranking that has remained remarkably stable over time (see Bogardus, 1951, 1958). The relative position of a given ethnic group on this dimension of social acceptability seems to be a function of the principal time of arrival of the group's ancestors (the earlier in American history, the higher the standing of the group) and the degree to which the group approximates the cultural attributes of white Anglo-Saxon Protestants.[1] In addition to such attitudinal studies of ethnic prejudice, a large number of studies of residential segregation of ethnic groups have found a generally parallel ranking of ethnic groups by their degree of segregation from each other (Duncan and Lieberson, 1959; Lieberson, 1963; Beshers, Laumann, and Bradshaw, 1964).

One of the major limitations of viewing ethnic groups simply in terms of a unidimensional rank order of relative social standing is that groups who share roughly comparable ranks in the ethnic status order in that they are equally "far" from the top groups in the system may also be *quite "far" from each other* despite their relatively similar ordinal positions on the unidimensional ranking scheme. Consider, for example, the case of the Jews and the Arabs, both of whom are relatively low in the general population's ranking of ethnic preference but are also quite far apart in their mutual orientations to each other.

Many studies have demonstrated that interpersonal attraction is a complex function of many factors, including physical proximity (for example, living in the same neighborhoods), the relative sizes of groups (which determine the differential opportunity to meet people of a given group), similarity of social attributes, notably socioeconomic status and religious preference, and more subjective personality characteristics and attitudes, including ethnic prejudices (McDavid and Harari, 1968: 127–50). In the analyses presented below, we explore the relative social distances between ethnic and other ascriptively defined groups in multi-dimensional spaces that permits us to portray graphically the resultant of these many factors affecting mutual attractions and repulsions among groups. We shall find that a man's ethnic group by itself is an inadequate specification of his ascriptive membership group and shall therefore proceed to consider the relevance of religious differences within ethnic groups in a further effort to account for the mutual attractions and repulsions of men on the basis of their social identities.

To review briefly the argument of the first chapter, the following definitions and assumptions underlie the analysis that follows: an individual's *social position* may be characterized by his group memberships and social attributes, such as his religious affiliation (including his denomination), ethnic origin, and occupational status. The *social structure* of a community can be defined as a persisting system of social relationships among social positions. Therefore, one way to describe this social structure is in terms of the differential likelihood of the formation of relationships among social positions (see Laumann, 1966: 1–5). Using this perspective, we shall attempt to portray the structure of intimate associations (social relationships) among ethnic groups, religious groups, and ethnoreligious groups.

THE SOCIAL STRUCTURE OF ETHNIC GROUPS

In the first two columns of Table 3.1 the percentage distributions of respondents and friends are shown by their ethnic origins.[2] The "percent

Table 3.1.   Percent distributions of respondents and friends by their ethnic origins and self-selection; ratios of self-selection and indexes of dissimilarity

Ethnic Group	Percent of Respondents	Percent of Friends	Percent Self-Selection	Ratio of Self-Selection	Indexes of Dissimilarity
German	22.1%	17.2%	27.5%	1.6	22.9
British (includes England, Wales, Northern Ireland)	12.9	15.7	34.5	2.2	21.1
Polish	11.1	11.8	40.8	3.5	30.4
Italian	4.8	5.5	24.3	4.4	26.0
Irish	13.2	10.3	25.0	2.4	18.3
French	7.8	4.5	12.3	2.7	17.8
Scotch	7.4	4.1	12.0	2.9	18.9
Dutch-Belgian	2.4	1.9	8.5	4.5	23.3
Scandinavian (includes Norway, Sweden, Denmark, Finland)	2.8	2.6	13.4	5.2	19.5
Russian	1.5	1.4	24.4	17.4	48.4
Slavic (includes Estonia, Lithuania, Bulgaria, Roumania, Latvia)	1.4	1.0	5.0	5.0	36.3
Hungarian	1.4	1.3	17.1	13.2	39.6
Armenian	0.6	0.8	11.1	13.9	32.8
Greek	0.6	0.7	11.1	15.9	39.6
Yugoslav	1.1	1.0	12.1	12.1	41.9
Jewish	0.6	0.9	27.8	30.9	68.0
Arab	0.7	0.8	38.1	47.6	58.5
Czech	1.1	0.5	6.3	12.6	27.2
Spanish (includes Spain, Portugal, Latin America, Mexico)	0.5	0.6	6.7	11.2	39.1
Nonwhite	1.0	1.2	–	–	25.9
American only	2.9	2.6	20.0	7.7	35.2
Do not know, not ascertained	2.0	13.4	36.6	2.7	37.1
Total	100.0[a]	100.0[a]			
N	(1013)	(2935)[b]			

[a] The index of dissimilarity of the percent distributions for respondents and friends is 16.7.

[b] The total N of 2935 departs from the expected 3039 cases (3 friends times 1013 respondents) because some respondents did not name three friends.

self-selection" (Column 3) refers to the percent of friends who are of the same ethnic group as the respondents. The "ratio of self-selection" (Column 4) indicates the degree to which the observed frequency of within-ethnic-group selection exceeds or is less than the expected frequency of within-ethnic-group selection by chance (parity equals 1.0), given the distribution of friends among the ethnic groups. The indexes of dissimilarity in Column 5 contrast the percent distribution of a given ethnic group's friends with the percent distribution of the ethnic groups of all friends reported by the sample. The index of dissimilarity (specifically, the sum of the positive percentage differences between two percent distributions) tells us the proportion of persons in one group or the other that would have to be redistributed so that the two percent distributions being compared would be identical (see Duncan and Duncan, 1955a).[3] These indexes may be regarded as measuring the degree to which the friendship choices of a given ethnic group depart from a chance distribution of choices by ethnicity—the larger the index, the greater the departure from chance (or, alternatively, the more segregated the group is from the rest of the population in its friendship choices).

Several additional features of the distributions of friendship choices by ethnicity should be noted. First, the self-selection ratio may be regarded as an index of the degree to which an ethnic group has maintained its distinctive "ethnic identity" or, alternatively, the degree to which an ethnic group has been assimilated into the native white population. Presumably, if an ethnic group manifested no tendency to select friends from their own group other than that of chance (a self-selection ratio equal to 1.0), the group would be completely assimilated (see Gordon, 1964; Beshers, 1962; Laumann, 1966). Nevertheless, some caution must be employed in interpreting this ratio as its maximum value is directly dependent on the relative size of a given group in the population. For example, if a given ethnic group comprises 50 percent of the population and chooses friends only from their own group, the maximum ratio of self-selection is 2.0. But if it comprised only 10 percent of the population, the maximum value of the ratio would be 10.0, five times as high. Consequently, we may expect and, in fact, we find a strong negative correlation (rank order) of $-.821$ ($p < .01$) between the size of the group in the sample and its ratio of self-selection; that is, the smaller the group, the greater the degree of in-group friendship choice. It should be recognized, however, that the high correlation arises partly from artifact and partly from substantive considerations, inasmuch as there is no reason for a group *necessarily* to overchoose friends from their own group simply because of its small size.

Secondly, the percentage of foreign white males of the total foreign stock from Country X in the Detroit SMSA in 1960 (see Table 3.2 below) is, as we might expect, positively correlated (.487, $p < .05$; .588 if Czechs are excluded) with the self-selection ratios; that is, the higher the percentage of foreign-born males in a given ethnic group, the higher the in-group friendship choice. This correlation between "recency of arrival" and self-selection could plausibly be interpreted as reflecting the

Table 3.2.   Socioeconomic characteristics of the 22 ethnic groups: Percent foreign born, mean rating of social standing, mean occupational status, mean family income, and mean school years completed

Ethnic Group	Percent Foreign Born, White Males[a]	Mean Social Standing of Group[b]	Mean Occupational Status[c]	Mean Family Income[d]	Mean Educational Attainment[e]
All countries	15.7%	—[j]	45.2	$10,177	12.0 yrs.
German	10.6	57.9	47.6	10,959	12.2
British (includes England, Wales, Northern Ireland)	17.0	65.5	51.1	10,921	12.0
Polish	13.3	44.3	34.2	9,838	11.7
Italian	18.4	50.1	43.8	9,526	12.2
Irish	9.8	61.8	43.8	9,722	11.9
French	13.5	55.0[f]	38.5	9,758	12.0
Scotch	20.7	59.2	44.0	10,909	12.1
Dutch-Belgian	20.1	57.5[g]	51.4	9,200	11.8
Scandinavian (includes Norway, Denmark, Sweden, Finland)	13.3	53.6[h]	61.7	9,750	13.7
Russian	18.8	36.0	65.0	12,500	15.4
Slavic (includes Lithuania, Estonia, Bulgaria, Roumania, Latvia)	28.9	42.8[i]	37.0	10,500	12.1
Hungarian	16.0	44.6	52.5	9,999	11.5
Armenian	—[j]	—[j]	25.0	14,999	13.3
Greek	27.2	41.4	45.0	9,999	12.1
Yugoslav	22.2	—[j]	65.0	11,875	12.3
Jewish	—[j]	46.4	69.0	12,500	15.4
Arab (includes UAR, Syria, Turkey, Lebanon)	18.2	—[j]	55.0	$ 9,250	12.0
Czech	13.2	42.5	57.5	9,750	13.4
Spanish surname	19.1	34.4[k]	25.0	10,833	12.0
Nonwhite	—[j]	—[j]	—[j]	—[j]	—[j]
American only	—[j]	—[j]	35.0	9,232	11.6
Do not know, not ascertained	—[j]	—[j]	17.5	9,100	11.6

[a] *Source:*   Table 99, Country of Origin of the Foreign Stock, by Nativity, Color, and Sex, for the State and for Standard Metropolitan Statistical Areas of 250,000 or More: 1960. *U.S. Census of Population, Final Report PC(1)-24D (Michigan): 1960.*

[b] *Source:*   NORC study by Hodge and Siegel (forthcoming).

[c] The current occupation of the respondent was first coded into the six-digit detailed occupation-industry code of the U.S. Bureau of the Census and then recoded by computer to the two-digit code of Duncan's Index of Socioeconomic Status (Duncan, 1961).

[d] Based on the sample respondents' reported total family income.

relative vitality of ethnic identification and orientations within given groups since a group comprised disproportionately of new arrivals from the Old Country might be thought to have its sense of distinctiveness as a group sustained and revitalized by them.

Table 3.2 presents a number of summary socioeconomic characteristics of the ethnic groups under consideration. Where available, we have reported in Column 1 the proportion foreign-born males of the total foreign stock (which includes the foreign born and native born of foreign parentage) from a given country of origin for the Detroit SMSA in 1960—presumably the higher the proportion foreign born, the more recent the "average" time of arrival of members of that nationality group. Column 2 presents the National Opinion Research Center's (NORC) national sample's ($N = 445$) evaluation of the relative social standing of the ethnic groups—the higher the number, the higher the social standing in the opinion of this sample.[4] Columns 3, 4, and 5 provide the ethnic group's mean family income, occupational status, and school years completed, based on information given by our respondents. All the information provided in this table reveals the considerable range of variation among the groups on various socioeconomic indicators and times of arrival.

For any pair of respondents' ethnic membership groups, the percentage distributions of their friendship choices among the 22 ethnic groups differ to a greater or lesser extent. If the two distributions of friendship choices were identical, it would indicate a minimum of dissimilarity or social distance with respect to friendship choices between the two groups. At the opposite extreme, if there were no overlap between the two choice distributions, the two groups would have a maximum distance from one another with respect to their choice distributions. The index of dissimilarity previously encountered can represent this distance between ethnic groups with respect to friendship choice distributions (see Blau and Duncan, 1967: 43–44, 67–69)[5] and shall serve as our proximity measure, as discussed in Appendix A.

Table 3.3 presents the indexes of dissimilarity for the twenty-two ethnic groups. Considerable dissimilarity appears in friendship choices

---

[e] Based on the sample respondents' reported school years completed.

[f] The French were ranked 59.1, while the French Canadians were ranked 50.9. We took a simple average of these two rankings.

[g] Only the Dutch were evaluated in the NORC study.

[h] Scandinavians are scored as the unweighted average of the following four groups: Danes (52.4), Finns (51.0), Norwegians (55.9), and Swedes (55.1).

[i] We had an evaluation only for the Lithuanians for the Slavic group.

[j] Not available.

[k] This is the unweighted average for four groups: Spanish Americans (47.6), Mexicans (25.0), Puerto Ricans (23.9), Latin Americans (40.9).

Table 3.3. Indexes of dissimilarity of friendship choices for 22 ethnic groups

Ethnic Groups	(1)	(2)	(3)	(4)	(5)	(6)	(7)	(8)	(9)	(10)	(11)	(12)	(13)	(14)	(15)	(16)	(17)	(18)	(19)	(20)	(21)	(22)
1. German	.00																					
2. British	.26	.00																				
3. Polish	.38	.41	.00																			
4. Do not know	.24	.27	.41	.00																		
5. Italian	.27	.32	.34	.30	.00																	
6. Irish	.32	.33	.38	.25	.28	.00																
7. French	.26	.28	.39	.27	.30	.33	.00															
8. Scotch	.26	.29	.41	.27	.26	.34	.24	.00														
9. Dutch (Holland-Belgium)	.22	.34	.47	.36	.37	.43	.24	.32	.00													
10. Scandinavian	.25	.31	.37	.29	.27	.29	.27	.29	.34	.00												
11. American only	.43	.41	.46	.32	.40	.40	.36	.43	.47	.41	.00											
12. Russian	.61	.63	.62	.52	.61	.62	.62	.61	.61	.59	.60	.00										
13. Slavic	.36	.51	.38	.40	.48	.52	.44	.44	.42	.45	.55	.61	.00									
14. Hungarian	.40	.41	.45	.45	.40	.40	.39	.37	.43	.35	.48	.66	.47	.00								
15. Nonwhite	.32	.30	.43	.18	.33	.40	.32	.31	.42	.30	.42	.56	.45	.38	.00							
16. Armenian	.39	.44	.43	.32	.38	.35	.44	.45	.51	.39	.47	.54	.48	.41	.31	.00						
17. Yugoslav	.36	.34	.47	.37	.39	.44	.24	.36	.36	.42	.44	.62	.45	.44	.41	.44	.00					
18. Greek	.48	.36	.54	.43	.44	.49	.40	.41	.44	.47	.58	.64	.56	.51	.40	.51	.43	.00				
19. Jewish	.29	.41	.52	.32	.43	.42	.34	.39	.31	.34	.49	.53	.42	.41	.38	.47	.46	.49	.00			
20. Arab	.69	.67	.68	.71	.62	.71	.58	.67	.65	.69	.57	.77	.79	.76	.72	.75	.52	.66	.81	.00		
21. Czech	.43	.56	.65	.52	.55	.58	.51	.41	.40	.49	.58	.72	.50	.44	.62	.56	.55	.62	.46	.85	.00	
22. Spanish surname	.56	.55	.56	.54	.50	.46	.50	.39	.63	.50	.61	.85	.70	.48	.48	.56	.56	.56	.56	.46	.56	.00

between German-Americans and Russian-Americans (.61) and between German-Americans and Arabs (.69), but relatively less dissimilarity appears between German-Americans and British-Americans (.26). By comparing the relative magnitudes of the indexes, the reader can determine the relative similarities of choice patterns among the different groups. The indexes for Arabs and Czechs with all other groups suggest, for example, that they are relatively isolated or segregated from all other groups with respect to their patterns of friendship choice. Since Table 3.3 has 231 entries that yield 26,565 possible paired comparisons, the need to simplify this task of analyzing the underlying structure of the table is apparent.

In order to obtain a clearer picture of the underlying structure, we submitted this matrix to smallest space analysis whose assumptions and rationale are extensively described in Appendix A. The coefficients of alienation for the best one-space, two-space, and three-space solutions were .322, .187, and .128, respectively—the latter two representing modestly acceptable fits of the data. Since the three-space does not provide an appreciably sharper picture of the structure of the data, Figure 3.1 presents the two-space solution only.

The general structure of the space may be conceived as forming a series of concentric circles in which the innnermost circle is comprised of the most assimilated groups, the British, Germans, Scots, Irish, and French—that is, principally northwestern European groups of the "Old Migration." The notable exception is the Italian group, which is predominantly comprised of more recent arrivals who are probably being "pulled" into the center because of their predominantly Catholic composition (note their close proximity to the Irish). The Poles are in the third ring,[6] in closer proximity to Slavic groups, which in general fall in the upper righthand quadrant of the space. By and large, groups from countries around the Mediterranean and Adriatic Seas are on the lefthand side of the space and groups from central and eastern Europe on the righthand side. The Jews and Arabs are at some distance from the center and on diametrically opposite sides of the space. This reflects the fact that, as lower status ethnic groups, they are often even more unlikely to associate with each other than they are to associate with the higher status groups.

Either the Germans or the British could be taken as the center point of the space. If the Germans are taken as the origin point, primarily because they are the largest subgroup of the old migration in the sample, we find that the NORC social standing rank order of ethnic groups (see footnote 1 and Column 2, Table 3.2) is correlated .754 with the Euclidean distances from the Germans; if the British are taken as the origin point, the correlation is .803. The correlation of the distance from Germans and the size of the group is .504 and the distance from the British and the size of the group is .608. The ethnic group's self-selection ratio is correlated .608 with its distance from the Germans and .677 with its distance from the British. Finally, the correlations between percent foreign-born males and distance from Germans and between percent foreign-born males and distance from the British are insignificant (.109 and .112 respectively).

Our efforts to determine the role of socioeconomic status, as indexed by the group's mean family income, occupational status, and school years completed (see Table 3.2 above), in structuring the space have been unsuccessful. There are no significant correlations of the socioeconomic status of the group and its distance from the center of the space as both

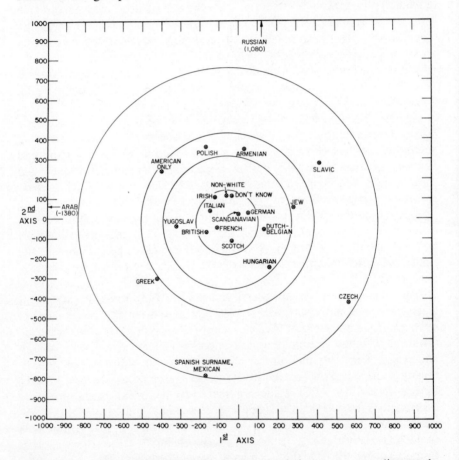

Figure 3.1 Graphic portrayal of proximities of ethnic groups, according to the indexes of dissimilarity data. Coefficient of alienation = .187.

centrally located (for example, the German and British) and peripherally located (for example, the Jewish and Czech) groups enjoy relatively high socioeconomic status while others in both regions (for example, the Italian and Arab) have relatively low socioeconomic attainments. In addition, an extremely important factor that determines the relative frequencies of friendship formation among the ethnic groups is common religious preference (see Kennedy, 1952; Herberg, 1955; Gordon, 1964). Indeed, whereas 69.9 percent of the sample have two or all three friends who share their broad religious preference (Protestant, Catholic, or Jewish), only 25.6 percent have two or all three of their friends drawn from the same ethnic group as their own. Now some groups, notably the Poles, Irish, and Italians, are relatively homogeneous with respect to their religious preference (and note that they also tend to be found in the same region of the space); other groups, such as the Germans and British, are more evenly split between Protestants and Catholics. Further, Protestants are differentiated internally with respect to denominational affiliations, which in turn reflect socioeconomic *and* ethnic differences in recruitment as well as differences in religious beliefs and practices (see Niebuhr, 1929; Gaustad, 1962; Demerath, 1965).

In view of these considerations, we were forced to pursue the analysis in two directions: first, we considered the structure of friendship formation among 15 religious groups and, second, we combined ethnic and religious attributes of respondents and friends and analyzed the structure of friendship formation among the resulting ethnoreligious groups. This latter analysis resolves many of the ambiguities of interpretation regarding the ethnic space reported here and it is to these analyses we now turn.

THE SOCIAL STRUCTURE OF RELIGIOUS GROUPS[7]

With over 200 recognized religious bodies, the United States would at first glance appear to rank high among the nations of the world in terms of its religious diversity. While the colonial period is a story of the settlement, growth, and geographical hegemony of a relatively few distinct religious groups, the nineteenth and early twentieth centuries are a continuing story of the arrival of new groups (for example, the Eastern Orthodox Communion with its national varieties), the breaking up of established groups into various factions divided on some often minor doctrinal issue, and even the rise of indigenous religious groups, such as the Mormons and Jehovah's Witnesses (see Niebuhr, 1929; Mead, 1963; Gaustad, 1962; Lipset, 1963a: 140–69). Many so-called religious differences were sustained by the fact that they were rooted in ethnic or linguistic differences (for example, between the Dutch and German Reformed or the various Lutheran groups). As these ethnic and linguistic differences moderated and disappeared in the course of assimilation, there often remained little rationale for continuing separate church organizations for doctrinally similar groups. For this and other reasons, some abatement in the proliferation of religious groups has occurred in recent years; moreover, the decline of some of the social sources of religious differentiation, accompanied by organizational pressures for unity, has resulted in a large number of mergers within and among Protestant groups (Lee, 1960) so that today a small number of denominations serve the majority of the Protestants.

Because of these developments many observers have concluded that religious differences in the population are more apparent than real (see Herberg, 1955; Williams, 1957; Lipset, 1963a). Robin Williams (1957: 344), for example, observes:

It is variously noted that much of religion has become a matter of private ethical convictions; that churches are active in secular affairs; that religious observances have been losing their supernatural or other-worldly character. It is said that religion in America tends to be religion at a very low temperature. . . .

Herberg (1955), drawing from Kennedy's (1944, 1952) description of ethnic and religious intermarriage trends in New Haven, has advanced the descriptive hypothesis that the religious differences that remain in the American population fall into three broad categories: Protestant, Catholic, and Jewish, and that differences within these broad groupings, especially to the extent that they arise from ethnic differences, are relatively residual and are slowly disappearing. Moreover, Herberg argues, the significance of these broad religious preferences lies in their social structural implications; that is, in determining who associates intimately with whom, rather than in any fundamental differences of religious outlook or values. In fact, among the three faiths, the growing tendency is to emphasize beliefs shared in common and to minimize their differences.

Glock and Stark (1965; Stark and Glock, 1968), on the other hand, contend that important differences among the denominations in their religious outlook and values still exist and these differences might still have considerable consequences for nonreligious attitudes, including those toward work, minority groups, and politics. Niebuhr (1929) and Demerath (1965) have also emphasized differences among the Protestant denominations but have traced them to the underlying differences in the social composition of their memberships. On the basis of their reasoning, we might expect structural differentiation within the three religious subcommunities, especially the Protestant.

The analysis in this section is addressed to an evaluation of the associational implications of these rival perspectives. That is, can the structure of intimate associations among religious groups best be characterized by Herberg's tripartite model or must one take into account differences within the three religious subcommunities that rest upon underlying social distinctions, as Niebuhr and Demerath contend, and upon differences in religious beliefs, as Glock and Stark suggest. We shall show that the relative proximities of religious groups (as defined by similarities in their patterns of friendship choices) are determined by three considerations: (1) the broad category of religious preference within which a given denomination is found, (2) the group's socioeconomic composition relative to others in the broad category, and (3) characteristics of its religious beliefs and organization.

Table 3.4 provides the same information for the fifteen religious groups[8] that Table 3.1 presented for ethnic groups. Again the last two columns of the table reflect the fact that religious groups differ considerably among themselves with respect to the extent to which they confine friendship choices to their own kind. Jews, Congregationalists, and certain of the more fundamentalist Protestant denominations are especially likely to practice homophily.

As we have already mentioned, many studies have shown that the religious groups differ considerably with regard to the socioeconomic composition of their membership (Niebuhr, 1929; Demerath, 1965) and their characteristic religious beliefs and behavior (Lenski, 1961; Glock and Stark, 1965; Stark and Glock, 1968). Protestant denominations, in particular, are known to vary considerably in both their socioeconomic compositions and their religious beliefs. Table 3.5 summarizes for our 15 religious groups a number of such indicators. These data rather dramatically reveal the similarities and differences among the various groups in terms of socioeconomic status and religious activities and beliefs. Given the distance-generating postulate discussed in the first chapter, that similarities in status and attitudes and beliefs are critical facilitating factors in the formation of intimate relationships, the similarities and differences reported in Table 3.5 will prove very helpful in interpreting the structure of intimate associations revealed in the smallest space analysis reported below. Parenthetically, we should note that comparisons of Protestants and Catholics in the aggregate reveal no appreciable differences between them in their socioeconomic composition (see Glenn and Hyland, 1967); but they do differ considerably in their proportions of men who attend church once a week or more (see Lenski, 1961: 48, who reported remarkably similar proportions for his 1958 Detroit sample) and who score high on the Devotionalism Scale (see footnote c, Table 3.5). Un-

fortunately, because efforts to determine subjective evaluations of the
relative standing of religious groups (comparable to the NORC (1947)
study of occupational prestige or the more recent study of the social standings of ethnic groups) have been unsuccessful,[9] the relative social standing
or prestige of religious groups can only be approximated for Protestant
groups by using their socioeconomic composition as an index of prestige.

As we did for the 22 ethnic groups, we submitted the matrix of indexes
of dissimilarity of friendship choices for the 15 religious groups (see

**Table 3.4. Percent distributions of respondents and friends by their religious
preferences and self-selection; ratios of self-selection and indexes of dissimilarity**

Religious Groups	(1) Percent Respondents	(2) Percent Friends	(3) Percent Self-Selection	(4) Ratio of Self-Selection (Col. 3 ÷ Col. 1)	(5) Indexes of Dissimilarity
Protestant groups					
Congregational	1.0%	0.5%	33.3%	33.3	41.5
Episcopal (Anglican)	3.3	2.6	20.4	6.2	29.1
Presbyterian	7.4	4.8	20.1	2.7	29.3
Nondenominational Protestant[a]	1.0	0.7	13.3	13.3	29.9
Methodist[b]	9.2	6.5	26.8	2.9	25.8
Lutheran	10.7	8.6	30.1	2.8	21.9
Protestant, no denom. specified	3.0	12.3	42.2	14.1	33.5
Baptist[c]	10.7	9.3	38.9	3.6	33.9
Church of Christ	1.6	1.2	33.3	20.8	50.5
Other fundamentalist sects[d]	1.6	0.6	17.4	10.9	45.5
Roman Catholic	42.1	41.4	62.3	1.5	21.6
Eastern Orthodox[e]	1.3	1.1	7.9	6.1	30.1
Jewish	2.8	3.6	79.5	28.4	76.4
No religious preference, other non-Christian	3.6	3.1	16.0	4.4	24.0
Not ascertained	0.7	3.8	30.0	42.9	47.0
	100.0	100.0			
Total N	(1013)	(2956)[f]			

[a] Includes nondenominational Protestant (explicitly reported as such), Unitarian, Christian (no further explanation), and Quaker groups.

[b] Includes Methodist, Evangelical and Reformed, Dutch or Christian Reformed, United
Church of Christ; 94 percent of this group were identified as Methodist.

[c] Includes American and Southern Baptist, Disciples of Christ, and United or Evangelical
Brethren; 97 percent of this group were Baptist.

[d] Includes Nazarene or Free Methodist, Jehovah's Witnesses, Assembly of God, Pente-
costal, Primitive Baptist, and other fundamentalist sects.

[e] Includes Greek, Russian, Roumanian, Serbian, and other Orthodox groups.

[f] The total N of 2956 friendship pairs departs from the expected 3039 cases (3 friends
times 1013 respondents) because some respondents did not name three friends.

Table 3.6) to smallest space analysis. The indexes for Congregationalists and Jews with all other groups suggest that they are relatively isolated or segregated from all other groups with respect to their patterns of friendship choice. The coefficients of alienation for the best one-space, two-space,

Table 3.5.   Socioeconomic and socioreligious characteristics of fifteen religious groups

Religious Groups	Total N	Socioeconomic Characteristics			Socioreligious Characteristics	
		Mean Family Income	Mean Occupational Status[a]	Mean School Years Completed	Percent Attend Church Once a Week or More[b]	Percent Highly Devotional[c]
Protestant groups	499	$10,117	45.3	12.0 yrs.	27.5%	32.7%
Congregational	10	17,500	82.7	16.5	40.0	30.0
Episcopal (Anglican)	34	13,000	59.9	13.0	20.5	20.6
Presbyterian	75	11,667	60.3	13.5	25.3	32.0
Nonden. Protest.	10	11,250	39.9	11.8	20.0	11.1
Methodist	93	10,703	45.0	12.1	22.8	31.9
Lutheran	110	10,375	42.9	12.0	33.6	41.3
Protestant, no denomination specified	32	9,727	48.8	11.5	9.4	21.9
Baptist	104	9,311	28.6	11.4	26.0	33.4
Church of Christ	16	8,636	23.3	11.5	56.3	31.3
Other fundamentalist sects	15	7,938	26.4	11.0	53.4	53.3
Roman Catholic	427	9,999	43.2	12.0	71.2	53.6
Eastern Orthodox	13	9,999	55.0	12.6	33.3	33.4
Jewish	29	14,688	65.0	15.7	3.4	17.2
No preference, other	38	10,357	55.0	12.1	0.0	5.2
Not ascertained	7	—[d]	—[d]	—[d]	—[d]	—[d]
Grand total	1013	$10,177	45.2	12.0	44.1	40.2

[a] See footnote c, Table 3.2.

[b] Respondents were asked: "Now referring to religion again, about how often, if ever, have you attended religious services in the last year?" For each group, we determined the proportion of people who answered "more than once a week" or "once a week." (See Q115, Appendix C.)

[c] "Devotionalism," following Lenski (1963: 25–26, 57–60), was measured by summing up the answers to two questions: (1) "When you have decisions to make in your everyday life, do you ask yourself what God would want you to do—often, sometimes, or never?" (2) "Which of these described most accurately how often you pray? a) more than once a day, b) once a day, c) once or twice a week, d) rarely, e) never." (See Q116 and Q117, Appendix C.) Respondents were considered highly devotional who said they prayed at least once or twice a week and considered God's wishes often or that they considered His wishes sometimes and prayed daily.

[d] Not calculated because the base is too small.

Table 3.6.   Indexes of dissimilarity of friendship choices for the 15 ethnoreligious groups*

Religious Groups	Religious Groups														
	(1)	(2)	(3)	(4)	(5)	(6)	(7)	(8)	(9)	(10)	(11)	(12)	(13)	(14)	(15)
Protestant groups															
1. Congregational	.00														
2. Presbyterian	.37	.00													
3. Episcopalian	.43	.25	.00												
4. Protestant (no denomination specified)	.42	.29	.44	.00											
5. Methodist	.38	.26	.32	.34	.00										
6. Lutheran	.45	.37	.36	.38	.33	.00									
7. Nondenominational Protestant	.40	.34	.41	.43	.36	.34	.00								
8. Baptist	.49	.39	.41	.42	.35	.43	.49	.00							
9. Other fundamentalists	.52	.50	.49	.50	.51	.51	.58	.26	.00						
10. Church of Christ	.59	.50	.61	.49	.50	.54	.50	.36	.40	.00					
Non-Protestant groups															
11. Roman Catholic	.50	.41	.38	.46	.42	.33	.43	.46	.55	.61	.00				
12. Eastern Orthodox	.56	.50	.35	.43	.51	.43	.46	.51	.61	.64	.21	.00			
13. Jew	.86	.79	.79	.82	.66	.81	.76	.80	.82	.84	.79	.79	.00		
14. No religious preference	.49	.41	.41	.45	.39	.33	.39	.48	.60	.59	.35	.32	.77	.00	
15. Not ascertained	.55	.55	.55	.46	.44	.55	.48	.60	.52	.45	.58	.44	.84	.49	.00

* The indexes presented in this table do not correspond to Table 3 with the same title in Laumann (1969b). Some time subsequent to publication of the article, we discovered that the wrong set of numbers had been inadvertently included as Table 3. Figure 3.2 in this chapter, however, is the same as Figure 1 in the article.

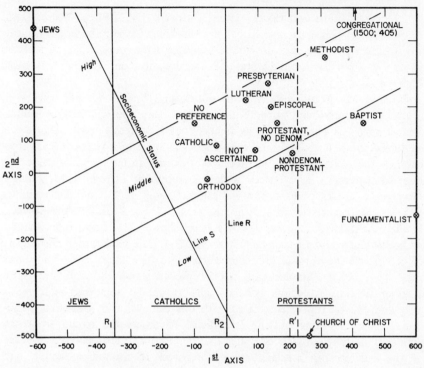

Figure 3.2 Graphic portrayal of proximity of religious groups, according to the indexes of dissimilarity of friendship choices. Coefficient of alienation = .180.

and three-space solutions were .283, .180, and .077 respectively—the latter two representing acceptable fits of the data. Since the three-space, a highly satisfactory fit, does not provide an appreciably sharper picture of the structure of the data, Figure 3.2 represents only the two-space solution. (It should be emphasized that the one-dimensional solution yields a *very poor* fit of the data matrix.)

The Jews and Congregationalists are shown to be completely isolated from the rest of the groups (this is reflective of the fact that these two groups have, as noted above, exceptionally high indexes of dissimilarity for all other groups). More generally, we can observe: First, the first axis may be divided by lines R_1 and R_2 into three parts which include only Jewish, Catholic, or Protestant groups. And within the Protestant region one can observe a gradient from the exceptionally "Protestant" denominations of Congregationalists, Baptists, other fundamentalists, and Church of Christ (to the right of the dotted vertical line R') to the more liturgically oriented denominations, which are closest to the Roman Catholic and Orthodox churches in religious belief and ritual (see Glock and

Stark, 1965; Stark and Glock, 1968; Gaustad, 1962; Mead, 1963; Demerath, 1965). Secondly, the groups are distributed along the line S according to their relative socioeconomic standing (the rank-order correlation of the group's mean family income and location on the line S is quite high (.817, $p < .01$)).[10]

Finally, we should take note of Glock and Stark's (1965) survey of church members living in the San Francisco Bay area concerning a number of religious beliefs, such as beliefs that God really exists, that Jesus is the Divine Son of God, and that Jesus was born of a virgin. The following are the percentage of members of denominations comparable to the ones in this study who agreed with the statement (1965: 91), "I know God really exists and I have no doubts about it.": Congregationalists (41%), Methodists (60%), Episcopalians (63%), Presbyterians (75%), Lutherans (78%), Baptists (80%), Catholics (81%), and other fundamentalist sects and Church of Christ (96%). The rank order correlation of groups on the vertical line R in Figure 3.2 with these nine groups was .929 ($p < .01$). (Similar rankings of groups would be obtained for a number of other religious beliefs.) Unfortunately, socioeconomic status also tends to be highly correlated with this dimension of Christian orthodoxy of beliefs, thus making it difficult to assess the extent to which similarity of religious beliefs rather than similarity of socioeconomic status of the membership are mediating the forces of mutual attraction and repulsion of religious groups.

In sum, the location of each group in a particular region of the space seems to be defined by the group's position on three facets, considered together.[11] The first facet reflects Herberg's tripartite religious division of the American social structure, but, by itself, is a very inadequate representation of all the information in Table 3.6. The second facet orders the groups in terms of their socioeconomic composition à la Niebuhr (1929) and Demerath (1965). The third facet is concerned with the differentiation of the Christian groups in terms of their religious beliefs and activities, with those denominations sharing certain liturgical and religious beliefs and an episcopal structure similar to Roman Catholicism being closer to the Catholics than the more "Protestant" groups, which emphasize a more congregational organizational structure.

THE SOCIAL STRUCTURE OF ETHNORELIGIOUS GROUPS

As noted above, many religious groups draw nearly all their membership from people of a given national origin, while others draw from a number of distinct nationality groups which, at least historically, often manifested considerable mutual antagonism (see Maynard, 1960). In the first set of religious groups, similarities of ethnic origin and religious affiliation are mutually reinforcing; in the second, they may be different and conflicting. A large body of sociological literature is devoted to an examination of the interplay of ethnic prejudice and hostility in patterning residential settlement, relative rates of socioeconomic assimilation, and even formal and informal relations in organizational settings (see Lieberson, 1963; Glazer and Moynihan, 1963; Gordon, 1964; Zaleznik et al., 1958). An interesting question thus arises: to what extent will ethnic differences override religious similarities in the formation of friendships? For example, will German Catholics prefer to associate with other Germans, even if they are Protestants, or with other Catholics, even if they are not German?

In order to answer such questions, we are faced with the difficult problem that there are many ethnic and religious groups in Detroit, and a simple permutation of the two attributes would generate too many groups with too small frequencies to sustain analysis. With an eye to maintaining reasonable numbers in substantively meaningful groups, we have summarized in Table 3.7 socioeconomic and socioreligious characteristics for 27 ethnoreligious combinations (see footnote a, Table 3.7, for details on the persons included in each group). It is readily apparent that Roman Catholics, as well as Protestants, are quite variable in socioeconomic characteristics and religious beliefs and activities when ethnic origin is taken into account.

Table 3.8 presents the matrix of indexes of dissimilarity for the 27 ethnoreligious groups; it was this matrix that was submitted to the Guttman-Lingoes (Lingoes, 1965a) computer routine. The coefficients of alienation for the best one-space, two-space, and three-space were .377, .202, and .132, respectively. Since the one- and two-space coefficients are unacceptably high, we shall use the three-space solution. Figures 3.3a, 3.3b, and 3.3c are the graphic representations of the three cross-sections of the three-space solution. The three-dimensional solution (see Figure 3.3d) may be conceived as three boxes, one for each broad religious category, stacked with the Protestant box on the bottom, the Catholic box in the middle, and the Jewish "box" (actually a single point located in an extremely isolated region of the space) on the top. The first (vertical) axis clearly segregates the three broad religious categories, with only one Protestant group—the Scandinavian Lutherans—and the Germans and Anglo-Americans with no religious preference being located in the Catholic box. As in Figure 3.2, one can readily see in Figure 3.3a (which shows a cross-section of the space in terms of the first and third axis) that the more "Protestant" groups of Anglo-American and German Methodists, Anglo-American and German Baptists, and German "Presbyterians" (of

Table 3.7.   Socioeconomic and socioreligious characteristics of 27 ethnoreligious groups

Ethnoreligious Group[a]	Total N	Socioeconomic Characteristics			Socioreligious Characteristics			
		Mean Family Income	Mean Occupational Status[b]	Mean School Years Completed	Percent Attend Church Once a Week or More[c]	Percent Highly Devotional[d]	Percent Third Generation or More[e]	Mean Subjective Ethnic Interest[f]
Protestant groups	499	$10,117	45.3	12.0 yrs.	27.5%	32.7%	82.4%	0.37
German Presbyterian*	25	14,999	58.8	13.8	40.0	24.0	92.0	0.29
Anglo-American Presbyterians*	70	12,639	65.0	13.7	22.2	33.3	84.7	0.42
Scandinavian Protestants	14	12,000	65.0	16.0	42.8	21.4	84.7	0.31
Slavic Protestants	12	12,000	59.9	12.5	25.0	8.3	25.0	1.00
German Lutherans*	57	11,635	43.1	12.2	38.6	47.4	71.9	0.49
German Methodists*	32	11,154	52.5	12.8	28.2	38.7	78.1	0.37
German Protestants	15	10,625	35.0	11.2	26.7	14.2	73.3	0.50
Anglo-American Methodists*	39	10,357	45.0	11.4	22.5	30.0	77.5	0.33
Anglo-American Prot., no denomination specified	26	9,999	55.0	11.6	3.8	23.0	88.5	0.05
French Protestants	28	9,999	38.8	11.8	25.9	40.7	92.9	0.12
German Baptists	27	9,250	29.2	11.5	37.0	34.6	74.1	0.27
Anglo-American Lutherans	29	9,100	27.5	11.7	20.6	28.6	79.4	0.13
Anglo-American Baptists*	80	8,941	26.5	10.2	30.0	32.9	91.3	0.11
Scandinavian Lutherans	12	8,500	46.7	12.5	33.3	41.7	66.7	0.80
Protestants, ethnic origin unknown*	33	8,286	26.7	9.5	16.7	30.0	76.7	1.08
Roman Catholic groups	427	9,999	43.2	12.0	71.2	53.6	58.4	0.79
Anglo-American Catholics*	33	12,167	37.0	11.2	60.7	56.2	72.7	0.57
Irish Catholics*	60	12,054	56.9	12.7	80.0	53.1	83.1	0.42
German Catholics*	78	9,944	45.3	12.2	70.9	50.6	81.3	0.41

Polish Catholics*	106	9,917	33.8	11.0	67.3	58.4	35.1	1.34
Italian Catholics*	54	9,700	40.8	12.0	60.0	37.8	25.5	0.94
Slavic Catholics*	38	9,647	39.9	12.3	65.8	54.0	26.3	1.18
French Catholics*	49	9,625	37.5	12.0	76.5	60.8	92.2	0.40
Catholics, ethnic origin unknown	9	—g	—g	—g	—g	—g	—g	—g
Eastern Orthodox	10	12,500	59.9	13.5	30.0	20.0	30.0	1.11
Jews*	29	14,688	65.0	14.8	3.4	17.2	17.2	1.93
Germans, no preference	14	9,750	9.9	12.0	—	—	71.4	0.19
Anglo-Americans, no preference	15	8,999	35.0	8.7	20.0	20.0	93.4	0.39

a In order to keep the frequencies for ethnoreligious groups at reasonable levels for analysis, both ethnic groups and religious groups were combined into larger categories. Ethnic groups were combined as follows: "Anglo-American" includes Americans, English, Scotch, Irish Protestants, non-French Canadians, and Welsh; "French" includes French and French Canadians; "German" includes German speakers (95 percent of the total), Dutch, and Belgians; "Italian" includes 50 Italians and 5 Spanish surnames (Mexican, Puerto Rican, Latin American); "Scandinavian" includes Norwegians, Danes, Swedes, and Finns; "Slavic" includes Russians, Czechs, Balkan states, Lithuanians, Estonians, Hungarians, Armenians, etc. "Poles" and "Irish Catholics" were not combined with any other group.

The religious groups were combined as follows: "Presbyterian" includes Presbyterians, Congregationalists, and Episcopalians; "Baptist" includes Baptists, Church of Christ and other fundamental sects; "Protestant" includes all other religious denominations not explicitly recognized in a given nationality group. "Jews" were treated as one group, regardless of national origin or preference (Conservative, Reformed) within Judaism; the "Eastern Orthodox" were also treated as one group regardless of national origin.

b See footnote c, Table 3.2.
c See footnote b, Table 3.5.
d See footnote c, Table 3.5.
e See Chapter 9, pp. 000–000, for explanation.
f The degree of subjective ethnic interest was measured by counting the number of "yes" answers to the following three questions: (1) "At Christmas or Easter, do you usually follow any traditions that are especially associated with (country of origin) ways of celebrating these holidays? (2) "Are you especially interested in what goes on today in (country of origin; for Jews, do you usually celebrate any Jewish holiday?)" (2) "Are you especially interested in what goes on today in (country of origin; for Jews, Israel) – that is, more than you are interested in most other foreign countries?" (3) "Do you especially like some (country of origin or Jewish) foods more than you like most other foreign foods?" (See Q109–Q112, Appendix C.)
g Not calculated because frequency base too small.
* See Chapter 8, p. 168, for explanation.

Table 3.8. Indexes of dissimilarity of friendship choices for 27 ethnoreligious groups

Ethnoreligious Groups	Ethnoreligious Groups								
	1	2	3	4	5	6	7	8	9
Protestant groups									
1. German Presbyterians	.00	—	—	—	—	—	—	—	—
2. Anglo-American Presbyterians	.35	.00	—	—	—	—	—	—	—
3. Scandinavian Protestants	.38	.37	.00	—	—	—	—	—	—
4. Slavic Protestants	.42	.41	.50	.00	—	—	—	—	—
5. German Lutherans	.52	.41	.55	.46	.00	—	—	—	—
6. German Methodists	.63	.62	.69	.65	.67	.00	—	—	—
7. German Protestants	.48	.36	.48	.38	.36	.64	.00	—	—
8. Anglo-American Methodists	.54	.40	.55	.38	.55	.62	.48	.00	—
9. Anglo-American Protestants, other	.54	.41	.50	.38	.42	.55	.30	.40	.00
10. French Protestants	.44	.31	.45	.39	.39	.54	.32	.48	.36
11. German Baptists	.65	.53	.66	.50	.51	.59	.46	.60	.43
12. Anglo-American Lutherans	.59	.48	.54	.49	.36	.66	.49	.56	.44
13. Anglo-American Baptists	.76	.66	.73	.62	.64	.68	.59	.64	.52
14. Scandinavian Lutherans	.65	.51	.68	.53	.55	.83	.50	.61	.51
15. Protestants, ethnic origin unknown	.56	.39	.47	.37	.43	.54	.34	.42	.26
Roman Catholic groups									
16. Anglo-American Catholics	.53	.39	.50	.47	.44	.60	.36	.50	.39
17. Irish Catholics	.56	.43	.54	.52	.47	.59	.41	.54	.45
18. German Catholics	.51	.37	.49	.45	.42	.67	.33	.49	.44
19. Polish Catholics	.66	.50	.60	.55	.48	.71	.45	.57	.48
20. Italian Catholics	.60	.39	.55	.44	.42	.56	.35	.51	.42
21. Slavic Catholics	.65	.55	.61	.44	.49	.75	.45	.55	.48
22. French Catholics	.64	.53	.56	.52	.50	.69	.35	.58	.40
23. Catholics, ethnic origin unknown	.59	.41	.49	.39	.45	.60	.30	.48	.34
24. Eastern Orthodox	.71	.64	.65	.58	.68	.90	.55	.69	.67
25. Jews	.74	.68	.75	.75	.64	.82	.63	.76	.66
26. Germans, no religious preference	.60	.50	.57	.38	.51	.67	.41	.51	.40
27. Anglo-Americans, no religious preference	.54	.48	.54	.41	.45	.68	.44	.51	.42

Table 3.8.   (Continued)

						Ethnoreligious Groups											
10	11	12	13	14	15	16	17	18	19	20	21	22	23	24	25	26	27
—	—	—	—	—	—	—	—	—	—	—	—	—	—	—	—	—	—
—	—	—	—	—	—	—	—	—	—	—	—	—	—	—	—	—	—
—	—	—	—	—	—	—	—	—	—	—	—	—	—	—	—	—	—
—	—	—	—	—	—	—	—	—	—	—	—	—	—	—	—	—	—
—	—	—	—	—	—	—	—	—	—	—	—	—	—	—	—	—	—
—	—	—	—	—	—	—	—	—	—	—	—	—	—	—	—	—	—
—	—	—	—	—	—	—	—	—	—	—	—	—	—	—	—	—	—
—	—	—	—	—	—	—	—	—	—	—	—	—	—	—	—	—	—
—	—	—	—	—	—	—	—	—	—	—	—	—	—	—	—	—	—
.00	—	—	—	—	—	—	—	—	—	—	—	—	—	—	—	—	—
.43	.00	—	—	—	—	—	—	—	—	—	—	—	—	—	—	—	—
.46	.57	.00	—	—	—	—	—	—	—	—	—	—	—	—	—	—	—
.57	.41	.68	.00	—	—	—	—	—	—	—	—	—	—	—	—	—	—
.42	.56	.52	.60	.00	—	—	—	—	—	—	—	—	—	—	—	—	—
.30	.41	.50	.42	.50	.00	—	—	—	—	—	—	—	—	—	—	—	—
.32	.48	.48	.60	.40	.38	.00	—	—	—	—	—	—	—	—	—	—	—
.35	.51	.49	.65	.47	.23	.23	.00	—	—	—	—	—	—	—	—	—	—
.37	.46	.52	.65	.38	.41	.26	.32	.00	—	—	—	—	—	—	—	—	—
.47	.56	.60	.64	.50	.47	.35	.38	.37	.00	—	—	—	—	—	—	—	—
.34	.43	.48	.56	.53	.36	.27	.33	.34	.34	.00	—	—	—	—	—	—	—
.51	.57	.56	.68	.47	.50	.40	.46	.34	.40	.41	.00	—	—	—	—	—	—
.44	.48	.52	.57	.46	.42	.32	.40	.36	.41	.38	.45	.00	—	—	—	—	—
.33	.42	.56	.52	.46	.27	.24	.32	.33	.40	.27	.40	.39	.00	—	—	—	—
.64	.69	.73	.75	.48	.61	.57	.61	.54	.55	.59	.38	.52	.56	.00	—	—	—
.69	.65	.72	.74	.73	.67	.65	.67	.65	.67	.67	.75	.64	.67	.72	.00	—	—
.43	.48	.52	.56	.44	.39	.37	.44	.35	.46	.36	.42	.39	.29	.50	.70	.00	—
.35	.53	.49	.65	.49	.38	.35	.33	.33	.47	.44	.42	.43	.39	.53	.69	.31	.00

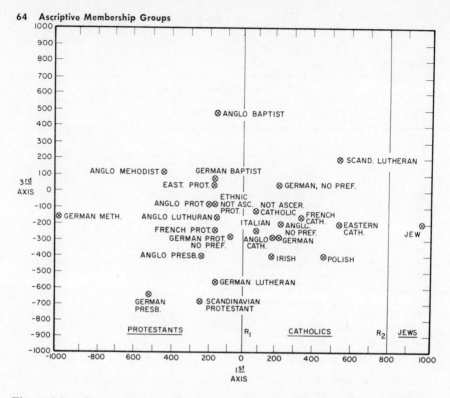

Figure 3.3a Cross section of the three-dimensional solution in terms of the first and third axes for all groups.

whom only a few are Episcopalians) are farther away from the Catholic groups than the Lutheran groups and the Anglo-American "Presbyterians" (of whom well over half are Episcopalians). The Catholic groups, despite their ethnic heterogeneity, form a relatively tight cluster in the center box, while the Jews are again quite isolated from all other groups.

Figure 3.3b and 3.3c portray cross-sections of the Protestant and Catholic boxes in terms of the second and third axes. For the Protestants (Figure 3.3b), the group's location on the line S has a rank-order correlation of .675 ($p < .01$) with the group's mean family income. All the groups below the line S are German, while groups above the line are Anglo-American groups (with two exceptions, the French and Eastern (Slavic) Protestants). Notice that the pair, Anglo-American and German Lutherans, fall on the line S in the high status sector but fall at some considerable distance from each other on the line C_1. This pattern may also be observed for the Anglo-American and German Methodists in the middle status sector and the Anglo-American and German Baptists in the lower status sector. More generally there is a rank-order correlation of

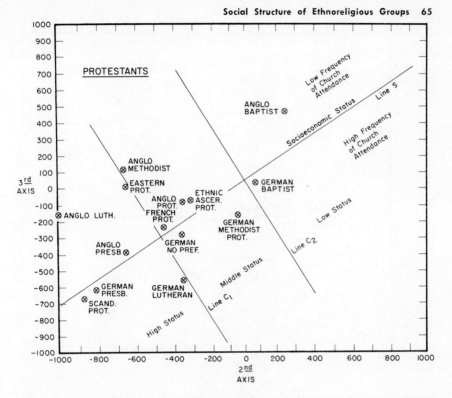

Figure 3.3b Cross section of the three-dimensional solution in terms of the second and third axes for Protestant groups only.

.618 ($p < .05$) between their location on the line C_1 and the proportion of the group who attend church once a week or more. Thus the socioeconomic status of the group appears to vary along the line S, while the line S divides the space into two regions of low and high church attendance, respectively. For the Catholics (Figure 4.3c), there is no relation between their location along line S and their mean family income; but it should be remembered that, except for the Irish and Anglo-American Catholics, there are no appreciable differences among them with regard to family income. They are, however, differentiated along the line C_1 according to their frequency of church attendance (.679, $p < .05$). It might also be noted that the more "ethnic" Catholic groups of Poles, Italians, Irish, and French are below the line S while Anglo-American and German groups (the most assimilated ethnic groups) are above the line.

For the entire set of groups (excluding the Catholics, ethnic group not ascertained, see Table 3.7), the rank-order correlation of their location along the line S and median family income is .449 ($p < .05$), but if the

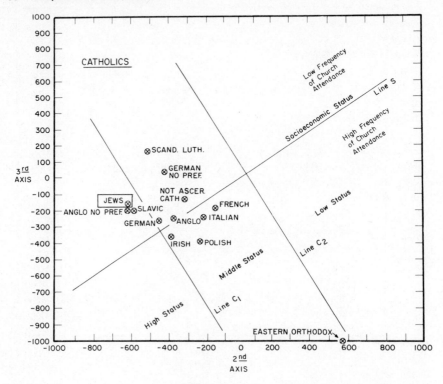

Figure 3.3c Cross section of the three-dimensional solution in terms of the second and third axes for Catholic and Jewish groups.

Eastern Orthodox (which have a twenty-rank discrepancy between their income rank and location on the line S) are also excluded,[12] the correlation rises to .658 ($p < .01$). And again (excluding the same two groups), the rank-order correlation of a group's location on the line C_1 and proportion attending church once a week or more is .622 ($p < .01$).[13] The rather consistent location of Anglo-American groups, whether Protestant or Catholic, above the line S, and the non-Anglo-American groups below the line S, suggest that an "ethnic" factor may be involved in distributing the groups in the space. But since Anglo-American groups, in general, also tend to have lower frequencies of church attendance relative to non-Anglo-American groups, there is some ambiguity with regard to interpreting this "third factor," to wit: is it a factor of ethnicity or religious involvement?

In brief, the location of each group in a particular region of the three-space seems to be defined by the group's position on three facets comparable to those identified in the two-space solution for religious groups:

(1) the tripartite religious division, (2) the socioeconomic composition of the group, and (3) its characteristic religious activities and beliefs which, in the ethnoreligious solution, seem to be confounded with an ethnic effect.

SUMMARY AND CONCLUSIONS

We have attempted to analyze the formation of friendship relationships among 22 ethnic, 15 religious, and 27 ethnoreligious groups, utilizing the relatively new technique of smallest space analysis. Certain anomalies in the interpretation of the ethnic solution forced us to consider the relevance of religious differences among ethnic groups. Three facets appear to account for the relative proximities of the 15 religious groups. First, there is confirmation of Herberg's hypothesis that the American social structure is divided into three religious groupings: Protestant, Catholic, and Jewish. Second, religious outgroup selection of friends follows the lines of similarity of socioeconomic status. And thirdly, similarity of religious beliefs and styles of worship may also be a factor, but some caution in accepting the relevance of this facet must be noted because of its relatively high association with the second facet, socioeconomic status—that is, groups with liberal religious beliefs tend also to be groups of high socioeconomic composition.

In order to assess the possible role of ethnic considerations in modifying this structure, we combined ethnic and religious attributes of respondents and their friends into 27 ethnoreligious groups. Again we found that the structure is differentiated into the three broad religious groupings and, within these groupings, along the socioeconomic status lines. There is, moreover, evidence that beyond these two facets, the structure is differentiated along a dimension of religious involvement (as indexed by the group's relative rate of church attendance), but that this may be confounded with an ethnic "effect" as the Anglo-American groups in general tend to have lower rates of church attendance than the other groups.

In sum, the results of the smallest space analyses, based, let us reemphasize, on a sample of *native* white men, clearly indicate that a single dimension by itself (presumably ordering the groups into Herberg's tripartite division) is totally inadequate for representing the structure of intimate associations among religious groups. (The coefficients of alienation, measures of the goodness of fit, are simply unacceptably large for 1-space solutions for either the 15 or 27 groups.) The rival "Niebuhr-Demerath" model which stresses the continuing significance of underlying social compositional differences among the various groups appears

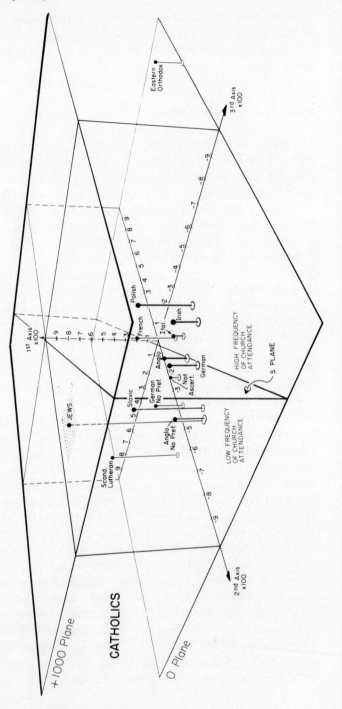

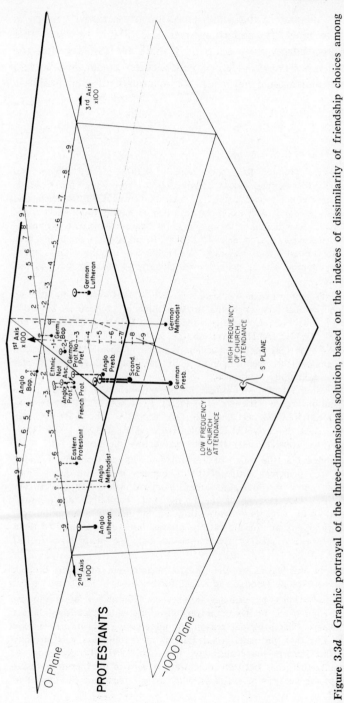

Figure 3.3d Graphic portrayal of the three-dimensional solution, based on the indexes of dissimilarity of friendship choices among 27 ethnoreligious groups. Coefficient of alienation = .132.

to represent more adequately the social structure of ascriptive groups in Detroit. Keeping in mind the underlying rationale of our approach that was sketched in the introductory chapter, I think we can say that the smallest space analyses have provided us with a better model than we had before of the multidimensional nature of the macrostructure of ascriptive groups.

NOTES

1. A recent National Opinion Research Council (NORC) survey (Hodge and Siegel, forthcoming), for example, asked respondents to sort some thirty ethnic groups in terms of their relative social standing. British, German, Dutch, Irish, and French ethnic groups—all early arrivals—were regarded as having the highest social standing; Polish, Czech, Scandinavian, Hungarian, and Spanish-American groups as having intermediate standing; and Mexican, Puerto Rican, Negro, and Japanese groups as having the lowest social standing. See Table 3.2 for the NORC mean evaluations of social standing for the groups corresponding to those included in this study.

2. The respondent's ethnic origin was determined by his response to the following question: "What nationality background do you think of yourself as having— that is, besides being American (Canadian)? (ACCEPT CLEAR ASSERTION OF 'ONLY AMERICAN NATIONALITY' WITHOUT PROBE. ALWAYS RECORD EXACT ANSWER.)" (See Q91 in the interview schedule, Appendix C.) Although we allowed the respondent to mention more than one nationality, this chapter considers only the first nationality mentioned.

For each of the three friends, we asked the respondent: "Do you happen to know the original nationality of (friend)? (REPEAT FOR EACH FRIEND. EN- COURAGE RESPONDENT TO 'GUESS' IF NECESSARY. IF 'AMERICAN', PROBE FOR 'ORIGINAL NATIONALITY BESIDES AMERICAN'.)" (See Q21, Appendix C.) Again we consider only the first nationality mentioned.

3. It might be noted that the index of dissimilarity between Columns 1 and 2 in Table 3.1 is 16.7. The principal source of the discrepancy in the two distributions arises from the "don't know" or "not ascertained" category, where only 2.0 percent of the respondents, but 13.4 percent of the friends fall. Typically, "don't know" responses are deleted from percentage distributions on the hopeful assumption that they are distributed randomly among the various groups, but we have included them here because our subsequent smallest space analyses will use them as a distinct category.

4. Each respondent was asked to sort 38 groups into ten categories, ranging from low to high social standing (Hodge and Siegel, forthcoming).

5. It should be noted that by utilizing indexes of dissimilarity we are trans- forming the original *asymmetric* matrix of percent distributions of friendship choices into a *symmetric* matrix. The principal reason for undertaking this transformation is to circumvent the fact that the matrix of conditional probabilities is very strongly affected by the relative sizes of the groups (see Bonacich, 1967; also Appendix A, pp. 238–240). Recently there has been an increasing concern in the literature (espe- cially that directed to the analysis of social mobility tables) regarding the impact of

size on the analysis of such tables (see Mosteller, 1968). Recognizing the possibility of artifactual results arising from size differences among rows and columns, Rogoff (1953) attempted to deal with the problem by calculating ratios of the conditional probabilities over the row (or column) marginal percentages (equivalent to our ratios of self-selection). But Duncan (Blau and Duncan, 1967: 90–97) has shown that these resulting ratios are still not independent of the marginals; given the cell entries and the total N, one can reproduce the marginal distributions. To date, there has been no generally satisfactory resolution of this problem. Even the indexes of dissimilarity that Blau and Duncan (1967: 67–75) and I employ are not completely free of these difficulties, but there is little question that the effect of size is substantially reduced when they are used.

For purposes of comparison, I calculated the smallest space solutions (see Appendix A) utilizing the conditional probabilities as the original data matrix (see Lingoes, 1965b). While it is true that the larger groups tended to be found toward the center of the space, it was also true that the substantive interpretations of the dimensions were identical to those we suggest for the solutions based on the matrix of indexes of dissimilarity. In short, our substantive conclusions were not materially affected whatever the original character of the original data matrix.

6.   The Detroit SMSA has an exceptionally high concentration of Poles when compared to other large SMSAs. Indeed among the twenty largest SMSAs, Detroit is tied for second place with Chicago in the percentage of Poles of the total foreign stock residing in the SMSA in 1960 (16.8 percent). It might be that the relatively high concentration of an ethnic group in a given city may be related to a higher rate of assimilation.

7.   The following sections are a revised version of a previously published article (Laumann, 1969b), reprinted with the permission of the *American Sociological Review* and the American Sociological Association.

8.   The respondent's religious preference was determined by his response to the following question: "Do you have a religious preference? That is, are you either Protestant, Roman Catholic, Jewish, or something else? (If Protestant: What specific denomination is that? If Jewish: Do you consider yourself Orthodox, Conservative, Reform, or none of these?)" (See Q89 in the interview schedule, Appendix C.)

For each of his three friends, the respondent was asked: "Do you know what (friend)'s religious preference is? (Where "Protestant," obtain denomination.) (See Q20 in the interview schedule, Appendix C.)

9.   The NORC national survey cited above (Hodge and Siegel, forthcoming) attempted such an evaluation of 21 religious groups, but was largely unsuccessful in interpreting the results.

10.   To determine a group's location on a particular line, such as the line S, one simply draws a perpendicular line from the line to the group.

11.   An interesting question arises concerning the extent to which the structure of intimate associations among religious groups, defined by friendship choice, would be similar to one defined by intermarriage choice. Because we asked the respondent about the religious preferences of his father and father-in-law, we are in a position to perform the same analysis on intermarriage choice. Several cautions arising out of the use of fathers' preferences should be noted. First, we are in effect looking at the structure of religious outchoice a "generation ago," when certain groups, especially Catholics, were of considerably lower socioeconomic status than today and may, indeed, differ in other respects as well. Second, Duncan (Blau and Duncan,

1967: 81–90) has shown that a representative sample of the population at a given point in time will not yield a representative sample of fathers a generation ago because of differential fertility and mortality (which affect the chances of a father being included in the "sample") and other factors (for example, 60-year-old men are reporting characteristics of fathers who were alive much earlier than the fathers of 25 year olds). Moreover, our sample is considerably reduced in size (from 2956 friendship pairs to 929 marriage pairs), which has the effect of increasing sampling errors arising from small frequencies in certain categories.

Limitations of space prevent us from reporting the table containing the relevant data matrix and the resulting solution. Suffice it to say that the marriage "picture" was almost identical to the one we obtained for the friendship data.

12. Eastern Orthodox is the only group that has an unusually "poor fit" in the three-dimensional solution. This may be due to some statistical aberration arising from the small number of people involved or from the fact that they are really different on a factor not captured in only a three-dimensional solution.

13. While frequency of church attendance appears to differentiate the groups on the line C, devotionalism (see Table 3.7) is uncorrelated with frequency of church attendance and location on the line C. As Lenski (1963: 22–28) has argued, devotionalism appears to tap a different aspect of religious involvement and orientation (that is, pietism) than frequency of church attendance, which apparently taps *associational* involvement in the religious group. Perhaps, therefore, it should not be surprising that frequency of church attendance can be meaningfully related to the structure of religious associations, while devotionalism is unrelated.

CHAPTER 4

The Social Structure of Occupations: The Role of Achievement-Based Criteria in Friendship Choice

ACHIEVEMENT-ORIENTED CRITERIA OF FRIENDSHIP CHOICE

The last chapter considered the structuring of men's friendship choices solely on the grounds of their ascriptive group memberships. It was assumed that ethnoreligious groups differ among themselves in their mutual attractiveness—that is, members of groups possessing similar attributes of social repute, cultural origins, ethnic and religious beliefs, and values will be drawn toward one another while members of dissimilar groups will tend to avoid one another. This chapter turns to an equally important basis for structuring friendship choices—that of achievement-oriented criteria. Here we will be concerned with the selection of friends on the basis of their similarities in occupational and educational achievements or, more broadly conceived, socioeconomic or worldly success. These bases for friendship formation focus on a man's performances—attributes that he has expended some effort to achieve—rather than on attributes to which he has been more or less "assigned" at birth.

Considerable theoretical and empirical attention has been directed to analyzing the patterning of sociometric choices by socioeconomic status (King, 1961; Riecken and Homans, 1954; Duncan and Duncan, 1955; Ellis, 1957; Curtis, 1963; Laumann, 1966). One general descriptive hypothesis, often advanced and supported, suggests that people tend to choose others for intimate relationships who are similar to themselves in various socioeconomic respects. The explanation for this pattern of equality in achievement rests on several considerations. First, relatively similar socioeconomic status facilitates intimate association by enabling *reciprocity* in the exchange of valued goods and services, such as visiting and dining in each other's homes (see Blau, 1956, 1964; Laumann, 1966: 133–34). Major discrepancies in the ability of friends to pay for mutual entertainments or for status display (for example, how one furnishes his living room, see Laumann and House, 1970) puts considerable strain on a relationship that is presumably premised on being *peers* (equals). Moreover, people of similar socioeconomic status share many values, problems, and experiences that provide bases for common interests. Finally, because there is ecological segregation of people according to their ability to pay for housing (Duncan and Duncan, 1955; Tilly, 1961), neighborhoods tend to be relatively homogeneous socioeconomically. Sheer physical propinquity in the neighborhood and at work facilitates the formation of intimate social relationships, but propinquity tends to juxtapose persons possessing similar socioeconomic characteristics. Consequently, the physical availability of persons with whom to become friends tends to be heavily influenced by similarities in achieved status. Because most studies have had only a limited number of cases for analysis, investigators have been constrained to measure socioeconomic status fairly crudely—often in terms of a simple dichotomy of manual and nonmanual occupations or, at best, in terms of four or five occupational categories. Such crude measurements tend to obscure the presence of "factors" differentiating occupations from one another other than their "prestige" or socioeconomic status that might be involved in determining the pattern of intimate association.

In an earlier attempt, Laumann and Guttman (1966) utilized smallest space analysis to describe the occupational associations of a sample of white men in Cambridge-Belmont, Massachusetts. Duncan's (1961) two-digit Index of Socioeconomic Status was employed to identify 55 occupational categories. Unfortunately, in order to build up a sufficient number of cases to sustain analysis, we were forced to combine the respondent's reports on the occupations of his friends, neighbors, father, and father-in-law—all persons likely to have some kind of relationship with the respondent but, nonetheless, all relationships varying considerably among themselves in their degree of intimacy and modes of formation. Moreover, the Index itself often put occupations of considerable heterogeneity into the same code category (see, for example, Haug and Sussman, 1968; Chapter 9, pp. 193–194 below), thus obscuring the underlying structure. Finally, we were not sufficiently alerted to problems arising from the differing numbers of people in the various categories—the so-called size effect (see Bonacich, 1967, but see Appendix A below, pp. 238–240). Despite these difficulties, we were successful in showing the unambiguous relevance of prestige differences *and* the probable relevance of bureaucratic and entrepreneurial differences among occupations in accounting for the relative proximities of occupations to one another (see Chapter 1, pp. 10–11).

In the present chapter we deal with some of these limitations: first, by limiting the analysis only to friends reported by the respondents;[1] second, by utilizing a new occupational code suggested by Blau and Duncan (1967: 26–29), but modified somewhat to permit explicit identification within various industry groups of those who are self-employed and those who are employees; and third, by manipulating the data in such a way as to reduce the size effect. As we shall see again, occupational prestige alone will not suffice to account for the relative locations of occupations. One must also consider the nature of the occupational activity: whether it takes place in a large-scale bureaucratic setting, such as an automobile assembly line, or in relatively small, autonomous work groups or alone.

THE SOCIAL STRUCTURE OF OCCUPATIONAL GROUPS

Utilizing the same indicators of within-group selection we employed to describe ethnic and religious group friendship patterns in the preceding chapter, Table 4.1 presents these measures for occupational friendship choice.[2] It is especially noteworthy that various self-employed groups, including self-employed professionals, proprietors and sales workers of various kinds, and the lowest skill groups, have unusually high indexes of dissimilarity for their choice pattern when compared to the total sample distribution of friends while managers and lower-level employees of bureaucracies (for example, clerical workers and operatives) manifest the weakest tendencies toward occupational exclusiveness in friendship selection (see Column 5). The former groups, then, are relatively more segregated or isolated from the general population than any of the other groups, at least with respect to their patterns of friendship selection. We might speculate either that these groups form more distinctive, homogeneous occupational subcommunities with associated styles of life and value orientations that make the members especially attractive to one another, or that their friendship choices are constrained because of the segregated ecologies of their work settings—that is, people from other occupational groups are not frequently found in their places of work. The last two columns of Table 4.2 provide some evidence that supports this speculation in that the occupational categories with unusually high indexes of dissimilarity (Column 5, Table 4.1) are also those that tend to have unusually high work hours per week (and therefore relatively less "free time" to spend with others not related to their occupational roles) and stronger preferences for entrepreneurial jobs (that might be taken to be indicative of distinctive occupational values).

To be sure, the 16 occupational groups differ considerably among

Table 4.1. Percent distributions of respondents and friends by their occupational categories and self-selection; ratios of self-selection and indexes of dissimilarity

Occupational Group	(1) Percent of Respondents	(2) Percent of Friends	(3) Percent Self-Selection	(4) Ratio of Self-Selection	(5) Indexes of Dissimilarity
1. Professional, technical, and kindred, self-employed	2.1%	2.7%	43.5%	16.1	52.3
2. Professional, technical, salaried	17.0	15.8	44.7	2.8	30.5
3. Managers and officials	10.1	10.9	28.0	2.6	24.0
4. Sales workers, other	3.2	3.3	10.9	3.3	30.6
5. Sales workers, self-employed	0.7	1.1	19.0	17.3	52.8
6. Proprietors	5.3	8.5	26.1	3.1	31.1
7. Clerical and kindred	6.1	5.5	15.3	2.8	16.5
8. Sales workers, retail and wholesale	2.1	2.9	23.7	8.2	41.6
9. Craftsmen, foremen, and kindred, manufacturing	14.0	11.4	25.4	2.2	23.8
10. Craftsmen, foremen, and kindred, other	6.5	9.2	26.7	2.9	23.2
11. Craftsmen, foremen, and kindred, construction	4.8	4.8	24.5	5.1	21.9
12. Operatives and kindred, manufacturing	14.8	10.7	25.7	2.4	26.4
13. Operatives and kindred, other	7.4	6.5	22.3	3.4	25.0
14. Service workers, except private household	4.0	3.9	32.7	8.4	33.6
15. Laborers, manufacturing	0.8	1.0	26.1	26.1	55.5
16. Laborers, other	1.0	1.6	10.0	6.3	41.8
Totals	100.0	100.0			
N	(1013)	(2874)*			

* The total N of 2874 friendship pairs departs from the expected 3039 cases (3 friends times 1013 respondents) because some respondents did not name three friends.

themselves on other measures of socioeconomic status, such as mean school years completed and mean family income, as well. Table 4.2 presents these means, together with other selected summary indicators of social differences, including the proportion Roman Catholic, the median number of employees at the place of work, median hours worked per week, and the proportion favoring entrepreneurial employment. The rank-order correlation between mean school years completed and mean family income is .752 ($p < .01$). Given the central assumption developed in the introductory chapter, that similarities in status and other attributes are critical facilitating factors in the formation of intimate relationships, the

Table 4.2. Selected socioeconomic characteristics of men in sixteen occupational categories

Occupation of Respondent	N	(1) Mean School Years Completed	(2) Mean Family Income	(3) Percent Roman Catholic	(4) Median Number of People at Work Place	(5) Median Hours Per Week Worked	(6) Percent Preferring Entrepreneurial Job[a]
Professional, self-employed	23	17+ yrs.	$17,188	43.5%	5[b]	55.8 hrs.	78.3%
Professional, salaried	170	15.5	12,240	32.9	500+	48.0	58.0
Managers and officials	101	13.1	12,586	44.6	500+	51.9	74.3
Sales workers, other	31	12.8	11,731	48.4	499	47.0	83.9
Sales workers, self-employed	7	14.1	13,125	28.6	1[b]	65.0	100.0
Proprietors	53	11.9	14,545	45.3	7[b]	58.5	88.7
Clerical and kindred	64	12.2	9,500	37.5	500+	46.9	62.5
Sales workers, retail and wholesale	22	12.4	9,813	31.8	75	52.5	86.4
Craftsmen, foremen, manufacturing	141	11.6	10,444	51.8	500+	49.0	63.8
Craftsmen, foremen, other	64	11.8	8,810	60.9	500+	47.9	60.9
Craftsmen, foremen, construction	48	10.9	10,435	41.7	48	47.5	70.8
Operatives, manufacturing	150	10.9	8,519	38.0	500+	47.0	56.7
Operatives, other	73	10.7	8,853	35.6	200	52.8	79.5
Service workers	39	11.8	9,250	43.6	500+	49.2	59.0
Laborers, manufacturing	8	10.0	5,667	25.0	500+	44.3	87.5
Laborers, other	10	11.7	6,600	70.0	499	46.0	50.0
Totals	1,013	12.0	10,108	42.5	500+	48.7	66.9

[a] Respondents were asked: "Now, picture two men: one who owns his own small business, and another who works in a large office. The office worker earns a steady income and works eight hours a day. Then he can forget his work and enjoy his leisure time. The other man runs his small business for much longer hours every day and so cannot take time out to enjoy life like the office worker. The small businessman can't be certain of his income, but he does have the chance to earn more than the office worker. If you had to choose, which of these kinds of work would you prefer?" (See Q57, Appendix C.)

[b] Respondents who were self-employed reported the number of people they employed.

Table 4.3.   Indexes of dissimilarity of friendship choices for 16 occupational groups

Occupational Groups	1	2	3	4	5	6	7	8	9	10	11	12	13	14	15	16
1. Professional, self-employed	.00															
2. Professional, salaried	.47	.00														
3. Managers and officials	.38	.33	.00													
4. Sales workers, other	.36	.39	.21	.00												
5. Salesworkers, self-employed	.52	.52	.41	.37	.00											
6. Proprietors	.41	.39	.25	.27	.28	.00										
7. Clerical and kindred	.50	.34	.27	.33	.46	.30	.00									
8. Sales workers, retail and wholesale	.39	.41	.25	.22	.43	.31	.40	.00								
9. Craftsmen, foremen, manufacturing	.59	.49	.42	.49	.50	.34	.32	.51	.00							
10. Craftsmen, foremen, other	.60	.50	.43	.49	.49	.32	.34	.48	.26	.00						
11. Craftsmen, foremen, construction	.63	.56	.44	.50	.53	.34	.38	.49	.31	.32	.00					
12. Operatives, manufacturing	.69	.57	.49	.56	.58	.42	.38	.58	.23	.30	.37	.00				
13. Operatives, other	.72	.61	.53	.60	.56	.42	.44	.62	.28	.29	.36	.20	.00			
14. Service workers	.58	.52	.43	.47	.55	.36	.42	.50	.43	.41	.44	.43	.48	.00		
15. Laborers, manufacturing	.71	.60	.58	.62	.67	.56	.37	.63	.42	.47	.50	.33	.44	.62	.00	
16. Laborers, other	.58	.50	.39	.46	.48	.28	.30	.45	.20	.20	.23	.27	.29	.40	.45	.00

similarities and differences reported in Table 4.2 will prove very helpful in interpreting the structure of intimate associations revealed in the smallest space analysis. A recent article by Glenn and Alston (1968) suggests, on the basis of a reanalysis of a number of national surveys, that occupational categories containing detailed occupations more homogeneous in status characteristics than the customarily employed crude occupational breakdowns (such as manual-nonmanual) can explain a considerably larger proportion of the variation in reported attitudes and behavior—their so-called "cultural distance among occupational groups"—than crude breakdowns that actually obscure differences. Differentiation among occupational groups, especially in terms of their educational attainments, is particularly useful in accounting for these differences.

The same reasons that justified our considering the matrix of indexes of dissimilarity between pairs of ethnoreligious groups as the original data matrix apply in the case of occupational groups as well. Table 4.3 presents these indexes of dissimilarity for the 16 occupational categories.

The coefficients of alienation for the best one-space, two-space, and three-space solutions were .270, .122, and .077, respectively—the latter two representing quite acceptable fits of the data. Since the three-space solution does not provide an appreciably sharper picture of the data, Figure 4.1 presents only the two-space solution.

Two facets apparently determine the relative proximities of the occupational groups to one another. The first facet appears to be relative social status, especially as indexed by educational attainment. The rank-order correlation of mean school years completed and location on the line E is .822 ($p < .01$), while the correlation of mean family income of the occupational groups and their location on the line E is .759 ($p < .01$).

The second facet might be identified with the relative size of the work place in which the occupational members are found, ranging from large-scale "bureaucratic" organizations to small work organizations, often including "entrepreneurial" types of work activities. The rank-order correlation between median number of employees at place of work and location on the line W, which is orthogonal to line E, is .597 ($p < .05$). One of the major reasons for this moderate correlation arises from the category of service workers who rank thirteenth in median number of employees at place of employment but only third on the line W. Obviously our indicator of median number of workers as reflecting large-scale work activities is misleading here insofar as most service workers, while employees of large organizations such as the utility repairmen for Michigan Bell Telephone Company (which employs 18,000 people), typically operate throughout the metropolitan area in very small work groups or alone. Disregarding this group, the rank-order correlation rises to .741

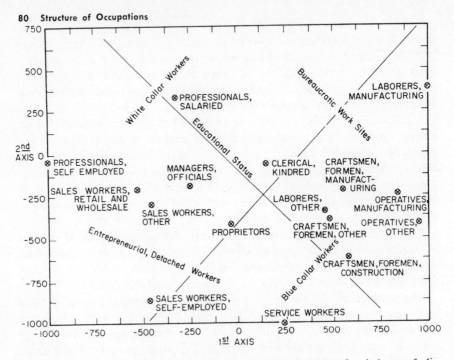

Figure 4.1 Graphic representation of the two-space solution for indexes of dissimilarity, occupations of friends. Coefficient of alienation = .122.

($p < .01$). Thus our account of this group's deviance adds to the credibility of our interpretation.

Rank-ordering the proportion of men in each occupational category who would prefer the job of the small businessman over that of the office worker (see last column of Table 4.2 and its footnote a) and correlating this with the category's position on line W, one obtains a coefficient of .368, which just fails to achieve significance. A considerable amount of the "error" arises from the "laborers in manufacturing" who rank sixteenth on line W (they obviously are concentrated in very large-scale work organizations—indeed, most are employed in automobile manufacturing) but third in the proportion preferring the small businessman's job over the office worker's. Since Chinoy (1955) and others have noted the widespread American dream of owning one's own business among automobile assembly line workers, perhaps this discrepancy between reality and fantasy should have been expected. (The correlation rises to .572 ($p < .05$) if this group of laborers is deleted from the analysis.) In any event, these results tend to support Laumann and Guttman's (1966) observation that occupational associations are structured by relative prestige or socioeconomic status *and* entrepreneurial-bureaucratic differences among occupations.

SUMMARY

In summary, the macrostructure of occupational groups may thus be seen to have at minimum a two-dimensional structure. The one-dimensional smallest space solution has an unacceptably high coefficient of alienation which suggests that one dimension—presumably socioeconomic status—fits the structure of the data matrix in hand very poorly indeed. The first dimension in the two-space solution corresponds more or less precisely to the relative prestige, social standing, income, and educational attainment of the occupational groups—in short, socioeconomic status; while the second somewhat less adequately corresponds to the predominant kind of work context and/or orientations to work of the occupational groups, especially as it relates to bureaucratic versus entrepreneurial work activities.

In a somewhat more speculative vein, it is here that we should discuss Marx's classic "theory" of the development of subjectively conscious economic classes (see Bendix and Lipset, 1966). Essentially deriving from his approach, we contend that only when people similarly circumstanced in their relationships to the means of production (or, to be sure, the ascriptive status structure) have opportunities for easy communication and extensive and more or less exclusive intimate interaction with one another, can one expect favorable conditions for the emergence of a consciousness of kind, or class consciousness, that transforms a potential class (*Klasse an sich*) into an actual class aware of and active in its own interests in competition with those of other classes (*Klasse für sich*). To the extent that other social forces (including other sources of social differentiation in the society) militate against the tendency to interact exclusively with other "class-" or "statusmates" on intimate terms, then the emergence of a fully crystallized class or status structure is forestalled. (Compare this argument with Marx and Engels' account of the absence of politically conscious trade unionism in the United States due to the differentiation of the working class into many competing and mutually hostile ethnic groups.)

As the results of the preceding chapter and this chapter show, patterns of association in the urban population are extraordinarily differentiated on both ascription- and achievement-oriented grounds. On the other hand, no group discussed in the analyses, whether occupational or ethnoreligious, manifests an overwhelming propensity to associate exclusively with others of their own group. On the contrary, all groups manifest more or less strong tendencies to have some intimate intercourse with members of the most disparate groups. As the next chapter will show, the average man is involved in relatively heterogeneously composed networks. It is considerations such as these that go far toward explaining the absence of rigidly differentiated social structures in the United States with correspondingly highly differentiated class and/or status subcultures. Group "boundaries" are simply too permeable—that is, are too often "breached" by members' choosing outsiders as intimates.

NOTES

1. Separate analyses of the occupational structure of associations of neighbors, fathers, and fathers-in-law in the Detroit data reveal quite clearly that they differ in some respects from one another in their underlying structure. By simultaneously considering all these different types of intimate associates, one merely confuses the results. (See also Blau and Duncan's (1967: 67–75) smallest space analysis of the father-son mobility table, based on a national representative sample collected by the U.S. Bureau of the Census in 1962.)

2. Occupations were first coded into the six-digit occupation-industry code of the U.S. Bureau of the Census. Then, following Blau and Duncan (1967), we collapsed the occupations into the sixteen-category code presented in Table 4.1. We departed from the Blau-Duncan scheme by deleting "farmers" and "farm laborers" categories (because our urban sample contained no such occupations) and by adding "self-employed sales workers."

CHAPTER 5

The Homogeneity of Friendship Networks

MICROSTRUCTURAL ANALYSIS OF FRIENDSHIP NETWORKS

As we turn our attention from the preceding two chapters' macro-structural concerns to the microstructural analyses presented in this and the next chapter, it will be useful to formulate more precisely what we mean by "friendship." Friendship *denotes* a voluntarily formed and maintained relationship between two persons who more or less mutually regard each other as having a special, affectively toned relationship of mutual trust and esteem. The specific content of social obligations and privileges will vary, depending upon the particular social positions that the persons occupy. That is, friendship *connotes* different things to adolescents and married adults, upper middle class professionals and working class automobile workers, men and women.

As I read the literature, three problematic aspects in the study of friendship relations have received special attention:

1. How and with whom are they formed?
2. How are they maintained?
3. What broader sociological and psychological consequences do they have?

The first question has generated considerable controversy between those social psychologists and personality theorists who emphasize personality need or value and interest *similarity* between friends versus those who emphasize need or value *complementarity* (see Albert and Brigante, 1962; Coelho, 1959). While the bulk of the literature on interpersonal attraction focuses on similarity of personality needs and attitudes among friends rather than on similarity of social roles, some more sociologically oriented researchers have demonstrated the extent to which friendships are formed among persons possessing similar social characteristics (see Curtis, 1963; Laumann, 1966; chapters IV and V). The issue of whether friends are attitudinally similar because they occupy similar niches in the social structure or because they mutually influence one another's views of the world has been relatively neglected probably due to methodological difficulties (for example, the need to observe systematically relations between friends over extended time periods; see also above, chapter 2, pp. 34–36). The second question has been especially attractive to "balance theorists" like Newcomb (1961) who attempt to formulate a processual account of the formation and maintenance of friendship ties (see Chapter 2, pp. 36–38). The third question has been of special concern to sociologists interested in the formation of vote intention (see Berelson et al., 1954) or other aspects of the process of personal influence and social communication (see Festinger, 1950; Katz and Lazarsfeld, 1955; Lazarsfeld and Merton, 1954; Kelman, 1958; Coleman et al., 1966; Katz, 1966).

All three questions tend to focus attention primarily on the dyadic relation between the focal actor (ego) and alter (friend) and the consequences of certain transactions between them. Deriving from certain formulations of Georg Simmel, a further question, usually only discussed theoretically, has occasionally been raised (Simmel, 1964; Laumann, 1966; Caplow, 1968; Mitchell, 1969; Granovetter, 1969) and deserves considerably more empirical attention than it has received to date: How can one most usefully describe the *structure* of a *set* of friends (or intimates) of ego and what implications do these structural characteristics have for ego's attitudes and behavior? Two of a number of possible characterizations of the structure of friendship networks are of special interest to us here: (1) the homogeneity of composition of the set of friends and (2) the connectedness of the set.[1] This chapter deals with the first; the second will be discussed in the next chapter. Both modes of characterization are "structural" in the sense that they derive from descriptions of the *relationships* among multiple actors—even if they are merely comparisons of the degree of "similarity" of the set of social positions comprising a given network—rather than "pure" attributes of the individual as in the case of his attitudes or incumbency in specific social positions. Of course, we shall treat these "structural characteristics" as attributes of an individual when we describe the characteristics of *his* particular friendship group and their associations with other features of his behavior and attitudes. But nonetheless it is probably worth keeping in mind the rather different character of these measures from those conventionally handled in survey studies (for example, attitudes).

The second mode of characterization in particular raises the critical shift, first stressed by Simmel, from dyadic to triadic and higher level interaction that more approximates "primary group level" interaction as traditionally conceived and all that that may imply (see Verba, 1961).

While there has been much sophisticated experimental work on small groups, usually artificially concocted from paid student "subjects" (see Hare, 1962), there has been remarkably little research done on small primary groups *in naturo* on large adult population cross-sections. The reasons for this neglect are fairly obvious given the practical difficulties of getting relevant and systematic information on such groups using a survey instrument. The following two chapters' discussion, then, must be treated as only a first approximation to such a study in which we have employed the strategy of treating respondents as "informants" on certain aspects of the structure of the groups in which they are involved. No doubt as we gain greater empirical experience, methods to measure better these and other, perhaps more critical structural features will be devised. We hope merely to demonstrate here the potential benefits in analysis to be derived from such developments.

FRIENDSHIP AND HOMOGENEITY

We find ourselves in an embarrassing theoretical position since we have little to guide us in deciding what is of general importance in determining the homogeneity of composition of a friendship network. There are many attributes that socially differentiate a population and that may, consequently, serve as a basis of mutual attraction or repulsion (see our discussion above of the distance-generating postulate, Chapter 1, pp. 4–5). But it is also likely that friendships are formed between persons who are similar (homogeneous) with respect to at least a given attribute they regard as especially relevant to their relationship (see Newcomb's (1961) discussion of common relevance noted in Chapter 2, footnote 8). In an important sense, then, homogeneity or similarity is in the minds of the participants rather than the beholder. But we must remember that friends, while mutually chosen on one or more attributes, are also the possessors of other social attributes, often associated with the one(s) of mutual relevance, that may become significant for the relationship if it persists through time. Precisely because friendship tends to be a functionally diffuse rather than a narrowly instrumental relationship, it is likely that over time other social features of the participants will become relevant to their interaction.

It is on the basis of this last consideration that we justify our proposal to explore "objective" homogeneity of friendship networks in terms of two types of social characteristics important in American society: (1) the more or less *ascribed* characteristic of ethnoreligious membership and (2) the *achieved* characteristic of occupation. It has almost become a commonplace to argue that ascriptive bases of solidarity (that is, the formation of social relationships among actors on the basis of their *qualities,* such as their sex, race, age, kinship or ethnic group membership, rather than on the basis of their *performances* or *achievements* (see Parsons, 1967; Litwak, 1965; Chapter 1 above, pp. 5–6) tend to weaken and disappear in the course of modernization and urbanization. Ascriptive orientations are presumed to maintain their vitality only among those parts of the urban population that are not fully assimilated into the modern mode of achievement-based criteria of intimate association as, for instance, among lower-class recently arrived ethnic groups (for example, see Gans' discussion (1962) of working class Italo-Americans in Boston's East End).

Mayhew (1968), however, has cogently argued against the assumption that ascriptive bases of soliarity are necessarily incompatible with meeting the functional requirements of highly differentiated social systems. He argues, for example, that:

. . . when an ascriptively defined group comes to have a range of usable capacities, well developed political leadership which is integrated with the polity at the societal level, extensive participation in a variety of roles, and extended horizons of loyalty, then ascription can come to play an important functional role within a highly differentiated society. This is a very important theoretical point for it weighs against the tendency to argue that participation breaks down ascription. We must argue against a unilinear model of evolution which would suppose that ascription and differentiation are mutually exclusive. On the contrary, the extensive participation of ascriptively defined groups in differentiated roles and institutions does not simply break down ascription: *it insinuates ascriptive elements into the institutional structure of modern society* in complex and variegated ways (1968: 177).

The reasoning of some theorists would thus lead us to predict that networks founded on ascriptive homogeneity should be negatively associated with networks founded on homogeneity of achieved characteristics—that is, homogeneity on one criterion of selection tends to imply heterogeneity on the other criterion of selection because of functional and other incompatibilities between these criteria. On the other hand, Mayhew would argue that, for ascriptive status groups whose members are distributed fairly widely across the range of the modern occupational structure, there is no necessary functional incompatibility between these two bases of friendship formation and, therefore, that we should expect no correlation, positive or negative, between the two bases of selection.

MEASURING HOMOGENEITY AND THE PLAN OF ANALYSIS

The preceding two chapters reported attempts to portray graphically the social structure of ethnoreligious and occupational groups in the

Detroit metropolitan area. The relative proximities of these groups were determined as a monotonic function of their differential similarity in their patterns of friendship choices across groups—that is, the more similar two groups' patterns of friendship choices, the shorter the distance between them in the space. In general, whether we consider ethnoreligious or occupational groups, the individual is most likely to find his friends within his own group—and, consequently, he may be regarded as having "zero" distance between himself and other members of his group. We propose to measure the homogeneity of a respondent's friendship group by simply summing the Euclidean distances (see Chapter 1) derived from the smallest space solutions for ethnoreligious groups (Chapter 3) and occupational groups (Chapter 4) between his membership group and those of his three friends. As we have argued throughout, the differentiation of these social structures is *multi*dimensional; the Euclidean distance retains this multidimensional feature. A man whose three friends are drawn exclusively from his own group will have maximum homogeneity—a sum of zero; while the larger the sum, the more heterogeneous the friendship network. This approach thus treats friendships between members of groups located at some distance from each other as being much more "dissimilar" than those which are considerably closer to each other on the assumption that such relationships, being more improbable, "unite" persons who are likely to be much more different from one another in important social respects and corresponding attitudes, values, and behavior. In other words, it attempts to take into account the fact that Scandinavian Lutherans, according to the smallest space analysis in Chapter 3, are in some sense more similar to German Catholics than they are to other Protestant groups, such as German Presbyterians. A more conventional analysis would on an a priori basis simply treat the Scandinavian Lutherans as more similar ("closer") to other Protestants than to Catholics.[2] In short, we are stressing here that we are letting the sample population itself "define" the social structures in which it is implicated rather than imposing such structures from a priori considerations of how the structures are differentiated.

In view of the fact that many studies have reported the greater significance of ethnic and kin concerns (ascriptive ties) among working class groups than higher status groups (see Bott, 1957; Dotson, 1951; Srole et al., 1962; Laumann, 1966; Adams, 1967a), we hypothesize that the homogeneity of ethnoreligious group memberships among friends will prove of greater importance to lower status groups. Other studies (Hyman, 1966; Kohn, 1969; Glenn and Alston, 1968) suggest that the middle class is more achievement oriented in its concerns; we, consequently, hypothesize that the homogeneity of occupations among friends will play a greater role among higher status groups. Such reasoning suggests that we should routinely explore the relations of our two measures of homogeneity within relatively more homogeneous socioeconomic groupings since we expect them to behave differently, depending on the socioeconomic category under examination. We shall, therefore, report the correlations of these measures and other variables for the total sample and three educational subcategories: some high school education or less ($N \approx 300$), high school graduates ($N \approx 300$), and some college or more ($N \approx 325$).

As we will make abundantly clear below, the composition of friendship networks is also strongly influenced by the fact that the man has a Protestant or Catholic religious preference. [Note, for example, that Catholics are more likely to have ethnoreligiously homogeneous networks than Protestants (see Table 5.1).] Consequently, we report the relations of our measures to the various other characteristics and attitudes within the subsamples of Protestants ($N \approx 490$) and Catholics ($N \approx 415$). We should note that these two religious categories are almost exactly matched in aggregate measures of socioeconomic status such as mean school years completed, family incomes, and occupational statuses (see Chapter 3, Table 3.5).

Much of our interpretation of the overall pattern of results turns on the notion that ethnoreligious homogeneity is reflective of a fundamentally ascriptive orientation to social relations and the world; while occupational homogeneity is reflective of a more achievement-oriented approach to social relations and the world. As noted before, theorists from Sir Henry Maine and Ferdinand Toennies to Ralph Linton and Talcott Parsons have tended to emphasize the fundamental incompatibility between these two orientations and to suggest a shift from ascription to achievement as societies "modernize." (But recall the caveat of Mayhew quoted earlier.)

There is, in fact, some slender evidence that our two measures are negatively correlated with each other ($-.066$, $p < .05$, total sample)— that is, men in homogeneous occupational networks have a very slight tendency to be in more heterogeneous networks with respect to ethnoreligious composition, and vice versa. But this is especially true among the high school graduates ($-.119$, $p < .05$) and to a lesser extent among men of some college education or better ($-.076$, NS). There is, however, no relationship among men who have attended only some high school or less ($-.005$, NS). These findings suggest that while there may be some incompatibility between ascriptive and achievement oriented criteria of friendship selection, especially among higher status groups, this incompatibility is obviously of only limited significance, otherwise the negative correlations would be much higher. Apropos to this last point, it is worth noting here that it is precisely in the lowest category of socioeconomic status that men of those ascriptive groups who are especially concentrated in the lower reaches of the occupational structure (for example, Polish Catholics and Anglo-American Baptists—see Table 3.7) have the largest number of opportunities to select others as friends similar to themselves on *both* occupational *and* ethnoreligious grounds if they wish to do so. But men of such groups who "make" it into the higher reaches of the socioeconomic hierarchy simply do not find themselves in an "opportunity structure of potential friends" from whom to select with ease those who are similar to themselves on both characteristics. To the extent that they wish to select friends similar to themselves occupationally, they must almost necessarily select people who differ from themselves ethnoreligiously simply because those similar to themselves on this characteristic are relatively rare at these levels. Thus Mayhew's qualification that essentially relates to the nature of the opportunity structure for choice confronting particular ascriptive groups is certainly consistent with these findings.

To give a brief overview of the analysis to follow, we shall first consider separately each homogeneity measure and its relationships to various demographic, social and attitudinal characteristics of the respondents, routinely controlling for educational and religious differences. In the concluding analytic section, we shall consider both measures simultaneously, that is, we shall identify the implications of men having completely homogeneous or heterogeneous networks on *both* occupational and ethnoreligious grounds as well as those who are in networks homogeneous on one measure but heterogeneous on the other. Since we want to present results bearing on a wide range of individual attributes and attitudes, we do not have the space nor the reader the patience to go into an *intensive* analysis of each attribute as it relates to the homogeneity measures—that is, where we would examine in detail alternative interpretations of the results bringing to bear additional controls to those routinely employed. Consequently, our interpretations of particular patterns of results must necessarily be regarded as only suggestive and what appear to us to be the most plausible given the theoretical assumptions sketched above.

HOMOGENEITY AND SOCIAL POSITION

Table 5.1 summarizes the product-moment correlations of these homogeneity measures with selected demographic and socioeconomic characteristics for the total sample, three educational categories and Protestants and Catholics. One might imagine that a man's age, being rather closely associated with fairly differentiated stages in the life cycle, would be related to the homogeneity of his friendship network. From one point of

Table 5.1. Product-moment correlations of ethnoreligious and occupational homogeneity measures and selected demographic characteristics of the respondents: for the total sample, three educational levels, and Protestants and Catholics

Educational Levels

Demographic Characteristic	Some High School		High School Graduates		Some College or More	
	Ethnoreligious	Occupation	Ethnoreligious	Occupation	Ethnoreligious	Occupation
1. Age	.019	.200**	.062	−.095	.036	.018
2. Religious Preference (Prot./Cath.)	−.296**	−.086	−.202**	.038	−.162*	.041
3. Generations in the U.S. (paternal line)	.193**	−.154**	.197**	−.081	.069	.017
4. Subjective class identification	−.069	−.049	−.046	−.013	−.026	−.202**
5. Occupation (Duncan)	.031	.049	−.087	−.072	−.051	−.174**
6. Total family income	−.004	−.085	−.076	−.088	−.066	−.100*
7. School years completed	—	—	—	—	—	—

Religious Preference

Demographic Characteristic	Protestants		Catholics		Total Sample	
	Ethnoreligious	Occupation	Ethnoreligious	Occupation	Ethnoreligious	Occupation
1. Age	−.079	.143**	.062	−.064	.014	.029
2. Religious preference (Prot./Cath.)	—	—	—	—	−.212**	−.040
3. Generations in the U.S. (paternal line)	.021	−.088*	.019	−.073	.149**	−.066*
4. Subjective class identification	−.055	−.093*	−.034	−.012	−.044	−.078**
5. Occupation (Duncan)	−.050	−.102*	−.028	.019	−.037	−.060
6. Total family income	−.123**	−.091*	.065	−.051	−.048	−.078*
7. School years completed	−.025	−.019	.064	.032	−.014	−.010

*$p < .05$.
**$p < .01$.

view, early adulthood is often associated with considerable geographical and job mobility that would presumably imply a wider range of opportunities to meet people of differing social backgrounds from whom to select intimates. Later on one might suspect that the more "settled" family life of the married man in his late thirties or forties would perhaps be associated with more homogeneous social environments—for example, living in fairly homogeneous suburbs so as to provide "good schools for school-age children" (Rossi, 1955). On the other hand, one could imagine that simply by virtue of living longer older men have accumulated more opportunities to meet and form friendships with people of differing social backgrounds. In our study, age is not related to the two measures of homogeneity for the total sample. But occupational heterogeneity is associated with older age among those having only some high school education or less. (Notice that this relationship almost reverses itself for high school graduates—older men appear to be associated with greater homogeneity of friendship networks.) Apparently the effects speculated above may have differing impacts on men variously situated in the "class" structure that more or less balance each other off in the total sample. Finally, we might note that only among Protestants is older age associated with occupational heterogeneity.

As one might have expected on the basis of a reading of the literature on Protestant-Catholic and ethnic differences (for example, Lenski, 1960; Gans, 1962; Suttles, 1968), Catholics are likely to have more homogeneous ethnoreligious networks than Protestants; but this relationship tends to weaken as we move from low to more highly educated groups. "Generations in the U.S. (paternal line)" refers to whether the respondent's father, grandfather, or great grandfather was born in the United States or abroad (respondents are all native born). Again, as might be expected, the more generations in the United States, the less likely the network is ethnoreligiously homogeneous. This is true for the total sample as well as the lower two educational categories, but appears to be no longer true among men of some college education or better. What is interesting here is that occupational homogeneity increases with generations in the United States. This suggests that as ethnic identifications are shed over the generations and, correspondingly, concern for maintaining ethnoreligious homogeneity declines, occupationally based considerations for friendship selection gain in importance.

The remaining four attributes of respondents reported in the table—subjective class identification, occupational prestige, total family income, and school years completed—might be regarded as tapping various aspects of a man's socioeconomic achievement. In only one case is ethnoreligious composition related to these indicators. But occupational homogeneity is frequently related, and especially among Protestants. With regard to subjective class identification (the respondent could assign himself to the upper, upper middle, middle, upper working, working, or lower class (see Q76 and Q77, Appendix C), the higher the class identification, the more homogeneous is the occupational composition of the friendship network. This is especially true for men with at least some college education. Similarly, the higher the prestige of the respondent's occupation (as indexed by Duncan's two-digit Index for Socioeconomic Status) and the larger his total family income, the more occupationally homogeneous is the man's friendship network. It is especially worth noting that occupational homogeneity is differentially distributed among Protestants on five of the six characteristics considered in contrast to no such differentiation among Catholics on either measure of homogeneity. Why should Protestants of higher socioeconomic status and longer nativity be particularly likely to be occupationally homogeneous in their friendship nets? Perhaps it may be due to the considerably weaker significance of ethnoreligious considerations in constructing friendship nets among such persons and a correspondingly stronger orientation to occupational differences per se. In any event Protestants and Catholics do seem to be implicated in rather different kinds of networks in respect to their bases of composition. As we shall see in the next chapter, they differ rather sharply in the connectedness of their networks as well. These findings tend to support our expectation mentioned above that friendship composition will respond to different considerations at different socioeconomic levels and among different religious groups.

HOMOGENEITY AND OTHER FEATURES OF FRIENDSHIP NETWORKS

While Table 5.1 summarizes the patterns of friendship homogeneity in terms of their relations to the conventional demographic and socioeconomic characteristics of the respondents, Table 5.2 considers the relationships of homogeneity to other features of the man's friendship network. The first four rows summarize in greater detail the relations of alternative measures of friendship homogeneity to the two measures employed in this chapter which we have already discussed in terms of the substantive validity of our derived measures (see footnote 2). Our measure of political homogeneity (row 5) is an effort to measure the extent to which the four individuals' political party preferences (ranging from Republican through independent to Democratic) are homogeneous. Noteworthy here is the fact that ethnoreligious homogeneity is consistently related to political homogeneity especially among high school graduates and Catholics (compare Berelson et al., 1954: 118–132); with the exception of the high school graduates, however, occupational homogeneity is, rather surprisingly, not related to political homogeneity.

A rather intriguing but, on further reflection, easily explicable result is the contradictory relations of the two homogeneity measures with the number of friends who are also relatives (row 6). Ethnoreligious homogeneity increases with the number of friends who are also relatives—this, of course, occurs because consanguineal kin (relatives by blood, such as brothers, fathers, cousins) especially are almost necessarily of the same ethnoreligious membership group as the respondent. On the other hand, occupational homogeneity decreases with the number of friends who are also relatives—this arises from the fact that in American society the assignment of occupational roles is rarely on a strictly kin basis—the kin group is, consequently, likely to be occupational heterogeneous (see Adams, 1967a). To the extent that a man chooses friends on kinship grounds, he will also be likely to choose people who are occupationally heterogeneous.

The places at which friends interact and the presence or absence of wives in the contact situation is differentially related to the two homogeneity measures as well. We asked the respondent to report where he regularly met each of his three friends—at his or their home or somewhere else (such as bowling alleys, bars, and the like) and at work or not. Ethnoreligious homogeneity was associated with a greater proportion of the friends being entertained in each others' homes; conversely, occupational homogeneity was associated with a smaller proportion of the friends being entertained in each others' homes. Almost as a corollary to this latter finding, occupationally homogeneous networks tend to be segregated by sex (see row 9). We asked the men whether they typically saw their friends with their wives present or not. Bott (1957), Gans (1962), Babchuk (1965), Adams (1967), and others have noted that working class couples tend to be involved in intimate friendship relations on a sex-segregated basis; middle class couples tend to associate with friends on a "husband-wife" basis. Note that the relationship of occupational homogeneity and sex segregation is especially strong for men of lower educational attainments.

Contrary to expectations that homogeneity should facilitate intimacy, we find the average reported closeness of friends is *negatively* related to occupational homogeneity (row 10)—that is, the more heterogeneous the friendship network occupationally, the more likely the respondent regards his friends as very close, personal friends. One plausible mechanism that might account for this surprising result is that work-based friendship nets (see row 8 above) tend to imply more superficial relations mediated by mere physical proximity and accessibility for large portions of the workday. The very ease with which these friendships are formed (and probably

Table 5.2. Product-moment correlations of ethnoreligious and occupational homogeneity measures and selected characteristics of the associational networks: for the total sample, three educational levels, Protestants and Catholics

| | Educational Levels | | | |
| | Some High School | | High School Graduates | |
Characteristics of associational network	Ethno-religious	Occupa-tion	Ethno-religious	Occupa-tion
1. Number of friends of same ethnic group[a]	−.468**	.026	−.363**	.039
2. Number of friends of same religious group (Prot./Cath.)[b]	−.055	.142*	−.107	−.017
3. Occupational prestige homogeneity, $100-\sqrt{\Sigma(F-R)^2}$ [c]	−.083	.543**	−.008	−.520**
4. Educational attainment homogeneity $100-\sqrt{\Sigma(F-R)^2}$ [d]	−.034	−.240**	.060	−.095
5. Political homogeneity, $10-\sqrt{\Sigma(F-R)^2}$ [e]	−.090	.065	−.215**	−.100
6. Number of friends who are also relatives[f]	−.055	.142*	−.107*	−.017
7. Number of home-based interactions[g]	−.140	.086	.050	.155**
8. Number of work-based interactions[h]	.036	−.079	−.017	−.190**
9. Joint vs. sex-segregated interaction[i]	.040	−.137**	.012	−.081
10. Average closeness of friends[j]	.035	−.028	−.005	−.182**
11. Average length of time known friends divided by age of respondent[k]	−.164**	−.066	−.183**	.171**
12. Interlocking-radial networks[l]	.024	−.010	.142*	−.041
13. Number of close friends[m]	−.058	.012	−.030	.040
14. Number of organizational memberships[n]	−.033	.012	−.075	−.027

* p less than .05.
** p less than .01.
[a] See Q21, Appendix C.
[b] See Q20, Appendix C.
[c] See footnote 1, Chapter 5, and Q18, Appendix C.
[d] See footnote 1, Chapter 5, and Q19, Appendix C.
[e] See footnote 1, Chapter 5, and Q22, Appendix C.
[f] See Q14, Appendix C.
[g] See Q26, Appendix C.
[h] See Q27, Appendix C.
[i] See Q29, Appendix C.
[j] See Q15, Appendix C.
[k] See Q16, Appendix C. The respondent reported the number of years he had known each of his three friends. We simply took the average number of years a man knew his three friends and divided by his age as a measure of the friendship net's duration.
[l] See Q25, Appendix C; see also Chapter 6.
[m] See Q12, Appendix C.
[n] See Q39, Appendix C; see also Chapter 7.

| Educational Levels | | Religious Preference | | | | | |
| Some College or More | | Protestants | | Catholics | | Total Sample | |
Ethno-religious	Occupation	Ethno-religious	Occupation	Ethno-religious	Occupation	Ethno-religious	Occupation
−.340**	.099	−.317**	.060	−.580**	.024	−.390**	.054
−.106*	.118*	—	—	—	—	−.086**	.071*
.027	−.647**	−.052	−.554**	−.039	−.583**	−.018	−.576**
.046	−.301**	−.019	−.232**	.086	.165**	.014	−.201**
−.090	−.045	−.064	−.071	−.126**	−.005	−.128**	−.033
−.106*	.118*	−.021	.044	−.096*	.155**	−.086**	.071*
−.082	.076	−.067	.100*	−.022	.146**	−.056	.102**
.107*	−.143*	−.025	−.137**	.053	−.163**	−.041	−.138**
.050	−.066	.065	−.118**	.043	−.067	.032	−.090**
.005	−.054	.025	.108*	.073	−.063	.011	−.089**
−.164**	.153**	−.134**	.125**	−.124*	.059	−.168**	.092**
.093	.065	.062	.013	−.002	.020	.083**	.003
−.030	.113*	−.079	.037	.010	.062	−.038	.051
−.075	−.143*	−.060	−.064	−.026	−.008	−.058	−.065*

broken as well) may mean that the affective ties are minimal as the basis for intimacy may be merely confined to the shared work environment. Friends who differ in occupations must be actively cultivated insofar as the man must expend his "free" time to seeing them (they are not "available" for interaction at coffee break), thus reflecting a higher valuation of their friendship.

A particularly intriguing result is the diverging pattern of relationships of ethnoreligious and occupational homogeneity with the average duration of the friendship (see row 11). While ethnoreligious homogeneity is associated with relatively longer average durations of the friendships, occupational homogeneity is associated with shorter durations. That is, friendship nets of long standing tend to be ethnoreligiously homogeneous and occupationally heterogeneous. One possible mechanism accounting for such a pattern would be the formation of close friendships while in school on the basis of ethnoreligious similarities. If these persist through time, divergencies in occupational achievement are likely to arise. Adolescent friends are likely to go into different lines of work when they "grow up" (even if their jobs do not differ so much in terms of their relative prestige, they certainly may differ in place and type of work). If the mutual attractions of friendship are strongly formed in earlier years and the partners continue to live in reasonable proximity to one another so that physical distances do not raise insurmountable obstacles to continued interaction, friendships of long duration would be expected to take on these diverging characteristics of homogeneity when we look at adult friendship patterns.

In addition, we found that ethnoreligiously homogeneous networks tend to be interlocking (rather than radial) networks (see row 12), that is, the respondent reported that at least two of his three friends were also friends of one another. Since the following chapter will discuss the important ways in which interlocking and radial networks systematically differ from one another, we shall merely note here the very suggestive fact that it is ethnoreligious homogeneity, the ascriptive basis of interaction, rather than the "achieved" occupational basis of homogeneity, which is related to this measure of microcommunity (*Gemeinschaft*) and the presence of a primary group of three or more persons.

When asked how many persons are regarded as close intimate friends of the respondent (see Q12, Appendix C), nearly 60 percent of the sample reported three or four friends or fewer, thus reflecting the "intensive" rather than "extensive" conception of the nature of friendship relations. (This fact, incidentally, provides a major part of the justification for focusing so much of our analysis on only the three closest friends of the respondent.) To the extent that certain respondents tend to hold an "extensive" definition of friendship—that is, many people are regarded as friends—we might infer that heterogeneity would characterize their friendship network. This inference is only supported for the occupational heterogeneity of men with some college education or more (see row 13).

An implicit assumption throughout this analysis has been that homogeneity in the composition of friendship networks should facilitate the development of proximate and generalized social support and consensus in the primary environment for ego's orientations toward and behavior in the world because the members of such networks are more likely to share common orientations and values than those in networks composed of men of highly dissimilar social positions (see Festinger, 1950; Laumann, 1966: 105–122; Chapter 6, pp. 113–116). Similarity of orientation and/or consensus among heterogeneous individuals who are, by virtue of that fact alone, likely to have differing perspectives toward the world is simply more unlikely. Consequently, we would expect social influence and control (for example, alters' sanctioning "deviant" attitudes or behavior of ego) in such networks to be less effective if for no other reason than the relative lack of consistency and coherence in the perspectives of the friends. The above reasoning is obviously premised on yet another assumption, repeatedly corroborated in this and other research, that social positions are differentially associated with given values and behavior. For instance, men of higher socioeconomic status are more likely to belong to voluntary associations than men of lower socioeconomic status (see Hausknecht, 1962; Chapter 7 below). In our sample, there is a correlation of .324 ($p < .01$) between a man's educational attainment, an indicator of socioeconomic status, and his number of organizational memberships (compare Chapter 7: p. 145). On the other hand, there is no significant relationship between Protestant/Catholic religious preference and number of memberships.

By combining the above considerations, one could then argue that homogeneity of associates at a given socioeconomic level (that is, a common level of social positions) should "amplify" the tendency to behave in the "characteristic" manner associated with that level—the case in point being participation in voluntary associations—because individuals of similar status positions (and correspondingly similar tendencies to behave or look at the world in certain ways) reinforce one another's inclinations to behave in the characteristic manner. On the other hand, men with heterogeneous associates are less likely to receive consensual primary social support and validation for these "characteristic" modes of behavior. More specifically, we are now in the position to predict that men of the highest educational attainment (that is, high socioeconomic status) in homogeneous friendship networks are *more* likely to belong to voluntary associations than men at this level with heterogeneous associates. Conversely, at the lowest educational level (that is, low socioeconomic status), men with homogeneous friendships are *less* likely to belong to voluntary associations than men in heterogeneous networks. There should be no such effects for ethnoreligiously homogeneous networks because religious characteristics, as noted above, are not associated systematically with this behavior pattern. And, in fact, the reader can observe in row 14 a shift in the direction of the correlation coefficients for occupational homogeneity and number of associational memberships, holding education "constant," that conforms, albeit rather weakly, to these expectations: +.012, −.027, and −.143, for the three educational groups, respectively. There is, however, no such pattern observable for ethnoreligious homogeneity.

HOMOGENEITY AND ATTITUDES

In this section, we would like to pursue further this question of the ways in which homogeneity of friendship networks is systematically related to the attitudes and behavior of respondents. In general, we expect, first, that ascription-oriented attitudes would be especially associated with ethnoreligious homogeneity and achievement-oriented attitudes with occupational homogeneity. Second, we expect that homogeneous networks will tend to foster and sustain more "extreme," clear-cut and consistent attitudes than heterogeneous networks for much the same reasons as sketched in the concluding remarks of the preceding section. Table 5.3 summarizes the results for eight selected attitudes.

First, let us consider attitudinal or behavioral measures that could reasonably be held to tap an ethnoreligious orientation. We should certainly expect that a homogeneous ethnoreligious network would either reflect greater subjective interest in ethnoreligious matters on the part of the respondent (who presumably would pick others as friends that share such interests) or help to sustain or induce such interests given time. Unfortunately, since we do not have data over time on friendship formation and attitudes, we cannot sort out the extent to which either or both of these processes (self-selection and reinforcement) are operative. At this point all we can do is establish the association. As can be readily seen for the four measures tapping ethnoreligious orientations, the pattern of association is, in every case, as expected. For frequency of church attendance and devotionalism (rows 1 and 2), we observe that both are positively related to ethnoreligious homogeneity and negatively (or not significantly) related to occupational homogeneity. A particularly intriguing result in this connection is the fact that occupational homogeneity is negatively

associated with high frequencies of church attendance and high devotionalism for persons of only some high school education or less. It is almost as if occupational homogeneity of friends, especially among the less
educated, implies a more secular orientation toward the world and a degree of estrangement from ethnoreligious concerns that tend generally to
characterize lower status men. Not surprisingly, an exceptional interest in
one's country of origin (row 3) and a preference to marry a person of the
same nationality group as one's own (row 4) are similarly positively
associated with ethnoreligious homogeneity, but unrelated to occupational
homogeneity. Parenthetically, our finding that ethnoreligious homogeneity declined with the number of generations in the United States (see
Table 5.1) is also congruent with this general expectation.

In attempting to tap achievement or performance orientations in the
respondent, we first asked the respondent his preference to belong to
informal social groups consisting exclusively of members of *his own social
class* or to groups with members drawn from *various social classes* (row 5).
In an earlier investigation (Laumann, 1966: especially Chapter 7), I
found considerable support for the notion that this question was related
to a man's *class consciousness* and *status awareness* (specifically, sensitivity to status differences among occupations). Indeed, I found in the
earlier study that a related measure of occupational homogeneity (see
Table 5.2, row 3) was positively associated with preference to associate
with members of the same social class. We again find such a positive
association in this study while ethnoreligious homogeneity is unrelated
to such a preference. Secondly, we asked respondents whether they would
discuss changing to a better but risky new job with their friends (row 6).
Willingness to discuss such a topic would presumably reflect shared
interests in occupationally relevant issues.[3] And again we find that men
in occupationally homogeneous networks were likely to discuss such an
issue with their friends but men in ethnoreligiously homogeneous networks were unlikely to do so.

In an earlier paper entitled "Open and Closed Structures" that was
written *before* the results of this study became available, Schuman and
I (1967) developed an extensive rationale for the proposition that there
should be a structural isomorphism or parallelism between personality
structure and social structure. Specifically, we hypothesized that "open-
minded" personalities (those with a high tolerance for ambiguity in social
life and openness to new experience without prejudgement—in Rokeach's
(1960) terms, nondogmatic flexibility in orientations toward the world)
should find especially congenial or at least nonthreatening "open" or
heterogeneous intimate networks (social structures composed of persons
from diverse, dissimilar social positions). Indeed, one might even suggest

Table 5.3.   Product-moment correlations of ethnoreligious and occupational homogeneity measures and selected attitudes: for the total sample, three educational levels, and Protestants and Catholics

| | Educational Level | | | |
| | Some High School | | High School Graduates | |
Attitudes	Ethno-religious	Occupa-tion	Ethno-religious	Occupa-tion
1. Frequency of church attendance[a]	.116*	−.134*	.196*	−.039
2. Devotionalism[b]	.084	−.121*	.090	−.017
3. Special interest in country of origin[c]	.179**	−.023	.230**	−.059
4. Preference to marry person of same nationality group[d]	.099	.058	.063	.032
5. Prefer members of informal social groups to be of same or various social classes[e]	−.087	.038	.007	.123*
6. Discuss making job change with friends[f]	−.137*	.122*	.021	−.003
7. Tolerance toward Communists[g]	−.100	.120*	.027	−.123*
8. Tolerance toward extremists of both left and right[h]	.076	.061	.035	−.237**

* p less than .05.
** p less than .01.
[a] See Q115, Appendix C.
[b] See footnote e, Table 3.4.
[c] See footnote f, Table 3.6.
[d] See Q113, Appendix C.
[e] See Q78, Appendix C.
[f] See Q59 f, Appendix C.
[g] Based on answers to five questions (Q47 or Q61), each coded as either a tolerant (1), neutral (2), or intolerant (3) response. See Chapter 6 and 7 for further discussion and Table 6.4, footnote a; Stouffer, 1955; Laumann and Schuman, 1967).
[h] Based on answers to ten questions (Q47 and Q61) each coded as either a tolerant (1), neutral (2), or intolerant (3) response. See Chapter 6 and 7 for further discussion and Table 6.4, footnote c; Laumann and Schuman, 1967.

| Educational Level | | Religious Preference | | | | | |
| Some College or More | | Protestants | | Catholics | | Total Sample | |
Ethno-religious	Occupa-tion	Ethno-religious	Occupa-tion	Ethno-religious	Occupa-tion	Ethno-religious	Occupa-tion
.183**	.027	.090*	−.002	−.002	−.082	.165**	−.051
.068	−.037	.056	−.008	.004	−.099	.082**	−.058
.197**	−.016	−.051	.020	−.106*	.046	.201**	−.018
.059	−.039	.050	.058	.113*	−.012	.074*	.022
.076	.061	−.037	.100*	.099*	.052	.004	.073*
−.064	.083	−.072	.040	−.067	.097*	−.064*	.066*
.061	.095	−.069	.044	−.055	−.003	−.042	.023
−.056	.113*	−.054	−.018	.032	−.047	.003	−.021

that such networks induce or at least sustain such orientations on the part of ego. Conversely, we hypothesized that "closed-minded" personalities with high intolerance for the unfamiliar and socially "different" (dogmatic prejudices highly resistant to change and a sharply dichotomized and often hostile sense of in-group–out-group relations) should find especially congenial or nonthreatening "closed" or homogeneous social networks where highly crystallized and firmly anchored social orientations may be fostered and mutually reinforced. Without going into the many complexities and difficulties in devising measures of "open-mindedness" here (see Laumann and Schuman, 1967; Rokeach, 1960; and Table 6.4, footnote a), suffice it to say that we devised what we regard as a more or less satisfactory measure of open-mindedness consisting of a ten-item scale in which the individual could express his willingness to extend basic civil liberties to political extremists of *both* the extreme right (Ku Klux Klansmen) *and* the far left (Communists).

Congruent with our expectations, we find in rows 7 and 8 that high school graduates in homogeneous occupational networks are more closed-minded and those in heterogeneous networks are more open-minded. Contrary to our expectations, however, is the apparent tendency for the least and most educated categories to be related in the opposite direction from that hypothesized—that is, homogeneity of network is associated with open-mindedness.

Several plausible ad hoc explanations for these contradictory results can be advanced. In general, education is positively correlated (.33 in our sample) with willingness to extend civil liberties to unpopular minorities (see Stouffer, 1955). The "some college or more" category includes men with only one or two years of college as well as those with postgraduate educations. The former tend to be much less open-minded by this measure than the latter. Since occupational homogeneity is also correlated with high socioeconomic status within this category (see Table 5.1, rows 4, 5, and 6), we can easily see why the relationship is probably spurious, arising from the uncontrolled educational variation. And, indeed, when we employ a more precise control for "education" in this category, the apparent "contradiction" to our hypothesis disappears.

We are on more shaky grounds in accounting for the apparent reversal among the least educated category. More precise control of the educational variation in the category does not make the reversed relationship disappear. Now note that it only achieves statistical significance for "tolerance for Communists" (row 7). We must not overlook the fact that Detroit is a single-industry, strongly unionized town. The United Automobile Workers (UAW), while never "soft" on Communists, has also never had quite the aversion for socialist and more left-wing politics that tends to characterize other American trade unions. It is possible that men in occupationally homogeneous networks in this predominantly working class category simply do not have such an aversive reaction to the Communist label as might be supposed. In any event, the high school graduate category—which is obviously completely homogeneous on the educational measure—provides strong support for the hypothesis and the relationship does not "disappear" when other relevant controls are introduced (for example, occupation, religion, and intergenerational occupational mobility). [Incidentally, we might just note in passing that a somewhat similar pattern of results was also obtained when we considered a three-item Dogmatism Scale derived from Rokeach (1960).]

I am at some loss to explain why this measure of open-mindedness is unrelated to our measure of ethnoreligious homogeneity beyond noting that ethnoreligious differences per se, once educational differences are taken into account (see Chapter 8, Table 8.1), are unrelated to differences in tolerance toward political extremists, while the various socioeconomic status indicators, including occupation, are consistently correlated with them. That is, intimate associations with others of similar ethnoreligious backgrounds is not likely to expose the person to prevailing attitudes for or against civil liberties for unpopular minorities.

We have already indicated our expectation that homogeneity of associates would foster more extreme, clear-cut, and consistent attitudes. In an earlier work, I presented the following rationale for such an expectation:

> The impact on one's economic and political beliefs of having associates of the same status should reinforce the beliefs characteristic of his status. On the other hand, having associations with people of status markedly different from one's own can be expected to produce cross-pressures on a man's economic and political beliefs. These cross-pressures should moderate the impact of a person's own status position as a determinant of his beliefs. For example, men in the upper occupational strata are likely to be economically conservative (and Republican in their party preference). Equal status association would tend to reinforce their conservatism, whereas unequal status association (especially since it would normally imply relations with lower-status persons) would tend to moderate their conservatism toward a moderate or more liberal position. Conversely, persons in the lower occupational strata are likely to be economically liberal (and Democratic in their party preference). Equal status contact will reinforce this tendency, while unequal status contact (because this usually implies interaction with higher-status persons) will moderate the liberal tendency toward a moderate or more conservative position. (Laumann, 1966: 134–35).

In this earlier study, based on a sample of white men living in Cambridge and Belmont, Massachusetts and employing a variant of the homogeneity index used here, I found that men high in "associational congruence"—equivalent to "homogeneity" here—were more likely to express definite

Table 5.4. Occupational homogeneity by strength of party preference: percent distributions, total sample

	Party Preference*		
	Strong Republican or Democratic Party Preference	Independent Preference or Only Slightly Inclined Toward Republicans or Democrats	Total
Homogeneous Occupational associates**	66.5%	33.5	100.0 (233)
Heterogeneous	55.3	44.7	100.0 (295)
Total	60.2	39.8	100.0 (528)
	$\chi^2 = 6.90, p < .01.$		

* Excludes men who expressed only "moderate" (or regular) preference for one or the other party.

** The distribution of scores on occupational homogeneity was split approximately at its median.

party preferences for *either* the Republican *or* Democratic party, while men low in associational congruence were more likely to be "independents."

This result is strikingly corroborated by the Detroit data, as can be seen in Table 5.4. (This pattern is also observable for each educational category. It is noteworthy that there was no relationship between degree of homogeneity and a man's preference for one or the other political party that was not qualified as being either strong or weak.) The association between "strong" party preference and ethnoreligious homogeneity, unfortunately, failed to achieve statistical significance although it was also in the direction reported for occupational homogeneity and "strong" preference.

Finally, our hypotheses did not fare so well for our three-item measure of economic liberalism-conservatism (see Table 8.1, footnote a). We were unable to detect any significant relationship between extremeness of liberal or conservative economic views and occupational or ethnoreligious homogeneity although the expected pattern was again observable.

These findings, taken in conjunction with those reported earlier (Laumann, 1966: 134–37), provide reasonably consistent, although by no means overwhelming, evidence supporting the hypothesis that homogeneity in one's intimate social milieu tends to "sustain" a certain consistency and definiteness in orientation toward the world. We should emphasize that it is not so much the *content* or substance of one's orientation (such as preference for one or the other political party) but the *form* of one's orientation that is affected by consistency of milieu.

ETHNORELIGIOUS AND OCCUPATIONAL HOMOGENEITY
CONSIDERED SIMULTANEOUSLY

To this point, we have examined the ascription- and achievement-based measures of friendship homogeneity by relating each by itself to other characteristics of the respondents. But an additional question must certainly be posed: what happens when one considers the two bases of homogeneity simultaneously? Surely we should expect that a man whose friends are similar to him on *both* ethnoreligious *and* occupational grounds is likely to be subjected to much more consistent and coherent social influences and control than one whose friends are quite dissimilar and differentiated with respect to one another in *both* crucial social respects simply by virtue of the former network's probable pyramiding of shared social perspectives among the participants. Further, one might expect differential consequences when men are in networks homogeneous on one factor but heterogeneous on the other. By splitting each measure's distribution of scores approximately at its median and cross-tabulating the resulting dichotomies, we can identify four "types" of friendship homogeneity. The two polar or "pure" types are, on one end, relatively *homogeneous* networks on both occupational and ethnoreligious characteristics of friends and, on the other end, relatively *heterogeneous* networks on both compositional factors. The two intermediate or "mixed" types are, of course, either homogeneous ethnoreligiously and heterogeneous occupationally or heterogeneous ethnoreligiously and homogeneous occupationally.

Without presenting all the details of the analysis here, I shall briefly summarize the most important results of the comparisons of these four types of friendship networks. Unless otherwise noted, the patterns described are statistically significant at the .05 level or less for each of the three educational levels and two religious categories considered above as well as for the total sample. Since the four types are not strictly ordered from pure homogeneity to pure heterogeneity—that is, we do not know the relative order of the two intermediate types along the dimension of conjoint compositional homogeneity—we employed cross-tabulations with Chi-square tests to determine statistical significance rather than the correlational technique employed in the preceding sections.

First, we found that pure homogeneity decreases with age while pure heterogeneity increases with age. There is also a tendency for occupationally homogeneous and ethnoreligiously heterogeneous networks to decline with age. There is, however, no consistent pattern for the other mixed category. As we suggested before, one can undoubtedly devise plausible ad hoc hypotheses emphasizing differences in stages in the life cycle to account for these age effects.

While there is no apparent association between the number of generations in the United States and pure homogeneity or heterogeneity, there are sharp differences between the two mixed categories—an example of an interaction effect. Men of the second generation favor ethnoreligiously homogeneous and occupationally heterogeneous networks while men of four or more generations in the United States favor occupationally homogeneous and ethnoreligiously heterogeneous networks. This is quite consistent with the hypothesized decline in ethnoreligious concerns and the hypothesized increase in occupational orientations over the generations mentioned before.

With regard to broad religious preference, Catholics are more than twice as likely as Protestants to be in pure homogeneous and *ethnoreligiously homogeneous,* occupationally heterogeneous networks; while Protestants are twice as likely to be in pure heterogeneous and *occupationally homogeneous,* ethnoreligious heterogeneous networks. One is tempted to recall here Durkheim's (1951) classic characterization of Protestant/Catholic differences in social orientations that emphasized the more individualistic (or egoistic) and secularized orientations of Protestants and the more collectivized (group-oriented) and religiously grounded orientations of Catholics (see also Weber, 1930).

In general, various measures of a man's socioeconomic status, including his occupational status, educational attainment, total family income, and subjective class identification, are not significantly related to the four types of homogeneity although there is a consistent tendency for men of higher socioeconomic status to be in pure homogeneous networks. One can only speculate here that such tendencies toward pure homogeneity among high status persons might greatly facilitate and sustain the development of coherent and consistent orientations toward the world and a characteristic style of life among "elite" groups. The fact that it is not a predominant tendency among such individuals (nor for that matter among people at the bottom of the socioeconomic hierarchy) may help to account for the relative failure to develop a sharply differentiated "social class" with a highly distinctive style of life at the top (or bottom) of the white stratification system in urban America (see Laumann, 1966).[4] It would be very interesting to have comparable information on smaller communities of the sort studied by W. Lloyd Warner (1953) and his associates who reported the existence of a sharply differentiated upper-upper (and lower-

lower) class with distinctive styles of life from the rest of the community. Could it be shown that such tendencies toward pure homogeneous networks at specific class levels are much more pronounced in such communities than in the large metropolis due perhaps to the greater or lesser differentiation of their respective social structures?

With respect to the various measures of social participation and other network characteristics, we found, consistent with our expectations (see next chapter), that interlocking networks are especially common in the pure homogeneous category and radial networks in the pure heterogeneous category. It is worth noting here that the two intermediate forms of homogeneity do not manifest consistent tendencies to associate with one or the other form of network connectedness. Perhaps the most intriguing finding in regard to social participation, however, concerns the relationship between the number of memberships in voluntary associations and network homogeneity. Men in pure homogeneous networks are much more likely to belong to three or more associations while men in pure heterogeneous networks are more likely to have no or only one membership. The association is accentuated among men with some college or more education. This finding is consistent with the expectation discussed above that persons who are anchored in a socially homogeneous space are facilitated or encouraged to participate in the characteristic activities of their social status. It is noteworthy, however, that the extent or size of a man's friendship network, whether the network is joint (interaction with wife present) or sex segregated, and the average frequency of interaction are not patterned in any significant way with the four types of network homogeneity.

In comparing the pattern of frequency of church attendance, devotionalism, and expressed interest in land of patrilineal origin by type of homogeneity with the pattern of distribution of Catholics and Protestants among the types of networks, one finds that they are remarkably similar. This would lead us to expect that it is the differential religious distribution that is accounting for the association of homogeneity and these attitudes and behavior rather than to the different types of homogeneity per se. Contrary to this expectation, however, these patterns *persist* in both the Protestant and Catholic subsamples. This means that these attitudes are associated with different types of networks *independent* of religious preference. Broadly consistent with the general pattern of results reported before, "pure" homogeneity among high school graduates is associated with "close-mindedness" and "pure" heterogeneity with "open-mindedness" while such associations either are not significant or are reversed for the other two categories. Finally, discussion with friends of making a job change, as might be expected, is especially likely among men who are occupationally homogeneous, but ethnoreligiously heterogeneous (presumably in such networks occupation was more likely to be the significant basis of the friendship).

CONCLUSIONS

We have presented a wide range of evidence in support of our contention that homogeneity of friendship networks is differentially distributed in the population on various social and demographic characteristics. Further, there appears to be systematic and theoretically meaningful differences between the two types of homogeneity in their pattern of relationships with a variety of attitudinal and network characteristics that plausibly conform to our notion that ethnoreligious homogeneity reflects an ascriptive orientation to the world while occupational homogeneity taps an achievement orientation. It is perhaps worth stressing here that religious differences appear in general to have a much stronger impact on the compositional homogeneity of a man's friendship network than his socioeconomic status characteristics. We might also highlight the fact that, contrary to the expectations of certain theorists, there appears to be no incompatibility between ascription and achievement-oriented criteria for selecting friends—the predicted negative correlation between these two kinds of homogeneity is only of negligible size (although admittedly significant, given the size of the sample). Moreover, one can more plausibly argue, with Mayhew, that these correlations, such as they are, are more likely to arise from differences in the "opportunity structure for friendship selection" at different levels of the social structure than from "functional incompatibilities" between the criteria of choice per se. While any given relationship between homogeneity and another variable is not of any appreciable size (the correlation coefficients are uniformly low), they do not disappear when appropriate controls are introduced and the overall trend and consistency of the results gives us some confidence in the belief that the character of network homogeneity is of some importance in understanding the men's view of the world.

Finally, we should reemphasize the fact that our measures of homogeneity derive in a systematic empirical manner from our macrostructural analyses of the social structure of ethnoreligious and occupational groups and not from a priori and impressionistic notions about the nature of social similarity. It is on this fundamental point that we hope that we have made a first step in introducing more empirical and theoretical rigor in examining the many interesting but primarily impressionistic speculations of various theorists and commentators on primary social environments.

NOTES

1. The rationale for picking these particular structural characteristics for study should become more apparent as we proceed to the analysis. Suffice it to say at this point that both have received considerable theoretical and empirical attention in the literature. In addition to their obvious theoretical importance, they have the further virtue of being relatively "easy" and appropriate to measure given our exclusive reliance on a survey instrument for data collection.

2. We might note in passing that both distributions of homogeneity scores are normally distributed with a slight skewing toward the homogeneity end of the continuum. Their means and standard deviations are approximately equal.

We have calculated several alternative measures of homogeneity and explored their relationships to our proposed measures. First, we simply counted the number of friends of the same ethnic group as the respondent. This count correlates .39 ($p < .001$) with our measure of ethnoreligious homogeneity and is uncorrelated (perhaps even negatively correlated) with our measure of occupational homogeneity. Second, we subtracted the respondent's occupational prestige score (Duncan, 1961) from those of his three friends, squared and summed the differences, took the square root of the resulting sum and subtracted it from 100 (compare Laumann, 1966: 114–16). This measure reflects the heterogeneous composition of the friendship network only in terms of prestige differences among the occupations and correlates .58 ($p < .001$) with our new measure of occupational homogeneity. A measure of educational homogeneity, utilizing the number of school years completed of respondents and his friends and calculated according to the formula employed in the occupational prestige index, correlated only .20 ($p < .01$) with our measure of occupational homogeneity. (Table 5.2 below summarizes these results.) These several correlations suggest that while there are substantial relationships among the measures, there also appears to be substantial variation in one measure that is not accounted for by the other.

3. Regarding the association between interest in and identification with one's occupation and friendship choice, we found in a study of engineers and technologists (see Rapoport and Laumann, 1964) that the greater an engineer's subjective commitment to engineering as an occupation, the more likely he reported all his best friends were engineers like himself. Conversely, the lower his identification with the occupation, the more likely he reported friends with occupations other than engineering [compare Lipset et al. (1956) discussion of the printers' occupational community]. Although somewhat crude given the relative heterogeneity of the occupational categories, we could consider the ratios of friendship self-selection within occupational groups (Table 4.1, Column 4) as reflecting the degree to which given occupational groups approximate occupational communities. By and large, professionals, self-employed and skilled groups—all groups relatively high on preference for entrepreneurial over bureaucratic occupations given a choice (see Table 4.2,

Column 6)—are much more likely to select friends among themselves (that is, they have higher ratios of self-selection) than clerical and other bureaucratically employed workers who seem to have the weakest tendencies toward self-selection and, inferentially at least, a lower interest in their occupational activities per se.

4. In a Warner-type study of Kansas City, with a population of some 850,000, conducted in the early 1950s, Coleman and Neugarten (1971) claim to have identified five *bounded* intimate interaction systems which they call "social classes" with distinctive styles of life; but, in my judgment, their evidence for this claim is neither adequate nor compelling. For a more detailed critique of this study, see my review (1972).

CHAPTER 6

Interlocking and Radial Friendship Nets: A Formal Feature with Important Consequences

THE STRUCTURE AND FUNCTION OF INTIMATE FACE-TO-FACE GROUPS

Intimate face-to-face interaction, whether in dyadic or larger group relationships, has long been recognized to be of crucial importance in the formation of an individual's basic personality or self-conception (see Brim, 1966: 3–49; McCall and Simmons, 1966), the development and maintenance of myriad attitudes toward the world,[1] the determination and social control of "appropriate behavior" (see Merton and Kitt, 1950; Kemper, 1968), and the maintenance of "motivational commitment to participate" through the provision of opportunities for release of emotional tension and for socioemotional support (see Bales, 1958; Parsons and Bales, 1955; March and Simon, 1958). Indeed, the intimate face-to-face group is often held to form the critical "primary environment" by which an individual is related to the larger society (see Verba, 1961: 17–60; Scheuch, 1965). (See Chapter 7 below for a fuller discussion of this last point.) One might reasonably argue that much of the research enterprise in social psychology has been devoted to the task of analyzing the specific mechanisms by which these various functions of intimate interaction are achieved.

While social scientists have long recognized the significance of the face-to-face group for individual behavior, until recently urban sociologists have lamented the disappearance of the small intimate group as a sustaining social force in the modern city. Louis Wirth, for example, in his classic essay (1938: 12, 20–21), "Urbanism as a Way of Life," observed:

. . . This is essentially what is meant by saying that the city is characterized by secondary rather than primary contacts. The contacts of the city may indeed be face to face, but they are nevertheless impersonal, superficial, transitory, and segmental. The reserve, the indifference, and the blasé outlook which urbanites manifest in their relationships may thus be regarded as devices for immunizing themselves against the personal claims and expectations of others.

The superficiality, the anonymity, and the transitory character of urban-social relations make intelligible, also, the sophistication and the rationality generally ascribed to city dwellers. . . .

The distinctive features of the urban mode of life have often been described sociologically as consisting of the substitution of secondary for primary contacts, the weakening of bonds of kinship, and the declining social significance of the family, the disappearance of the neighborhood, and the undermining of the traditional basis of social solidarity. All these phenomena can be substantially verified through objective indices. . . .

In effect then, urban sociologists have tended to infer microstructural characteristics of social networks based on inferences from large-scale changes in society as they shift from *Gemeinschaft* (or rural community) to *Gesellschaft* (or urban society).

But perhaps beginning with Bott's (1957) highly suggestive analysis of the closely knit and intensive kin and friend *networks* of some 20 working and middle class families in London, a number of authors have contributed intensive case studies of the social networks of various populations living in fairly circumscribed urban neighborhoods.[2] One of the fundamental implications drawn from these studies has been to suggest that in heavily populated, even economically depressed sections of the city, residents enjoy much more vigorous and vital informal social networks than has hitherto been assumed, and these networks perform many of the same important social functions attributed to them by anthropologists studying nonurban societies.

With the "rediscovery" of social networks in urban society and, admittedly, to some extent independent of this development, a number of writers have attempted to develop more formal, theoretical treatments of the properties of social networks as communication systems and as mechanisms by which individuals may be linked into the larger society.[3] While some important advances have been made in developing the theory of networks (see discussion in Chapter 1 above), one major constraint on such a venture, in my opinion, has been the relatively limited cross-sectional and comparative data available on urban populations in general. Case studies are excellent vehicles for developing interesting new working hypotheses, but they are of considerably more limited value in identifying the general features of the phenomenon from the idiosyncratic features of the specific case. For example, it is important to know the extent to which closely-knit networks are a special feature of settled working class populations of particular ethnic backgrounds (the groups most often studied in these case studies) and the extent to which they are commonly found throughout the social structure without regard to socioeconomic status or ethnicity. The findings reported below, together with those of the last chapter, should provide us with more suitable "fixes" on the general features of informal urban networks at least for the white population.

INTERLOCKING AND RADIAL NETWORKS: SOME EXPECTATIONS

Deriving from certain suggestions of Georg Simmel and others, the preceding chapter directed our attention to the "formal" property of friendship networks with respect to their compositional homogeneity as it relates to a variety of demographic, social, and attitudinal characteristics of our sample. In this chapter we shall be concerned with the extent to which the set of three friends and the respondent form an interrelated group. In gathering information on the respondent's three closest friends, we also determined which of the three "nominated" friends were good friends of one another (see Q25, Appendix C). We were thus in a position to characterize the friendship network of our respondents as being radial or interlocking (see Harary, Norman, and Cartwright, 1965). A *radial* network is one in which ego (the main respondent) engages in three *discrete* dyadic relations with his friends inasmuch as they are not friends of one another and do not have common interaction among themselves, while an *interlocking* network is one in which at least two of the friends are good friends of one another and have common interaction with ego. Diagrammatically these networks may be represented as in Figure 6.1:

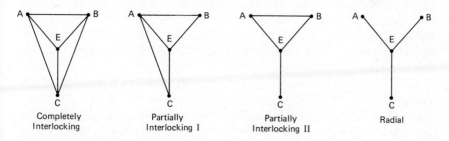

Completely Interlocking	Partially Interlocking I	Partially Interlocking II	Radial

Figure 6.1 Types of friendship networks. E = ego or main respondent; A,B,C = friends A, B, and C; ——— = friendship link.

Although many features of our inquiry must be frankly exploratory, we do have a number of general expectations that will guide our analysis. In general, we expect an interlocking network to be composed of a set of individuals who are alike in a number of important social respects on the grounds that similarity of social attributes tends to imply similarity of social attitudes and personality characteristics and therefore mutual attraction (see Laumann, 1966). These similarities facilitate the development of *common* intimacy since an extensive, common set of values, interests and concerns are likely to be shared among the members of the net (compare Newcomb, 1961; Davis, 1963: 451–59; Rosow, 1957; Shils, 1951). A salient characteristic of an intimate face-to-face relationship, especially when voluntarily created and dissolved without institutional constraint as in marriage (friends in a sense continuously *choose* each other), is the minimization or at least strict regulation of heated conflict and dissension among the participants. Friendship may almost be defined as a consensual relationship. Similarity of religious or political views, for example, would tend to reduce the potential for conflicting attitudes and opinion that are usually of some importance to most people and therefore likely to play a role in social intercourse. Moreover, people sharing relatively similar positions socially are also more likely to share common physical locations at work and in private life (compare literature on residential segregation by occupation and ethnicity including Duncan and Duncan, 1955b; Lieberson, 1963; Laumann, 1966). Sheer physical proximity should facilitate the weaving of more interconnected networks—that is, friends of ego are simply more likely to encounter one another as well so that intimate relations between them can develop.

Radial networks, on the other hand, may be formed on some more specialized basis (for example, a common interest in chess, work activities, sports). There is little need for uniformity of opinions across the set of persons inasmuch as they do not interact with other than ego and he can tailor the interactional exchange to fit a particular dyadic relationship. Consequently, the alters *can* be considerably more differentiated or heterogeneous in important social respects although, of course, they do not *have* to be so differentiated.

People in radial networks are, moreover, likely to have a relatively lower affective involvement and commitment to their relations with alters because the set of common interests and concerns is likely to be more severely circumscribed and limited by virtue of the greater likelihood of differing statuses comprising the networks. The exchange of intimate information about oneself is more problematic when there is uncertainty about the evaluative standards that may be employed by alter who is different from ego in important social respects. Persons of very different status attributes are likely to have differing standards for evaluating the same information (see Berelson et al., 1954, on cross-pressures on vote intensions; Turner, 1965). Consequently, relations in radial structures are likely to be weaker in affective involvement and more functionally specific, while relations in interlocking networks are likely to be much more affective and functionally diffuse.[4]

We may further expect that the successful maintenance of a radial network is inherently more difficult and complicated for the individual than maintenance of an interlocking network because of the probable need to balance conflicting demands and expectations. Consequently, we expect that, holding educational attainment constant, persons in radial networks are likely to have greater intellectual capabilities than persons in interlocking networks.

Networks having high emotional involvement for the individual, a relatively monolithic set of expectations (due to the commonalities of the components), and high frequencies of contact should be more effective mechanisms of social influence and control on ego than those that are "disorganized" with respect to given social perspectives and relatively lacking in personal involvements. Moreover, an ego in an interlocking network must in some sense "confront" at least two significant others who are likely to be in communication with one another concerning his manifest behavior and attitudes. Their positions as "social control agents" should be more effective by virtue of this potential for coalition formation (two against one) that is simply nonexistent in dyadic interaction (see Simmel, 1950; Caplow, 1969; the classic social psychological experiments of Asch (1956) and Sherif (1936) investigating the impact of majority opinion on ego's perceptual judgments; Proshansky and Seidenberg, 1965). As a result, we should expect attitudes of persons in interlocking networks to be more "decisive" and expressive of the characteristic content of given social positions than those of persons in radial networks.[5] For example, persons in interlocking networks should be more likely to have explicit identifications with political parties than those in radial networks, given the expectation that interlocking networks are likely to be more politically homogeneous than radial networks. In short, interlocking networks should serve as more effective group anchors for opinions and attitudes than radial networks for much the same reasons as sketched in the last chapter (pp. 97–105) for the efficacy of homogeneous networks as "anchors" for opinions and attitudes.

In a more speculative vein, we argue that radial networks are in some sense more flexible and, consequently, more adaptive to the demands of a modern industrial society that is undergoing continuous social change and in which many of its personnel are likely to be highly mobile, both geographically and socially. The formation of friendship ties on functionally more specific criteria may facilitate an individual's adaptation to new social circumstances (compare Eisenstadt, 1954; Blau, 1956; Whyte, 1956). Consequently, socially mobile persons should be more likely to have radial networks. Interlocking networks should be associated with more localistic and ascriptive orientations of ego and should be rooted in long-term neighborhood associations and ascriptive ties of kinship and common ethnoreligious backgrounds [see Gans' (1962) description of intimate relations among working class Italo-Americans; Bott, 1957]. To summarize our speculations in terms of the pattern variables, radial networks are more likely to be functionally specific, universalistic, affectively more neutral, and performance or achievement oriented; while interlocking networks are more likely to be functionally diffuse, particularistic, affective, and quality or ascription oriented.[6]

The schematic diagram in Figure 6.2, a modified version of Figure 1.1 in the introductory chapter, attempts to summarize our model of the hypothesized interrelationships among various features of an individual's personality and social position, structural characteristics of his non-kin-based "primary environment" and attitudes toward politics, ethnic identity, and work that might be presumed to be especially responsive to his experiences in his current social environment. I shall again informally characterize the model as a "path diagram" (see Duncan, 1966b) as it follows the logic and conventions of path analysis (see Chapter 1, pp. 12–13). It is worth stressing here that it is not a path diagram because a number of the variables and their interrelationships violate some of the basic assumptions underlying linear regression analysis and, consequently, we could not estimate the path coefficients for the model from the data we will be considering. Nevertheless, we believe the model will provide a useful theoretical overview for integrating the complex set of findings to be discussed below.

With these general considerations and expectations in mind, we shall attempt to answer three general questions:

1. Are interlocking and radial networks differentially distributed in the population with respect to demographic, socioeconomic and personality characteristics of respondents?

2. Do these networks differ systematically with respect to their composition (that is, similarity or dissimilarity of social attributes of the participants), frequencies and sites of interaction and levels of intimacy?

3. Do men involved in these networks differ with respect to selected characteristic attitudes?

Just as was briefly alluded to in the preceding chapter, there is a fundamental ambiguity in our data regarding the appropriate explanatory model linking the type of friendship network to other characteristics of the respondent. On the one hand, a "self-selectivity" model would suggest that the relationship between the type of network and another variable

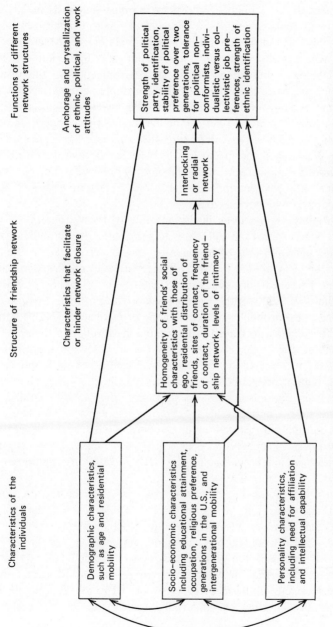

Characteristics of the individuals

Structure of friendship network

Functions of different network structures

Demographic characteristics, such as age and residential mobility

Socio-economic characteristics including educational attainment, occupation, religious preference, generations in the U.S., and intergenerational mobility

Personality characteristics, including need for affiliation and intellectual capability

Characteristics that facilitate or hinder network closure

Homogeneity of friends' social characteristics with those of ego, residential distribution of friends, sites of contact, frequency of contact, duration of the friendship network, levels of intimacy

Interlocking or radial network

Anchorage and crystallization of ethnic, political, and work attitudes

Strength of political party identification, stability of political preference over two generations, tolerance for political non-conformists, individualistic versus collectivistic job preferences, strength of ethnic identification

Figure 6.2 A hypothetical model for the structural-functional analysis of interlocking and radial networks.

117

is mediated by certain perduring features of the personality of ego. That is, a man with certain characteristic ways of looking at the world creates a social network that supports his outlook. Indeed his associates may meet an important need for social validation of his points of view. On the other hand, a "structuralist" model would place primary emphasis on the characteristics of the *current* social environment of ego to which he reacts and by which his attitudes are formed and maintained. Macrostructural processes, which place very sharp constraints and limitations on active individual choice in "creating" his social environment, are the principal determinants of these characteristics. For example, occupational activity or the social ecology of the neighborhood in which the individual lives willy-nilly involves him in physical contacts and social opportunities to meet prospective friends. His values, attitudes, and habits become congruent with those expected in the group in which he has become involved. Each model obviously implies quite different causal processes. Yet our survey data provide little information to enable one to determine which model is more appropriate in a given case.

My theoretical predilections incline me toward the "structuralist" point of view, in which forces typically beyond the control of the individual are regarded as providing the determinative causal force, rather than the converse notion, in which the individual essentially creates his primary environment to reflect his preexisting needs and orientations. There is no doubt that the "real world" is probably a mixture of these two processes in which there are probably even cybernetic or feedback relations between them. But the schema portrayed in Figure 6.2 is reflective of the structuralist presumption; the reader is warned that the cross-sectional nature of the data precludes an explicit test of this presumption just as it did for our analysis of homogeneity and its correlates in the preceding chapter. Of course, there is no reason why social forces must neatly parallel each other in any case. Contingencies making interlocking networks likely may be quite randomly distributed among socioeconomic status levels while the attractiveness of one type of network over another may vary more directly with personality characteristics such as need for autonomy and world views.

Before turning to the findings, it is useful to describe the distribution of types of networks for the entire sample. Table 6.1 indicates that 27 percent of the men are in completely interlocking networks (all three friends are good friends of one another) and another 42 percent have at least two friends who are good friends of one another. Only 31 percent are in completely radial networks. The entire analysis described below was first performed on these three types of networks: completely interlocking, partially interlocking, and radial (see Figure 6.1). Rarely were

Table 6.1.   Types of friendship networks. (Answers to Q25: "Of your three best friends, how many of them are good friends with one another?") Percent distribution

	Percent
All three of them (completely interlocking)	27 ⎫
Partially interlocking I (AB, AC; BA, BC; or CA, CB)	2 ⎬ 69
Partially interlocking II (AB, AC, or BC)	40 ⎭
None of them (radial)	31
Total	100

Total N	988
Not ascertained	12
No friends reported	13
Sample total	1013

there any significant differences between completely and partially interlocking networks when compared to radial networks. One might almost conclude, with Simmel, that the mere presence of tryadic rather than dyadic relations would appear sufficient to raise qualitatively different processes of interaction. Consequently, for the purposes of this chapter, the completely and partially interlocking networks will be treated as a single category.

AN ASIDE ON METHOD: MULTIPLE CLASSIFICATION ANALYSIS

For much of the analysis which follows, we shall be regarding the connectedness of the network as a dichotomous dependent variable. We shall examine this variable's relationship to a number of demographic and social characteristics including religious preference, educational attainment, occupation, age, and so on. Not only are these independent variables correlated among themselves (which poses questions about each variable's relationship to the dependent variable "net" of the effects of the other variables that may be correlated with the independent variable under examination), but also some of these variables are qualitative (for example, religion) rather than continuously ordered along some scale (for example, family income). Consequently, multiple regression analysis, which assumes among other things the presence of linear relationships among the independent and dependent variables, is inappropriate.

The major analytical tool to be employed is the technique of multiple classification analysis (Hill, 1959; Pelz and Andrews, 1961; Morgan et al., 1962; Andrews, 1963; Andrews, Morgan, and Sonquist, 1967), a multivariate technique that can be used to examine the relationship between a predictor (independent) variable and a dependent variable or the relationships between each of a set of predictor variables and a dependent variable holding the effects of the remaining predictors constant (see Chapter 1, p. 17). As noted in Chapter 1, while operating in principle similar to multiple regression techniques with respect to its additive assumptions (see Fennessy, 1968), multiple classification analysis is the analysis of variance with unequal cell entries (reflecting the correlations among the independent variables being considered). Its advantage over multiple regression techniques is that the predictor variables may be in a form as weak as the nominal level of measurement. The two major constraints of multiple classification analysis are that the dependent variable must be an interval scale (a dichotomy is such a scale), while no predictors should be so highly correlated that there is complete overlapping on any categories.

To determine the relationship between an independent and a dependent variable, the computer routine yields (in addition to the N and the percent of the total) the mean value of the dependent variable—in this case, a proportion—for each category of each predictor variable, thus allowing one to see whether the relationship is positive, negative, or curvilinear. The program also yields an eta coefficient (or correlation ratio), the square of which indicates the proportion of the total variance in the dependent variable accounted for by the effect of each predictor variable considered by itself. When multiple predictors are used, the program yields an adjusted mean giving the mean value of the dependent variable for each category of the predictor, controlling for the effects of the remainder of the set of predictors.

Other output includes an adjusted multiple correlation coefficient, which, when squared, yields the proportion of variance in the dependent variable accounted for by all of the predictor variables considered simultaneously, the total sum of squares, the total explained sum of squares, and the residual sum of squares. From these statistics, a variety of F tests can be computed (see Andrews, Morgan, and Sonquist, 1967: 99–100, for computing formulae) to test the statistical significance of various summary statistics, such as the correlation ratio and the net increment of an additional variable in the multivariate model.

FORM OF NETWORK AND SOCIAL POSITION

Turning to the first of the three general questions posed above, we can determine from Table 6.2 that only two of the seven demographic and

Table 6.2.   Correlation ratios (etas) of selected demographic and social characteristics of respondents and their involvement in an interlocking or radial network

Demographic and Social Characteristics[a]	Etas
Number of generations in the U.S. (paternal line) (2)	.005
Age (4),	.071
Broad religious preference (4)	.114*
Ethnic group (7)	.122*
Educational attainment (6)	.089
Occupation (7)	.061
Proportion of life spent in Detroit (5)	.088

* $p < .01$.

[a] The number of categories employed in each predictor variable is reported in the parentheses.

social characteristics of the respondents considered was significantly related to the type of network—namely, that of broad religious preference and ethnic group membership (but this latter relationship *disappears* when broad religious preference is controlled). Holding all the other predictor variables "constant," 75 percent of the Catholics and 77 percent of the Jews were in interlocking networks while only 63 percent of the Protestants and 62 percent of the "other" religious category were in closely knit networks. Not only are there no zero-order effects of the other variables on the type of network favored, but all of them together make no significant contribution to the explained sum of squares once the net effects of religious preference are taken into account.

This is a puzzling and important result as one would certainly expect that a man's ethnic group membership, relative socioeconomic standing, and age would also be of some importance in determining the form of his friendship network. First, it is noteworthy that it is Catholic religious affiliation per se that affects the type of network and not the recency of arrival of the man's family (generations in the United States) or specific ethnic affiliation. Many descriptive studies of the behavior of working class members of various ethnic and racial groups [including those of Whyte (1943), Gans (1962), Liebow (1967), and Suttles (1968)] have stressed the intensive and closely knit nature of their interpersonal relationships. Surely we would have expected to find that second-generation Americans would be more likely to have interlocking networks since they manifest stronger ethnic-based affiliations than later-generation Americans (see preceding chapter on the correlation of homogeneous ethnoreligious friendship groups and generations in the United States).

Second, we would have supposed that younger men in their twenties would have closer and more interconnected ties with friends than older men who are more involved with family and occupational responsibilities and presumably have less time to devote to activities with friends. (See Chapter 2 above that reports younger men as having closer ties with friends than older men.) While the pattern of net effects on age does conform with this expectation, it is not strong enough to be statistically significant.

Third, these same observers and others (for examples, Bott, 1957; Young and Willmott, 1959) would also suggest that working class men should be more likely to form more tightly knit networks than middle and upper middle class men because their friendships are more likely to be neighborhood based, making interlocking networks more probable. But neither educational attainment nor occupation is related to the differential formation of interlocking and radial networks. That is, a strong majority of men (69 percent) at every class level (however indexed) appear to form closely knit networks. Finally, we would expect that the longer a man lived in one place, the more likely that time alone would enable his intimate associates to come to know one another. Apparently the weaving of closely knit networks requires relatively little time to be completed. (An examination of the pattern of net effects of the proportion of life spent in Detroit does conform with this "opportunity" hypothesis, but is not of sufficient magnitude to achieve significance. Men of less than five years' residence in Detroit do appear to be somewhat less likely to be in interlocking networks than men of longer residence.)

As a final observation on "background" characteristics, we should note our speculation that intergenerational occupational mobility should be associated with the type of friendship network on the grounds that substantial upward or downward movement in occupational status from father to son (the respondent) involves major changes in the nature of social contacts available to an individual and should lead to a more socially heterogeneous set of friendships, some of which were formed at the man's status of origin and some at his status of destination. The formation of an interlocking network should be more difficult for the socially mobile (see Eisenstadt, 1954; Blau, 1956). But we found that there was simply no zero-order or higher order (with education and religion controlled) relationship between intergenerational mobility and the type of network.

In arguing that the successful maintenance of a radial network is inherently more difficult and complicated for the individual than the maintenance of an interlocking network because of the greater need to balance conflicting demands and expectations arising from a more heterogeneous set of friends, we concluded above that, net of educational differences, persons in radial networks are likely to have greater intellectual capabilities than persons in interlocking networks. We measured "intellectual capabilities" with the 13-item Similarities Subtest of the Wechsler Adult Intelligence Scale (see Q70, Appendix C),[7] contrasting those who scored in the bottom third of the distribution with those in the average and above average thirds. The zero-order correlation ratio is .080 ($p < .02$) with men scoring in the bottom third being more likely to be in interlocking networks. While just failing to achieve statistical significance when educational and religious differences are taken into account, the pattern remains. For high school graduates alone (where this measure of intellectual functioning is of great importance because educational achievement cannot vary by definition), 85 percent of the men scoring in the lowest third were in interlocking networks while only 67 percent of the men in the upper two-thirds were in interlocking networks ($p < .001$).

FORM OF NETWORK AND OTHER FEATURES OF INTIMATE INTERACTION

We may now turn to the second general question: do these networks differ systematically with respect to their composition (similarity or dissimilarity of social attributes of the participants), frequencies and sites of interaction, and levels of intimacy? Each of these network characteristics may be expected to affect the manner in which ego's friends influence his values and attitudes. Table 6.3 summarizes the zero-order correlation ratios.

With the exception of the number of friends who live in the respondent's

Table 6.3.   Correlation ratios (etas) of selected features of friendship networks and their interlocking or radial character

Features of Friendship Networks[a]	Etas
Number of friends residing in the neighborhood (3)	.070
Number of persons regarded as friends (3)	.122*
Ethnoreligious homogeneity (5)	.159*
Occupational homogeneity (5)	.130*
Political party homogeneity (3)	.111*
Average frequency of interaction (3)	.194*
Number of home-based interactions (4)	.203*
Number of work-based interactions (4)	.162*
Average level of intimacy (5)	.123*
Average duration of friendship (5)	.129*

* $p < .01$.
[a] The number of categories employed in each predictor variable is reported in the parentheses. See footnotes to Table 5.2 for definitions of measures.

immediate neighborhood, each of our measures of different features of the friendship network are significantly related to whether or not the network is closely knit. Even when both religious and educational background characteristics are controlled, *all* of the significant zero-order relationships continue to be significant. Apparently propinquity per se does not facilitate the formation of closely knit networks; but the more friends entertained in the home or seen regularly at work, the more interlocking the networks are likely to be.[8] It is especially noteworthy that interlocking networks are exceptionally likely to be composed of members who are similar to one another in ethnoreligious group memberships, occupational activities, and political party preferences while radial networks are likely to be more heterogeneous in these three respects (see Table 5.2 also). As we predicted in our introductory remarks, interlocking networks will be composed of people who are similar to one another in important social respects, while radial networks will be less likely to be socially homogeneous. Similarity on important social attributes among a set of persons should at least facilitate the formation of such networks.

Various subanalyses were performed to determine whether each type of compositional homogeneity contributed independently to the formation of interlocking networks, once religious and educational background differences and all the other measures of homogeneity were controlled. While ethnoreligious and political party homogeneity made significant net contributions to the explained sums of squares when all the other variables were taken into account, occupational homogeneity, rather surprisingly, failed to make significant net contributions. (This result was also reported in the preceding chapter on the basis of a somewhat different analytic technique. It is perhaps worth stressing again that it is ascription-based rather than achievement-based homogeneity that seems especially congenial to the emergence of interlocking nets.)

Interestingly enough, the more persons a man counts as his friends, that is, the more extensive his friendship net, the more likely he is himself in an interlocking net and the more likely he reports that his three friends are very close personal friends—that is, the more intensive are his reported friendship relations.[9] Men in radial networks, on the other hand, tend to report fewer friends in general and these are not regarded as especially close personal friends. Finally, as expected, we find that the greater the proportion of one's life one knows his three "best" friends, the greater the likelihood that they form an interlocking network.[10]

We can summarize the results to this point by saying that interlocking networks are more likely to be homogeneous in the important social respects of ethnoreligious group membership, occupational activity (only zero-order effects), and political party preference, to involve greater feel-ings of intimacy and emotional involvement, to involve greater frequencies of contact, and to have, on the average, existed for a longer proportion of one's life than radial networks.

These features, separately or in combination, would certainly seem to encourage a more functionally diffuse relationship among the men in closely-knit networks. To distinguish among types of friendship bonds, we asked the following question:

Q59. Now, here's a list of several problems that might come up in a person's life. (Present card.) Some people would ordinarily want to discuss some of these with their friends; others would ordinarily prefer not to. In each, *if this were* a problem for you, would you ordinarily discuss it with your friends, or would you ordinarily rather not? What about

		Discuss	Not Discuss	Total Sample
a.	What kind of new car to buy?	64.3%	35.7	100.0
b.	Who to vote for President?	52.5	47.5	100.0
c.	Troubles between you and your wife?	9.8	90.2	100.0
d.	Difficulties at work with your boss?	43.9	56.1	100.0
e.	A serious personal medical problem?	44.5	55.5	100.0
f.	Whether to change to a better but risky new job?	66.2	33.8	100.0

The problems were selected to vary in degrees of intimacy and yet to be salient to people at all socioeconomic levels. The marginals reported suggest that we were rather successful in the first objective, and none of the items was found to be significantly correlated with socioeconomic status.

Perhaps most noteworthy here is the fact that less than two-thirds of the sample as a whole were willing to discuss with their "closest" friends such a matter as what new car to buy. And less than 10 percent would discuss marital difficulties with their closest friends. The many ethnographic studies, based on relatively long-term participant observation, of friendship relations among selected subpopulations cited above at least give one the impression that friendship relations tend to be very intensive and intimate and, indeed, in many cases even become assimilated into the kinship networks through the extension of "fictive" kinship (for example, making a close family friend a godparent or having the children call him "uncle"). While our data are by no means strictly comparable to studies such as these, I nevertheless believe it reasonable to conclude that adult friendship relations among white urban men tend, on the average, to be rather circumscribed affairs in which there are relatively restricted exchanges of intimate content [see Schneider (1969) for somewhat similar findings for the German city Osnabrück].

In any event, we found rather unexpectedly that while a simple count of the number of topics discussed with friends was not significantly related to the type of network, specific topics of an "intimate" character were more likely to be discussed in closely knit networks than in radial networks. These included discussions of difficulties with the boss, personal medical problems, marital difficulties, and changing to a better but risky new job.

FORM OF NETWORK AND ATTITUDES

We may now turn to our third general question: do men involved in the two types of networks differ with respect to selected characteristic attitudes? In general, we can answer this question in the affirmative.

With regard to a man's subjective interest in his own nationality group,[11] we find that greater interest in one's own nationality group is related to having an interlocking network of friends. This is especially true for high school graduates and Catholics—for Protestants, there is no such relationship but then, Protestants, as a group, tend to have very weak identifications with their countries of origin.

Perhaps one of the most intriguing set of results arises from examining the relationship between type of network and a man's occupational preferences. If our reasoning regarding the nature of the differences between radial and interlocking networks is plausible, then we could hypothesize that men in radial networks should prefer more individualistic, autonomous, and "risky" sorts of occupations than men in interlocking networks. This expectation is borne out by our finding that, controlling for religious and educational differences, men in radial networks are more likely to prefer, if they had a choice, being the owner of a small business over being an office worker (see Question Q57, Appendix C) and being a skilled mechanic over having a clerical job (Question Q58, Appendix C).

Our introductory discussion also suggested that we should expect interlocking networks to serve as more effective social anchors for an individual's attitudes, leading to more well crystallized attitudes on various issues characteristic of given social positions. This hypothesis is supported by our finding that men in interlocking networks are much more likely to have definite preferences for either the Republican or Democratic party, while men in radial networks are much more likely to be politically independent ($p < .02$). In addition to asking about the respondent's party preference, we asked about the party preference of his father. We divided the respondents into those who had the same party preference as their fathers and those who had switched preferences (including switching to "independent"). While 68 percent of the men in interlocking networks had the same party preference as their father's, only 57 percent of the men in radial networks had the same party affiliation as their fathers ($p < .001$). These zero-order effects persist even when educational and religious differences are taken into account and also when intergenerational occupational mobility is controlled.

Finally, if interlocking networks are especially effective group anchors for attitudes and especially likely to facilitate the emergence of crystallized attitudes and to support and maintain them, then we could expect men in interlocking networks to be more intolerant toward political extremists ("close-minded") while men in radial networks should be more tolerant toward political extremists ("open-minded") (see related discussion in Chapter 5, pp. 99–103). This expectation is supported in the results reported in Table 6.4.

To summarize these results, we have presented evidence that men in interlocking networks are likely to manifest greater subjective interest in their nationality group, to prefer relatively secure "bureaucratic" white-

Table 6.4.   Tolerance for political extremists and type of friendship networks

Total Sample	Intolerant To Both	Tolerant to Klan, Intolerant to Communists	Tolerant to Both	Total
Interlocking	44%	23%	33%	100% (363)
Radial	30	30	40	100% (148)

Tolerance for Political Extremists[a]

χ^2 7.92, 2 d.f., $p < .02$, Total $N = 511$[b]

[a] Briefly, we measured "tolerance for political extremists" on the basis of ten items. Five items (see Q47 and Q61, Appendix C) were selected from Samuel Stouffer's (1955) unidimensional scale, "Willingness to Tolerate Non-Conformists," relating to the willingness to extend basic civil liberties to Communists. We added five exactly parallel items dealing with the Ku Klux Klan. In order for a man to score high on open-mindedness, he had to answer all ten items (for both Communists and Klansmen) in a tolerant direction, for example, be willing to allow an admitted Communist (and a Ku Klux Klansman) to make a public speech in his community. A "close-minded" individual could be intolerant either toward both Communists and Klansmen or toward one and not the other. See also Rokeach (1960). This measure of open-closed mindedness is modestly correlated (+.30) with a subset of three items drawn from the 40-item Rokeach Dogmatism Scale. Men scoring high on our three-item Dogmatism Scale (see QS3, QS8, and QS10, Appendix C) were also disproportionately likely to be in interlocking networks.

[b] The reduced size of the total sample N to 511 results from the deletion of cases who had intermediate scores on the measure of open-closed mindedness. See Laumann and Schuman (1967) for the rationale for this procedure.

collar occupations over occupations demanding greater risk, self-autonomy, and greater time spent at work-related activities. Finally, they are likely to have more intergenerationally stable and crystallized political preferences and greater intolerance for extremist minorities of the left and right.

It is perhaps worth stressing the point that the impact of participation in interlocking networks is not so much on the specific content or direction of attitudes—for example, leading men to favor the Democratic party over the Republican party—but rather, the impact is in terms of the degree of commitment to given views or to their stability over time. Interlocking networks facilitate the possibility of given views resonating through the network and receiving more frequent mutual reinforcement from significant others. Thus just as in our discussion of homogeneity, we must stress that the relationship between connectedness and attitudes is one premised on their *form* rather than their *content*.

DISCUSSION

Despite the fact that we have presented wide-ranging evidence that the type of network is differentially associated with many demographic and socioeconomic characteristics and attitudes of the respondents, it is, of course, still true that, while statistically significant, none of the relationships are of exceptional strength in the sense of manifesting high correlation ratios. Perhaps, however, it is to be expected that correlations would be low in an area of such empirical complexity. Despite the qualifications that must be introduced when discussing given results, it is still worth noting that one can make sense of the overall pattern of results in terms of our introductory comments suggesting that the comparison between interlocking and radial networks will tend to parallel the classic comparisons between primary and secondary groups, *Gemeinschaft* and *Gesellschaft,* mechanical and organic solidarity, and the four pattern variables. This overarching conceptualization of the differences between interlocking and radial networks does, we feel, reduce considerably the need for proposing a number of ad hoc explanations of the results.

In view of the multiplicity of significant relationships reported, there is considerable theoretical and empirical promise in pursuing a more detailed examination of how these networks come to be formed and how they function once in existence. Since a substantial majority of urban white men at every class level are involved in interlocking networks, one might speculate that this has considerable functional significance, among other things, for the relative political stability of the system. From a comparative point of view, it would be especially interesting to determine whether this proportion varies in systematic ways from city to city, society to society, or among racial groups; and, further, if variable, whether the structure of people's primary environments could be linked to characteristics of the relevant political systems (see Scheuch, 1965).

NOTES

1. Festinger (1950: 272–73) argues, for example, that when opinions, attitudes, or beliefs have no firm anchorage in physical reality, a person seeks a basis for the subjective validity of his opinions in his social reality, that is, in the fact that they are shared by members of some reference group. "An opinion, a belief, an attitude is 'correct,' 'valid,' and 'proper' to the extent that it is anchored in a group of people with similar beliefs, opinions, and attitudes." For a recent formalization of these propositions, see Davis (1963).

2. The more recent contributions to this growing literature are Young and Willmott's (1959) study of the working class London suburbs of Bethnal Green and Greenleigh; Gans' (1962) study of Italo-Americans in the predominantly working class East End of Boston; Liebow's (1967, especially pp. 161–207) study of Negro streetcorner men in Washington, D.C.; Adams' (1967a) study of kinship in Greensboro, North Carolina; and Suttles' (1968) study of the social structure of a slum area in Chicago.

3. For a selected bibliography, see Rapoport, 1953, 1963; Katz, 1966; Henry, 1958; Davis, 1963; Adams, 1967b; Granovetter, 1972; Travers and Milgrim, 1969; Mitchell, 1969a).

4. We are using the terms functional specificity-diffuseness, affectivity, and so forth, essentially as Talcott Parsons (1951) defines them in his discussion of the pattern variables.

5. Following a similar line of argument Brim (1966: 7) observes:

. . . . Personality processes have been analyzed with concepts which do not articulate with analyses of the outside social structure, and what is needed are personality concepts which permit easy and direct movement from characteristics of the social organization to its consequences for personality. For example, if a man lives in a highly differentiated complex social structure, one can describe the effects on his personality using the concept of heterogeneity of his significant reference figures. Similarly, where he is involved with persons who make conflicting and unresolvable role demands, the concept of identity confusion permits one to move directly from the existence of conflict in the objective social order to its consequences for personality.

6. In the *Division of Labor,* Emile Durkheim distinguished two fundamental ways in which a social structure may be integrated: mechanical and organic solidarity. In a mechanically integrated structure (the earlier, more "primitive" type), integration is based on the fact that all the units are fundamentally alike; while in an organically integrated structure (such as modern industrial society), integration is based on the interdependence of the functionally differentiated units.

Of course, Toennies' distinction between *Gemeinschaft* and *Gesellschaft* parallels this distinction, while Talcott Parsons' well-known *pattern variables* are a decomposition into their essential elements of these global dichotomies. The comparison of primary and secondary groups is also similar to the above distinctions. Our characterization of interlocking and radial networks is derived from the notion that interlocking networks more closely approximate the classic conceptions of the primary group, while radial networks more closely approximate the classic conceptions of the secondary group. (See also Davis, 1963: 444.)

7.   The employment of this particular subtest has several advantages. It is relatively simple, short, reliable, and nonthreatening to administer as part of a basic survey interview situation. It correlates highly (.81) with the total Wechsler Scale (Wechsler, 1955), according to basic standardization information and has a split-half reliability of .85, thus providing about as good a brief measure as one can obtain of what psychologists consider functional intelligence in America today.

8.   But for the ten percent of the sample who reported that they only met all three or at least two of their friends in eating, drinking, and/or sports establishments and *not* in their homes, 93 percent of this group had interlocking networks. This group is overwhelmingly drawn from the working class.

9.   Another piece of evidence supporting the notion that men in interlocking networks are likely to form more intensive and affective relations with their friends is the correlation ratio of .113 ($p < .01$) between a personality measure of need Affiliation and interlocking or radial networks. Men high on need Affiliation [measured by summing responses to the following questions: S16, S19, S21, and S24 (see Appendix C)] are especially likely to be in interlocking networks.

10.   We asked the respondent to estimate how many years he knew each friend. We then averaged the estimates for the three friends and divided by the respondent's age so that we have a measure of the average proportion of the respondent's life he has known his three "best" friends.

11.   See footnote f, Table 3.6.

PART TWO

Substance: Attitudes and Values

CHAPTER 7

Voluntary Association Membership and the Theory of Mass Society

STEPHEN J. CUTLER

SOCIAL PARTICIPATION AND THE THEORY OF MASS SOCIETY

As has been stressed throughout Part One of this volume, central to an understanding of the social structure of urban areas are the related questions of the nature and consequences of an individual's involvement in various types of social networks. On the one hand, it has been shown that the nature of interaction in urban social networks (that is, in the primary zone, see Chapter 1, p. 7) is not nearly and generally as impersonal, segmented, and isolated as many earlier accounts of urbanism would suggest (see Wilensky and Lebeaux, 1965: 115–33; Chapter 6 above). On the other hand, some have argued that even involvement in "second- and higher-order" social networks (that is, where ego is linked to another by a mediating chain of others who are known to ego personally or to one another, see Chapter 1, pp. 7–8) may be viewed as having positive functions not only for the system as a whole, but for the individual as well. Indeed, one such theoretical perspective, the theory of mass society, holds that the existence of and interaction in a network of intermediate, secondary relations provide one of the major bulwarks against structural atomization of the individual, alienation, and divisive tendencies in the system. In the present chapter, the theory of mass society is reviewed, particularly as it relates to the salutary effect of voluntary association membership, and

This research was supported by a pre-doctoral fellowship from the Horace H. Rackham School of Graduate Studies, University of Michigan. I wish also to acknowledge the helpful suggestions made by Edward O. Laumann, Albert J. McQueen, James L. Walsh, and David R. Segal.

a number of derivative propositions are tested concerning whether voluntary association membership does, in fact, play the integrative role ascribed to it by mass society theorists.

Mass man, or the individual in mass society, is said to be marked by a number of behavioral and psychological characteristics. First, he is alienated in a psychological sense from himself and from the larger system (Fromm, 1955). Devoid of a sense of power in political, social, and economic affairs, the mass man is also said to be divorced from the dominant normative and value systems of his society. So conceived, he either withdraws out of a feeling of frustration and becomes apathetic or is prone to attempt to assuage his futility by embracing ideological movements which are able to provide him with a sense of integration as well as a sense of efficacy. Ideologically, then, the chief concern of mass society theorists lies in their identification of these characteristics with a propensity to engage in direct, activist solutions to felt problems through the vehicle of totalitarian movements (Kornhauser, 1959: 16; Arendt, 1968: 22).

The primary structural factor identified by theorists of mass society and mass behavior is atomization. Where individuals are unrelated to one another beyond implication in familial networks, when they are not integrated into meaningful, secondary group relations, when there is a loss of "community," the processes conducive to the emergence of mass behavior are said to be put into motion.

> People become available for mobilization by elites when they lack or lose an independent group life. . . . The lack of autonomous relations generates widespread social alienation. Alienation heightens responsiveness to the appeal of mass movements because they provide occasions for expressing resentment against what is, as well as promises of a totally different world. In short, *people who are atomized readily become mobilized.* Since totalitarianism is a state of total mobilization, mass society is highly vulnerable to totalitarian movements and regimes. (Kornhauser, 1959: 33)

Additionally, to the degree that power is concentrated, whether at the national, regional, local, or organizational level, the possibility of influencing it is said to be substantially reduced. Furthermore, as the basis for decision making becomes increasingly removed from scrutiny, the understanding of both issues and processes is diminished and the possibility is heightened of apathy toward or alienation from the society.

Counteracting such tendencies is the existence of and membership in second-order intermediate groups, of which voluntary associations would be the major example. Specifically, such groups are seen as having the following consequences for the stability of the society as a whole and for the integration of individual members into it:

1. Voluntary associations assist, first, in the distribution and acquisition of influence and power over wide sectors of society. Association members, therefore, by virtue of both strength in numbers and access to greater resources than the uninvolved individual, should be in a relatively better position to exert influence. To the extent that the association's program of influence is met or potentially attainable, membership in voluntary associations should be associated also with a lesser sense of alienation and futility and thereby should reduce the need for militant action from beyond the legitimate channels of influence. Thus, Hunter (1963: 519) observes that "the better organized groups do have some voice in community affairs and with such a voice, the individual may feel some security even if his own voice is not actually heard."

2. The existence of voluntary associations, via interest representation, can act as a force for either social change or the maintenance of the status quo (Smith, 1966a: 484–86; Coleman, 1957; Rose, 1954: 51). On the one hand, change induced by associations might maintain the flexibility of a society that might otherwise be subject to destructive strains brought on by excessive rigidity (Coser, 1956); on the other hand, the notion of the interplay between veto groups suggests that proposed social change inimical to the interests of an association stands some chance of being effectively challenged (Riesman, 1951: 213ff).

3. To the extent that participation in voluntary associations is segmental (or single-stranded, see Chapter 1, p. 8), involving only one or a few of an individual's total constellation of social roles while other role obligations are distributed elsewhere in the system, the possibility of any given association approaching totalitarian control over its membership is structurally constrained. Furthermore, given such segmental participation, and to the degree that social roles are dispersed rather than being concentrated within the scope of any one association, social conflict along one line of cleavage deriving from a convergence of interests is also less likely (Smith, 1966a: 487).

4. Voluntary associations also exercise socialization and social control functions (Lopata, 1964: 207–10; Eckstein, 1966: 280–83). Rose (1954: 51), for example, contends that voluntary associations socialize their members by teaching democratic practices, and that the ". . . associations *provide a sense of satisfaction with modern democratic processes* because they help the ordinary citizen to see how the processes function in limited circumstances, of direct interest to himself, rather than as they grind away

in a distant, impersonal, and incomprehensible fashion." In addition, association membership supposedly

> . . . provides factual knowledge of events; tends to promote insight into and understanding of the significance of events; and a knowledge of, as it were, the mechanics of government and society generally. Since the association is part of the political and social processes of the society it may also help train future social leaders and serve as a channel for their emergence into the society (Hausknecht, 1962: 10; see also Lipset et al., 1956: 82–91).

5. Finally, as a locus of interaction and a mechanism for the satisfaction of expressive and socioemotional needs, associations implicate their members in networks of interpersonal relations that serve to promote fellowship. "While often formed for some specific impersonal function, the voluntary association provides a latent function of increasing a man's meaningful, primary relationships and so compensates for alienation." (Gerson, 1965: 150).

Support for mass society theory comes from a variety of quarters. Smith (1966a), for example, finds a lack of interest group activity to be associated with totalitarian political regimes and the presence of interest group activity to be associated with political stability. Extremist behavior in Iran (Ringer and Sills, 1952) and rioting in Watts (Ransford, 1968) were found to be concentrated among the least integrated elements of the community. Moreover, a sense of political competence was shown to be related to membership in voluntary associations (Almond and Verba, 1965: 255–56) as was factual knowledge, awareness of social problems, and involvement in public services (Hausknecht, 1962: chap. 6). Similarly, Maccoby (1958) concludes that voluntary association members are more likely to be, to remain, or to become voters, and that such participation is also related to positive and nonfatalistic attitudes toward the social environment.

A number of studies also examine the relationship between voluntary association membership and various components of alienation. Erbe (1964), for example, finds that association members are less alienated than nonmembers, while Neal and Seeman (1964) find that workers who do not belong to labor unions are more likely to feel powerless to effect outcomes in society than union members. Among a group of welfare recipients, Levens (1968) notes that involvement in association activities was related to lower fatalism as well as to greater perception of control over events and engagement in political activity designed to alter life circumstances. Approximating a test of the theory is a series of articles (see, for example, Seeman and Evans, 1962; Seeman, 1963; Seeman, 1966) in which alienation, taken as the independent variable, is related to lower degrees of control-relevant learning and fewer efforts taken toward mastering one's destiny.

Even given this rather impressive support, there are nevertheless both empirical and theoretical critiques of the position taken by mass society theory. Seeman (1967), in a study of Swedish workers, notes that involvement in voluntary associations and occupational communities does little to reduce work-related alienation, while Olsen (1965) and Aberbach (1968) find that social participation variables do little in accounting for alienation after socioeconomic status is considered.

Other critiques either question or specify some of the basic assumptions of mass society theory. There are, first, those who challenge writers such as Fromm and Nisbet with respect to their descriptions of the "massifying" consequences of urbanization and the life styles associated with urbanism. In brief, their argument is that the quality of urban life is not nearly so impersonal and isolated as has been suggested (see Chapter 6 above). Not only has the urban family not lost all of its functions, but the extent of informal neighboring relations appears to be more extensive than depicted in many characterizations of urban areas (Sussman and Burchinal, 1962; Adams, 1967a; Bell and Boat, 1957; Dotson, 1951). Still others maintain that the conditions producing the alienative consequences associated with mass society are differentially distributed in urban areas, and that the integrative functions supposedly best performed by voluntary associations can also be performed by other social mechanisms (Selznick, 1963; Greer, 1956; Greer and Orleans, 1962; Bell, 1962: chap. 1; Janowitz, 1952; Segal and Meyer, 1969).

A further focus of criticism deals more directly with voluntary associations and raises the question of whether in fact they can or do perform the functions attributed to them by mass society theorists and under what conditions they are best able to play that role. For example, Greer (1957; see also Holden, 1965) maintains that voluntary associations are relatively unimportant because of limited membership and lack of involvement on the part of the members, while Rose (1954: 68) suggests that any factors that act to reduce a member's involvement in or commitment to the association impede the effective functioning of the association as an intermediate group. Others (Mills, 1959; Nisbet, 1953: 266–67; Olsen, 1968) have argued that voluntary associations themselves may be structurally parallel to the conditions of the larger (mass) society and as such act to reinforce rather than to mitigate alienative consequences. For instance, Raphael (1965) notes that a dispersed membership is an impediment to the democratic (as contrasted with the oligarchic) functioning of labor unions, while a spatially concentrated membership facilitates interaction and communication among the members and provides the basis for the viable functioning of the informal networks which Lipset et al. (1956) have seen as being of such consequence for the existence of union democracy.

A final set of concerns of critics of mass society theory postulates that rather than acting to minimize conflict, intermediate groups may actually facilitate or heighten the possibility of conflict. Gusfield (1962), for example, maintains that extremist behavior in a pluralistic system may well come from disenfranchised, doomed, or defeated groups that refuse to accept compromise solutions. Putnam locates such an argument in the context of the community:

> Group members are more exposed to dominant community norms and are more sensitive to these opinions. . . . In a community where prejudice or antagonism to democracy was widespread, the network of community associations would tend to propagate these anti-democratic attitudes, and organizational membership would not have the effect of stimulating support for democratic norms. If the hypothesis is correct, it constitutes an important qualification of the "pluralist" thesis (1966: 654).

Finally, Pinard (1968), in an extensive criticism of mass society theory, suggests that certain groups may exert neutral or mobilizing effects in contrast to the restraining effects usually attributed to intermediate groups.

In sum, then, central to the theory of mass society is the existence of and membership in intermediate groups of which voluntary associations are seen as being of critical significance. Such associations are said to be a vital factor in the political and structural integration of the society as a whole and in the integration of individuals into the society. The absence of voluntary associations, on the other hand, or lack of membership in them where they exist, is said to have negative consequences for the stability of the society and its social and political order as well as for the social-psychological characteristics of the nonmembers. In light of this, our first objective is to determine whether differences that might be expected between members and nonmembers, based on the general theory, do in fact occur. Thus the general empirical question guiding the analysis is as follows:

> Viewing voluntary associations as intermediate groups and association membership as involvement in a network of such intermediate relations, will we then find association members manifesting certain social-psychological characteristics associated with mass society to a lesser extent than nonmembers?

However, the review of critiques of mass society theory suggests a number of qualifications to the general theory. First, association membership per se may be insufficient to mitigate mass society characteristics.

More than membership itself, the quality or nature of participation may be a factor of some consequence in determining whether the alleged benefits of membership actually accrue to the members. Second, owing to such factors as size, formalization (Chapin and Tsouderos, 1955), membership dispersion, and possible oligarchic tendencies in voluntary associations, the association itself may have mass structural characteristics and thus be of little real benefit to the members. On the other hand, the presence of informal networks within voluntary associations is offered as a parallel to what the existence of intermediate groups means for the larger society. In view of these considerations, we will examine the importance of membership involvement and the existence of informal, peer, or primary group ties within the association. The general empirical question to be raised here is:

Does the role of voluntary associations as intermediate groups differ under variable conditions of membership involvement and the existence within the association of friendship networks?

Finally, there appears to be considerable evidence to indicate that voluntary associations do not act in a singular fashion. Given differing contexts, it is suggested that some associations may work in a manner completely contrary to that proposed by mass society theorists. In view of this, a third area of inquiry will engage our attention:

Are there differences between members of different types of voluntary associations in the extent to which the social-psychological predispositions characteristic of mass society are in evidence?

HYPOTHESES AND MEASUREMENT

Insofar as the consequences of voluntary association membership suggested earlier are structural in nature, facilitating the overall integration of the larger system, our data are largely inapplicable except by inference. To the extent, however, that membership in voluntary associations is said to have social-psychological consequences that are hypothesized to differentiate members from nonmembers, a number of items in the interview schedule are available for specific tests of this more general proposition. After consideration of the measurement of voluntary association membership, we then take up the delineation of certain social-psychological variables which, consistent with the theory of mass society, should be related to association membership, and, finally, the operationalization of certain qualifications to the general theory of mass society.

Voluntary Association Membership

Membership in voluntary associations is determined by the responses to Q39, Appendix C, with the distribution of memberships for the total sample, by the number of associations to which the respondent belongs, given in Table 7.1.

While approximately 83 percent of the sample belongs to one or more voluntary associations, a number of considerations would suggest that this figure is not unduly distorted given the parameters of the universe from which the sample was drawn. First, other studies of urban males also find a similarly high proportion of membership (Bell and Force, 1956). A second consideration is the relatively high proportion of labor union members in the Detroit area: for our sample, 39.7 percent indicate such membership.[1] Third, the particular form in which the item on association membership was asked (closed ended, with an extensive list) is clearly one that would facilitate recall (see Wright and Hyman, 1958: 286; Babchuk and Booth, 1969: 32). Finally, the major exclusions of urban females, the foreign born, and persons over 65 years old would tend to increase the overall membership rate in comparison with samples more representative of the total urban population (Hausknecht, 1962: chap. 3).

For the purpose of the first set of hypotheses, the number of voluntary association memberships will be considered, first, as a dichotomy comparing those who belong to one or more associations with those who belong to no associations and, second, by the number of associations to which a respondent belongs with membership in four or more being the upper limit.

Table 7.1. Distribution of number of voluntary association memberships

Number of Memberships		N	Percent
None		168	16.6
One		286	28.2
Two		245	24.2
Three		148	14.6
Four	(or more)	69 (166)	6.8 (16.4)
Five		52	5.1
Six		22	2.2
Seven		13	1.3
Eight		6	.6
Nine		2	.2
Ten		2	.2
Total		1013	100.0

Powerlessness

Among the social-psychological consequences of nonmembership in intermediate groups, perhaps that one most consistently cited by theorists of mass society is alienation. The concept of alienation, however, has been shown, both on the conceptual and empirical levels (Seeman, 1959; Neal and Rettig, 1967), to be a multifaceted notion involving a number of distinguishable dimensions. The following three items from our data would seem to tap most closely Seeman's dimension of powerlessness, that is, "the expectancy or probability held by the individual that his own behavior cannot determine the occurrence of the outcomes, or reinforcements, he seeks" (Seeman, 1959: 784):

S1.   Planning only makes a person unhappy since plans hardly ever work out anyway.

S8.   There have always been good times and bad times, and there is nothing anybody can do to change that. That is the way it is, and if you are smart, you will take it as it comes and do the best you can.

S11.   Nowadays with world conditions the way they are, the wise person lives for today and lets tomorrow take care of itself.

Based, then, on the assumption that the greater availability of channels of influence through association membership will lead to a higher expectancy of outcome control and based on the relationship between membership and alienation found in previous research, our first hypothesis is that *Powerlessness will be negatively related to voluntary association membership.*

Dogmatism

The second dependent variable derives from the notion that one of the social-psychological characteristics of those prone toward extremist, totalitarian movements (that is, the mass man unintegrated into meaningful group relations) is a dogmatic rigidity in belief and thought (Lipset, 1963: 178; Kornhauser, 1959: 73). If, then, dogmatism is characteristic of those prone to embrace authoritarian and/or extremist movements and if such a proneness is also characteristic of the unintegrated mass man, we would be led to expect that *Dogmatism will be negatively related to voluntary association membership.*

As a measure of dogmatism, we use the following three items drawn from Rokeach's (1960) dogmatism scale:

S3.   In this complicated world of ours, the only way we can know what's going on is to rely on leaders or experts that can be trusted.

S10. There are two kinds of people in the world, those who are for the truth, and those who are against the truth.

S12. To compromise with our political opponents is dangerous because it usually leads to the betrayal of our own side.

Tolerance of Ideological Nonconformity

The final set of dependent variables can be used to test a specific hypothesis examined by Kornhauser (1959: 67):

If it is true that those who are socially isolated feel less bound to employ legitimate methods in community controversies, then we would expect to find a close association between community involvement and support for civil liberties in the United States (where civil liberties are institutionalized norms). Support for civil liberties may be interpreted as a belief in the importance of using legitimate methods, rather than direct action against opponents, in carrying on social conflict.

Kornhauser takes as support for this proposition findings from Stouffer's (1955) analysis of tolerance of Communism in which community leaders are shown to be more willing to extend civil liberties to Communists than nonleaders. Included in our schedule was a set of five items taken from Stouffer's analysis. In addition, recognizing that these items dealing with Communism tapped only tolerance of leftist ideological nonconformity, a parallel set of items concerning members of the Ku Klux Klan was also included, allowing us to consider tolerance of rightist ideological nonconformity as well. The actual items are given below (see Q47 and Q61 in Appendix C; Chapter 5, pp. 99–102, and Chapter 6, pp. 127–128):

1.   Suppose there is a man who admits he is a Communist (Ku Klux Klansman). Suppose the admitted Communist (Ku Klux Klansman) wants to make a speech in your community, should he be allowed to speak or not?

2.   Should an admitted Communist (Ku Klux Klansman) be put in jail?

3.   Suppose he's a teacher in a high school. Should he be fired or not?

4.   Suppose he is a clerk in a store. Should he be fired or not?

5.   Now I would like you to think of another person. A man who has been questioned by a Congressional Committee about his suspected Communist (Klan) sympathies, but who swears under oath he has never been a Communist (Klansman). Suppose he's a teacher in a high school. Should he be fired or not?

Based, then, on the considerations given above, we would expect that *Tolerance of leftist and tolerance of rightist ideological nonconformity will be positively related to voluntary association membership.*[2]

Involvement in Voluntary Associations

As suggested earlier, it has been argued that the alleged benefits of voluntary association membership might not be forthcoming under the condition of token or passive membership. Almond and Verba (1965: 260), for example, find that political competence is higher among active association members than among inactive members. A somewhat parallel finding from the literature on aging suggests that the mere fact or quantity of membership may not be as important as its quality. In a study of the adjustment and adaptation of older persons, Lowenthal and Haven (1968) find that while adjustment to old age is associated with the frequency of interaction, the strength of the relationship is somewhat greater when such interaction is of an intimate nature involving the presence of alters who could be characterized as confidants. Considerations such as these, then, lead us to the following hypothesis:

Under the condition of high membership involvement in voluntary associations, a) powerlessness and b) dogmatism will be lower and c) the tolerance of ideological non-conformists will be greater than under the condition of inactive or passive membership.

To determine the nature of association involvement, we use the following item asking each respondent to indicate, for each association in which he noted membership, his estimate of the strength of his involvement:

Q40. Would you say you are very involved or not very involved in (specific association)?

For purposes of presentation, the primary measure of association involvement is a simple count of the number of associations in which the respondent indicated that he was very involved.

Friendship Networks in Voluntary Associations

That voluntary associations may themselves have structural characteristics parallel to those identified by mass society theorists at the societal level and thereby actually serve to reinforce rather than to mitigate the alienative consequences ascribed to mass society was pointed out as a key criticism of mass society theory. Support for this idea comes from a variety of sources. Spaulding (1966), for example, notes that the attachment of students to clubs and organizations is greater when their friends are also members, and further, that membership in any sub-unit is related to a higher degree of attachment to the parent organization than where no sub-unit memberships exist. More to the point, in a study of nursing personnel, Pearlin (1962) finds powerlessness among nursing personnel to be somewhat lower among those who share an extra-work friendship relation with their co-workers. In other words, the existence of primary networks within an organization can be postulated to be a mechanism that performs functions similar to those performed by the existence of voluntary associations within the context of the larger society, to wit, to facilitate the integration of the member into the association and thereby into the larger system as well. Given that data are available on the existence of friendship networks within the association, the following hypothesis is offered:

Where friendship networks exist within voluntary associations, a) powerlessness and b) dogmatism will be lower and c) tolerance of ideological nonconformists will be greater than where the member is not involved in such networks having their locus within the association.

Consistent with the substantive concerns of the survey, information was gathered about friends of the respondents. In the series of items on association membership, the respondent was asked to indicate whether he met any of the three friends cited earlier in the interview at meetings of each association in which he cited membership:

Q41. Do you usually meet any of the three friends you mentioned in meetings of (specific association)?

Again, major reliance is placed on a count of the number of associations to which his friends also belong.

Nonintegrative Effects of Association Membership

The final concern of this chapter will be an attempt to evaluate the functionalist position generally taken by mass society theorists. Specifically, proponents of the pluralist thesis view the existence of intermediate groups as a stabilizing force to the virtual exclusion of their possible divisive consequences. By way of example, Pinard (1968: 684) would alert us to the possibility that intermediate groups may have very diverse effects:

. . . what constitutes a major shortcoming of mass society theory is its failure to recognize that secondary groups may exert neutral or mobilizing functions. It may be empirically true that a large number of organizations in affluent societies will usually exert restraining effects, but not all organizations under any circumstances will do so. There are always certain components of the intermediate structure which exhibit a diffuse orientation of alienation vis-a-vis most or all features of the larger society, and there are certain other components which are alienated against specific aspects of the society, that is, which perceive their subjective interests as well as their norms and goals in harmony with those of a social movement. Obviously, such groups will stimulate rather than restrain participation in social movements.

In brief, there would then seem to be some justification for examining the relationships between membership and the dependent variables for each of the kinds of voluntary associations included in the study. In so doing, we pose the frankly exploratory question of whether membership in certain kinds of associations may have little effect on the dependent variables or even, perhaps, an effect opposite to that which would be anticipated on the basis of mass society theory.

ANALYSIS OF THE DATA

The major analytical tool to be employed is the technique of multiple classification analysis. The reader is referred to the preceding chapter for a fuller exposition of its assumptions and the various summary statistics it produces.[3]

FINDINGS

Before examining the first set of hypotheses, a word concerning the nature of controls is in order. Powerlessness, dogmatism, and tolerance of ideological nonconformity have all been shown to be related to various measures of socioeconomic status. This, too, is the case among our respondents (Table 7.2) with all correlations being in the expected directions and significant at the .05 level at least.[4] Similarly, both membership in voluntary associations and the number of such associations to which one belongs are also consistently related to measures of socioeconomic status. For our sample, for instance, the product-moment correlation between education and the membership/nonmembership dichotomy is .116 ($p < .01$) while that between education and the number of voluntary association memberships is .324 ($p < .01$). In view of this, a most specific question informs the first set of hypotheses: Does voluntary association membership (or the number of memberships) have an effect on the dependent variables above and beyond that of education?[5]

To restate briefly the first set of hypotheses, we expect that association members, in comparison with those who do not belong to voluntary associations, should be lower on the powerlessness and dogmatism indexes

Table 7.2.   Matrix of product-moment correlations of selected socio-economic items and dependent variable indexes

Index	Education[a]	Occupational Status[b]	Family Income[c]
Powerlessness	−.347	−.276	−.265
Dogmatism	−.419	−.287	−.192
Tolerance (leftist)	.325	.276	.087
Tolerance (rightist)	.175	.172	.092

[a] See Q87, Appendix C. Responses were collapsed into the following categories: (1) less than high school graduate, (2) high school graduates, (3) some college and college graduates, and (4) postgraduate education.

[b] The respondent's current occupation was coded into the two-digit code of Duncan's Index of Socioeconomic Status (Duncan, 1961). This code was then collapsed into five categories: (1) 01–19, (2) 20–39, (3) 40–59, (4) 60–79, and (5) 80–96.

[c] See Q125, Appendix C. Responses were collapsed into the following four categories: (1) $6,999 and under, (2) $7,000–9,999, (3) $10,000–14,999, and (4) $15,000 and above.

and higher on the tolerance of ideological nonconformity indexes. To begin with, each of the dependent variables was significantly related to the combined or multiple effects of association membership and education. However, examination of the gross effect of the membership/nonmembership dichotomy clearly indicates that these relationships are due largely to the effect of education alone (Table 7.3, row A). Specifically, the magnitude of the eta coefficients, the differences between the category means for the gross effect of association membership on each of the dependent variables, and the F tests for the zero-order effects of membership alone as a predictor all pointed to the absence of significant relationships. In other words, for neither the gross nor the net effect of association membership do we find a significant difference between members and nonmembers. On the other hand, the effects of education on the dependent variables are strong and consistent in that these relationships are significant by the F tests and in the expected directions for both gross and net effects.

Consideration of the number of voluntary association memberships does little to change this conclusion (Table 7.3, row B). Significant relationships, by the F test for multiple effects, were found between the combined effect of the number of associations to which the respondent belongs and education and each of the dependent variables, although these too would appear to be largely the result of the effect of education. Thus in examining the gross effects of the number of memberships, we found that the differences at the extremes were in the predicted direction for each dependent variable, that the powerlessness and dogmatism scores decreased

Table 7.3. Summary of gross and net[a] effects of voluntary association membership variables on the dependent variables

	Dependent Variables			
	Powerlessness		Dogmatism	
Membership Variables	Gross	Net	Gross	Net
A. Member/nonmember dichotomy	NS	NS	NS	NS
B. Number of association memberships	$p < .001$	NS	$p < .001$	NS
C. Number of associations in which the respondent is very involved	$p < .001$	NS	$p < .05$	NS
D. Number of associations to which one or more of the respondent's friends also belong	$p < .001$	$p < .05^b$	$p < .01$	NS
	Leftist Tolerance		Rightist Tolerance	
	Gross	Net	Gross	Net
A. Member/nonmember dichotomy	NS	NS	NS	NS
B. Number of association memberships	$p < .05$	NS	NS	NS
C. Number of associations in which the respondent is very involved	NS	NS	NS	NS
D. Number of associations to which one or more of the respondent's friends also belong	NS	NS	NS	NS

[a] Controlling for education.
[b] Reduced to nonsignificance when controlling for the effects of education and income.

while the tolerance scores increased as we moved from one to four or more memberships, and that, with the exception of rightist tolerance, these relationships were significant by the F test for the gross effects of the number of association memberships. However, with the introduction of education as a control, the net effect of the number of association memberships is reduced to a nonsignificant level in all cases where a significant zero-order relationship had existed. On the other hand, the effect of education on the dependent variables is unchanged when the net effects of this variable, controlling for the effects of the number of memberships, are considered. In sum, then, *virtually no evidence is found to indicate that membership in voluntary associations or the number of associations to which a person belongs has any independent effect on the dependent variables.*

If, however, we view integration into intermediate groups as the crucial variable, what is then needed are measures more refined than membership or the number of memberships so that the nature or quality of participation in voluntary associations may be determined. Thus token membership and the possibility that voluntary associations may have "mass" structural conditions parallel to those proposed to describe the larger, mass society have been suggested earlier as two of the qualities that may be of some importance in understanding the role of voluntary association membership. Therefore, we turn to a consideration of the effects of differences in involvement in voluntary associations and the presence of intermediate (friendship) groups.

As might be expected, involvement in voluntary associations, like membership and the number of memberships, is related to measures of socioeconomic status. Among the association members in our sample, we find a product-moment correlation of .274 ($p < .01$) between education and the number of associations in which the respondent is very involved (with involvement in three or more being the upper limit).[6] Given this relationship between education and involvement as well as those between education and the dependent variables,[7] we again focus on whether involvement in voluntary associations has an independent or net effect on the dependent variables.

While the combined effect of the number of voluntary associations in which the respondent is very involved and education was significantly related to each of the dependent variables, in Table 7.3, row C, we see again that these relationships are due primarily to the effect of education. Although the zero-order relationships between involvement and the dependent variables were in the expected directions, and significant by the F test for gross effects in the case of powerlessness and dogmatism, in no instance do we find significant net effects when education has been introduced as a control.

Similar results prevail when we examine the effect of the presence of friendship networks in voluntary associations. For purposes of discussion, the results to be given here refer to the number of associations to which the respondent belongs and to which one or more of his friends also belong, with two or more associations being the upper limit given the distribution.[8] Also, given the correlation of .180 ($p < .01$) between education and the number of associations in which friends are present, the educational attainment of the respondent was again entered as the standard control variable.

While the combined effect of the two predictors was significantly related to each of the dependent variables, and differences in the predicted directions were noted in the case of all four dependent variables, in only one case is there a significant relationship for the net effect of the number of associations in which the respondent's friends are present (Table 7.3, row D). The relationship with dogmatism, significant at the zero-order level, is reduced to nonsignificance when controlling for education, while neither leftist nor rightist tolerance show significant relationships even at the zero-order level. Only in the case of powerlessness would there appear to be an independent effect of being an association member when friends are also in the association.

Since the use of education as a control has been predicated on its being a rough measure of socioeconomic status and recognizing the probable slippage involved in using it as the only measure, the relationship between the number of associations in which the respondent has friends and powerlessness was reexamined entering family income as a predictor also in order to allow for a more adequate assessment of the effect of the socioeconomic factor.[9] However, with this addition, the net effect of the number of associations in which friends are present is reduced to nonsignificance while both education and family income are significant for both gross and net effects at the .001 level. In sum, then, the basis for the observed relationship between the number of voluntary associations to which friends also belong and powerlessness would still appear to be more directly attributable to the effect of socioeconomic status. More generally, the results presented here fail to provide any support for the two qualifications to the theory of mass society that were offered.

In the absence of support for the stated hypotheses, we turn to an examination of the relationships between memberships in various kinds of associations and the dependent variables in order to determine whether any effects, not seen when all associations are considered together, are in evidence. The procedure to be employed is both exploratory and inductive, to a great extent necessitated by the inherent indeterminacy in knowing the structural characteristics of many of the associations in which the respondent has indicated membership. To take a set of contrasting examples for illustrative purposes, description of the category "sports groups" as a rather small, nonhierarchical, nonpolitical association in which there is likely to be considerable congruence between the goals of the group and the reason the individual joined is probably a valid assessment. On the other hand, the category "business and civic groups," in the absence of precise information on the organizational characteristics of the particular association within this category to which the respondent belongs, would encompass a wide range of possible associations with a much greater likelihood of variation along such dimensions as size, the nature of recruitment and reasons for joining, and the goals and ideological commitment of the association. If treatment of all voluntary associations in an undifferentiated fashion involves the possibility of obscuring effects that may be visible upon a more detailed examination of associations taken individually, this possibility would also exist if we elected to construct hypotheses based on typologies of associations in the absence of such descriptive data. While eschewing the establishment of predictions, therefore, would seem reasonable, it should also be emphasized at the outset that, by the same token, the findings must be regarded with some caution and as tentative in nature.[10]

Employing education once again as the standard control,[11] the relationships between the combined effect of membership in the thirteen kinds of associations and education and powerlessness were all significant by the *F* test for multiple effects. The gross and net effects of membership on powerlessness did point to some interesting differences among the kinds of associations. Significant relationships, for both gross and net effects, were found between powerlessness and membership in the following associations: labor unions, fraternal organizations and lodges, neighborhood improvement groups, youth groups, professional groups, and political clubs and organizations. In the case of labor unions, however, members were significantly higher on the powerlessness index than nonmembers while in the other cases for which net effects were in evidence, members were significantly lower on the powerlessness index.

Among members of business and civic groups, country clubs, and parent-teacher associations, significant relationships for the gross effect of membership were found although these were reduced to a level of nonsignificance for the net effects of membership controlling for education. Finally, significant relationships at neither the gross nor the net level were seen among the members of sports teams, charity or welfare groups, church-connected groups, and veterans' organizations.

Following the procedure employed earlier, the six voluntary associations in which membership was found to be independently related to powerlessness were subjected to a more intensive analysis using family income and the respondent's Duncan occupation score as predictors in addition to education in order to allow more adequately for the operation of the socioeconomic factor.[12] The net effect of membership in the six kinds of voluntary associations was examined in the first instance, controlling for the effects of education and income and, then, for the effects of education, income, and occupation. The final results, as described below, remained basically the same no matter which set of controls was employed. In brief, in the case of membership in neighborhood improvement associations and professional groups, while the direction of the relationships was sustained with the additional controls, the finding that members of these two associations have lower powerlessness scores than association members not belonging to these kinds of groups was reduced to a nonsignificant level. However, in the case of members of fraternal organizations and lodges

$(p < .025)$, youth-serving groups $(p < .05)$, and political clubs and organizations $(p < .05)$, membership appeared to entail lower powerlessness scores regardless of the socioeconomic controls employed, while in the case of members of labor unions, the net mean powerlessness scores were still significantly higher for members $(p < .001)$. Membership in at least four of the thirteen kinds of associations, therefore, would appear to be related to powerlessness beyond the effect contributed by socioeconomic status.[13]

The findings with respect to membership in the thirteen kinds of associations and dogmatism may be considered somewhat more summarily. In all thirteen cases, the inclusion of education and membership as predictors yielded relationships with dogmatism that were significant at the .001 level by the F test for multiple effects. Examination of the gross and net relationships, however, pointed to an independent effect of membership in only one case.[14] The gross mean dogmatism scores were significantly lower for members of political clubs and organizations than for association members who do not belong to this kind of association. Furthermore, membership in political clubs and organizations was still significantly related to dogmatism when the net effect of membership, holding education constant, was considered. Finally, the significance of the relationship was still maintained $(p < .05)$ for the net effect of membership even with the addition of occupational status and family income as controls over the relationship.[15]

The findings with respect to tolerance of both leftist and rightist ideological nonconformity are also such that they may be taken up in summary manner.[16] Considering, first, tolerance of leftist ideological nonconformity, we found that in only one of the thirteen comparisons was there a net relationship between membership and leftist tolerance: members of veterans' organizations were more intolerant of leftist ideological nonconformity than association members not belonging to this kind of group. Not only was the gross relationship significant, but the net relationship, controlling for education, was also sufficiently large to be significant by the F test for the net effect of membership in veterans' groups. Furthermore, neither the addition of income nor the addition of income and occupation to education as controls reduced the relationship to nonsignificance $(p < .025)$.[17]

The findings are much the same with respect to tolerance of rightist ideological nonconformity. In only one case, members of church-connected groups being lower on the rightist tolerance index than nonmembers, was there a significant relationship $(p < .05)$ with the dependent variables after the introduction of all socioeconomic controls.[18] Significant zero-order relationships were found for membership in four associations (labor unions, veterans' organizations, professional groups, and political associations) but these were reduced to nonsignificance when the net effects of membership, controlling for education, were considered; no significant relationships were found for membership in the eight remaining associations.

It would seem that a number of conclusions can be drawn from this analysis of the effects of membership in different kinds of associations. First, the role of socioeconomic status, as it has been throughout, was of critical importance in understanding the observed relationships. In brief, membership in the various kinds of voluntary associations is differentially distributed along socioeconomic dimensions, and since the dependent variables are also related to socioeconomic status, this situation is able to account for the observed effect of membership in the majority of cases.

Second, assuming the validity of those few relationships that were sustained independent of the effect of the socioeconomic controls, there would appear to be support for the contention that voluntary associations cannot be treated in an undifferentiated manner. Findings such as these, however limited, indicating that membership in certain associations has effects opposite to those that would have been expected on the basis of mass society theory, corroborate the notion of critics of mass society theory that voluntary associations and/or membership in such associations may have very diverse consequences.

Finally, with respect to the findings themselves, that members of labor unions were high on powerlessness calls to mind two salient features of union membership. On the one hand, membership in labor unions is among the least voluntaristic of any of the associations included in the analysis. On the other hand, the organizational structure of many labor unions is such that power is concentrated far from the individual or local levels. In this sense, then, it may be that the relative powerlessness of union members is a reflection of their position in a microcosmic mass system. By way of contrast, political groups, fraternal organizations, and youth-serving groups, membership in which was related to lower powerlessness and dogmatism, would all appear, at face value, to be characterized by a much greater degree of voluntarism.

Somewhat easier to explain are the relationships between membership in veterans' organizations and leftist tolerance and membership in church-connected groups and rightist tolerance. Given the composition of the items making up the indexes, it is not surprising that the patriotic ideology of veterans' groups should be reflected in a low degree of support for the civil liberties of Communists while a similar argument would prevail for members of church-connected groups given not only the racial but the religious sentiments espoused by the Ku Klux Klan.

DISCUSSION

The primary purpose of this chapter has been both to examine a proposition central to the theory of mass society and to evaluate a set of qualifications to that general proposition. On the whole, the findings yielded little support for the hypotheses concerning the effects of membership in voluntary associations. Specifically, examination of both a simple membership/nonmembership dichotomy and the number of associations to which the respondent belonged indicated no residual or independent effects of membership on the dependent variables beyond that contributed by education alone. Although the number of associations to which the respondent belonged proved to be a better predictor than the simple dichotomy at the zero-order level, in no instance were significant relationships with the dependent variables sustained when the effect of education was introduced. Similarly, the hypotheses concerning the extent of association involvement and the presence of friendship networks fared little better. In only one case, that between the presence of friends and powerlessness, was there a significant relationship beyond the zero-order level. This relationship, too, was reduced to nonsignificance when family income was combined with education as a control.

Finally, examination of the relationships between membership in thirteen kinds of voluntary associations and the dependent variables yielded some evidence of residual effects of membership. Thus membership in labor unions was related to high powerlessness while membership in fraternal organizations and lodges, youth-serving groups, and political clubs and organizations was related to low powerlessness. Membership in political associations was also related to lower dogmatism while membership in veterans' organizations and in church-connected groups was related to low tolerance of leftist and rightist ideological nonconformity, respectively. Despite these latter findings, however, the majority of significant zero-order relationships between membership in a given association and one of the dependent variables were reduced to nonsignificance with the introduction of the socioeconomic controls.

The major and most important conclusion, then, is that the effects of membership in voluntary associations are largely an artifact of the differential distribution of membership along socioeconomic lines. The overwhelming weight of the evidence, in other words, suggests that the effect of membership in voluntary associations for our sample, even under what were considered to be the optimal conditions of high involvement and the presence of friendship networks, is negligible with the possible exception of belonging to a few particular kinds of associations. To conclude, then, let us try to account for the lack of support for the hypotheses both in terms of the kind of data that would seem essential for a more definitive test of these and related hypotheses and, more importantly, in terms of alternative explanations.

One major factor limiting the possibility of generalizing from these results to the entire population is the exclusion from the sample of certain segments of the population. One might argue, with Selznick (1963: 20), that the conditions of and thus responses to mass society are not evenly distributed in a highly differentiated society. Perhaps most important in this connection is the absence of data on nonwhites. Clearly, such an analysis would provide not only a comparative assessment of the role of intermediate group membership for a group rather low on socioeconomic status dimensions but also the opportunity to measure more directly, both attitudinally and behaviorally, the proneness to militant, extremist behavior that is at the very heart of mass society theory. In brief, by focusing only on the white community as we have done, the possibility remains that we have overlooked an area of the system in which mass society theory may have greater explanatory power.

Furthermore, the little evidence that existed for any effect of membership in voluntary associations strongly points to the need for a differentiated view of both the nature of membership and the characteristics of the associations.[19] Given that this would seem to be the most fruitful approach to the analysis of association membership as it relates to the theory of mass society, detailed data of the following kind are considered critical:

1.   Information on the nature of the member's total involvement in the association (for example, length of membership, proportion of meetings and functions attended, time spent on association activities beyond attendance at meetings, offices held by the respondent, attendance at regional or national meetings, extra-association activities with fellow members, and so forth);[20]

2.   Information on the characteristics of the associations (for example, size, ease of member involvement in decision making, extent of the association's hierarchical structure, election procedures, the goals and purposes of the association, methods of recruitment, and so forth);

3.   Information on why the respondent joined and what he views as the major benefits of membership.

While this enumeration is more suggestive than exhaustive, the inclusion of such variables would serve the basic function of allowing one to categorize associations along important theoretical dimensions and to construct typologies with some precise knowledge of both the nature of the association and the respondent's involvement in that association.

On the other hand, it is well to recall some observations made earlier that may help to account for the very limited effects of association membership that were seen in the analysis. First, the responsiveness of voluntary associations to their members may be quite minimal, particularly among the larger, more powerful associations. Attributing this to their changing organizational characteristics, Olsen (1968: 329) notes that

> . . . the more significant [associations]—such as labor unions, political parties, professional associations, and business organizations—are becoming so huge, formalized, and complex that ordinary members can exercise no more control over their activities than over the national government. On the national level, these kinds of organizations can and do influence the government and hence give the society a semblance of pluralism, but they do not provide an organized channel through which individuals can act collectively to make their interests felt on the national level.

Indeed, this interpretation is entirely consistent with the relationship we noted between membership in labor unions and high powerlessness.

Second, there are many indications that a comparative historical treatment of the importance of voluntary associations would be of considerable value. Viewed from a systematic perspective, for example, such associations exist in and interact with an environment that is subject to change and which, therefore, may affect their role. Hausknecht (1962: 125) implicitly adopts such a perspective when he argues that, aside from the area of civil rights, the significance of voluntary associations as a force in social change has declined as affluence has risen and as the major and innovative goals of associations have been met. Similarly, Pinard (1968: 608-9) suggests that the role of voluntary associations may be more prominent when "sources of strain" that act to mobilize and to direct association activities are present in the environment. In brief, we would contend that a more detailed examination of the social context in which voluntary associations function may well disclose that they are less operative as integrative mechanisms and, therefore, of considerably less importance in terms of mass society theory than may have formerly been the case.

Furthermore, and not unrelated to the last point, support has been received for the notion that linkages into other social networks may serve the same purpose. Summarizing an analysis of influences on political attitudes, Segal and Meyer (1969: 232), in noting the viability of the neighborhood and the local community as sources of integration, conclude that

. . . other forms of association . . . especially residence in the local community, can serve to integrate the individual into the political order and thus provide bases for diversity which are absent from Kornhauser's model of mass society.

In sum, then, our findings clearly indicate that certain social-psychological variables thought to be related to voluntary association membership are more properly attributed to education in particular and to socioeconomic status in general. Furthermore, the kinds of criticisms of mass society theory cited above and elsewhere in the analysis make abundantly clear the appropriateness of an extensive and critical reassessment of the general significance of voluntary associations and association membership.

NOTES

1.   The inclusion of labor unions can be contested on the grounds that "closed-shop" policies are inconsistent with the voluntary nature of associations. Thus if the element of *voluntarism* is of critical importance in the study of voluntary associations, it would make some sense to leave out membership in labor unions. On the other hand, if membership in *intermediate groups* is of primary importance, there would then seem to be some justification for considering union membership. This latter argument is accepted for the purpose of this analysis.

2.   Summary indexes for the three powerlessness and three dogmatism items were constructed by assigning scores of from 1 to 4 to the responses from "strongly disagree" to "strongly agree." The sum of the scores for each set of three items was then divided by 3, yielding a mean powerlessness and a mean dogmatism score for each respondent (only those who answered all three items on each index were included). The range of scores, therefore, is from 1.0 (representing low powerlessness and dogmatism, respectively) to 4.0 (indicating high powerlessness and dogmatism). On the tolerance items, those expressing an intolerant response were coded 1, those giving a qualified response were coded 2, and those giving tolerant replies received a score of 3. Total scores for each respondent from the five Communist items and from the five Ku Klux Klan items were obtained and a mean score for each respondent on each index was computed (again, only for those who answered all five items). On these two indexes, then, the range of scores is from 1.0 (low tolerance) to 3.0 (high tolerance). For a fuller discussion of the validation of the indices, see Cutler (1969: 56–65).

3.   The form in which our dependent variables have been constructed is neither dichotomous nor at the interval level of measurement. An independent assessment of how this might alter the findings and conclusions was undertaken by examining a number of the relationships using the component items of the dependent variables in dichotomous form. The results of that analysis are entirely consistent with the conclusions reached based on the use of the summary indexes as dependent variables. Although the use of ordinal level data in this case would not appear to pose any

complications of a substantive nature, therefore, the reader is cautioned about the resulting limitations in interpreting the data.

4. While the use of product-moment correlations and the associated tests of significance in this instance and in other cases throughout the analysis is in violation of the assumptions of simple random sampling and interval level data, their use for descriptive purposes is more defensible (Hays, 1963: 510). Nevertheless, it is well to keep in mind as we proceed that these statistics are, strictly speaking, useful only as descriptions of the relationships *in these data*.

5. Education is to be the only control variable used in conjunction with the analysis at this stage since the results are not substantially changed with the inclusion of other socioeconomic measures entered alone or in combination. Also, both for reasons of economy of presentation and the nature of our primary interest, tables detailing multiple effects and the relationships between education and the dependent variables are not included here. The interested reader will find the detailed tables in Cutler (1969).

6. Two aspects of this stage of the analysis might be noted prior to a discussion of the findings. First, education is, once again, the only socioeconomic control used. Preliminary analysis employing other socioeconomic controls, either alone or in combination, disclosed no substantive alterations in the results. This is also the case with involvement in voluntary associations. While the data to be discussed here use the number of associations in which the respondent is very involved, this is only one of a number of variables that could be used. Other involvement variables that were constructed ranged from the number of associations in which the respondent was very involved as a simple proportion of his total number of memberships to more complicated interaction variables designed to examine the number of associations in which the respondent was very involved at each level of total memberships. In brief, these analyses led to conclusions which would differ in no way from those to be discussed here.

7. The product-moment correlations between education and powerlessness, dogmatism, and leftist and rightist tolerance, for association members, are −.380, −.439, .345, and .185 respectively, all significant at the .01 level at least.

8. Separate analyses employing this independent variable in other forms failed to yield any evidence that would contradict the findings to be discussed here.

9. The product-moment correlation between family income and the number of associations in which friends are present is .133 ($p < .01$) while that between family income and powerlessness is −.276 ($p < .01$).

10. There is still another problem with the proposed analysis that should be brought to the reader's attention. Should we find that membership in certain kinds of associations bears a significant relationship to any of the dependent variables, given multiple memberships, some question would necessarily remain as to whether the observed effect is the product of membership in that particular association, the consequence of membership in another voluntary association to which the respondent also belongs, or finally the joint product of membership in the total set of associations to which he belongs. One possible way of resolving this difficulty would, of course, be to examine the relationship among respondents who belong to only one association in order to determine how membership in that particular association alone relates to the dependent variables. Such a course is adopted whenever possible, although, unfortunately, this method is largely unsatisfactory in our case in that for 12 of the 13 associations with which we will be concerned (members of ethnic

groups and community centers are being excluded from the analysis given the small number of respondents indicating membership in these associations as are the two "other" categories included in the check list of associations), the number of respondents with membership in that association alone is under 30, while in ten of the associations, the number of respondents with that membership alone is less than 20. For this reason also, the findings to be discussed here must necessarily be construed as far more suggestive than definitive.

11.   Education was unrelated only to membership in veterans' organizations. In the remaining cases, the relationships were significant and, with the exception of membership in labor unions, positive. We might note here that owing to the results of the following analysis, extensive tabular presentations would hardly seem warranted. The interested reader is referred to Cutler (1969: chap. 6) for a complete summary of the data on which the following discussion is based.

12.   Both income and occupation are significantly related to powerlessness as they are to membership in the six kinds of associations. Also, the F tests for the multiple effects of the inclusion as predictors of membership, education, and family income on the one hand and membership, education, family income, and occupation on the other hand are all significant at the .001 level.

13.   For two of these four associations, there was a sufficiently large number of respondents who indicated membership in only one association so that a more detailed examination of the effect of membership in the given association by itself could be undertaken. In both cases, education, family income, and the Duncan occupation score were used as controls. Thus, respondents who belonged to a labor union and no other associations had the highest net mean powerlessness score; respondents belonging to a labor union as well as one or more other associations occupied an intermediate position; finally, those association members not belonging to a labor union had the lowest net mean powerlessness score. On the other hand, those respondents belonging only to a fraternal organization or lodge had the lowest net mean powerlessness score; those who belonged to this kind of association as well as one or more other associations were in the intermediate position; and those association members not belonging to a fraternal organization or lodge had the highest net mean score on the powerlessness index. Both relationships were significant by the F test for net effects at the .01 level and both may be construed as yielding additional, suggestive evidence that the effects we have observed, for these two cases anyway, are not solely attributable either to socioeconomic status or to simultaneous membership in other associations.

14.   Significant gross effects but nonsignificant net effects were found for membership in labor unions, business or civic groups, parent-teacher associations, country clubs, and professional groups. Neither the gross nor the net effects of membership were significant for the remainder of the associations.

15.   The product-moment correlations between family income and the Duncan occupation score and dogmatism are both significant at the .01 level while the F test for the multiple effects of each set of socioeconomic variables with membership in political groups is significant at the .001 level.

16.   The multiple Rs for the relationships between education and membership in the thirteen kinds of associations and both leftist and rightist tolerance are all significant at the .001 level.

17. For the remaining associations, significant gross effects were found for membership in labor unions, professional groups, political clubs and organizations, and neighborhood improvement groups. The net effect of membership in these associations was reduced to a nonsignificant level when education was introduced as a control. Finally, membership in the remaining eight kinds of associations showed no significant relationships to leftist tolerance at even the zero-order level.

18. In this instance, we were again able to examine the relationship in more detail considering the effect of multiple memberships. Thus, respondents who belonged to church-connected groups and no other voluntary associations had the lowest net mean score (controlling for education, income, and occupation) while those members not belonging to church-connected groups had the highest score. Significant at the .05 level by the F test for net effects, this finding would suggest that the observed effect can be attributed with a greater degree of assurance to membership in this kind of association.

19. The same may be said for the dependent variables. While every indication is that those used in the analysis tap theoretically important dimensions, it is clear that a much wider range of variables (for example, political participation and knowledge, facets of alienation other than powerlessness, and so forth) is needed for an adequate empirical assessment of mass society theory (see Neal and Abcarian, 1969).

20. In our own case, even in the absence of these more objective measures of association involvement, two studies (Smith, 1966b; Dean, 1958), which find a very high relationship between self-reported and observed participation, would lead us to place some confidence in the respondents' assessments of their involvement.

CHAPTER 8

A Reexamination of the Status Inconsistency Hypothesis

EDWARD O. LAUMANN AND DAVID R. SEGAL

INTRODUCTION

The preceding chapters have been primarily concerned, at the macrostructural level of analysis, with describing the social structure of an urban community in terms of the interrelationships among ethnoreligious groups and among occupational groups and, at the microstructural level, with the implications of certain "formal" properties of a man's informal social networks for his attitudes and behavior. A recurring reference point has been the manifold consequences of men's being located at specific points on the achievement-based hierarchies of socioeconomic status, including educational attainment, occupational status and family income, and in the ascription-based, multidimensional structure of ethnoreligious group membership. In this chapter, we shall sharpen our focus on the implications of a man's simultaneous location in the several structures of social esteem by examining a "theory" that has as its principal focal point precisely such concerns.

THE STATUS INCONSISTENCY MODEL

It has long been recognized in sociological theory that in complex societies an individual's position in one social ranking or status system does not necessarily determine or coincide with his location in other status systems (see Weber, 1953; Sorokin, 1947). While there is a tendency for

---

* This chapter is a revised version of Laumann and Segal (1971), reprinted with the permission of the journal and the University of Chicago Press.

"different types of status to reach a common level" over time (Benôit-Smullyan, 1944: 160; compare Kimberly, 1970), at any given point in time there are always individuals whose several statuses are highly inconsistent. Since Lenski reintroduced the notion of discontinuities among status systems in his theory of status crystallization or status inconsistency (Lenski, 1954), a wide range of studies have been undertaken to examine the possible correlates and consequences of such discontinuities (see Geschwender, 1967).

The basic model implicit in the literature is a straightforward one. Through processes of social mobility and social change, people with lowly evaluated ascriptive status characteristics, such as race, religion, and ethnicity, succeed in raising their positions in status systems based upon achievement, such as those of educational attainment or occupational prestige (see Segal and Knoke, 1968). This necessarily creates inconsistencies between their relative ranks in the achieved and ascribed status systems, both being conceived as essentially unidimensional in structure.

A person in such a situation is assumed to define his social position in terms of his higher status and will expect deference and other status-linked behavior from others to conform to the privileges befitting such higher status (Galtung, 1966). People interacting with the inconsistent individual, perhaps in the interest of maximizing their own relative power in the relationship, however, may define him in terms of his lower status, and hence his deference expectations will be frustrated (Lenski, 1966: 87). Empirical research suggests that, in fact, people will judge the status inconsistent individual not in terms of his lower status but in terms of the average of his several statuses (Himmelfarb and Senn, 1969). The net result, however, will be the same. Lower status will be attributed to him by others than he attributes to himself.

Lenski suggests that individuals in such a situation will be subjected to disturbing experiences in social encounters and will in fact experience difficulty in establishing rewarding patterns of social interaction (Lenski, 1956). The literature suggests that there are a variety of behavioral and psychological responses to such stress. Jackson (1962) sees it causing psychological disturbance. Goffman (1957) sees it leading to desires to change the distribution of power in society, presumably to restructure society in a way that will make the lower status of the status inconsistent individual less relevant. Lenski (1954, 1967) demonstrates a relationship between status inconsistency and Democratic party support (historically this party, at least nationally and in the nonsouthern regions of the United States, has been more oriented to "social change" favorable to disvalued minority groups than the Republican party), as well as with liberalism with regard to socioeconomic issues.

CRITICISMS OF THE MODEL

Four major types of criticism have been directed at the status inconsistency model. *First,* the assumed underlying dynamic, namely, disruption of social relations as a function of status inconsistency, has never been empirically demonstrated. Lenski (1956) presents only inferential evidence in support of this proposition, and Bauman (1968) presents data that suggest that status inconsistent people may actually have more satisfying social contacts than do people who are status consistent.

Second, some critics have argued that when the main effects of the individual statuses are taken into account first, the statistical "interaction" effect due to status inconsistency has no explanatory power (Brandmeyer, 1965; Treiman, 1966) or only minimal power (Fauman, 1968) with regard to the dependent variable.

Third, the effects attributed to status inconsistency have been interpreted by some researchers as being due to ethnic group membership. One variant of this criticism is concerned with the main effects of ethnic status as a variable in the stratification system, and in this wise, this argument is merely a specification of the above mentioned point (Kelley and Chambliss, 1966). Indeed, Lenski (1954) has argued that the most important inconsistencies for explaining liberalism are those that occur between low ethnic status and high financial, educational, or occupational status; and Segal (1969) has shown that the political effects of status inconsistency are in general manifest only when the low ascriptive status of the inconsistent individual is socially visible (compare Box and Ford, 1969). Another variant of explanations in terms of ethnicity takes a more subcultural bent. From this perspective, the relative social ranking of the ethnic groups is not important. Rather, primacy is placed upon their subcultural traits affecting political attitudes and sociability patterns (see Glazer and Moynihan, 1963; Parenti, 1967; Wolfinger, 1965). It should be noted that while one of the chapter's authors anticipated finding evidence of status inconsistency effects in our data, the other author felt that our results could be adduced to demonstrate the persistence of subcultural factors.

Fourth, on methodological grounds, it has been argued that although some statistical interaction effects have been demonstrated between status variables with regard to some presumed effects of status inconsistency, any "interaction" effect cannot simply be equated with an inconsistency effect (Blalock, 1967b; Hyman, 1966; Mitchell, 1964). Blalock (1966a, 1966b, 1967a) suggests in this regard that a priori specification of main effects as well as the expected magnitude and direction of interaction effects is necessary in identifying which interaction effects are attributable to inconsistency.

QUESTIONS FOR INVESTIGATION

The present chapter attempts to confront four unresolved questions raised in the above discussion:

1. Can the presumed effects of status inconsistency upon social relations and political attitudes be replicated on an all white, native-born sample, or are these factors so dependent upon racial and nativity differences that they will be absent in a situation where race and nativity do not vary?

2. Do individuals who are objectively status inconsistent actually experience less intense social relationships and less frequent social contacts than do people who are status consistent? That is, do the specific forms of statistical interaction among objective status variables suggested by the theory of status inconsistency tell us something about social relations above and beyond what we know can be attributed to the main effects of the status variables, giving us a basis for inference regarding the subjective processes involved?

3. Are there interaction effects on social participation and political attitudes apart from those attributable to status inconsistency?

4. If there are such effects, can they be attributed to the persistence of ethnoreligious or subcultural differences?

Since our sample is exclusively white, we were assured that if inconsistency effects were discovered, they could not be due to racial differences. At the same time, the fact that the sample was native born assured us that if we did discover ethnoreligious differences within the white sample, they would be attributable to persisting subcultural differences and not to differences between immigrants and native-born Americans.[1]

STATUS DIMENSIONS

Previous research has shown that the most important status inconsistencies are those between an achieved status and an ascribed status (Segal and Knoke, 1968). Education was utilized as the achieved status dimension in this analysis. Education is in general highly correlated with other achieved statuses; in our sample the correlation between education and occupational status was .61. At the same time, the main effects of education on attitudes and social participation have repeatedly been demonstrated to be, in general, greater than the main effects of income or occupation for the population as a whole (see, for example, Hodge, 1970).

Race, religion, and ethnicity are the most commonly analyzed ascriptive bases of social status.[2] Race was precluded from the present analysis by the nature of the sample, and the utility of religion in and of itself has recently been called into question. Specifically, Gockel (1969) and Goldstein (1969) have argued that status differences among members of various American religious groups are predominantly functions of educational, occupational, and regional differences in their compositions, rather than of religious differences per se (compare Warren, 1970a, 1970b). But, as Chapter 3 demonstrated, the structure of friendship choice can in fact be described as following systematic differences among ethnoreligious groups that are not entirely reducible to differences in socioeconomic composition but reflect religious *and* ethnic factors as well. These findings, as noted before, are quite consistent with research on the persistence of ethnic differentiation in America (see, for example, Parenti, 1967; Kantrowitz, 1969; Greeley, 1971), and with Miller's (1968) findings with regard to political variables which suggest that ethnic and religious factors must be looked at concurrently.

On the basis of these considerations, we defined our ascriptive status variable in terms of the positions of the 15 largest ethnoreligious groups on the first axis in Chapter 3, Figure 3.3a. (See Appendix 8.A of this chapter for the actual rank order.) The rank-order correlation of this measure with Hodge and Siegel's (forthcoming) ethnic status index was .668 ($p < .01$).[3] The correlation with the mean occupational status of group was only .248 (NS), indicating that our measure of ethnoreligious status was not simply an artifact of differences in socioeconomic status (see also Lasswell, 1965: 340–48). The careful reader will have noted that this nonsignificant correlation is almost necessary since the first axis of the three-dimensional solution is nearly orthogonal (that is, uncorrelated) to the second axis which was identified in Chapter 3 as being related to the differing socioeconomic composition of the groups. The twelve other groups considered in Chapter 3 were omitted due to insufficient numbers to sustain the type of analysis employed below.

We viewed the propositions of Segal (1969) and Box and Ford (1969) regarding the visibility of ascribed status as a potential refinement of the status inconsistency model. If visibility were not a requisite for the processes assumed by the model, we would expect to observe inconsistency effects for all low-status ethnoreligious groups as education increased. If visibility were a necessary condition, on the other hand, then on the basis of Segal's findings, we would expect only the Jews, as the most visible low-status group, to manifest consistently the hypothesized effects of status inconsistency. We must point out that both the theory of status inconsistency and the data with which we confront it are concerned with ascribed status in a heterogeneous community.

Status inconsistency may also have somewhat different effects on one's relations with his own ethnoreligious group than it does on his relations with members of other groups. The highly educated Jew, for example, may not be accorded deference on the basis of his education by non-Jews, but he will have high status within the Jewish community because of his adherence to the value placed on scholarship by that group.[4] The highly educated black, on the other hand, may both be refused deference by the white community and be alienated from the black community because of the difference between the modal level of education in that community and his own level. The intersection of the effects of subcultural patterns and the effects of the structure of the larger community needs to be explored more intensively than we are able to do with the data available to us.

THE ANALYTIC MODEL

Alternative hypotheses derived from the theory of status inconsistency, on the one hand, and the assumption of persisting subcultural differences, on the other, were operationalized in terms of the equation:

$$Y_{ki} = a_k + b_k x_{ki} + e_{ki} \qquad (8.1)$$

where Y_{ki} is a measure on individual i in group k which may manifest the hypothesized effect of status inconsistency, for example, disrupted social relations or political liberalism; a_k is the intercept of ethnoreligious group k on the ordinate: b_k is the regression slope for ethnoreligious group k; x_{ki} is the educational attainment of the ith individual in group k; and e_{ki} is the error term.

At the first level of analysis, we were concerned with whether differences in political attitudes and social relations were attributable to educational differences, to ethnoreligious differences, or to both. If both variables have an effect on the dependent variable, we would then be concerned with whether those effects were simply additive or whether statistical interaction occurred. Finally, if interaction effects were detected, we were concerned with whether these effects were of the specific type predicted by status-inconsistency theory or whether they would be attributable to nonstatus characteristics of the groups included in the analysis (see Hodge and Siegel, 1970). For example, Poles as a group have been shown to have disproportionate tendencies to own real estate (see Wood, 1955; Wilson, 1964; Wolfinger, 1965; Parenti, 1967). As achieved status increases among the Poles, they will presumably purchase more property and may become increasingly anxious about the security of their property. We might, therefore, find hostile attitudes toward groups perceived to be threats to property values (Negroes, for example) increasing as a function of achieved status but attributable to subcultural rather than inconsistency factors (see Greeley, 1968, who showed that Polish Catholics have the highest anti-Negro sentiments of Catholic groups tested).

Our statistical analysis had three objectives. First, we evaluated the differences among the slopes of the regression lines for the fifteen ethnoreligious groups by calculating the ratio of variance between slopes to variance within groups as a means of detecting the presence of interaction effects. Essentially this test (Hald, 1952: 580) determines whether the set of slopes of the ethnoreligious groups, b_k, varies appreciably around the common slope, $\bar{b}$. Second, we determined whether the 15 regression lines were identical (coincident) or different from one another (Hald, 1952: 579–84). That is, the first test merely establishes whether the slopes, b_k, are equal. It could be that the within-group relations of education to the dependent variable for each of the 15 groups were equivalent, but that the regression lines themselves were not identical but parallel to one another (that is, with significant differences among the a-intercepts). Parallel lines would indicate the presence of group differences, *net of the educational differences* among the groups. Finally, the regression slope for each ethnoreligious group was compared to the weighted average of all 15 slopes, using a method developed by Tukey (Acton, 1966: 184–87), to test for the significant departure of any specific group slope from the common slope. Several groups might deviate significantly from the common slope while all the others did not. Such a situation, especially if the deviating groups were numerically small, would not necessarily result in a significant F ratio on the first test, but would be identified by the Tukey Test.

The expectation was that if there actually were interaction effects due to status inconsistency, then, as a general pattern, for high ethnoreligious status groups such as German Presbyterians and Anglo-American Methodists the value of the dependent variable would decrease as education increased and the two statuses became increasingly consistent. The pattern for lower ethnoreligious status groups, on the other hand, would be deflected from this pattern.

This expectation is presented graphically in Figure 8.1a, where the interaction effect is indicated by the difference between b_1 and b_2. As a function of the groups involved, this would indicate either inconsistency

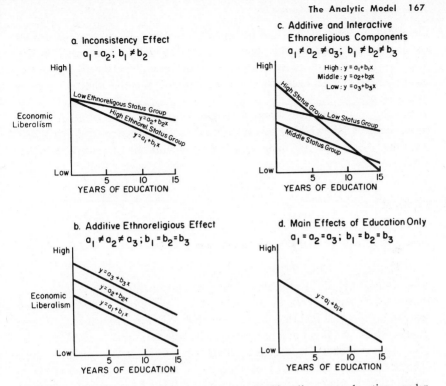

a. Inconsistency Effect
$a_1 = a_2;\ b_1 \neq b_2$

c. Additive and Interactive
Ethnoreligious Components
$a_1 \neq a_2 \neq a_3;\ b_1 \neq b_2 \neq b_3$

High : $y = a_1 + b_1 x$
Middle : $y = a_2 + b_2 x$
Low : $y = a_3 + b_3 x$

High Status Group
Low Status Group
Middle Status Group

Low Ethnoreligous Status Group
High Ethnorel Status Group
$y = a_2 + b_2 x$
$y = a_1 + b_1 x$

b. Additive Ethnoreligious Effect
$a_1 \neq a_2 \neq a_3;\ b_1 = b_2 = b_3$

$y = a_3 + b_3 x$
$y = a_2 + b_2 x$
$y = a_1 + b_1 x$

d. Main Effects of Education Only
$a_1 = a_2 = a_3;\ b_1 = b_2 = b_3$

$y = a_1 + b_1 x$

Economic Liberalism
High — Low
YEARS OF EDUCATION
5 10 15

Figure 8.1 Hypothetical regression of economic liberalism on education, under varying conditions of ethnoreligious effects.

effects or interactive subcultural effects. If b_1 and b_2 were not significantly different but a_1 and a_2 were different—that is, the lines were parallel—this would indicate the presence of additive ethnoreligious group effects. This outcome is represented graphically in Figure 8.1b. We shall note here that these additive effects need not be related to the social status of the groups.

Figure 8.1a in fact reflects an ideal typical set of findings which, while useful for purposes of exposition, would be unlikely to be approximated by a body of data. A more likely outcome, if status-inconsistency effects were operating, would be that the slopes of the several regression lines would be increasingly deflected from the pattern observed among high-status groups as social distance from those groups increased, but that the pattern would be confounded by main effects attributable to ethnoreligious group differences, reflected in differences in the a-intercepts. This kind of outcome is presented in Figure 8.1c. Here again, the additive ethnoreligious component is indicated by the significance of the differences among a_1, a_2, and a_3, and the presence of interaction due to status inconsistency is indicated by the significance of the differences among b_1, b_2, and b_3. This sort of pattern, but with any other status ordering of the groups, would indicate interaction effects due to factors other than status inconsistency.

Finally, our statistical analysis might have yielded no ethnoreligious component at all, whether additive or interactive. Such a situation where the only effects are the main effects of education is presented in Figure 8.1d.

FINDINGS

Status Inconsistency and Ethnoreligious Group Differences

In Chapter 3, Table 3.7 presents for the 27 ethnoreligious groups summary indicators of differences in their socioeconomic composition, attitudes, and behavior with respect to religious and ethnic matters. For the regression analysis reported below, we shall consider only the 15 largest groups which are identified in that table by asterisks next to their names.* (See also Appendix 8.A of this chapter.) Within each broad religious category, groups are ordered by their mean family incomes (which, as is easily seen, is almost equivalent to ranking them by their mean number of school years completed and their mean occupational status as well). Not only are there highly significant differences among the 15 groups remaining, net of group differences in educational achievements, with respect to our measures of ethnic and religious behaviors and orientations; but these differences are not simply attributable to the obvious differences between Protestant, Catholic, and Jewish groups considered in their respective aggregates. That is, there are generally significant differences (net of educational differences) among Protestant and among Catholic groups considered separately, especially for frequency of church attendance and subjective ethnic interest.

The basic findings relevant to our discussion of the theory of status crystallization versus the theory of ethnic of subcultural differences are summarized in Table 8.1.

We have divided the dependent variables into two sets.[5] The first set

---

* For the reader's convenience we list the groups here: Protestant groups include German Presbyterians, Anglo-American Presbyterians, German Methodists, German Lutherans, Anglo-American Methodists, Anglo-American Baptists, and Protestants, ethnic origin not ascertained; Catholic groups include Irish, Slavic, German, French, Italian, Anglo-American, and Polish Catholics; and Jews.

includes five measures intended to tap various aspects of a man's orientation to political and economic issues—it being assumed in the literature (see Fauman, 1968; Goffman, 1957) that "liberal" orientations (specifically, preference for the "underdog," the worker, in labor-management disputes and active governmental support in guaranteeing job opportunities, Democratic party preference, and civil libertarianism) are especially likely to be expressed by status-inconsistent individuals. We further reasoned that a man's condition of status discrepancy on two important ranking dimensions in our society might make him especially concerned with social status matters per se, that is, concerned with how other people regarded him. As the first column in the table shows, high educational attainment is associated with conservative economic ideology, Republican party preference, willingness to grant civil liberties to Ku Klux Klansmen and Communists, and low status concern.

The second set of dependent variables is intended to tap various aspects of a man's social participation in intimate primary groups and secondary or voluntary associations. The theory of status crystallization leads one to expect that status-discrepant individuals are likely to be subject to considerable strain in engaging in social relations with others because their social ambiguity—by which they may be accorded high or low deferential treatment depending on which status dimension others choose to regard as more important in the interactional context—creates anxiety concerning their preferred status treatment (naturally they would always like to be treated in terms of their more highly evaluated status). Consequently, a status-discrepant man is expected to avoid membership in voluntary associations that are broadly recruited (that is, include members who are not also members of the disvalued status), to be less involved in those voluntary associations in which he is a member, and to prefer friendship groups that are strictly comparable to him in status attributes (thus, such an individual would prefer kin-based and ethno-religiously homogeneous friendship networks). We might also expect that the reported closeness of friendships, the frequency of interaction with friends, and the duration of friendships would be adversely affected for such individuals as manifestations of their "defensive," ego-protecting posture toward social relations.

The alternative theory of ethnic differences would simply maintain that ethnoreligious groups will differ on both sets of measures, once socioeconomic differences in their composition are taken into account, because each has a unique cultural and historical relationship to American society that mediates their members' relation to it. Thus given the different times of arrival of the various ethnoreligious groups and cultural and other peculiarities of their European and American experiences (see Handlin, 1959; Higham, 1955; Lieberson, 1963; Abramson, 1969), we should

Table 8.1. Tests for differences among various regression parameters for fifteen ethnoreligious groups for selected political and social attitudes and measures of social participation, regressed on educational attainment

Dependent Variables	(1) Product-Moment Correl. (r)	(2) Test for Differences Among Slopes, bs	(3) Test for Differences Among Intercepts, as	(4) Groups Deviating Significantly from the Common Slope, $\bar{b}$, According to the Tukey Test	
				Steeper Than Common Slope	Flatter Than Common Slope
Political and social attitudes:					
Economic ideology[a]	.26*	NS	$F = 2.58$, $p < .05$	Anglo-American Methodists, Protestants, Origin N.A.	German Presbyterians, Jews
Party preference[b]	−.23*	NS	$F = 10.43$, $p < .001$	Anglo-American Catholics	German Presbyterians, Jews
Tolerance for Ku Klux Klan[c]	−.18*	NS	NS	None	None
Tolerance for Communists[c]	−.30*	NS	NS	None	None
Status concern[d]	−.20*	NS	NS	German Presbyterians, Jews, Protestants, Origin N.A.	Irish Catholics, Slavic Catholics
Social participation:					
Number of memberships in voluntary associations[e]	.39*	NS	NS	None	None
Degree of associational involvement[f]	.03	NS	$F = 2.94$, $p < .05$	None	None
Average closeness of friendships[g]	−.11*	NS	NS	None	None
Average frequency of interaction[h]	−.01	NS	NS	None	None
Average duration of friendships[i]	−.02	NS	$F = 2.05$, $p < .10$	Anglo-American Baptists, Polish Catholics, Jews, Protestants, Origin N.A.	German Presbyterians, German Methodists, Anglo-American Catholics
Number of work-based friends[j]	−.02	NS	NS	None	None
Number of kin-based friends[k]	−.13*	NS	NS	Slavic Catholics, Jews	Anglo-American Catholics

Mean ethnoreligious homogeneity[l]	−.05	NS	$F = 32.147$, $p < .001$	None	None
Mean occupational homogeneity[l]	−.00	NS	NS	Jews	None

* $p < .01$.

a Based on answers to three questions, Q3, Q46, and Q60, Appendix C. See Laumann, 1966: 182–84, for details on index construction. The range on this index was from 1 (liberal) to 7 (conservative).

b Party preference was coded on a 7-point scale from "strong Republican" (1) through "independent" (4) to "strong Democrat" (7). See Q80, Appendix C.

c See Chapter 5, Table 5.3, footnote h.

d Based on the summation of two Likert-scale items, S7 and S14 (Appendix C), each with five response categories. The range of this index was from 0 (low status concern) to 8 (high status concern).

e The respondent was presented with the following list of voluntary associations and was asked to indicate to which ones he belonged: church-connected groups (but not church itself) (19.1%), labor unions (39.3%), veterans' organizations (10.7%), fraternal organizations or lodges (22.7%), business or civic groups (9.6%), parent-teacher associations (15.8%), community centers (1.7%), organizations of people of the same nationality (2.4%), sport teams (16.6%), country clubs (5.9%), youth groups (scout leaders, etc.) (8.3%), professional groups (13.9%), political clubs or organizations (5.5%), neighborhood improvement associations (10.9%), charity or welfare organizations (4.6%), and others (specified) (20.4%). (Percentages in parentheses are proportions of total sample who belong to given type of organization.) See Chapter 6, pp. 149–52.

f For each organization in which the respondent indicated membership, he was asked whether he was very involved or not very involved in the activities of the organization. See Chapter 7, p. 143.

g For each of the three friends mentioned by the respondent, he was asked whether he was (1) a very close, personal friend, (2) good friend, or (3) acquaintance. See Q15, Appendix C.

h For each of the three friends, the respondent was asked Q28, Appendix C.

i For each of the three friends, the respondent was asked how many years he had known the friend. We determined the proportion of a man's life he had known the friend by dividing the number of years he had known the friend by the age of the respondent. See Chapter 5, Table 5.2, footnote m.

j For each of the three friends, we asked the respondent Q27, Appendix C.

k For each friend, we asked the respondent whether the friend was a relative (consanguineal or affinal) of his. See Q14, Appendix C.

l See Chapter 5, pp. 86–87.

expect differences among the groups with regard to many social attitudes and modes of social participation. A number of studies (for example, Glazer and Moynihan, 1963; Wilson and Banfield, 1964; Dahl, 1961; Parenti, 1967) have suggested, for example, that certain groups, such as the Irish Catholics, have especially strong ties to the urban-based Democratic party as a result of their concentrations in urban ghettos of our eastern cities in the mid-nineteenth century.

The last four columns of Table 8.1 present the summary results of our regression analysis. As noted above, we calculated the regression equation, $Y_{ki} = a_k + b_k x_{ki}$, where x_{ki} is the number of school years completed by each man, for each of the fifteen ethnoreligious groups. We first determined whether the slopes, b's, were significantly different from the common slope, $\bar{b}$, for the men irrespective of ascriptive group membership. As is apparent in a glance at Column 2, all of the F tests failed to indicate significant differences among the slopes. Considering this evidence alone, we would be forced to conclude that the relationship of educational attainment to the various dependent variables, as measured by the slopes of the regression lines, do *not* differ among the 15 groups—that is, there are no detectable patterns of interaction effects of education and ethnoreligious group on the dependent variables. As noted before, the theory of status crystallization at the least implies the presence of statistical interaction effects and, more specifically, interaction effects that are patterned such that lowly evaluated status groups are expected to be deflected from the "normal" relationship of, for instance, conservatism with high status toward more liberal positions. Unfortunately for the theory, however, we do not find any significant interaction effects according to this first test (in Column 2).

Our hypothesis of ethnic group differences, however, fares much better. While it may be true that all the groups manifest similar relationships of educational attainment to the dependent variable, it is still quite possible that the groups significantly differ among themselves with regard to their tendency to be high or low on the dependent variable, even when the effects of their differences in educational composition are taken into account. For example, Irish Catholics, on the average, tend to be more inclined to the Democratic party than German Methodists, although their within-group relationship of education to party preference is the same. In the regression analysis this would be reflected by the two groups having parallel rather than coincidental regression lines, that is, the a's or Y-intercepts would be significantly different. As Column 3 indicates, five of the F tests for determining the presence of noncoincident regression lines are statistically significant. With respect to political and social attitudes, Jews and Catholic groups of the recent or "new migration" generally tend to be more heavily Democratic in party preference and economically

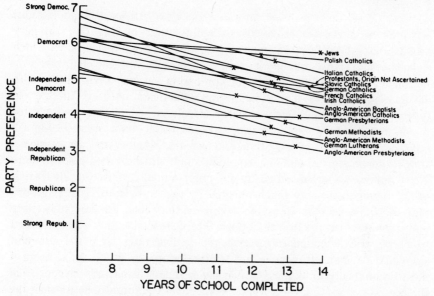

Figure 8.2   Regression lines of political party preference by educational attainment, for the 15 ethnoreligious groups.

liberal than "old migration" Protestant and Catholic (for example, French and Anglo-American) groups. Due to limitations of space, we have included only one graphic portrayal (see Figure 8.2) of the regression lines—that of political party preference and educational attainment for the 15 ethnoreligious groups; but the patterns observed here are generally replicated for the other four measures of political and economic views. Note that the status ordering of the ethnoreligious groups in terms of partisanship at the high end of the education dimension is almost exactly what we would expect in terms of status-inconsistency theory. It is the processes producing this ordering that make explanations in terms of status inconsistency theory questionable. Rather than finding ethnoreligious status to be related to the deflection of regression lines, we find that in some instances the lines for high and low groups are almost parallel—German Presbyterians and Jews, for example—while some low-status groups such as Italian Catholics manifest deflections *toward* the lines observed for higher-status samples.[6] The observed status ordering, then, must be explained in terms of the initial ordering of groups; that is, on the intercepts at the ordinate, as much as in terms of regression slopes.

With respect to our measures of social participation, Jews and new-migration Catholics did not differ greatly in their involvement in voluntary associations from old-migration Protestants and Catholics. They were, however, more likely to have kin-based and ethnoreligiously homogeneous networks as alternative areas of sociability, thus making the voluntary associations relatively more important to the old-migration groups, which lacked these ascription networks (see Appendix 8.A of this chapter).

Column 4 reports the results of comparing specific group slopes with the common slope to detect significant differences, utilizing Tukey's (in Acton, 1966: 184–87) technique for calculating confidence intervals for the discrepancy between the group slope and the common slope. Column 2 reported the results of a test that determines whether the set of slopes varies appreciably around the common slope. In the latter case, if there are a number of groups that do not differ among themselves, the test is likely to fail to be very much affected by the presence of several groups that do in fact differ from the common slope but are not sufficiently numerous to affect the overall pattern. The Tukey technique was developed to permit the detection of specific group departures from the common slope. To facilitate discussion and interpretation, the groups in Column 4 have been divided into those which have slopes significantly steeper than the common slope and those which have slopes significantly flatter than the common slope.

There were eight dependent variables for which we found significant deviations of group slopes from the common slope. Most of the groups so identified have few members; consequently, caution should be exercised in drawing conclusions. There is one readily observable pattern, however. German Presbyterians and Jews both appear to deviate rather regularly from the common slope and in the same way, in contrast to a somewhat more varied set of Protestant and Catholic groups. These latter have middling achieved status as groups (see Table 3.7) and usually deviate in the opposite direction from the German Presbyterians and Jews.

It is especially noteworthy that German Presbyterians and Jews both enjoy the highest mean occupational and educational status and family income of any group in the sample—that is, on achievement-based criteria, they are the two most favored groups in the Detroit metropolitan area. Moreover, they enjoyed these highly favored achieved statuses over two generations, with their fathers also the highest in mean educational and occupational status (see Chapter 9). While most other Protestant and Catholic groups manifested considerable upward intergenerational mobility, these groups were already at or near the top of the achieved status system a generation ago.

But what is of signal importance in this context is the fact that German Presbyterians, as white Anglo-Saxon Protestants (WASP's), enjoy exceptionally high ascriptive status, while Jews are at the bottom of the white ethnoreligious hierarchy of social status (see above discussion on ethnoreligious group ranking). Yet the relationship between achieved socioeconomic status, as measured by education, and various attitudes and behaviors are similar for these two groups and differentiate them from the rest of the population. In the cases of economic ideology and party preference, higher socioeconomic German Presbyterians and Jews are less likely to be economically conservative and Republican than high socioeconomic status members of other groups.[7] While the theory of status crystallization would predict such patterns for Jewish high achievers, such patterns for German Presbyterians are completely contrary to the theory's predictions.

Certainly a plausible inference from the theory would be that highly status-discrepant individuals would have higher status concern than status-consistent individuals. But another blow to the theory might be seen in the fact that among both Jews and German Presbyterians the negative relationship between education and status concern is high, relative to other groups. That is, the regression slopes for these two groups are steeper than the common negative slope for the sample as a whole.

Most of the groups identified as having slopes significantly higher than Jews and German Presbyterians with respect to economic ideology, party preference, and status concern are of middle rather than high or low achieved status and have had unusually high rates of upward intergenerational mobility (see Chapter 9). It is higher socioeconomic status members of these groups who are more likely to be economic conservatives and Republicans and to express high status concern. In a purely speculative vein, we suggest that perhaps the status insecurity engendered by such intergenerational mobility may be seen to promote more conservative political and economic attitudes in an effort to protect recently acquired gains (see Lopreato, 1967). For groups such as Jews and German Presbyterians, who tend to have greater intergenerational status stability, such defensive measures are not seen as particularly relevant.

To summarize the results to this point, we have shown that while there are substantial differences among ethnoreligious groups on a number of political and social attitudes and characteristic modes of social participation, net of group differences in educational composition, we have also suggested that the theory of status crystallization affords little if any explanatory power in accounting for the pattern of differences among groups. The sole exceptions to this generalization are status-inconsistent Jews, who behave in large part the way the theory of status inconsistency predicts that they should. Since our so-called theory of subcultural differences merely asserts the presence of group differences without specification of their form, we can only conclude that the observed patterns (see Appendix 8.A of this chapter) should provide useful clues for the construction of a model of ethnoreligious group differences which would have to be tested on other sample populations.

THE IMPACT OF STATUS CONCERN

In the course of our review of the literature on status crystallization, we concluded that one possibly important intervening variable linking a man's objective condition of status discrepancy to his subjective view of the world and social behavior would be his degree of awareness of or concern for status that would presumably make him more or less sensitive to the status-linked behavior and attitudes of others. In an earlier work (Laumann, 1966: 105–22), the senior author observed: "The phenomenon of *differential status awareness* is an important attribute of stratification systems in its own right that may have significant consequences for processes occurring within the status system and its relation with other institutional subsystems, such as the political or economic system." (1966: 106) While the measure of differential status awareness employed in this earlier study was derived from the respondents' differential tendencies to discriminate subjectively among men in various occupations as possible partners for intimate social relationships (such as fathers-in-law, friends, and neighbors), it is highly likely that this measure would be positively related to the measure of status concern employed in this chapter. In general, it was found that:

. . . status-sensitive men tend to be those who identify themselves as members of the upper and upper-middle classes or those who derive from ethnic groups that have more recently arrived on the American scene. They are likely to desire their intimate associates to be of comparable status to themselves and are likely to succeed in confining their relations to such persons. Moreover, their theories of the basis of the class structure emphasize its hierarchical character. They are themselves upwardly mobile and aspire for upward mobility for their children . . . they express stronger political party preferences for either the Democratic or Republican parties and have more extreme and well-defined economic ideologies of either a liberal or conservative persuasion. (Laumann, 1966: 121)

Indeed, using a measure of status crystallization comparable to Lenski's (1954), it was even found that status-discrepant men tended to be more status sensitive.

One might reasonably speculate that men with high status concern should manifest the effects of status discrepancy prescribed in the theory of status crystallization more clearly than those who were unconcerned with such matters. To test this speculation, we performed an analysis similar to that described above for a subsample of those men who scored roughly in the upper third on our measure of status concern [see Table 8.1, footnote d, $(N = 364)$]. Table 8.2 summarizes the results for the Tukey test for identifying groups deviating from the common slope. Despite the sharply reduced sample sizes of the various groups (which should decrease the number of significant results due to increased sampling variability), we found that there were significant group differences for all but one of the dependent variables (in contrast, note that eight of the dependent variables in Table 8.1 showed no significant results). This suggests that the presence of high status concern is itself an important precondition for eliciting interaction effects of educational attainment and ethnoreligious group membership. In the case of the first set of attitudinal variables, there are no changes in the pattern of group departures from the common slope when compared to the total sample although there were some groups added to the list. We now, moreover, observe significant group departures from the common slope for the two measures of tolerance toward extremist groups of the right and left.

But perhaps the most noteworthy and puzzling results occur for our second set of measures relating to social participation. For all but one of our measures, we observe groups deviating from the common slope; this suggests the presence of significant interaction effects of educational attainment and group membership for men high in status concern. Unfortunately, the pattern of departures defies any summary generalization beyond the negative conclusion that the pattern predicted by the theory of status crystallization does *not* manifest itself for any of the dependent variables. It is not at all clear, for example, why German Lutheran and French Catholic men high in status concern should manifest significantly stronger relations between education and the number of memberships in voluntary associations while Anglo-American Baptist and German Methodist men, among others, should manifest significantly weaker relationships between education and associational memberships than the relationship obtained for the sample as a whole. It is certainly plausible to argue that if there are persisting differences among men of differing ethnoreligious groups in the ways in which they handle interpersonal relationships, they would be especially likely to manifest themselves among those members who are highly concerned with status. And in fact we do find that our measure of status concern is positively associated with subjective ethnic interest and traditional values concerning the family,[8] another measure presumed to be linked to the retention of strong ethnic orientations. But again, in the absence of a well-established model of ethnoreligious group differences that is based on a comparative study of these groups, we are left at the rather unsatisfactory point of asserting that the differences reported here should provide useful guidelines in developing such a model.

Table 8.2. Groups deviating significantly from common slope, $\bar{b}$, according to the Tukey test for men with high status concern

Dependent Variables	Product-Moment Correl. (r)	Groups Deviating Significantly from the Common Slope, $\bar{b}$, According to Tukey Test	
		Steeper Than Common Slope	Flatter Than Common Slope
Political and social attitudes:			
Economic ideology	.29**	German Lutherans	German Presbyterians, Jews, French Catholics
Party Preference	−.24**	German Lutherans, German Methodists, Anglo-American Catholics	German Presbyterians, Jews, German Catholics, Protestants, Origin N.A.
Tolerance for Ku Klux Klan	−.16**	German Methodists, Anglo-American Catholics	German Presbyterians, Italians Catholics, Slavic Catholics, Protestants, Origin N.A.
Tolerance for Communists	−.21**	German Methodists, Protestants, Origin N.A.	German Presbyterians
Social participation:			
Number of memberships in voluntary associations	.30**	German Lutherans, French Catholics	Anglo-American Baptists, German Methodists, Anglo-American Catholics, Jews, Protestants, Origin N.A.

	Correlation		
Degree of associational involvement	−.26**	None	Jews
Average closeness of friendships	−.04	German Methodists, Irish Catholics, Protestants, Origin N.A.	Anglo-American Methodists, Anglo-American Catholics
Average frequency of interaction	.03	German Presbyterians, German Methodists, Anglo-American Catholics, Protestants, Origin N.A.	Anglo-American Methodists, Slavic Catholics
Average duration of friendships	−.11*	Anglo-American Methodists, Jews	Irish Catholics
Number of work-based friends	−.08	None	German Methodists, Anglo-American Catholics, Slavic Catholics
Number of kin-based friends	−.37**	None	None
Mean ethnoreligious homogeneity	−.04	Jews, Protestants, Origin N.A.	Anglo-American Baptists
Mean occupational homogeneity	.03	None	German Lutherans, Slavic Catholics, Protestants, Origin N.A.

* $p < .05$.
** $p < .01$.

SUMMARY AND CONCLUSIONS

Our data clearly provide a basis for rejection of a general status inconsistency phenomenon among urban white men such as that proposed by Lenski. There is no overall pattern of statistical interaction between ethnoreligious group membership and education with regard to either political attitudes or social participation. At the same time, there are significant interaction effects involving particular ethnoreligious groups that indicate subcultural differences in political orientations and sociability patterns. It is especially noteworthy that such effects are common among Jews since previous research has suggested that because of their social visibility Jews should be especially prone to the stresses of status inconsistency. At the same time, the similarity of interaction effects among German Presbyterians and Jews suggests that the stability of high achieved status in these groups across generations and the relative homogeneity of these groups may be more parsimonious explanations of their similarities than is the theory of status inconsistency, which in fact would lead us to expect differences in the very areas in which similarities have been observed. However, the patterns we have observed among the Jews in our sample, taken together with Segal's earlier results on nonwhites, suggests that similar behavior on the part of members of these two minority groups may well explain previous results that have been taken as supportive of the status-inconsistency argument. Moreover, as we have shown in Figure 8.2, it is possible for apparent effects of inconsistencies between low-ascribed and high-achieved statuses to emerge on the basis of social dynamics other than those assumed by the theory of status inconsistency. Specifically, it is the persistence of traits characteristic of ethnic subcultures that leads to these results.

The incidence of statistical interaction effects increased in our data when we confined our analysis to men who scored high on our index of status concern. These interactions once again failed to fit the pattern predicted by the theory of status inconsistency. They do point to the necessity of rejecting an overly simplistic "melting-pot" theory of ethnic assimilation and recognizing the cultural pluralism of American society.[9]

NOTES

1. As a test of the assumption of persisting differences, we analyzed our data controlling for generational differences (second generation versus third or more generations, see Chapter 5, p. 91). While we observed general differences, they were not consistent in direction, and did not suggest the atrophy of subcultural differences. See also Chapter 9.

2. Age is an additional ascriptive status that comes under frequent scrutiny. Smith (1969) has in fact argued that age is an important intervening variable in understanding the effects of status inconsistency. In controlling our analyses for age, we found main effects attributable to age. These effects, however, formed no coherent pattern across ethnoreligious groups.

3. While the correlation between Laumann's ethnoreligious status ranking and Hodge and Siegel's ethnic states index (see Chapter 3, Table 3.2) was not perfect, we are pleased with its magnitude. The former involves objective interaction patterns, while the latter reflects subjective choices. It is comforting to know that the two are related. The departure from unity may be attributed to the facts that subjectively each group ranks itself first, after which there is consensus on the relative ranking of other groups, and the Hodge-Siegel Index includes only ethnic designations while the Laumann Index takes into account religious differences as well.

4. Our data suggest that neither retreat into nor withdrawal from the ethnoreligious community is a common response to status inconsistency. That is, status inconsistency is not related to the ethnoreligious homogeneity of social contacts. Although the level of ethnoreligious homogeneity varied among the groups we analyzed, as indicated by significant differences among the a intercepts (Table 8.1), we found no significant differences among the regression slopes.

5. In Appendix 8.A of this chapter, we have provided the means and standard deviations for all the dependent variables for the 15 groups. The variables are defined in the footnotes to Table 8.1.

6. Rank-order correlations were computed between the ethnoreligious status ranks for the 15 groups (see Appendix 8.A of this chapter) and their regression slopes for each of the 14 dependent variables. These correlations can be taken as summary measures of the presence of the patterns we would expect if status-inconsistency effects were operating. If these effects were present, we would expect the rank-order correlations to be positive in sign; that is, the highest-ranked groups would have the steepest slopes and the lowest-ranked groups the flattest slopes. Contrary to this pattern, we found that only two of the fourteen correlations—number of voluntary association memberships and average duration of friendships—were significantly different from zero at the .05 level. One significant difference from zero would have been anticipated on the basis of chance alone.

7. As can be seen in Figure 8.2, however, it should be noted that Jews as a group are more likely to have Democratic party preferences than German Presbyterians as a group, who tend to be independent Republicans. Both groups, however, have roughly equal means on the economic ideology scale.

8. Family traditionalism was measured by a three-item scale, including S2, S5, and S13, Appendix C. See Goldberg and Litton, 1968.

9. It is noteworthy that while our data do not support the melting-pot view of assimilation, neither do they support Borhek's (1970) alternative model of the breakdown of ethnic group cohesion. Borhek suggests that formal education is the most important determinant of both the homogeneity of friendship choices and the expression of assimilationist attitudes. While we have not dealt directly with the latter variable, we have regressed ethnoreligious homogeneity on education for each group and for the total sample. While we did find main effects due to ethnoreligious group membership, that is, significant differences among intercepts, we found the zero-order correlation between education and homogeneity to be statistically insignificant. Moreover, there were no significant differences among the regression slopes of the fifteen groups tested.

Appendix 8.A.   Means and standard deviations on selected socioeconomic characteristics, political and social attitudes, and measures of social participation for the fifteen ethnoreligious groups[a]

| | | | Socioeconomic Status Characteristics | | | |
| | | | School Years | | Occupational Status[c] | |
Rank on Ethnoreligious Status Scale[b]	Group	Total Number	$\overline{x}$	s	$\overline{x}$	s
Protestant						
1	German Methodists	32	12.8	3.24	50.4	25.37
2	German Presbyterians	25	13.8	2.94	58.0	24.92
3	Anglo-American Methodists	40	11.4	3.21	46.5	25.68
4	Anglo-American Presbyterians	72	13.7	2.83	59.2	21.65
5	German Lutherans	57	12.2	3.30	49.9	24.90
6	Anglo-American Baptists	80	10.2	3.08	36.0	22.93
7	Protestants, Origins N.A.	32	9.5	3.81	32.0	18.86
Catholic						
8	Italian Catholics	55	12.0	3.00	44.1	23.24
9	Anglo-American Catholics	33	11.2	3.83	43.3	27.65
10	Irish Catholics	65	12.7	2.93	51.1	21.63
11	German Catholics	81	12.2	2.75	48.6	23.62
12	French Catholics	51	12.0	3.19	41.2	22.92
13	Slavic Catholics	38	12.3	3.25	45.5	25.27
14	Polish Catholics	111	11.0	3.55	39.6	22.87
15	Jews	29	14.8	2.84	63.4	24.22
Total		801	12.0	3.18	46.3	23.42

Selected Political and Social Attitudes and Measures of Social Participation											
Economic Ideology		Party Preference		Tolerance for				Status Concern		Number of Associations	
				KKK		Communist					
$\bar{x}$	s	$\bar{x}$	s	$\bar{x}$	s	$\bar{x}$	s	$\bar{x}$	s	$\bar{x}$	s
4.81	1.71	3.88	2.18	1.41	.45	1.59	.43	4.21	1.86	2.2	1.92
4.46	1.38	4.00	2.48	1.49	.46	1.54	.54	3.96	2.21	2.7	1.77
3.93	1.70	3.54	2.18	1.37	.50	1.89	.62	4.51	2.14	2.3	1.37
4.81	1.65	3.19	2.00	1.42	.44	1.62	.55	3.85	2.34	2.4	2.14
4.35	1.51	3.73	2.14	1.36	.38	1.64	.50	4.27	2.02	2.1	1.72
3.97	1.45	4.58	2.12	1.51	.55	1.95	.60	4.88	2.06	1.6	1.39
3.57	1.28	5.38	1.94	1.38	.44	1.84	.68	5.50	2.18	1.5	1.17
3.76	1.70	5.54	1.88	1.53	.48	1.81	.55	4.98	2.24	2.1	1.59
4.06	1.27	4.73	2.05	1.53	.49	1.75	.57	4.59	1.78	2.2	1.87
4.19	1.41	4.77	2.00	1.48	.43	1.80	.63	4.28	2.17	2.5	1.82
4.27	1.44	4.95	1.94	1.46	.49	1.72	.56	4.71	2.15	1.8	1.69
3.71	1.54	4.92	2.13	1.49	.37	1.88	.57	4.53	2.33	1.9	1.57
3.84	1.73	5.11	2.07	1.42	.47	1.65	.60	4.65	2.20	1.8	1.60
3.69	1.55	5.72	1.72	1.56	.57	1.87	.58	4.81	2.35	2.1	1.63
3.86	1.63	5.79	1.29	1.46	.44	1.36	.38	3.69	2.71	3.6	2.18
4.08	1.54	4.70	1.99	1.47	.48	1.76	.57	4.54	2.20	2.1	1.70

Appendix 8.A.   Means and standard deviations on selected socioeconomic characteristics, political and social attitudes, and measures of social participation for the fifteen ethnoreligious groups[a] (Continued)

| | | | Selected Political | | | |
| | | | Degree of Association Involvement | | Average Closeness of Friends | |
Rank on Ethnoreligious Status Scale[b]	Group	Total Number	$\bar{x}$	s	$\bar{x}$	s
Protestant						
1	German Methodists	32	174.1	51.7	1.4	.47
2	German Presbyterians	25	175.9	50.6	1.4	.49
3	Anglo-American Methodists	40	154.7	50.2	1.3	.41
4	Anglo-American Presbyterians	72	178.9	50.4	1.4	.44
5	German Lutherans	57	180.5	49.2	1.6	.45
6	Anglo-American Baptists	80	176.5	52.7	1.5	.49
7	Protestants, Origins N.A.	32	166.7	51.3	1.6	.48
Catholic						
8	Italian Catholics	55	175.5	112.6	1.3	.43
9	Anglo-American Catholics	33	177.7	51.1	1.6	.50
10	Irish Catholics	65	176.9	52.0	1.6	.49
11	German Catholics	81	182.8	98.6	1.5	.55
12	French Catholics	51	163.8	52.1	1.5	.43
13	Slavic Catholics	38	184.0	47.8	1.6	.48
14	Polish Catholics	111	172.6	51.4	1.6	.46
15	Jews	29	189.3	130.5	1.5	.48
Total		801	175.5	67.4	1.5	.47

and Social Attitudes and Measures of Social Participation

Average Frequency of Interaction		Average Duration of Friendships		Number of Work-Based Friendships		Number of Kin-based Friendships		Mean Homogeneity			
								Ethno-religious		Occupation	
$\bar{x}$	s	$\bar{x}$	s	$\bar{x}$	s	$\bar{x}$	s	$\bar{x}$	s	$\bar{x}$	s
3.0	1.15	12.9	6.40	.45	.78	.38	.61	99.7	23.9	49.7	30.5
2.8	1.22	13.6	8.10	.46	.93	.28	.54	67.1	22.0	38.8	26.0
3.2	1.34	17.3	11.46	.49	.78	.28	.65	52.8	18.7	49.2	20.5
3.0	1.15	14.2	8.06	.39	.72	.31	.60	43.5	17.5	46.2	25.6
3.4	1.19	15.6	9.15	.29	.57	.70	.89	46.2	21.3	53.3	30.0
2.7	1.32	11.8	6.69	.56	.90	.48	.70	66.9	32.1	45.4	27.2
3.2	1.17	11.0	6.45	.83	1.07	.47	.76	32.9	21.7	33.1	28.9
2.6	1.22	13.8	8.77	.50	.87	.53	.86	34.0	18.4	53.1	27.8
3.1	1.65	14.6	9.75	.55	.90	.47	.62	28.8	13.7	49.5	26.4
2.9	1.27	12.7	6.70	.55	.90	.40	.68	33.7	21.3	46.7	29.8
2.8	1.38	12.6	7.36	.62	.93	.52	.73	33.7	17.0	42.1	26.4
3.1	1.23	16.0	7.60	.29	.54	.55	.78	42.2	15.9	46.5	28.6
3.2	1.36	15.4	9.28	.33	.76	.70	.85	50.4	21.9	55.9	26.0
3.0	1.22	14.6	8.22	.32	.71	.60	.85	31.9	23.9	46.5	26.6
2.7	1.21	15.8	11.54	.33	.73	.46	.86	24.2	44.5	40.3	37.4
3.0	1.27	14.0	8.26	.46	.81	.49	.75	43.9	22.9	46.7	27.7

[a] Variables are defined in the footnotes to Table 8.1.

[b] Rank on the first axis of the three-dimensional smallest space analysis of ethnoreligious groups, Chapter 3, Figure 3.3a.

[c] See footnote a, Table 2.2, Chapter 2.

CHAPTER 9

The Persistence of Ethnoreligious Differences in the Worldly Success of Third- and Later-Generation Americans

THE DIFFERENTIAL WORLDLY SUCCESS OF MINORITY GROUPS

Over the years considerable attention has been given to the differential educational and occupational achievements of ethnic and racial minorities in the United States (see Handlin, 1954; Gordon, 1964; Nam, 1959; Lieberson, 1963; Taeuber and Taeuber, 1968; Duncan and Duncan, 1968; Thernstrom, 1969; Featherman, 1971). Some groups, such as the eastern European Jews, have been noted for their exceptionally rapid movement up the socioeconomic status ladder while other groups, such as the Poles and Negroes, have been notably less successful.

Three broad varieties of explanations or theories for the differential success of minority groups have been formulated. The first type of explanation focuses on a nationality group's competitive advantages or disadvantages deriving from certain features of its culture. For example, it has often been suggested that the Jews' high evaluation of education has greatly facilitated their meeting a critical prerequisite for access to high status occupations (see Slater, 1969, for a critical examination of this view). Weber (1930) and others (McClelland et al., 1958; Lenski, 1963; Rosen, 1959) have suggested that certain Protestant groups are especially likely to inculcate a this-worldly asceticism and need for achievement in their communicants that is highly likely, however unintentionally, to lead to worldly success (see Featherman, 1971, for a recent critical look at one aspect of this argument).[1] And finally, it has been argued that the traditionalistic peasant orientations of southern Italian and Polish immigrants made them especially ill fitted to their new urban environment (see Banfield, 1958).

The second type of explanation stresses the differing times of arrival of various groups such that northwestern European groups were especially favored over southern and eastern European groups simply because they have had a longer time to acclimate to American conditions. In addition, they possessed certain cultural features, such as Protestant religious preferences, that were more acceptable to the native "majority" American of British Protestant ancestry, who comprised the bulk of the settlers in the first 200 years of the nation's existence. The third type of explanation notes that discriminatory practices against specific minority groups, especially with regard to access to higher level educational and occupational positions, were practiced by "majority" Americans. Nearly every immigrant group has been subjected to such practices with greater or lesser intensity (see Higham, 1955) and with corresponding consequences for their socioeconomic success.

While each of these explanations doubtless has some merit and all are not mutually exclusive, they all would seem to have one important implication that will be of special concern in this chapter. As minority groups become more fully assimilated into the host society and culture with each succeeding generation, differences in group educational and occupational achievements will inevitably disappear as whatever distinctive features of the groups for facilitating or hindering educational and occupational achievement moderate and disappear over time. This is especially likely in view of the fact that the period of mass immigration, whereby group identities could be sustained and revitalized by fresh recruits from the Old Country, is essentially over. This fact is caused primarily by the passage of restrictive immigration laws beginning in the mid-1920s.

Recently Duncan and Duncan (1968) have presented unusually rich data, based on an enormous national sample, that document once again the presence of nationality group differences in educational and occupational achievements. One must concede that, with their introduction of certain controls, the differences appear to be rather modest in size (Duncan and Duncan, 1968: 360). There is, however, the distinct possibility that these differences might be underestimated because of the rather heterogeneous categories they were forced to employ. They were constrained by their data (collected by the U.S. Bureau of the Census) to consider only differences in national origin for first (immigrant) and second generation (sons of foreign stock) Americans. Since they did not have information on specific religious preferences, they could only infer (admittedly with considerable plausibility, see Beshers et al., 1964) that the favored position of Russian Americans, for example, could be attributed to their predominantly Jewish religious preference. They also report the rather anomalous finding that German Americans are underachievers. One might suspect that an inability to differentiate among Protestants and Catholics within the German group might mask important differences within this nationality group. Several recent studies (compare Gockel, 1969; Gold-smith, 1969; Chapter 3; Schuman, 1971; Warren, 1970b) have noted, moreover, that the tripartite division of religious preference into Protestant, Catholic, and Jew may cover up more than it reveals, especially for the highly differentiated Protestant denominations. Thus there is good reason to suspect that the identification of meaningful *ethnoreligious* groups would be of considerable assistance in developing an explanation of group differences in worldly success, especially if one wants to assess the relative merits of the notion of cultural pluralism as opposed to the theory of the melting pot (compare Gordon, 1964). Finally, any theory that stresses subcultural differences (see Chapter 8, for example) would have to demonstrate the successful transmission of these differences into the third generation (native sons of native parentage of foreign grandparent(s)).

This chapter has two principal objectives: first, to discover if, once we identify a set of ascriptive membership groups for the native white population (specified simultaneously in terms of the principal country of origin of one's ancestors and one's detailed religious preference), we can demonstrate differences among the groups in the degree to which educational achievement and occupational prestige are transmitted from fathers to sons; and second, to find out whether these differences can be shown to persist for third and later generation members of these groups.

SOME PRELIMINARY CONSIDERATIONS

Since the entire study was originally conceived as an exploration of ethnoreligious differences in values, attitudes, and behavior in an urban population, considerable pains were taken to measure the key variable of ethnoreligious group membership. In addition to asking the respondents to indicate their *subjective* identification with a country of origin—to which they were permitted to respond with multiple countries (see Q91, Appendix C), we also asked them to indicate the country of birth of their parents, grandparents, and great grandparents (this last question was asked only if the first two sets of ancestors were all born in the United States or Canada) (see Q93–98, Appendix C). While we do some violence to our data by ignoring for this analysis the matter of multiple countries of origin for the 39 percent of the sample who reported them, we are assuming that the individual's first country mentioned is his principal country of origin. While well over 60 countries of origin were reported by our respondents in addition to a number of religious denominational preferences, we have, for analytic purposes, grouped these into the 15 ethnoreligious groups considered in the preceding chapter.

The number of generations in the United States is determined by the response to the set of questions on the country of birth of the respondent's ancestors. Respondents in the third and later generation are at the minimum those, both of whose parents were born here or in Canada.

THE ANALYTIC MODEL

Following the reasoning in Blau and Duncan (1967: 140–47, 163–77), we propose to examine the intergenerational transmission of the achieved characteristics of educational achievement and occupational status by the application of regression analysis. The correlation coefficient is a summary statistic by which we can indicate the degree to which the respondents' educational and occupational statuses covary with those of their fathers— that is, the higher the coefficient, the higher the "transmission" of the fathers' socioeconomic characteristics to their sons.[2] For our purposes, we are especially concerned with determining whether the regression slopes b_k for our set of ethnoreligious groups appreciably vary around the common slope for the total sample. Since this concern is formally identical to those posed in Chapter 8, I shall employ the same analytic model described there (pp. 165–68):

$$Y_{ki} = a_k + b_k X_{ki} + e_{ki} \qquad (9.1)$$

where Y_{ki} is the number of school years completed *or* the occupational prestige score (Duncan, 1961) of respondent i in group k, a_k is the intercept of ethnoreligious group k on the ordinate, b_k is the regression slope for ethnoreligious group k, X_{ki} is the number of school years completed *or* occupational prestige score of respondent i's father in group k, and e_{ki} is the error term.

FINDINGS

As one can readily see from Table 3.7 (Chapter 3), there is considerable variation among the Protestant groups on mean school years completed, mean occupational status, and mean total family income, while Catholic groups, with one or two notable exceptions, appear to be much more tightly clustered on these measures. With regard to the summary indicators of socioreligious characteristics, there is considerable variation within the Protestant and Catholic groups with regard to church attendance and devotionalism. But all the Protestant groups are predominantly composed of third- and later-generation Americans while the

Table 9.1. Summary of tests for common slope, identity of regression lines, and specific group departures from the common slope, for the total sample, second generation, and third and later generations

Achieved Status	(1) Total No.	(2) Common Slope $(\overline{b})$	(3) Test for Common Slopes	(4) Test for Identity of Lines	(5) Tukey Test — Above the Slope	(5) Tukey Test — Below the Slope
				Total Sample		
Education	798	.405	$F = 3.213$, $p < .01$	$F = 2.967$, $p < .01$	German Presbyterians, Irish Catholics, Jews	German Lutherans, Anglo Baptists, Polish Catholics, Protestants, Origin, N.A.
Occupation	801	.271	NS	NS	—	—
				Second Generation		
Education	185	.417	$F = 3.445$, $p < .01$	NS	German Catholics, Jews	—
Occupation	223	.234	NS	NS	—	Anglo Catholics
				Third and Later Generations		
Education	530	.372	$F = 2.673$, $p < .01$	$F = 3.364$, $p < .01$	German Presbyterians, Irish Catholics, French Catholics	German Lutherans, Polish Catholics, Slavic Catholics, Protestants, Origin N.A.
Occupation	550	.256	NS	$F = 2.300$, $p < .05$	Anglo Catholics	Italian Catholics, Slavic Catholics

Catholic groups are split between those who are predominantly third- and later-generation Americans, including the Irish, Germans, French, and Anglo-Americans, and those who are predominantly second-generation Americans, including Slavs, Italians, and Poles.

The basic findings relevant to the degree to which the fifteen groups[3] vary among themselves in transmitting education and occupational status from fathers to sons are summarized in Table 9.1. The first column reports the total number of cases included in the regression analysis for the total sample, second generation subsample, and third and later generation subsample. The common slope for each analysis appears in the second column. Column 3 reports a test that determines whether the slopes b_k are significantly different from the common slope $\bar{b}$ reported in Column 2, for the men irrespective of ascriptive group membership. In the case of the regression of sons' school years completed on fathers' school years completed, we note that the slope b_k significantly varies around the common slope for the total sample and both subsamples. This result would support the hypothesis that the ethnoreligious groups do in fact differ among themselves in the degree to which there is intergenerational transmission of educational achievement (compare Featherman, 1971). But there is no support for such an hypothesis with regard to the intergenerational transmission of occupational status. Column 4 reports the F tests to determine whether the regression lines are coincident or parallel, given that the slopes are equal. For the educational regression analyses, we can reject the hypothesis that the lines are identical. In the case of occupational status, however, only among third- and later-generation Americans can we reject the null hypothesis that the lines are identical.

Column 5 reports the results of comparing specific group slopes with the common slope to detect significant differences, utilizing Tukey's (Acton, 1966: 184–87) technique described in the preceding chapter. Following the format developed in the preceding chapter, the groups in Column 5 have been divided into those that are significantly above the common slope and those that are significantly below the common slope.

The evidence appears fairly clear that certain groups, most notably the German Presbyterians, Irish Catholics, and Jews, are most successful in transmitting educational achievements from father to son while other groups, especially the German Lutherans, Anglo-American Baptists, Polish Catholics, and Protestants, origin not ascertained, are decidedly less likely to transmit educational advantages (or disadvantages) across generations. (See Tables 9.2 and 9.3 for detailed summaries of the regression parameters for the third- and later-generation subsample.) The three groups most successful in transmitting educational advantage are precisely the three who rank among the top groups in worldly success (see the first

Table 9.2. Regression parameters for fathers' and sons' educational attainment, for fourteen ethnoreligious groups three or more generations in the United States

Ethnoreligious Group	Total Number	Sons' Mean School Years Completed	Fathers' Mean School Years Completed	Gross Change Intergenerationally	Slope (*b*)	Correlation (*r*)
Protestant:						
German Presbyterians	23	13.9	9.2	4.7	.558	.393
Anglo-American Presbyterians	61	13.8	11.1	2.7	.259	.164
German Lutherans	41	13.3	8.1	5.2	.049	.030
German Methodists	25	13.2	8.6	4.6	.434	.275
Anglo-American Methodists	31	11.5	6.6	4.9	.439	.394
Anglo-American Baptists	73	10.2	6.3	3.9	.281	.246
Protestants, Origin N.A.	23	9.0	5.4	4.6	.168	.259
Catholic:						
Slavic Catholics	10	14.1	9.0	5.1	.139	.118
Italian Catholics	14	13.9	10.2	3.7	.470	.166
Irish Catholics	54	12.7	9.3	3.4	.612	.419
German Catholics	65	12.2	9.2	3.0	.430	.291
French Catholics	47	12.2	7.3	4.9	.571	.421
Polish Catholics	39	11.6	7.8	3.8	.000	−.000
Anglo-American Catholics	24	11.2	9.6	1.6	.482	.369

Note: Common slope $\bar{b}$ for all groups $= .372$

three columns of Table 3.7). Conversely, the groups who were least successful in transmitting educational advantages were typically ranked near the bottom of the socioeconomic ladder.[4]

In an effort explicitly to explore the assumption that the subgroups composing broad ethnic (for example, German and Anglo-American) and religious (for example, Roman Catholic and Protestant) categories are essentially similar to one another with regard to the intergenerational transmission of educational and occupational status, we calculated the relevant F tests for common slopes and identity of lines separately for the four German-American, five Anglo-American, seven Roman Catholic, and seven Protestant groups for the total sample and third generation and later subsample. In the case of the educational regression analyses, all the F tests were highly significant while the tests for the occupational regres-

Table 9.3.   Regression parameters for fathers' and sons' occupational prestige, for fourteen ethnoreligious groups three or more generations in the United States

Ethnoreligious Group	Total Number	Sons' Mean Occupational Status	Fathers' Mean Occupational Status	Gross Change Intergenerationally	Slope (b)	Correlation (r)
Protestant:						
German Presbyterians	23	60.6	53.5	7.1	.258	.255
Anglo-American Presbyterians	61	60.2	53.2	7.0	.237	.265
German Lutherans	41	55.6	33.8	21.8	.277	.265
German Methodists	30	50.5	39.6	10.9	.217	.239
Anglo-American Methodists	34	46.3	28.0	18.3	.183	.145
Anglo-American Baptists	79	36.3	23.8	12.5	.263	.250
Protestants, Origin N.A.	24	25.2	22.7	2.5	.131	.214
Catholic:						
Slavic Catholics	10	48.8	28.9	19.9	−.219	−.092
Italian Catholics	14	44.8	23.5	21.3	−.034	−.017
Irish Catholics	55	50.4	43.5	6.9	.284	.306
German Catholics	66	48.6	39.9	8.7	.231	.221
French Catholics	48	40.7	35.2	5.5	.283	.255
Polish Catholics	40	41.9	28.3	13.6	.167	.149
Anglo-American Catholics	24	42.7	43.8	−1.1	.581	.542

Note: Common slope $\bar{b}$ for all groups = .256

sion analyses were not significant except for the five Anglo-American groups. These results would seem clearly to imply that assumptions about the internal homogeneity of such broad social categories are incorrect and that these group differences do persist into the third and later generations.

The problem of interpretation is considerably complicated by the fact that while we consistently find group differences in educational transmission persisting into the third generation, we find less consistency with regard to group differences in the transmission of occupational status. There is some reason to believe, however, that the failure to find such differences with regard to occupation may be due to our measure of occupational status, the Duncan Index of Socioeconomic Status, which is a highly reliable indicator of prestige differences among occupations but is relatively insensitive to functional differences among occupations of

Table 9.4. Occupational percent distributions of the ethnoreligious status groups, grouped by approximately equal means on the Duncan Index of Socioeconomic Status

Ethnoreligious Status Group	Mean Duncan Index	Professional, Self-Employed	Professional, Salaried	Managers and Officials	Self-employed, Sales and Proprietors	Clerical and Retail Sales	Craftsmen and Foremen	Operatives, Laborers	Total
(58.0–63.4)									
1. Jews	63.4	17.9	21.4	17.9	21.4	0.0	10.7	10.7	100.0
2. Anglo Presbyterians	59.2	1.4	30.6	16.7	22.2	8.3	7.0	13.9	100.0
3. German Presbyterians	58.0	8.0	28.0	8.0	12.0	16.3	8.0	20.0	100.0
(48.0–51.1)									
4. Irish Catholics	51.1	1.5	21.5	13.9	15.4	3.1	21.5	23.1	100.0
5. German Methodists	50.4	6.3	28.1	6.3	9.4	6.3	18.7	25.0	100.0
6. German Lutherans	49.9	3.6	21.4	8.9	12.5	12.5	14.3	26.8	100.0
7. German Catholics	48.6	1.3	13.9	13.9	11.4	10.1	32.9	16.5	100.0
(40.0–47.0)									
8. Anglo Methodists	46.5	0.0	20.0	12.5	7.5	17.5	12.5	30.0	100.0
9. Slavic Catholics	45.5	0.0	18.4	13.2	2.6	5.3	34.2	26.3	100.0
10. Italian Catholics	44.1	3.6	10.9	9.1	12.7	7.3	34.6	21.8	100.0
11. Anglo Catholics	43.3	12.1	9.1	9.1	6.1	3.0	24.2	36.4	100.0
12. French Catholics	41.2	2.0	9.8	7.8	13.7	2.0	29.4	35.3	100.0
(39 and below)									
13. Polish Catholics	39.6	0.9	10.9	8.2	8.2	4.6	35.5	31.8	100.0
14. Anglo Baptists	36.0	0.0	8.8	7.5	1.3	6.3	31.3	45.0	100.0
15. Protestants, N.A.	32.0	0.0	6.3	3.1	0.0	9.4	34.4	46.9	100.0

Table 9.5. Indexes of dissimilarity of the occupational distributions of ethnoreligious groups, grouped by approximately equal means on the Duncan Index of Socioeconomic Status*

	(58.0–63.4)					(48.0–51.1)		
	1	2	3		4	5	6	7
1	—	21.5	31.9	4	—	16.5	15.2	18.4
2		—	21.5	5		—	13.8	27.7
3			—	6			—	23.6
				7				—

	(40.0–47.0)						(39 and below)		
	8	9	10	11	12		13	14	15
8	—	22.4	30.9	30.2	30.4	13	—	14.9	19.9
9		—	16.1	25.7	22.1	14		—	8.2
10			—	23.1	14.5	15			—
11				—	13.5				
12					—				

* The numbers in the rows and columns refer to the ethnoreligious groups as listed in Table 9.4.

approximately equal socioeconomic status. As Table 9.4 demonstrates, ethnoreligious groups having essentially equal means on the Duncan Index do in fact differ in their distributions across occupational categories that might be taken as evidence that the groups seem to be transmitting different orientations toward occupational activities. Table 9.5 attempts to summarize these differences by presenting the indexes of dissimilarity between the occupational distributions within groups having essentially identical means. For example, in the case of the highest status set of groups, 21.5 percent of the Jews would have to be redistributed among the occupational categories for them to have an identical distribution to that of the Anglo-American Presbyterians—despite the fact that they only differ by 4.2 points on the Duncan Index. A similar index of dissimilarity is obtained for Anglo-American and German Presbyterians who differ by only 1.2 points. Needless to say, since the sizes of the subgroup samples are quite small, considerable caution should be exercised in interpreting these results.

DISCUSSION

Because of the excessively small number of cases in many of the groups, one should be very cautious in drawing conclusions about specific groups from this sample. With this caveat in mind, however, it does seem useful to speculate about the meaning of the results, especially in the light of the results reported by Duncan and Duncan (1968) on a much larger national sample.

Duncan and Duncan (1968: 357–58) report:

> The survey results reveal fairly substantial differences among national-origin groups with respect to both educational and occupational achievement. Especially distinguished by high achievement are the Russian-Americans, who outrank not only the other minorities, but also the native-of-native majority. The lowest achievement is recorded on the part of native Americans whose fathers were born in Latin America, most often in Mexico. It is neither of these groups which most closely resembles the third-generation in achieved status, however, but rather the Irish, the Canadians, the Germans, and the "other Europeans," such as Czechs. Moreover, were a measure of vertical mobility to be constructed by subtracting from the mean achievement score of respondents the corresponding mean score for their family heads, the group of "other European" origin would outrank Russian-Americans with respect to occupational mobility; and German-Americans would appear to be low achievers in the educational sphere.

The authors subsequently speculate that the unusual achievements of the Russian-Americans may be attributed to the large proportion of Jews in this group. Our results strongly support their hypothesis in that the Jews (predominantly of Russian extraction in our sample) are unusually high achievers. But perhaps it is even more interesting to note that our third-generation Slavic Catholic group (also principally of Russian origin) also manifests unusually high upward mobility.

While they note that German Americans appear to be underachievers (once their starting points are taken into account), we can suggest that this may be more specifically due to the underachievement of German *Catholics* who comprise 42 percent of our sample of third- and later-generation German Americans. Third-generation German Lutherans, on the other hand, have been unusually upwardly mobile, both educationally and occupationally (see Tables 9.2 and 9.3, also see Schuman, 1971: 42). Anglo-American groups manifest similar variability in amounts of mobility and intergenerational transmission of educational and occupational status.

More generally we believe that these data, together with those reported in the preceding chapter, are certainly consistent with the notion that more or less ascriptive membership groups in the native white population are continuing to provide important subcultural variations in the behavior and attitudes of third- and later-generation Americans. Future research must give considerably greater and more careful attention to the identification of relevant subgroups. It seems abundantly clear that overly simplistic categorizations of membership groups that rely exclusively either on presumed ethnic origin *or* broad religious preference are more likely to mislead than to enlighten us.

NOTES

1. Having participated in the design and execution of our Detroit Area survey, Howard Schuman (1971) was especially interested in replicating some of the findings reported by Gerhard Lenski in *The Religious Factor* (1963), which was based on data gathered in the Detroit Area Study eight years before, particularly as they related to hypothesized differences between Protestants and Catholics with respect to their beliefs and values relevant to economic advancement. Lenski argued that these reported differences could be derived from Max Weber's thesis concerning the relevance of the Protestant Ethic to the rise of modern capitalism. Save for one important exception, the differences between white Protestants and Catholics found in the 1958 Detroit Area Study were not replicated in our 1966 study, thus casting some serious doubt on the validity of Lenski's findings at least as they relate to aggregate comparisons of Protestants and Catholics. Schuman does, however, find evidence (p. 42) that Protestants of different denominations do differ among themselves in the degree to which they hold certain work values. But this finding is, unfortunately, complicated by the fact that the ordering of differences in the 1966 Detroit sample does not appear to conform to any obvious deduction of the ordering implied by Weber's discussion that Calvinist Protestants—in his discussion the closest embodiment of the Protestant Ethic as an ideal type— should disproportionately embrace the work ethic while Lutherans—in his terms relatively close to Catholics—should be underrepresented in holding these values.

The range and complexities of the results are such that they cannot be adequately summarized here. The reader is thus encouraged to read the original article itself and Lenski's reply (1971).

2. Naturally the mechanisms by which this transmission of status is effected are of considerable interest, but must be left untreated here at least in an explicit fashion due to the lack of relevant data. As noted in the first chapter, transmission of most ascriptive status positions—age and sex roles are obvious exceptions— follows strict inheritance and, consequently, a perfect correlation should at least theoretically obtain between father's and son's status. Historically there have been many societies in which occupational roles have had many more strictly ascriptive features than they have today and even today there are certain roles—for example, small businessmen and farmers (see Blau and Duncan, 1967: 41)—which have strong tendencies toward ascriptive transmission from fathers to sons.

The intergenerational transmission of achieved statuses, however, is clearly much more problematic since, by definition, entry into an achieved status is on the basis of an individual's performances or "effort." Thus we are really speaking elliptically when we talk of fathers transmitting achieved statuses to their sons. What we mean by such an assertion is that the son has certain socialized capacities, values, attitudes, claims on financial and other resources including the social contacts of the father and, probably most important of all, educational opportunities that he received by virtue of being born into a particular family of orientation. As an adult, *he* must in some sense convert these capacities, orientations, training, and so forth into relevant performances in order to gain access to statuses comparable to those of his father. The father's educational attainment and occupational status must, then, be regarded as fairly crude *indicators* of the typical kinds of socialization experiences, educational opportunities, and so forth, to which the son is likely to be exposed. Of course, in addition, there is "real" inheritance from the father of genetically determined, innate capacities (intelligence, for example (see Eckland, 1967; Lasswell, 1965; Jensen, 1969)) that obviously have important impact on the son's capacities to perform.

3. While we used all 15 groups for the total sample regression analysis, we were forced to use only seven groups in the regression analysis of second generation members because of insufficient numbers in the other eight groups. Only the Jewish group had to be dropped from the set of 15 groups in the third- and later-generation subsample because of insufficient numbers.

4. In a similar analysis, Blau and Duncan (1967; compare Duncan, 1968) have shown that the intergenerational transmission of educational status is somewhat lower and occupational status much lower for blacks, a group ranked at the bottom of the socioeconomic ladder, than for whites.

CHAPTER 10

Urban Social Structure: Some Conclusions and Prospects

To attempt to present here a pleasingly concise, theoretically relevant summary of the empirical content of the preceding chapters would in all likelihood prove to be a futile and redundant exercise. The three theoretical vantage points sketched in the first chapter have hopefully provided a certain consistency and coherence to the thrust of our analysis. But there have been many occasions when we have indulged our curiosity in elaborating an empirical finding because of its intrinsic interest and not because it contributed to a particular theoretical point.[1] Our theoretical preconceptions have served, then, to orient us to particular questions and modes of interpretation and no doubt have occasionally blinded us to equally plausible, perhaps even more parsimonious, alternative explanations of the results. In this chapter, we can only hope to highlight some of our most important results, stressing their relevance to particular theoretical or hypothetical formulations, and to sketch some alternative explanations of the central findings that might deserve more attention than we have given them.

Of the many issues that were discussed, perhaps the formulation of a theoretically relevant, empirically sensitive method for describing social structure and the resulting descriptions of American urban social structures will prove to be the most promising and worthy of further work. Our primary objective was to provide a systematic description of the patterning of social relationships among analytically distinguishable social categories (aggregated social positions). The macrostructural analysis was focused on two particularly crucial vantage points from which to view American social structure: the structures of intimate relations among (1) ascriptively-grounded ethnoreligious groups and (2) achievement-based occupational categories. The resulting descriptions are in terms of multidimensional spaces, although there was nothing in our methodology (smallest space analysis) that necessitated such results. That is, the technique permits the identification of unidimensional structures as well; our data, however, could not be adequately represented by such simple structures.

Several more simplified unidimensional models of American urban social structures that have been proposed in the literature enjoy broad acceptance. The Herberg model of the Triple Melting Pot (we are here clearly oversimplifying his position for expository purposes) would imply that white Americans confine intimate relations to their respective broadly defined religious categories: Protestant, Catholic, and Jewish. Moreover, these three subcommunities are in turn alleged to be only modestly internally differentiated in terms of socioeconomic, socioreligious, and ethnic considerations—the last, in particular, being of declining significance in the wake of the white ethnic groups' complete assimilation into American society. For some purposes this unidimensional model is justified (and our own results clearly support the critical importance attached to these three categories in channeling intimate interaction). Nevertheless, the point remains that a more accurate representation of what people in fact do in choosing others for intimacy requires a more complex model—one that takes into account both socioeconomic and socioreligious differentiation within these broad categories. This is quite clearly the case for Protestants and, to a lesser extent, for Catholics. We had an insufficient number of Jews in the sample to examine differentiation for them, but I strongly suspect that future work on a more adequate sample of Jews classified in terms of their respective subcommunities (Orthodox, Conservative, Reform, and "secularized" or nonreligiously grounded ethnic affiliation) would find such differentiation among them as well. The analytic utility of a more refined classification of ethnoreligious groups is clearly demonstrated when one considers the results of our examination of 15 ethnoreligious groups for the effects of status inconsistency and differences in worldly success in contrast to the results obtained when only the three broad subcommunities are considered as in Schuman's (1971) replication of Gerhard Lenski's *The Religious Factor*.

With respect to the occupational structure, a unidimensional model emphasizing differentiation in terms of occupational prestige and socioeconomic status enjoys almost universal acceptance, especially in sociological studies of stratification. While this assumption of unidimensionality has rather consistently proved of value in many sorts of investigations, our own data indicate that it too is insufficient to account for the patterning of intimacy among occupational groups. We propose that a bureaucratic-entrepreneurial dimension crosscuts the prestige dimension and is associated with rather important differences in occupational values and preferences that are even manifested in whom one prefers to be with on a basis of intimacy. This interpretation is supported by an earlier investigation by Guttman and myself employing data from Cambridge, Massachusetts. Essentially the same structure was observed despite differences in the occupational coding schemes employed.[2] Again it is worth noting that an oversimplified conception of the occupational structure may obscure more than it reveals.

Despite the empirical plausibility of these descriptions of the Detroit ethnoreligious and occupational structures, one must still treat these results with some caution. In order to employ the technique of smallest space analysis, we made a series of assumptions about the data (for example, how to collapse and aggregate detailed information on ethnoreligious preferences and occupations, whether to employ indexes of dissimilarity rather than conditional probabilities to obtain a matrix suitable for analysis) and postulates about interpreting the resulting spaces (for example, the distance-generating postulate of Chapter 1). We have, in fact, examined some of the more obvious alternative assumptions and strategies and found the technique to be quite robust—that is, it yields remarkably similar "dimensional pictures" despite what would appear at first glance to be important differences in the way the input matrices are constructed. Nevertheless, the technique itself is new and has not been extensively employed for analyzing such problems as we have set for it. Clearly, we need replication of these results on other sample populations, employing somewhat different assumptions, before we can place complete confidence in the results. As we acquire greater familiarity with the technique and its limitations and greater facility in analyzing data such as we have considered, we shall be in a much better position to move on to the fascinating questions of comparing social structures, both in space and time, in order to identify more precisely than has been possible before the systematic ways in which structures may be similar or dissimilar, stable or changing. Once structures can be adequately described and measured, we can then move with greater confidence into the almost virgin field of structural dynamics.

Shifting from this macrostructural to a microstructural focus, we have attempted to analyze certain structural features of a man's personal network, taking into account in the first instance the results of the macrostructural analyses. Both the homogeneity in the composition of a man's friendship set (as measured by distances between ego's and friends' membership groups established in the macrostructural analyses) and the connectedness of the network (that is, interlocking or radial) were shown to vary systematically in: (1) their distributions across the population classified in terms of various social characteristics; (2) their associations with other important features of the networks themselves (such as their degree of intimacy, functionality, and customary place of interaction); and (3) their associations with certain of ego's orientations toward the world as well as the "form" of his attitudes—that is, their consistency, definiteness, openness, and stability over time.

Religious differences were found to have especially strong impact on the form of a man's friendship networks. In fact, this is one of the few occasions when the simple crude distinction among Protestants, Catholics, and Jews manifested such consistent associations with other characteristics that simply did not disappear when appropriate "controls" were introduced. Catholics and Jews are especially likely to have ethnoreligiously homogeneous, interlocking networks while Protestants tend to favor occupationally homogeneous, ethnoreligiously heterogeneous, radial networks. These differences do not appear to be attributable to the "greater ethnicity" and more recent generation of arrival of Catholics, but to "Catholicness" per se. These findings strongly suggest some important perduring differences among religious communities in their inculcation of preferential modes of social intercourse that penetrate well beyond their manifest differences in religious belief systems to the ways in which men organize their social life.

Moreover, one can draw a number of suggestive parallels between the pattern of associations between these structural attributes and other attitudinal and social characterisics of ego and the patterning that might be expected to be associated with *Gemeinschaft* versus *Gesellschaft* or primary versus secondary groups when these classic sociological dichotomies are equated to homogeneous versus heterogeneous or interlocking versus radial networks. These parallels must be regarded merely as suggestive because the clarity and rigor with which one may deduce implications of these dichotomies for individual behavior and microstructure is greatly impaired by their relatively abstract formulation for rather different analytic purposes.

At least two important objections can be raised to this microstructural analysis. First, we have confined ourselves to a structural analysis of only three contact points (the three friends) out of the typically much larger personal networks that include relatives in the nuclear and extended family and other friends and acquaintances. How can one realistically argue that he has adequately characterized the structural characteristics of a man's total social ambience (personal network) under such a restriction? Second, it is well known that relatives play a much more important role in many people's lives than their so-called closest friends (see Adams, 1967a; Schneider, 1969). Should not the characteristics of relatives have been more systematically considered?

Several considerations, however, make these objections much less serious. First, relatives *outside* the nuclear family could be and were in-cluded among the three closest friends when the respondent so regarded them (see wording of Q13 and Q14, Appendix C). Second, as men-tioned in Chapter 5, a substantial majority (over 60 percent) reported that they regarded only three or four persons or fewer as really close personal friends and only a small minority thought that six or more persons could be so regarded. In other words, the three-person cutoff is by no means as unrealistic and arbitrary as might appear at first glance. While most people probably maintain social contacts on a relatively regular basis with many more than three persons, it is not immediately clear why we should expect that these other persons are substantially different in social characteristics from the closest intimates and would be likely to exert effective influences substantially at variance with those of the more in-timate circle. Finally, the results reported in Chapter 6 on interlocking and radial networks suggest, as Simmel argued long ago on theoretical grounds, that it is the simple fact of being in a dyadic (one to one) versus a tryadic (two against one) net which seems to "create" the differences observed in the impact of network connectivity on ego's attitudes and be-havior. That is, no significant differences were found between those men who had three friends potentially allied against them (were in completely interlocking nets) and those who had only two of their friends known to one another (were in only partially interlocking nets). By extension one could argue that increasing the number considered in the personal net-work would not substantially change the results. In any event, future research explicitly addressed to such questions can establish the relative merit and importance of these objections. What I hope has been accom-plished with the research reported here is to establish the "promise" of additional work on the structural attributes of personal networks.

The efforts of my colleagues and my efforts to provide support for a series of more substantively oriented and controversial hypotheses about American urban society have been notably less successful. The "real world," unfortunately, proved to be considerably more Procrustean than these hypothesized simplifications and complications of reality would permit. We have already alluded to the oversimplification of the Triple Melting Pot hypothesis as an account of the differentiation of intimate association among ethnoreligious groups, although it is by no means a bad first approximation, as well as to the need to consider other features of occupations than simply the axis of socioeconomic status or prestige. Cutler's effort to find support for some important derivative hypotheses from Kornhauser's theory of mass society, which relates forms of social participation to various political structures, is by and large completely un-successful. His results suggest that the role attributed to voluntary associations in maintaining a pluralistic structure, at least insofar as it relates to their benign effects inculcating and/or supporting certain congruent social psychological orientations in the population at large, has been grossly exaggerated. A much more parsimonious explanation in terms of certain personal socioeconomic characteristics, most notably education, almost entirely accounts for these hypothesized effects. It should be clear, however, that these negative results do not speak at all to the possibly important role voluntary associations play in sustaining a pluralistic political structure at the macrostructural or societal level where these organizations (rather than individuals) are regarded as the units of analysis in the larger political structure.

Given the special concern of this study in delineating the persisting character of religious and ethnic diversity in values, attitudes, and social participation in American society, we were particularly disappointed by our relative lack of success in replicating and extending a significant source of inspiration for our work—Lenski's seminal investigation applying Max Weber's thesis regarding Protestant and Catholic differences in economic and work orientations. As Schuman (1971) demonstrates, the simple dichotomy Protestant-Catholic lumps together highly heterogeneous subgroups, especially among the Protestants, that tends to submerge real differences among them—a result certainly to be anticipated given our smallest space results for ethnoreligious groups. Schuman shows, moreover, that five of the six comparisons between Protestant denominations are as large as the original Protestant-Catholic difference. Unfortunately, these differences among Protestant groups do not seem to correspond very closely to what a careful reader of Max Weber would have anticipated, since the more "Calvinistic" Presbyterians score closest to the Catholics while the "pietistic" Lutherans are unexpectedly high in giving the classic Protestant Ethic response (see footnote 1, Chapter 9). From these results then, it would seem that considerably more work needs to be done in conceptualizing and identifying the bases of religious differentiation and their nonreligious correlates in the United States. The classic Weberian model appears clearly inadequate in this contemporary context.[3] While I have neither the space nor all the relevant information to enter into such a model construction here, it occurs to me that one promising way of constructing a more appropriate model for the American case would be to attend closely to the distinctive historical experiences of the various religious denominations in the United States, particularly their interrelationships with other denominations and the relative privileged or disprivileged status of their average members (see footnote 3). The differences we observe among ethnoreligious groups today (see, for example, Appendix 8.A of Chapter 8) are the distillates of this historical process as well as the resultants of their contemporary situations and may provide useful clues for the construction of such a model. One thing appears certain, however: taking into consideration all the results reported in Chapters 8 and 9 and elsewhere on the existence and persistence of important ethnoreligious differences, we have presented sufficient evidence to warrant such an effort.

A natural bridge linking our interests in ascribed and achieved statuses is the hypothesis of status inconsistency. Attracting considerable theoretical and research attention over the past 15 years, this hypothesis holds that one can account for important differences in political attitudes and social participation by determining whether an individual enjoys congruent or incongruent ascribed and achieved statuses. Despite the attractiveness of such an hypothesis, especially since it seems to go beyond "common-sense" understandings and implies interesting psycho- and socio-dynamics that tend to fascinate many sociologists and social psychologists, we were unable to find any satisfactory evidence for its operation in our sample population, employing what we regard as a more adequate methodology for its detection than has usually been the case. To be sure, we found convincing evidence for the importance of ascriptive ethnoreligious group membership *and* of achieved socioeconomic status in accounting for our sample's political attitudes and social participation. And, indeed, there were some complex and significant interactions to be discerned in the interplay of these two attributes as well. But, unfortunately, practically none of the interactive effects, such as they were, could plausibly be attributed to status-inconsistency effects per se, with the possible exception of the case of the Jews. Since German Presbyterians, a high-status WASP group, tended to manifest rather similar patterns as those of the Jews—a complete contradiction in terms of the hypothesis— one is left with the distinctly uncomfortable feeling that the status-inconsistency hypothesis enjoys greater theoretical elegance than efficacy and relevance in explaining empirical phenomena.

Actually, if we were to reject the status-inconsistency hypothesis as being unsupported, we are perhaps left better off than before because, on the basis of our results, we are probably justified in adopting a much simpler "additive" model that simply postulates additive effects for both socioeconomic status and ethnoreligious group membership without the added complication of specifying an "interaction" term (that is, effects of the specific combinations of ascribed and achieved statuses). Basically the statistical model for the status-inconsistency hypothesis requires such a term; and, indeed, this term, according to the hypothesis, must have a specific form—it cannot be equated to any interaction term one pleases. Thus two important results of Chapter 8's analysis are, first, to simplify the complexity of analysis by eliminating the need for a complicated model of statistical interaction and, second, to provide further evidence that ethnoreligious group membership per se has effects on important social behavior in addition to or independent of the effects of socioeconomic status. Nevertheless, our appeal in Chapter 8 to the importance of "subcultural differences" merely names the problem which remains—the formulation of a coherent model of ethnoreligous group differences. The differences reported there provide an initial configuration of the nature of such a model. But given the small sample bases and resulting statistical instabilities in estimating characteristics for a number of groups, it would be premature to place much confidence in all the details of this configuration or profile of group differences. They merely represent starting points for testing on more adequately sized samples.

We have had many occasions to allude to the current fashion of downgrading the importance of differences in the population that are rooted in ethnoreligious groups. Most commentators on the American scene are prepared to recognize the continuing importance of subcultural differences in explaining the social behavior of certain groups, most notably the Jews, blacks, and persons of Spanish surname (especially of Puerto Rican and Mexican extraction). Even here, however, many investigators tend to ascribe such differences to a fundamentally economic base especially for the latter two groups, that is, the disprivileged occupational roles that the typical members of these groups are constrained to play resulting in the so-called "culture of poverty"—rather than to subcultural differences per se. For the native-born white population, subcultural differences rooted in ethnoreligious groups are often held to be of minor importance, destined to disappear in the third and later generations. It is in this context that our findings, based precisely on such a sample population, regarding the persistence of differences in religious beliefs and activities, political, economic and work orientations, modes of social participation and worldly success among third- and later-generation Americans becomes all the more remarkable. *While it would be quite foolish for us to exaggerate the magnitude of these differences and to conclude that the American urban scene is a mosaic of highly differentiated, self-contained nationality-religious groups, it would be equally foolish for us simply to dismiss them as being of little or no importance in accounting for the vitality and heterogeneity of contemporary urban life.*

Just consider for a moment the massive forces to which these groups have been subjected in order to bring about total acculturation and assimilation of the white population at least. Certainly mass public education and the mass media have played a major and continuing role attempting to "purge" foreign, non-American identifications and behavior patterns. The

1950s and subsequent years have witnessed the near demise of most ethnic-oriented institutions (such as the ethnic newspapers and the ethnic-based fraternal associations like the Sons of Italy or the German Männerchöre) that served to transmit and maintain ethnic identifications and value orientations. Hardly anyone (aside from persons of Spanish surname) can speak or use regularly in daily life the language of his country of origin. All that remains to maintain differences have been the informal but by no means impotent socialization mechanisms of the family and the patterns of association with others of like mind who may be chosen for intimate relationships. Certainly ethnoreligious differences have been somewhat transmuted and transmogrified in the course of Americanization with religious commonalities tending to become more important than ethnic ones. But their continued vitality, even if in highly modified form, despite the relative disappearance of formal supportive institutions and the almost exclusive reliance on informal mechanisms for transmission and maintenance, presents fascinating questions to the student of society. What functions do these "subcultures" perform for the individual? for the larger society? What mechanisms have been especially important in their maintenance? Can these mechanisms be expected to become less effective in the future?

To this point in our discussion of status groups, we have been stressing those features of their associated *styles of life*[4] that have to do with their distinctive, or perhaps more accurately, their *inclinations* to favor certain value orientations, attitudes, modes of social participation and related behavior. But it is worth mentioning in this connection that these groups also appear to have rather pronounced preferences for different material styles of life as manifested in their living room decors. As House and I (1970) demonstrate in a study of the styles and contents of living room furnishings and decoration,[5] the data for which were gathered by a checklist inventory of 53 objects or characteristics to be observed in the living rooms of our Detroit Area respondents (see HH1-HH12, Appendix C), the patterning of material styles of life can by no means be comprehended as a simple function of family income—that is, the higher the income, the more and perhaps better quality the objects in the living room. In addition, there are important crosscutting considerations of "taste" as well that are not simply a function of one's socioeconomic standing but one's status group membership as well. Upper working class and lower middle class Catholics, for example, are found to favor "traditional ethnic" living room decors while their highly successful, intergenerationally mobile brethren tend to prefer modern decors. On the other hand, well-to-do, occupationally successful Protestants whose fathers also were of high occupational status—that is, "upper class" WASPs, tend to have traditional living room furnishings and decors. Again we must emphasize that given styles cannot be said to be the exclusive monopolies of particular status or class groups but are at best mere propensities to prefer one style over another, without overly sharp demarcations between groups. In other words, the dominant tendency is to blur distinctions, to move rather fluidly from one to another style, indeed to mix styles almost without compunction. Some of this blurring in patterns probably arises out of the basic crudity of the checklist inventory itself. Rather powerful analytic techniques were required to tease out the underlying order or pattern in living room furnishings. While these limitations of our analysis should not be minimized, we should not overlook this evidence of the differentiation of material life styles along ascriptive and socioeconomic group lines.

We may summarize much of the foregoing discussion with the following rationale for our model of urban pluralism: the degree to which an ascribed or achieved "group"[6] manifests distinctive or different behavior patterns—styles of life—from those of other groups may be seen to be a function of at least two considerations. The first consideration is the distinctiveness of the typical member's social role either with respect to the "inheritance" of particular designs for living (the cultural heritage of a status group) or with respect to his relationship to the societal division of labor (class grouping). The second is the permeability of the boundaries that integrate the group with or isolate it from others in terms of intimate access. The extent to which a given inclusive community structure is pluralistic may thus be defined as a function of the degree to which it may be differentiated into groups that manifest more or less distinctive styles of life and, *as a necessary corollary,* associated tendencies to choose intimates from within the group and limit intimate transaction with out-group members—or, in other words, the degree of social structural differentiation as we have been using the term. We regard social structural differentiation as a necessary corollary of cultural differentiation (different styles of life of different groups) because it provides the crucial structural mechanism by which group differences may be developed and sustained. It is difficult to imagine how groups could develop and maintain distinctive styles of life—or, indeed, what we would mean by "group" at all—without such a minimal structural underpining.

From the wide range of evidence presented here, neither in social behavior nor in material style of life can we say that there are sharp and radical differences to be found between one group and another. The distinctions among groups, whether identified as occupational class or ascribed status groupings, tend to merge, almost imperceptibly, into one another. One explanation for this phenomenon of graded differences, derived from this model's assumptions, is that no economic or status grouping in Detroit, with the possible exceptions of the Jews and the blacks, maintains or have maintained for them such sharp and exclusive boundaries between themselves and other groupings so as to preclude the penetration of "outside" influences into the very intimate networks of the group in question. Even an individual who himself deals exclusively on an intimate basis with ingroup members is likely to include others in his personal network who have outgroup members in their intimate circles; that is, they are likely to be connected "once removed" to the outside by intimate links through their secondary networks. Thus our earlier analysis of friendship choices among groups shows quite clearly that while there are in practice marked tendencies to favor members of one's own occupational or ethnoreligious group for intimate relationships, there are still many "outgroup" members of one sort or another included in these intimate circles as well.

Of course, in addition, the entire community in a fully modern society is subjected more or less uniformly to the messages of the mass media, however selectively attended to, that would also serve to disseminate common models for behavior and, consequently, blur group differences. Thus the "model" of urban pluralism that we see developing for the American case must necessarily take into account the relatively high permeability of the boundaries between groups and the corresponding tendencies toward fusion of groups. In fact, the Triple Melting Pot hypothesis is premised precisely on this line of reasoning. This is in sharp contrast to the accounts we have of the situations in societies with rigid status orderings as in the Indian caste system (see Weber, 1958; Leach, 1967; Lewis, 1958; Blunt, 1931; Hsu, 1963) or in more strictly class-ordered societies as in early modern England or France (see Stone, 1965; Moore, 1966; Barber and Barber, 1965) where permeability among groups is alleged to have been much less than it is today in modern metropolises.[7]

To what extent is Detroit itself typical of modern American metropolises in its "form" of urban pluralism? Would we observe similar modes of differentiation in cities in other parts of the country and of different size? To the extent that they are dissimilar, what factors account for the dissimilarities? Is there some critical (absolute) number of persons of a given group that must be available for intimate interaction in a given locale before the group can sustain its distinctive characteristics? When a group is substantially below this critical threshold, does it tend to become absorbed into adjacent groups—that is, what really happens when one speaks of assimilation? Would we find smaller communities of the sort studied by W. Lloyd Warner and his associates to be less complexly differentiated—that is, tending toward unidimensional structures—at the same time that we observed sharper differences among status and class groups along their respective single dimensions, which is to say that class and status boundaries are more sharply drawn in such communities (see Laumann, 1966)? A careful reading of Warner's work tends to imply such a result. One might even offer the hypothesis that unidimensional structures are especially likely to lead to more rigid stratification systems while multidimensional or complexly differentiated structures mitigate against such a development. What would we find in other cultural settings and in societies at different stages of modernization? In order to pursue comparative questions and hypotheses such as these, we clearly must obtain systematic and comparable data of the sort we have considered here on the nature of intergroup access for different times and places. This is the task that lies before us.

NOTES

1. There are many tables in the book that are simply packed with data about ethnoreligious or occupational groups that were barely mentioned even in passing. These data have been included for two reasons: first, to permit the skeptical reader or one with a different set of theoretical biases to pursue alternative explanations and, second, to provide an opportunity to formulate comparative differences and similarities among these groups that might be tested in other sample populations.

2. In a recently completed dissertation analyzing the impact of family background and college experiences on occupational value orientations of male college students at the University of Michigan in 1962–1963, Jeylan Mortimer (1970, 1972) shows that occupational differences of fathers along this axis explain important differences in their college sons' occupational values and career choices. Given the generally high occupational origins of the large sample ($N = 2250$), Mortimer was able to use a 13-category occupational code that made fairly fine distinctions among high-status occupations. A smallest space analysis of profiles of occupational choice by father's occupation clearly revealed a first axis corresponding to our bureaucratic-entrepreneurial dimension.

3. Since Weber's thesis was originally intended as an historical hypothesis relating the rise of capitalism in the sixteenth and seventeenth centuries to the spread of the Protestant Ethic and since Weber himslf disclaimed its necessary relevance to the maintenance of capitalism once it was established, it is probably incorrect to expect his thesis to have much relevance in accounting for contemporary differences among religious subcommunities. [Incidentally, this historical thesis has been the subject of considerable controversy among economic historians (see Samuelsson, 1957).] This is especially likely given the peculiarities and idiosyncracies of subsequent historical developments of the various subcommunities in the United States during the nineteenth and twentieth centuries (see Mead, 1963; Gaustad, 1962; Niebuhr, 1929; McLoughlin and Bellah, 1968). For example, American Catholicism experienced a rather unusual historical situation (in contrast to its typical European

experience) in never having enjoyed the favored status of being the established church and being a relatively persecuted minority religion in a Protestant-dominated country whose members were heavily concentrated in the lower reaches of the socioeconomic hierarchy (see Maynard, 1960). One would certainly expect, and it in fact occurred, that these special historical circumstances elicited adaptive responses from the Catholic leadership and laity that would help them accommodate to the special demands of their new environment. Not the least important of such responses was to adopt some of the more salient characteristics and orientations of their Protestant neighbors. In short, American Catholicism is in a number of important respects quite different from European Catholicism—the empirical object of Weber's thesis—and closer to its American Protestant counterparts.

4.   To avoid any misunderstanding at this point, we note again that *style of life* has been regarded throughout the book as comprehending all the value, normative and behavioral elements that relate to the way an individual or group organizes its daily life and routines, including those of work, politics, family, status and class relations, religion and leisure.

5.   If there ever was any question in our minds regarding the popular sensitivity to the issues raised in this study of living room decor, it was quickly resolved by the response to a public airing of the study. An earlier version of the article was read on September 4, 1969, at the Annual Meetings of the American Sociological Association in San Francisco. A bastardized summary of the findings appeared the same day on the *front page* of the Los Angeles *Times* rivaling in length the coverage of Ho Chi Minh's death. Subsequently the "story" was picked up by major urban newspapers, magazines, radio and television, and was disseminated coast-to-coast, even appearing, to our knowledge, in newspapers in Canada, Japan, and the Union of South Africa! The authors were deluged with letters from a broad assortment of people making comments on the findings and requesting copies of the report, as well as with requests to appear on national television to discuss the results. Many people expressed real personal anxiety whether they had "successfully passed" the sociological test of "good taste." Perhaps the *piecé de resistance* of the whole affair was the Los Angeles *Times'* publication in December of an article in its Sunday supplement providing housewives with decorating hints for "hiding the TV set in the living room" so that sociologists and others wouldn't conclude that their families were "working class." With such evidence of touching an exposed social nerve, it is truly remarkable that sociologists have been so negligent in exploring this obvious avenue for studying status-linked behavior.

6.   Perhaps a word or two is necessary here about our usage of the term "group" with which I must admit we have taken some unusual liberties. Needless to say, "group" has been used at many points in the text in an exceptionally broad sense to denote the most inclusive set of persons who manifest disproportionate tendencies to form intimate relationships among themselves and to maintain a set of characteristic attitudes and behavior patterns that vary considerably in degree of specificity and breadth of activities covered from one "group" to another. Perhaps it would have been more accurate to have used the term "quasi-group" or even "category" since the boundedness of our notion is much less than is conventionally connoted when group is used to refer only to a set of persons who are mutually oriented to one another and explicitly self-conscious of common group membership. The borderline between the term "social category," which may minimally refer to a set of persons, all of whom may be completely unrelated to one another, but who

happen to share a given social characteristic of interest to the observer (that is, it has no necessary self-conscious existence in the minds of the members of the set and is completely amorphous) and a "quasi-group" is quite ill defined; and to some extent the distinction may be regarded as simply a matter of analytic convenience. On many occasions I wanted to connote something more structured and interrelated than the term "category" tends to imply. In these cases I have tried to indicate by the context the broader sense in which the term is being used.

7. All that has been said here obviously only applies with any force to the white population from which our sample was drawn. Given the near total exclusion of the black community from intimate access to the white community (only two out of some 3000 friends reported by our sample were black in a metropolitan area in which nearly one in five is black; see Farley and Taeuber, 1968, for black-white residential segregation indexes), one may only speculate that we have here the "best" ingredients for the development and/or persistence of important subcultural differences between white and black communities (compare Siegel, 1970, for a counter-argument on this point).

APPENDIX A

Social Distance as a Metric:
A Systematic Introduction to
Smallest Space Analysis

DAVID D. MCFARLAND AND DANIEL J. BROWN

INTRODUCTION

This appendix is concerned with the formal foundations of social distance and other spatial concepts as applied to sociology, and with the computational procedures used to analyze sociological data in this manner. Since sociologists constitute the intended audience, the discussion is in terms of *social* distance, even though the material covered is of much broader applicability and, indeed, was developed primarily by psychologists and mathematicians.

The initial sections review the sociological literature with respect to the concept of social distance—or, more precisely, several different concepts of social distance used by different authors. Since the utility of a social distance concept depends on an analogy with physical or spatial distance, this leads to a discussion of the various properties of physical distance and other distance-like functions that are called "metrics" in the mathematical literature. It is shown that such indices as the Bogardus scale do not share certain important properties of physical distance, so that the intended analogy is not valid.

The concept of a "proximity measure" is introduced to solve this problem. A proximity measure is related, by certain monotonicity condi-

This appendix is largely based on a working paper by the senior author, who gratefully acknowledges partial support of this project from The Population Council and the National Science Foundation (GS-1929). During the junior author's work on this appendix he was supported by a Canada Council fellowship, which is also gratefully acknowledged.

tions, to another function that is a metric and does share the properties of physical distance. Thus such indices as the Bogardus scale can be treated as proximity measures and can be manipulated to yield other sets of numbers for which the analogy with physical distance is valid. The latter part of the chapter is devoted to a nontechnical explanation of the computerized procedures which are available to perform such manipulations, and the appendix ends with a discussion of the relationship of such procedures to the goals of the sociological research in which they are applied.

A SHORT HISTORY OF SOCIAL DISTANCE

Over four decades ago Pitirim A. Sorokin made the following observation concerning social distance and related concepts:

Expressions like "upper and lower classes," "social promotion," "N. N. is a climber," "his social position is very high," "they are very near socially," "right and left party," "there is a great social distance," and so on, are quite commonly used in conversation, as well as in economic, political, and sociological works. All these expressions indicate that there is something which could be styled "social space." (Sorokin, 1927: 3)

He went on to say that there had been few attempts to deal systematically with "social space" and such related concepts as "social distance." In the meantime, however, a number of such attempts have been made. This section will be a brief and incomplete history of the development of the concept of "social distance," with emphasis on (1) different meanings which have been attached to the term, (2) quantification thereof, and (3) development of a clear analogy with physical or geometrical distance.

Although Sorokin (p. 9) traces "social space" and related concepts back to the social physics of the seventeenth century, contemporary concern with "social distance" seems to have much more recent roots. Perhaps the earliest of these is the work of Simmel (1908) who neither attempted to quantify "social distance" nor clearly related its properties to those of physical distance. Emory S. Bogardus (1925 and later work) quantifies his idea of "social distance," but in his work the analogy with physical distance is subdued, if present at all. In fact, his "social distance scale" values lack certain basic properties of physical distance. On the other hand, Sorokin (1927) clearly states the analogy with physical distance but makes no attempt to quantify the concept. The combination of the two in a single work—quantification *and* clear analogy with physical distance —first appeared in a paper by Laumann and Guttman (1966) some 40 years after the two components had appeared separately. (However, this is not to say that no empirical regularities had been found relating physical distance to one or another type of social distance whose definition had been made without any explicit analogy to the definition of physical distance. Such empirical regularities, as opposed to analogies of definitions, appear in, for example, Duncan and Duncan, 1955b.)

In the meantime, however, interest in social distance had by no means waned. A large number of papers appeared that applied Bogardus-type scales in different parts of the world. Other works attempted to evaluate and improve the Bogardus scale (for example, determining reliability, modifying the scale to make it more sensitive to small social distances), and to further clarify the concept, as in distinguishing sources of different types of social distance. Substantively, the applications were primarily to relations between ethnic groups and not to "social distance" in a more general context. (For a somewhat more detailed review of the developments mentioned in this paragraph, see Laumann, 1966; 23 ff.)

Simmel's (1908) discussion of social distance concerned "The Stranger," whom he described as having elements of both nearness and distance. The nearness comes from features held in common with the observer, and the distance comes from the observer's awareness that the features held in common are common to all men or at least to large groups of men. Simmel's use of the concept does not lend itself either to quantification or to a clear analogy with physical distance since in his usage two people can simultaneously be "near" and "distant." His concept of social distance actually seems to be a mixture of two different concepts: features held in common, and the degree of specificity or generality of these common features.

Yet an analogy with physical distance is apparently involved, otherwise the term "common features" would suffice and there would be no reason to introduce terms like "near" and "distant." But the analogy, if present, was not made explicit. For one thing, physical distance is quantified in inches and miles but Simmel made no attempt to quantify his idea of social distance, or to represent it geometrically as the distance between physical points.

Bogardus, with whose name the term "social distance" is probably most frequently associated, constructed the first scale to measure social distance in 1925, and a revised scale a few years later (Bogardus, 1925; 1933). He constructed 60 attitude items such as, "I would admit _____ to my street as a neighbor," "I would marry _____," and "I would exclude _____ from my country." A panel of "experts" rated each of these items by the amount of *sympathetic understanding* expressed, on a seven-point scale. The average rating for each item was calculated, and a scale was constructed using only those seven items whose ratings were closest to the integers one through seven—an attempt to construct an equal-interval scale.

Although the instructions to the raters were in terms of sympathetic understanding, Bogardus called the result a Social Distance Scale rather than a Sympathetic Understanding Scale. In this regard he was undoubtedly influenced by Robert E. Park who had previously used the term "social distance" with respect to racial attitudes and "degrees of understanding and intimacy which characterize personal and social relations generally" (1924: 339). Apparently both Park and Bogardus felt that the use of the word distance would set up an analogy with spatial distance, thereby yielding more insight into certain aspects of social relationships. But the analogy, if present, was not made explicit by Bogardus. In fact, it could not possibly have been: his scale values violate certain properties of physical distance. For example, while the distance from an object to itself is zero, the Bogardus scale (with scores from one to seven) does not permit a respondent to have a Bogardus scale value of zero from his own ethnic group. This problem with the analogy could be easily overcome, by rescaling from zero to six; but the analogy has much more serious difficulties, as we shall see.

Sorokin (1927) makes the analogy with the geometrical distance between physical points quite explicit in his discussion of social distance. In fact, he discusses physical space at the same time he discusses social space (and points out that two people who are physically close may be socially distant, as a gentleman and his servant, and vice versa, as the rulers of two different countries). "Euclid's geometrical space is space of the three dimensions. The social space is space of many dimensions . . . ." (Sorokin, p. 7). Just as the location of a point in geometrical 3-space is determined by values of three coordinates, so a man's location in social space is determined by the values of many coordinates, among them "family status, the state of which he is a citizen, his nationality, his religious group, his occupational group, his political party, his economic status, his race, and so on . . . ." (Sorokin, p. 5). These and other coordinates determine both the social position of individuals and the social distance between any pair of individuals:

> The greater the resemblance of the positions of the different men, the nearer they are toward each other in social space. The greater and more numerous are their differences in these respects, the greater is the social distance between them. (Sorokin, 1927: 6)

Sorokin made no attempt to quantify his idea of social distance, to arrive at a numerical value for the social distance separating two men. He did not even specify how the discrepancies on the various coordinates should be weighted and combined to yield social distance. Yet, in listing some of the coordinates he was clearly taking steps in that direction.

Laumann and Guttman (1966) used a concept of social distance that was even more clearly related to physical distance than was Sorokin's and that, unlike Sorokin's, was quantified. Their first step was to construct a geometrical representation of the social space; then the social distance between two groups was calculated from the coordinates of each in the space. Thus their social distance values, unlike those of Bogardus, do satisfy the various properties of physical distance. Their concept of social distance is given in terms of a monotonicity condition: the higher the social distance between two groups, the lower the probability that a man in one of these groups will have "important others" (father, father-in-law, close friend, neighbor) in the second of the two groups.

In constructing the social space they first specify its dimensionality (or at least a trial dimensionality). The distance function used is the usual Euclidean distance, the square root of the sum of squared discrepancies along the various dimensions. Then a computerized procedure, "Smallest Space Analysis," is used to construct a social space (to assign coordinates along the various dimensions to each of the groups) in such a manner that violations of the monotonicity condition are minimized. A "coefficient of alienation" is used as an index of how badly the goal of monotonicity is violated by any particular configuration of social coordinates. If the violations are considered excessive, an improved fit can be found by going to a social space with a higher number of dimensions. This technique will be discussed in detail in a later section.

METRICS, PHYSICAL DISTANCE, AND SOCIAL DISTANCE

Properties of Metrics

As pointed out in the first section, sociologists have realized for many years that some of the quantities with which they deal bear a resemblance to physical distance. Mathematicians, too, have noticed quantities other than physical distance that also have distance-like properties. This led them to analyze these properties abstractly, so that their results apply to any quantities having these properties, and not only to physical distance itself. Such a distance-like quantity is called a *metric,* and a set of objects together with a metric defined on it is called a *metric space.* Metric spaces are treated in standard mathematics texts (for example, Royden, 1963: ch. 7; Kelley, 1955: ch. 4).

The most frequently used metric is the Euclidean distance function. Distances between physical locations are ordinarily given as Euclidean distances, except when there are obstacles which prevent measurement of distance along the straight line between two physical locations. (Examples of such obstacles are buildings, which prevent one from diagonally crossing a city block, and the earth itself, which prevents one from traveling in a straight line to China.) For example, if a person places a mark on a sheet of paper, and places a second mark three inches to the right of and four inches below the first mark, the distance between the two marks, both as calculated from the Euclidean distance formula, and also as measured by a ruler, will be $\sqrt{3^2 + 4^2} = 5$. The general formula for calculating Euclidean distance will be given below, along with the formulae for certain other metrics.

A metric is a function which, to each pair of objects, attaches a number to be interpreted as the distance from the first to the second object. But not just any assignment of numbers to pairs of objects will qualify as a metric. A metric is defined as a relation with the following seven properties:

M1   Its domain (the set to each member of which a number is assigned) is the set of *ordered pairs* of elements from some well-specified underlying set. The elements of the underlying set, which might be individuals, ethnic groups, and the like, in the case of social distance, are often referred to abstractly as "points."

M2   Its range (the set of numbers which may legitimately be assigned) is the set of *nonnegative* real numbers.

M3   It is a *function;* to each ordered pair from the domain it attaches only one number, not several, from the range. (It need not be one-to-one, however; the same number may be attached to two or more ordered pairs.) This number given by the metric may be thought of as the abstract distance from the first to the second of the two objects in the ordered pair. Some notation is required to complete the definition. Let a, b, and c denote generic elements of the underlying set, and let $M(a, b)$ denote the distance from the first element to the second.

M4 $M(a, a) = 0$. This is the *reflexive* property, which requires that the distance from any object to itself be zero.

M5 $M(a, b) = M(b, a)$. This is the *symmetry* property, which requires that the distance from the first object to the second must be equal to the distance from the second object back to the first.

M6 $M(a, b) \leq M(a, c) + M(c, b)$. This is called the *triangle inequality*. This condition may be illustrated by attempting its violation: it is impossible to draw a triangle with one side longer than the sum of the lengths of the two other sides.

M7   If $M(a, b) = 0$, then $a = b$. This assumption states that when the distance between any two objects is zero, they are really not two distinct objects, but only two different names for the same object.

The relation M is a metric if and only if it meets all of these seven conditions.

As indicated earlier, the Euclidean distance function is the most frequently used metric. It is a special case of a more general class of metrics, known as the Minkowski metrics, which differ from one another in the exponent used. The general formula for the Minkowski metric with exponent p is:

$$d_p(a, b) = \left[\sum_i |x_{ai} - x_{bi}|^p \right]^{1/p} \qquad (A.1)$$

where $1 \leq p \leq \infty$, a and b are any pair of objects, and x_{ai} is the value ascribed to object a on dimension i. The vertical bars denote absolute values.

The Minkowski metric with the exponent $p = 1$ is, from equation A.1, simply the sum of the discrepancies on the various dimensions, where only the magnitude and not the sign of each discrepancy is considered. Another metric, which differs from this one only by the constant factor of $\frac{1}{2}$, is the "index of dissimilarity" which is frequently used in sociological work. With an exponent of $p = 2$, the Minkowski metric becomes the familiar Euclidean distance function,

$$d_2(a, b) = \left[\sum_i (x_{ai} - x_{bi})^2 \right]^{1/2} \qquad (A.1a)$$

the square root of the sum of squared discrepancies.

Strictly speaking, the expression on the right side of equation A.1 is undefined for $p = \infty$, so a separate definition is required for that case. The natural thing to do in such a situation is to determine whether equation A.1 has a limit as p approaches ∞ and, if so, to define d_∞ as being equal to that limit. It can be shown (Royden, 1963) that the limit does exist, and is equal to the largest of the discrepancies along the various dimensions. Thus the definition in equation A.1 is extended to include the case $p = \infty$ as follows:

$$d_\infty(a, b) = \max_i |x_{ai} - x_{bi}|. \qquad (A.2)$$

In words: the metric d_∞ assigns to each pair of objects a distance equal to the largest of their discrepancies on the various coordinates. Although the most frequently used exponents for Minkowski metrics are 2, 1, and ∞, other values are occasionally used;[1] likewise, although the Minkowski family of metrics includes the most frequently used metrics, other metrics are occasionally used (Beals et al., 1968).

To avoid the possibility of confusion, it should be pointed out that the word "metric" (and even more frequently, "nonmetric") occurs in the social science literature with a different meaning, as an adjective whose meaning appears from context to be "measured on at least an interval scale." Thus ordinal scale variables are sometimes referred to as "nonmetric variables," and methods for analyzing ordinal scale variables are sometimes referred to as "nonmetric techniques" (for example, Guttman, 1968).

Two simple examples will show that "metric," as defined above, and "quantity measured on at least an interval scale" are quite distinct. The simple dichotomy, "same/different," which has no quantitative aspirations whatever, yields a metric whose function rule is:

$$M(a, b) = \begin{cases} 0 \text{ if } a \text{ and } b \text{ are the same} \\ 1 \text{ if } a \text{ and } b \text{ are different.} \end{cases}$$

It is easy to show that this function is, in fact, a metric, by verifying each of the seven conditions above. This example shows that a metric need not involve an interval scale, nor even a nontrivial ordinal scale.

On the other hand, a quantity measured on an interval scale need not be a metric. Height, weight, income, and the like—which form not only interval scales but ratio scales as well—are not metrics. Each of these is a function of an *individual* person or object, not a function of *pairs* of objects as required by condition M1 in the definition of "metric." Thus a quantity measured on an interval scale need not be a metric.

The source of the use of "metric" as an adjective is the fact that interval scales do give rise, in a very natural manner, to metrics (noun). If v_a and v_b denote the values of objects a and b on an interval scale, one can easily verify that the seven properties in the definition of (the noun) "metric" are satisfied by the function

$$M(v_a, v_b) = |v_a - v_b|$$

where the bars denote absolute values. (Here distances are attached to pairs of scale values, v_a and v_b, and thus indirectly to the underlying objects, a and b). This is the "natural metric" of the scale v.

If we consider a set of numbers as forming an interval scale, we make use of this natural metric arising from the scale. For example, if we are thinking in strictly monetary terms, the difference between $10 and $11 is identical to the difference between $10,000 and $10,001, namely a difference of one dollar. But discussions of "utility" in economics and elsewhere point out that an additional dollar "means more" to a man with only ten dollars than it does to a man with ten thousand dollars, so that the two differences are not subjectively equal. From this subjective viewpoint, the metric defined above should be ignored, and the numbers should not be treated as forming an interval scale.

In sociology there are similar examples, such as the number of children a woman has. The difference between one child and two children and the difference between four children and five children are identical, namely a difference of one child. However, women in a survey (Goldberg and Coombs, 1963) reported that they felt the difference (in pleasure and trouble to the mother) between having one child and two children would be much greater than the difference between having four children and five children. Thus from the women's subjective viewpoint this metric should be ignored, and the variable "number of children" should not be treated as forming an interval scale. In fact, Goldberg and Coombs went on to construct a new scale for "number of children," a scale whose natural metric *does* correspond to the subjective differences reported by the women in the survey.

Now that the distinction between "metric" and "quantity measured on an interval scale" has been made, we need to state two more definitions before discussing the seven properties which define a metric in terms of their validity for physical distance.

Definition. A *metric space* consists of a set of points, say a, b, etc., together with the set of distances between the various pairs of points, $M(a, b)$, $M(a, c)$, and so forth (see Royden, 1963: 109).

A metric space with a small number of points is often most conveniently specified by a square matrix whose rows and columns correspond to the points, and whose cell entries are the interpoint distances. For example, one particular metric space is specified by the matrix:

$$\begin{array}{c} & \begin{array}{ccc} A & B & C \end{array} \\ \begin{array}{c} A \\ B \\ C \end{array} & \left[\begin{array}{ccc} 0 & 3 & 5 \\ 3 & 0 & 4 \\ 5 & 4 & 0 \end{array} \right] \end{array}$$

Notice that not just any square matrix will do: it must be symmetric and have zeros on the diagonal (this is easily determined by visual scanning) and the entries must also satisfy the triangle inequality (this can be checked only by performing the relevant calculations).

Definition. A *dimensional representation* of a metric space consists of a set of points, a, b, and so forth, a set of coordinates for each point, say x_{a1}, x_{a2}, . . . , x_{an} for point a, and a function by which the distance between any two points can be determined from the coordinates of the two points.

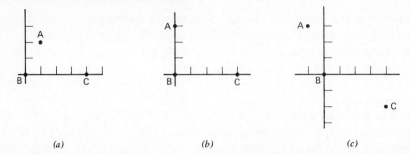

Figure A.1   Configurations of points that give different visual impressions can, when analyzed in terms of different metrics, yield identical interpoint distances. Configuration (a) under the city block metric, d_1, configuration (b) under the Euclidean metric, d_2, and configuration (c) under the maximum discrepancy metric, d_∞, all yield the same interpoint distances: $d(A,B) = 3$, $d(B,C) = 4$, and $d(C,A) = 5$.

(We are not aware of any previous formal definition of this term. However, our definition is consistent with its usage in the literature; see especially Tversky, 1966.) Once the coordinates are known, the points can be plotted on graph paper for visual inspection of their configuration.

The relationship between metric spaces and dimensional representations thereof is not one-to-one. There is usually more than one possible dimensional representation for a given metric space. For example, the metric space given in the matrix above could be given the dimensional representation: $A = (1, 2)$; $B = (0, 0)$; $C = (4, 0)$; where $M(a, b) = \Sigma \, |x_{ai} - x_{bi}|$; this is plotted in Figure A.1a. But a second—and equally valid—dimensional representation of the same metric space would be: $A = (0, 3)$; $B = (0, 0)$; $C = (4, 0)$; where $M(a, b) = [\Sigma(x_{ai} - x_{bi})^2]^{1/2}$; this is plotted in Figure A.1b. And a third—equally valid—dimensional representation is: $A = (-1, 3)$; $B = (0, 0)$; $C = (4, -2)$; where $M(a, b) = \max |x_{ai} - x_{bi}|$, the notation "max" referring to the largest of the values found by inserting the various values of i—in this case, $i = 1$ and $i = 2$. This is plotted in Figure A.1c.

Note that although the three different dimensional representations given above are equally valid, they give rather different visual impressions of the relationships between the points. But this is a matter for consideration in a later section; we now turn to a discussion of physical distance to show that it does, in fact, satisfy the seven properties used to define "metric."

Properties of Physical and Social Distance

Property M1.   Physical distance is always distance *from* one location *to* another location, thus it involves a pair of locations. We sometimes speak of the distance *to* a single location, but such an expression would be meaningless without the implicit understanding that we really mean the distance *from* the location of the person speaking *to* the location in question.

Property M2.   Physical distance can be a positive number (from one location to a second distinct location) or zero (from one location to itself), but can never be negative.

Property M3.   The distance between two physical locations is a single number that is unique (once the unit of measurement is determined), and is conventionally taken as the shortest possible distance traversed in going from one location to the other. (Some maps follow a different convention, taking distance along expressways; regardless of the convention followed, distance is always given as a unique number.)

Property M4.   The distance from any location to itself is zero.

Property M5.   Physical distance is symmetrical: The distance from location a to location b is the same as the distance from location b back to location a.

Property M6.   Physical distance satisfies the "triangle inequality" (whose name comes from the fact that no side of a triangle can be longer than the sum of the lengths of the other two sides). The distance traveled in going directly from location a to location b will be no greater (and may be considerably less) than the distance traveled in going indirectly from location a to location b by way of location c.

Property M7.   If the physical distance from location a to location b is zero, then "location a" and "location b" must simply be different names for the same location.

Thus we see that the abstract mathematical properties of a metric agree with the familiar properties of distance between physical locations. Our interest, however, is neither in abstract metrics nor in physical distance, but rather in a quantifiable notion of "social distance." But, as pointed out above, the only apparent reason for the use of the term "social *distance*," rather than some other term such as "sympathetic understanding," is the utility seen in making an analogy with physical distance. Laumann (1966: 5) makes this quite explicit in his justification of the use of the term "distance" for the social phenomenon he studied:

. . . the concept of distance is "relationally fertile" in the sense that it suggests by its connotations a number of new hypotheses and methods of analysis that otherwise might have been overlooked.

But analogies can be dangerous: conclusions drawn by analogy may be invalid if the analogy is not correct. Hence if we are to make use of an analogy with physical distance, it is important to ascertain that what we call "social distance" does, in fact, have the same properties as physical distance. This is the reason for considering the properties of physical distance, and metrics in general, in some detail.

Bogardus and his followers have been, by far, the most prolific of the numerous authors using the term "social distance." Yet the Bogardus social distance scale is subject to the dangers mentioned above: the analogy between physical distance and the Bogardus social distance is not valid. The Bogardus social distance is not a metric, failing to satisfy three different properties of physical distance and other metrics.

Property M4 requires that the distance from any object to itself be zero. But it is not possible for a subject responding to a Bogardus questionnaire to give a rating of zero to his own social group, the only ratings available being the integers from one to seven. Hence the Bogardus social distance from one group to a second group (calculated as the average, over all respondents in the first group, of individual social distances from the respondent to the second group) cannot possibly satisfy property M4. As stated earlier, however, the impossibility of a zero Bogardus distance from a group to itself could be overcome by a simple transformation (using the scale values zero through six, rather than one through seven).

But such a modification of the scale would only make it *possible* for the scale to satisfy property M4; it would not guarantee that the property would be satisfied, as it must in order to yield a metric. It then becomes an empirical question. Our intuition suggests that some members of many groups, the black trying to make his way in a white world of business, the second generation immigrant trying to become fully assimilated, and so on, would *not* rate themselves as close as the scale permits to the groups of which they are members, and hence that even a modified (0 to 6) Bogardus scale would not yield a distance of zero from a group to itself.

It turns out that our intuition here is correct. Laumann (1966: 42), using a scale similar to that of Bogardus, found that respondents in each of five self-identified classes rated a list of occupations so similarly that, regardless of the respondent's class, the social distance from the respondent's class to the high prestige occupations was smallest, and the social distance from the respondent's class to the low prestige occupations was greatest. Thus the ratings made by working class respondents were such that their social distance to the working class occupations in the list was higher than their social distance to any other occupations in the list. So even if a Bogardus type scale were transformed to give a social distance of zero to the closest group, the distance from a given group to itself would not be zero.

Property M5 requires that distance by symmetrical. But there is no logical reason why Bogardus type social distances must be symmetric, since the determinations of the two distances (from the first group to the second, and from the second group to the first) are experimentally independent, one based on ratings made by persons in the first group, and the other based on ratings made by persons in the second group. So the symmetry of Bogardus type social distances also becomes an empirical question. But only a brief examination of the data cited earlier (Laumann, p. 42) is required to observe a marked lack of symmetry.

Property M6 requires that distances satisfy the triangle inequality: that the distance from one group directly to a second group be no greater than the distance from the first group indirectly to the second group by way of a third group. Again there is nothing about the manner in which the Bogardus scale is constructed which would require this condition to be satisfied. And again it is made highly suspect by experimental independence: two of the distances in the triangle (from group 1 to groups 2 and 3) are based on ratings made by the first group, while the third distance (from group 3 to group 2) is based on ratings made by the third group.

The use of categories that lack strict comparability makes Laumann's (p. 42) data inappropriate for testing this property empirically. But this is really irrelevant. We cannot prove that a particular function is a metric by merely citing examples where it did satisfy the properties of a metric; in order to be a metric a function must be such that the satisfaction of these properties follows automatically from the very way in which it is calculated, as is the case with physical distance. Hence the Bogardus social distance scale does not provide a satisfactory analogy between social distance and physical distance; it fails to have several important properties of physical distance.

A second attempt at quantifying social distance (Beshers and Laumann, 1967) will be discussed only briefly, since it has the same types of shortcomings we have seen in the Bogardus scale. Another reason for the brevity is that it has been exposed only in a single recent paper, unlike the Bogardus scale which is the basis for an exceptionally large volume of work published over a period of four decades. This notion of social distance is based on mean first passage times from the theory of Markov chains (Kemeny and Snell, 1960). Assuming intergenerational social mobility operates as a Markov chain (an incorrect assumption, incidentally; see Hodge, 1966; McFarland, 1970) one can ask how many generations would be required, on the average, for a family line which is initially in one specified social class to reach a second specified social class. (This question, as posed, assumes that each man has precisely one son, that family lines retain their identity rather than either branching or terminating; this is one of the reasons the Markov chain assumption is incorrect; see Duncan, 1966a.)

This formulation of social distance does not satisfy property M4, that the distance from any object to itself be zero. This, however, is merely an artifact of the convention adopted in Markov chain theory for defining the mean passage time from a given state to itself. The convention used is to define it as the mean time required to leave the state and subsequently return. An equally reasonable convention—and one by which mean passage times would satisfy property M4—would be to define the mean passage time from any state to itself as zero, since the process is already in the state in question. But such a modification would not make the mean passage time a metric since it also violates property M5, the symmetry property. This is easily seen by counterexamples (Beshers and Laumann, 1967: 227).

Lest this section end on a pessimistic note, we should remark that quantities such as the Bogardus scale and the mean passage time, which are not metrics themselves, can be manipulated to yield new functions which are metrics, and for which the analogy with physical distance would be valid. The method will be covered more fully in a later section, but here we will remark that it is formally identical to the procedure mentioned earlier with regard to the work of Laumann and Guttman (1966). First, a monotonicity condition is proposed: the higher the social distance between two groups, the higher their Bogardus scale ratings of each other (or mean passage times). Next, a computer program is used to construct a social space (assign coordinates to each of the groups) in such a manner that violations of the monotonicity condition are minimized. Then distance in the resulting social space is a metric, and it reflects more-or-less (depending on the extent to which monotonicity must be violated) the Bogardus scale ratings (or mean passage times) on which it is based.

TWO CONCEPTS OF SOCIAL DISTANCE

The time has come to point out explicitly that Sorokin and Bogardus had rather different things in mind when they used the term "social distance." According to Sorokin (1927: 5) two persons are close to each other in social space when they have similar countries of citizenship, nationalities, religions, occupations, political parties, economic statuses, races, and so on, regardless of whether each could stand to have the other as a neighbor, co-worker, or in-law. Bogardus (1933), in contrast, measured his concept of social distance in terms of the type of social interaction likely to take place between two persons (or more precisely, between members of two groups): small social distance is characterized by such social interactions as marriage and having each other as friends; intermediate social distance by interaction as co-workers, neighbors, or speaking acquaintances; and large social distance by unwillingness to have each other in the same neighborhood or even the same country.

Some examples that point out the substantive difference between the two social distance concepts are the following: two businessmen who are fiercely competing with each other may be very close according to the Sorokin concept of social distance, but very far apart according to the Bogardus concept. Two socialite women who are feuding have the same possibility. On the other hand, a married couple of mixed ethnic or socioeconomic background exhibits the opposite possibility, the mates being very close according to the Bogardus concept of social distance, but far apart according to the Sorokin concept.

In addition to this difference of substantive meaning, there is an important methodological difference: concepts of social distance such as that of Sorokin are easily and directly translated into metrics, while concepts such as that of Bogardus can be translated into metrics only in a roundabout manner, using such techniques as the smallest space analysis mentioned earlier and to be covered later in more detail.

It will be convenient to have some terminology for this distinction between types of social distance when we consider a variety of possible indices of social distance. For this purpose we will use the terms "interaction" and "similarity."

According to an *interaction* notion of social distance, low distances should be assigned between individuals or groups who are likely to be involved in such social interactions as living near each other, seeing each other socially, intermarriage, having friends or relatives in the other group, moving from one group to the other, or merely approving of each other. High distances should be assigned where such social interactions are unlikely.

According to a *similarity* notion of social distance, low distances should be assigned between individuals or groups who are similar on such attributes as occupation, income, education, ethnicity, entire pattern of social contacts, entire pattern of attitudes, group pattern of mobility, and group pattern of residence. High distances should be assigned where such attributes are dissimilar.

Thus in our terminology the Bogardus concept of social distance will be of the "interaction" type, while the Sorokin concept of social distance will be of the "similarity" type.

However, we need to make one more distinction. We have until now been using the term "dimension" in two different senses: (1) as an axis along which one of the coordinates of a geometrical point is measured, as when x_{a1} is the coordinate of point a on the first dimension, and (2) as a numerically measured attribute of the real-world object to which the geometrical point corresponds, as when the first dimension is a person's income, the second is his number of years of formal education, and so forth.

In the "similarity" type of social distance, there will be a one-to-one correspondence between attributes of the real-world objects (persons, groups, and so on) and the axes along which the corresponding geometrical points will be plotted, since the axes are determined directly from the attributes; in this case there is no harm in using the same term for both concepts. However, in the analysis of "interaction" type social distances, the axes are determined by a procedure which does not involve these attributes directly; there need not be a one-to-one correspondence between axes used in the dimensional representation and attributes of the objects. In fact, one frequently ends up with axes for which no substantive interpretation can be found, while the attributes one would expect to affect social distance appear in the dimensional representation as concentric circles, wedge-shaped patterns, or other configurations.

Thus it becomes important to distinguish between the two different senses in which the term "dimension" has been used. We will do so by restricting our subsequent use of the term "dimension" to its usual mathematical meaning, and introducing a new term to cover its substantive meaning: a *dimension* is an axis along which one of the coordinates of a geometrical point is measured; a *component* of social position or of social distance is a numerical attribute possessed by the real-world objects being considered. Although the latter runs counter to established usage (Sorokin's, in particular), the distinction we make will be helpful.

THE CONCEPT OF A PROXIMITY MEASURE

We have seen that such indices as the Bogardus scale do not possess certain important properties of physical distance, and hence that the analogy between such indices and physical distance is not valid. To avoid invalid analogies one should, strictly speaking, avoid using the term "social distance" to describe such indices.

However, all is not lost. Although the values of such indices as the Bogardus scale do not, themselves, qualify as social distances, it can nevertheless be extremely useful to think of them as systematically related to other sets of numbers which *do* qualify as social distances. In order to pursue this possibility we now introduce the concept of a proximity measure.

Shepard (1962a: 125 ff) noted that there are a number of different types of numerical relationships between pairs of objects which, although they do not have the properties of metrics, are usefully conceptualized as being systematically related to distance. For example, two stimuli in a psychological experiment may be considered "near" each other if they produce similar response patterns in a subject; in this case "nearness" has the meaning of substitutability. A second type of example given by Shepard, where substitutability considerations are inappropriate, involves association: the word *butter* is often associated with the word *bread,* but their relationship (or that of their referents) is one of complementarity rather than one of substitutability. As a generic expression to cover both types of relationships Shepard proposes the term *proximity;* a set of numbers describing the degree of such relationships among pairs in a set of objects is called a *proximity measure.*

Such measures may be viewed as related to metrics. They may be described in terms of metric properties, as in Table A.1.

Table A.1. Properties of a proximity measure

Metric Property	Description	Proximity Measure Requirement
M1	Ordered pairs: (a, b)	*Must hold*
M2	Nonnegative numbers: (≥ 0)	Need not hold
M3	Function: (unique number from the range)	*Must hold*
M4	Reflexive: $M(a, a) = 0$	Need not hold
M5	Symmetric: $M(a, b) = M(b, a)$	Need not hold
M6	Triangle inequality: $M(a, b) \leq M(a, c) + M(c, b)$	Need not hold
M7	Same object: if $M(a, b) = 0$, then $a = b$	Need not hold

Moreover, proximity measures may be considered as either directly related to distance (large proximities corresponding to large distances) or inversely related to distance (large proximities corresponding to small distances). Bogardus-type scales, for example, while they are not metrics, may be treated as the former type of proximities. The correlation coefficient and its nonparametric analogs may be treated as the latter type of proximities, with high correlation corresponding to small distance. For example, Laumann and House (1970) in a study of living room furnishings, begin by correlating indicator variables (that is, variables with the values: 1 for presence, 0 for absence) of the various types of objects in living rooms, and use these correlations to arrive at a type of social distance, but here the distances are between different types of living room objects and attributes, rather than directly between persons or groups.

As defined above, proximity measures do not necessarily possess many specific mathematical properties, such as those defining a metric. And proximity measures themselves are not powerful tools of analysis, precisely because they are not well-behaved functions with known mathematical properties. The main purpose of this appendix is to show how proximity measures can be manipulated to yield other, more powerful, sets of numbers. In particular, these manipulations will yield: (1) a social distance function that *is* a metric, and (2) a dimensional representation of the objects in question, permitting analysis of the configuration or pattern formed by the set of objects.

PROXIMITY MEASURES AND METRICS

One could impose the assumption that the proximity measures are identical to the social distances between the objects in question. Under that assumption each violation of the triangle inequality (M6), for example, would constitute an "error" in the data, and one would have to "correct" the data in some manner to make them satisfy the triangle inequality and the other properties of a metric. The noun "error" and the verb "correct" appear in quotation marks with good reason: it is not that the sample was not representative of the relevant population, that the respondent misinformed the interviewer, that the interviewer inadvertently recorded the wrong response, that the clerk miscounted in tallying responses, or anything of that nature; the "error" is merely that the data—no matter how accurately collected—do not fit the theoretical assumption being imposed on them. Corrections (without quotation marks) for the other types of errors (without quotation marks) are an entirely different matter; the issue here is "errors" arising in a disagreement between the data and certain theoretical assumptions being imposed on them.

In analyzing data we would like to "let the data speak for themselves" as much as possible. But at the same time we would like to use techniques of sufficiently high power to extract information that would not be apparent in a mere scanning of the data. If our assumptions are too strong our conclusions will depend more on the assumptions than on the data; but if they are too weak no conclusions will be forthcoming. The ideal is to impose moderately strong assumptions: sufficiently strong to permit us to extract substantially more information from the data than would be possible by mere inspection, but sufficiently weak that our conclusions appropriately reflect the data, rather than being little more than a restatement of the assumptions we imposed on the data. Perhaps the most useful rule of thumb is to use the weakest possible assumptions that permit extraction of the kind of information one wants from the data.

As we already saw, the use of such proximity measures as the Bogardus scale values would run into serious difficulty, requiring numerous "corrections" of the data, if we imposed the assumption that the proximities are identical to the corresponding distances from a metric. But proximity measures may be related to metrics in a variety of weaker manners, requiring less "correction" of the data.

One may, for example, wish to impose the following weaker assumption on the data: the proximity from any object to itself is to be ignored (often the data will not even include anything that could be interpreted as self-proximity), but all other proximities are monotonically related to (have the same rank order as) the corresponding social distances. If two or more social distances are equal, it would be assumed that the corresponding proximities are either tied or of adjacent ranks.

Under the stronger assumptions discussed earlier—that the proximities are identical with the corresponding social distances—it constituted an error, a violation of metric property M4, whenever the proximity from an object to itself was any number other than zero. But under this weaker assumption the proximity from an object to itself is merely ignored, not counted as "error."

Under the stronger assumptions, it constituted an "error," a violation of metric property M2 or M7, whenever the proximity from one object to a distinct object was zero or negative. Both zero and negative proximities are permissible under the weaker assumption, since adding an appropriate constant to each proximity—which is a monotonic transformation—solves the problem.

Under the stronger assumptions, it constituted an "error," a violation of metric property M5, whenever the proximity measure was not symmetric. Under these weaker assumptions the two proximities, say $r(a, b)$ and $r(b, a)$, may be unequal as long as they have adjacent ranks.[2]

Under some conditions (compare footnote 2) it may be reasonable to treat the nonsymmetry of proximities as "error" even though the weaker assumption now under consideration does not force us to do so. If that seems prudent, then it is natural to treat $r(a, b)$ and $r(b, a)$ as two estimates of the same quantity, differing only because of random error, and replace each of them with their mean, which is apt to be a better estimate than either of the two separate estimates (Kruskal, 1964a: 21; Kruskal also suggests a second, more complicated way of handling non-symmetric proximities). Although we would still be treating some of the data as "error," there would have been even more "error" had we imposed the stronger assumption instead.

Under the stronger assumptions it constituted an "error"—and an extremely serious one—whenever proximities failed to satisfy the triangle inequality (M6). But under the weaker assumption of monotonicity, proximities that violate the triangle inequality are perfectly admissible. This assertion, unlike the previous ones, is not intuitively obvious. It follows, however, from the following theorem: any proximity measure which is symmetric (M5) can be transformed into a metric by the addition of a suitably chosen constant to each proximity (after a change of sign, in the case of proximities inversely related to distances), which is a monotonic transformation.[3]

CONDITIONAL PROXIMITIES

Even weaker assumptions than monotonicity are possible. In particular, in certain substantive problems it is not at all clear that nonsymmetry of proximities should constitute "error"; in fact, intuition often suggests the opposite. For example, Coombs (1964: 404) writes, "We may expect that the proportion of times (a blindfolded subject trying to identify cigarette brands) reports brand B when smoking brand A will not be the same as the proportion of times he reports brand A when smoking brand B."

This type of consideration leads to the concept of *conditional proximity matrices* as alternative to symmetric proximity matrices (Coombs, ch. 19). A conditional proximity matrix is interpreted as follows: the entries in any one row of the matrix, say row i, reflect the *relative* distances from the ith object to each of the other objects, apparently in the sense of being monotonically related to the social distances from the ith object to each of the other objects. But this monotonic function relating proximity to distance for row i may differ from the monotonic functions for other rows, so that the rank order of all the proximities from the entire matrix may differ considerably from the rank order of the corresponding social distances.[4]

Let us see how much difference it might make whether a matrix is treated as a conditional proximity matrix. We will consider a simple example of a matrix which is symmetric (so it can be treated both ways) and compare the two sets of restrictions on the distances that result when the proximities are treated as completely monotonic, or conditionally monotonic, with distances. Let the matrix of known proximities and the matrix of unknown distances be as follows:

$$r = \begin{bmatrix} 0 & 2 & 4 & 6 \\ 2 & 0 & 1 & 5 \\ 4 & 1 & 0 & 3 \\ 6 & 5 & 3 & 0 \end{bmatrix} \qquad \text{(A.3a)}$$

$$d = \begin{bmatrix} - & U & V & W \\ U & - & X & Y \\ V & X & - & Z \\ W & Y & Z & - \end{bmatrix}. \qquad \text{(A.3b)}$$

If we treat the proximities as *completely* monotonic with distances, this yields the following complete rank order of distances:

$$X < U < Z < V < Y < W. \tag{A.4}$$

This, incidentally, is all the information the data give about the distances, if we require only that the distances be completely monotonic with the given proximities.

If, in contrast, we treat the proximities as conditionally monotonic with distances, we must analyze each row separately. From the first row we have $U < V < W$; from the second row, $X < U < Y$; from the third row, $X < Z < V$; and from the last row $Z < Y < W$; and this is all the information the data give about the distances if we require only that the distances be conditionally monotonic with the given proximities. But this information is insufficient to determine the complete rank order of the distances; the reader may verify that the inequalities from the four rows, taken together, determine the partial order as in Figure A.2, where the distance at the upper end of a line is larger than the distance at the lower end of a line. When the data are treated as conditional proximities, the ordering of the distances V and Y is undetermined, as is the ordering of the distances U and Z. Thus the given proximities, when treated as conditional proximities, are compatible with any of the following rank orders:

$$\begin{aligned}
X < U < Z < V < Y < W \\
X < U < Z < Y < V < W \\
X < Z < U < V < Y < W \\
X < Z < U < Y < V < W.
\end{aligned} \tag{A.5}$$

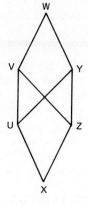

Figure A.2 Partial order of distances under conditional monotonicity.

The conclusion to be drawn from our example is true in general: the assumption of conditional monotonicity is even less restrictive than the assumption of complete monotonicity. However, there is no simple formula for the number of different permissible rank orders of the distances, or other indices of how much less restrictive the conditional monotonicity assumption is. For example, the reader may verify that if 1 and 2 are interchanged in the conditional proximity matrix of equation (A.3a), only two, rather than four, different rank orders of distance are permissible:

$$
\begin{aligned}
U &< X < Z < V < Y < W \\
U &< X < Z < Y < V < W.
\end{aligned}
\qquad (A.6)
$$

The assumption of conditional monotonicity places fewer restrictions on the ordering of the distances. This, in turn, has obvious qualitative implications for the problem discussed earlier, of proximities with a marked lack of symmetry resulting in a large number of tied distances: the fewer restrictions made on the ordering of the distances, the less that problem will arise.[5]

The motivation for a conditional matrix might be the desire to move to the perceptual level and to consider distances (or at least their rank order) from each person's point of view. However, this approach might be expanded by considering the entire matrix from the perspective of one individual or group, rather than just a single row as stated above. Implementation of individual-specific matrices would run the risk of lack of information on the part of respondents, since the proximity of any other two people may be unknown to the perceiver. Perhaps a method could be utilized whereby information of reduced certainty (as indicated by the perceiver) could be permitted progressively lighter impact on the solution to the dimensional problem. The notion of establishing social distance on a perceptual basis as opposed to an "actual" one was first mentioned by Poole (1927). He suggested that distances between racial groups as perceived by themselves should be termed "subjective" while cultural differences obvious to an observer should be called "objective."

Next let us attempt to give a precise meaning to the notion of "relative distance," and determine how it would be possible for nonsymmetric relative distances to arise from a metric space whose distances are (by definition) symmetric.

RELATIVE DISTANCE

A reasonable definition for the concept of relative distance might be as follows:

Let the set of distances $d(a, k)$, from point a to each of the other points, k, be ranked from smallest to largest. Then the *relative distance from a to b* is equal to the rank of $d(a, b)$ in this set of distances.

We are not aware of any previous definition, but this is consistent with the usage in the literature. Note that relative distance as defined here is an ordinal-level concept; we explored the possibility of giving a quantitative definition, namely $d(a, b)/\Sigma d(a, k)$, but we could find no rationale for the assumption that human behavior should be in terms of such a quantitative relative distance, although this alternative definition is also consistent with the usage of the term in the literature.

Relative distances, as we have defined them, need not be symmetric. The relative distance from b to a is equal to the rank of $d(a, b)$ among the set of distances $d(k, b)$, which need not be the same as its rank among the set of distances $d(a, k)$. We will illustrate this with an example involving four points, the *distances, d*, being given in the matrix:

$$
\begin{array}{c}
\quad\ \ A \ \ B \ \ C \ \ D \\
\begin{array}{c} A \\ B \\ C \\ D \end{array}
\left[
\begin{array}{cccc}
0 & 6 & 7 & 8 \\
6 & 0 & 2 & 3 \\
7 & 2 & 0 & 4 \\
8 & 3 & 4 & 0
\end{array}
\right] = d.
\end{array}
\qquad (A.7)
$$

Such a configuration of points is shown in Figure A.3. The *relative distances, r*, from the row point to the column point, are given in the matrix:

$$
\begin{array}{c}
\quad\ \ A \ \ B \ \ C \ \ D \\
\begin{array}{c} A \\ B \\ C \\ D \end{array}
\left[
\begin{array}{cccc}
- & 1 & 2 & 3 \\
3 & - & 1 & 2 \\
3 & 1 & - & 2 \\
3 & 1 & 2 & -
\end{array}
\right] = r.
\end{array}
\qquad (A.8)
$$

Note that there are three violations of symmetry in the matrix of relative distances. In particular, $r(A, B)$ and $r(B, A)$ are at opposite extremes of the relative distance scale, with values of 1 and 3, respectively. But this makes sense geometrically, as reference to Figure A.3 shows: from the viewpoint of someone located at point A, point B is the closest other point; but from the viewpoint of someone located at point B, point A is the most distant other point. The distance between A and B is the same in both cases, namely $d(A, B) = 6$, but in one case it is being compared with one set of distances, $d(A, C) = 7$ and $d(A, D) = 8$, while in the other case it is being compared with a different set of distances, $d(B, C) = 2$ and $d(B, D) = 3$.

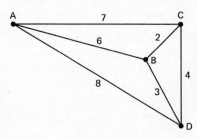

Figure A.3 A three-dimensional pyramid-shaped figure, drawn only approximately to scale, to illustrate the discussion in the text of conditional proximity and relative distance concepts.

So it makes sense, mathematically, to speak of "relative distances" which are not distances in the strict sense (where "distance function" and "metric" are synonyms) since they are not symmetric, but which are related to the underlying distances (from a metric) by conditional monotonicity as described above. But it remains to be seen what, if any, behavioral data are appropriately viewed as conditional proximities which are related to social distances by conditional monotonicity. To that problem we now turn, in the substantive context of friendship patterns.

THE FRIENDSHIP EXAMPLE

Sociologists often work with data in a form suggestive of the possibility of treating them as conditional proximities. In particular, a cross-classification table is often transformed into a stochastic matrix—one with nonnegative entries and each row summing to unity—by dividing each entry of the original matrix by the sum of the entries in the same row (for example, Laumann and Guttman, 1966; McFarland, 1969). The entries of such a stochastic matrix are then often described as conditional probabilities or estimates thereof. Once the data are in this form it is tempting to try statements of the form: if the conditional probability of b given a is greater than the conditional probability of c given a, then the distance between a and b is less than the distance between a and c (see Laumann and Guttman, 1966). The latter, of course, is not a statement of fact; rather, in the lack of an independent definition of social distance, it must be taken as merely an indication of what the writer in question chooses to mean when he uses the term "social distance," a partial definition of the term as he uses it.

Consider the results of a survey in which respondents are asked to name their three best friends, or to name other associates or relatives. An exhaustive list of groups (religious, ethnic, occupational) has been made, and the data to be interpreted or explained are the entries in a cross-classification of the respondent's group by the group of which a person he names is a member. With data of this type Laumann and Guttman (1966) chose to define social distance as being conditionally monotonic with the numbers they interpreted as conditional probabilities of friend's group given respondent's group. (It turns out that nothing is gained by initially transforming frequencies into conditional probabilities, since this is also a conditional monotonic transformation; the social distance matrix is a conditional monotonic transformation of the conditional probability matrix if and only if it is a conditional monotonic transformation of the original cross-classification table.)

It appears that the basis of measurement of social distance is somewhat variable. Clearly, in the absence of conventions, Laumann and Guttman were free to define friendship operationally in any manner which appeared suitable. Yet it could be that they have in fact combined two or perhaps three conceptually distinct forms of association: those of family, friends, and neighbors. An upwardly mobile respondent, for example, could obtain new friends and neighbors more congruent with his own new status, but would ordinarily be unable to do anything that would produce corresponding changes in the statuses of his relatives. Furthermore, the inclusion of neighbors seems to require the assumption that physical distance largely coincides with interaction, and this is clearly violated in many neighborhoods, especially among apartment dwellers.

We shall now make some theoretical assumptions about the behavioral process generating the data, and determine how well the Laumann-Guttman meaning of "social distance" fits in with the resulting theory. First, assume that there is some underlying social space of which the respondents are aware (though perhaps not consciously), and which is perceived the same way by the various respondents (actually, completely identical perception of the social space is not necessary, as will become apparent below). Then assume that any given respondent rank orders the various groups according to their social distances from his own group. He chooses as many friends as possible from his own group; then he chooses as many additional friends as possible from the group with the smallest social distance from his own; then from the group with the second smallest social distance; and so forth, until his quota of friends is filled. (Compare the theory of intervening opportunities; Stouffer, 1940.) The term "as many as possible" requires further explanation. If there were no restrictions or constraints, any respondent could choose all his friends from his own group. However, this may not be possible, either because the group is small or because his residence and employment locations make it unlikely for him to meet many members of the group with sufficient frequency to establish friendship.

This is a set of theoretical assumptions that could be imposed on the friendship data in order to interpret the latter in terms of social distances between groups. In particular, it specifies a type of inverse ordinal relation between the social distance to a group and one's propensity to choose a friend from that group, namely that persons in socially distant groups are second (or higher) choices, and are only selected when persons in closer groups are not available.

From this set of theoretical assumptions we can deduce conclusions about the relation of the data to the underlying social distances: if the various constraints on the formation of friendships in a particular group (for example, group size, opportunity to meet members of various groups) are the same for all groups or are included in the determination of a given group's position in the social space, then the matrix of social distances is a conditional monotonic transformation of the matrix of friendship choice frequencies or, what is equivalent, of the matrix of numbers interpreted as conditional probabilities. If not, the matrix of social distances need not be a conditional monotonic transformation of the data.

THE PROBLEM OF GROUP SIZE

The constraints other than group size are, presumably, part of what we mean by social position or social distance, so that part of the conclusion is agreeable. But the various groups will not ordinarily be of equal sizes, so we are forced to conclude one of the following: (1) the effect of group size is cancelled by other constraints; (2) group size is one of the components determining the social position of a group; (3) our theory of the effect of social distance on friendship choice behavior is incompatible with the Laumann-Guttman characterization of social distance.

Conclusion (1) seems highly implausible, so we will consider only the other alternatives. Bonacich (1967), in a comment on the Laumann-Guttman paper, asserts that the Laumann-Guttman characterization of social distance is in error, as if the issue were a factual matter which has a correct answer. But it is not. It is a matter of definition: Do we or do we not wish to include group size as a component of whatever it is we want to call "social distance"? That is the issue. If we wish to include group size in our concept of social distance there is no problem; if not (assuming our theory is correct) the Laumann-Guttman characterization of social distance must be reformulated. But there is no correct answer. All we can do is explore the consequences of choosing one answer or the other.

Suppose first that we decide that, as we wish to use the term, the social distance between groups *ought* to include a group size component. The justification would be that group size is, after all, often a major determinant of social interaction patterns, and hence should be included in what we mean by "social distance." This decision may have a negative consequence. An exceptionally large group, unless it is actively boycotted, will be chosen with exceptionally high frequency by members of the various other groups. An exceptionally small group, unless it is actively sought out, will be chosen with exceptionally low frequency by members of the various other groups. Thus the decision to include group size as a component of social distance is tantamount to an a priori decision that the large groups will be located near the center of the social space and the small groups near the periphery. This effect may be so pronounced as to mask the effects of other determinants of friendship patterns and to preclude their identification from the resulting configuration of social positions. Thus if we decide to include group size as a component of social distance the analysis may be relatively uninformative, since we already know group size is important without going to the trouble of analyzing the data, and its inclusion may prevent the discovery of other components of social distance.

But the other alternative also has difficulties. Suppose, then, that we decide, as Bonacich (1967) did, that group size should *not* be included in social distance. In this case the Laumann-Guttman data should be reanalyzed after "controlling for" group size. But there is the catch! We cannot "control for" group size unless we have a theory about the manner in which group size affects patterns of friendship; we are not able to remove the effects of differential group size unless we have a theory telling us how large these effects are.

Unfortunately, the method proposed by Bonacich does not succeed in "controlling for" group size in any reasonable sense of the expression. Group size affects the cross-classification table in two different manners: an effect on the composition of a (presumably representative) sample of respondents, and an effect on the frequency with which group members are listed as friends by any one given respondent. The Bonacich method "controls for" the latter in a certain sense, but does nothing about the former type of effect.

The only method we have found that seems likely to succeed in "controlling for" group size in some sense, on the one hand, and corresponds to a plausible theory about the effects of group size, on the other, is a modification of the iterative procedure given by Deming (1943) for quite different purposes. The procedure in question, which has been discussed more recently by Mosteller (1968) as of wide applicability, is one for simultaneously adjusting a given matrix to a specified set of row marginal totals and a specified set of column marginal totals, while leaving unchanged the association between the row variable and the column variable. (This description is incomplete, as association may be defined in various manners; for details see Mosteller, 1968.)

The problem in our case is to adjust the given friendship matrix into another matrix with different marginal totals, the latter matrix to be interpreted as the matrix that would have been obtained under the hypothetical condition where all groups are of equal size. The needed modification of the procedure described above would be an additional restriction on the adjustments. Each row and its corresponding column would require the *same* adjustment factor, one to adjust for group size as it results in large groups doing a disproportionate amount of the choosing, and the other to adjust for group size as it results in large groups constituting a disproportionate number of the individuals available to be chosen. The details of such a modified adjustment procedure—and, indeed, even its feasibility—remain to be explored.

THE DIMENSIONAL REPRESENTATION OF PROXIMITIES

In this section we consider a number of computerized iterative techniques for finding a dimensional representation of a set of data when the distances themselves are unknown and are to be determined simultaneously with the coordinates of the configuration of points. The information that is known and utilized consists only of the order relations one seeks to impose on certain (perhaps all) pairs of distances. These latter constraints on the distances arise from the goal that the social distances be completely or conditionally monotonic with the corresponding proximities making up the data (for example, Bogardus-type scales or friendship frequencies).

The number of dimensions required for the dimensional representation is unknown; its determination is part of the analysis. Considerations of parsimony and the desirability of being able to plot the configuration (which is extremely difficult in three dimensions and impossible in four or more dimensions) yield a second goal: to keep the number of dimensions very low.

These two goals—imposing desired order on distances and keeping dimensionality low—will often conflict. It is seldom possible to impose all the given order relations on the distances when the points are restricted to a two-dimensional space. The larger the number of points involved, the more likely the two goals are to conflict.

It should be emphasized that, contrary to the impression given in a casual reading of some reports on these techniques [for example, Lingoes, 1967: "The distances between points . . . were forced to be monotonic with . . . (a specified proximity measure)"], the given order relation between distances is treated as a *goal to be approximated,* and not as an absolute restriction to be completely enforced in all cases. In other words, in order to achieve a suitably low dimensionality we are willing to forgo, if necessary, the possibility of imposing *all* the given order restrictions on the distances. Nor is such a compromise without merit. Any given set of data includes a certain amount of random "noise," and it is quite conceivable that some of the given inequalities were reversed by the "noise," the corresponding "true" inequalities going in the opposite direction. Random sampling is one, but by no means the only, source of such "noise."

A third goal is to achieve a dimensional representation which makes substantive sense; that is, a dimensional representation in which objects (persons, groups) lying in one part of the space have properties (ethnicity, SES, degree of urbanization) similar to those of nearby objects and differing systematically from the corresponding properties of objects lying in other parts of the space. As "blind" computational procedures, none of the programs under discussion can incorporate this type of goal. It is imposed after the analysis. Presumably the researcher discards any dimensional representation for which no substantive interpretation can be found, or else the entire substantive problem is viewed as requiring further study, perhaps by different methods.

COMPUTATIONAL PROCEDURES

The computational procedures to find a dimensional representation are iterative in nature. Iterative procedures may be characterized as refinements on trial-and-error procedures: make a guess, determine how good it was, make another guess, determine how good it was, and so on. What distinguishes iterative procedures from trial-and-error (and this distinction makes a world of difference) is that in iterative procedures the successive guesses are made according to a systematic formula, which is designed to make each guess an improvement over the preceding guesses. After a sufficient number of iterations the successive guesses should become more and more alike, as convergence is approached, whereupon further improvements in the guesses will be negligible. When (or if) such a situation arises it is time to stop performing the iterations and print out the latest and best guess.

This is how iterative procedures are intended to operate. But two different problems may arise: (1) the successive guesses may continue to fluctuate, rather than converge, or (2) the successive guesses may converge, but to a wrong answer. Both of these possibilities should be kept in mind when iterative procedures are used. It is often quite difficult to prove that a given iterative procedure will always converge to the correct answer, or even that it will always converge at all; thus computer programs are sometimes made available when little is known of their convergence properties aside from the fact that they did converge on the examples used to de-bug them.

With this background we proceed to discuss the various procedures available for the dimensional representation of proximities. The programs all have certain general features in common. We will first give a general description that would apply, with only minor changes, to any one of the available programs (see Gleason, 1967); afterwards we will discuss some of the differences between the various programs.

First a certain function (for example, Euclidean distance) is specified, presumably on the basis of a priori theoretical considerations, by which the interpoint distances are to be calculated from the coordinates of the various points. As another preliminary, an order relation (partial or complete), which we desire to impose on the interpoint distances, is specified on the basis of proximity data. Then a sequence of steps is performed iteratively:

(1) An integer, n, is chosen for the dimensionality of the space during the current iteration. (2) A trial configuration (a set of coordinates in n dimensions for the various points) is specified. (3) The trial configuration is evaluated in terms of how well it satisfied ordering of interpoint distances, whether it could be collapsed into a space of fewer dimensions without violating the specified ordering, and so forth. (4) If the current configuration is deemed satisfactory, the iterations stop and the results are printed. (5) If the current configuration is not satisfactory, the details of its shortcomings are used to calculate a new trial dimensionality and/or configuration, hopefully an improvement, and the iterative process is continued.

As noted above, this description does not completely fit any one of the programs; rather it is an attempt to formulate a single description in general terms which is approximately applicable to each of the programs.

DIFFERENCES AMONG ITERATIVE PROGRAMS

The various programs differ in the details of each of the steps listed above: which types of distance functions can be used, what types of order relations can be specified, how dimensionality is determined initially, how the initial configuration is determined, the precise criteria used in evaluating a given configuration, and the formula used to calculate an improved configuration for the next iteration. Only a few of these differences can be covered here; for a complete and accurate description of any specific program the reader can only refer to the relevant literature. For specific programs see the following entries in the bibliography: Gleason, Guthrey, Guttman, Kruskal, Lingoes, McGee, Roskam, Shepard, Torgerson, F. Young.

We will, however, discuss a few differences.

The Initial Breakthrough

Although a considerable amount of earlier work was done on multidimensional scaling in psychology (see Torgerson, 1958, ch. 11, for one line of development, and Coombs, 1964, chs. 21–22 for another), the big breakthrough in multidimensional scaling came in a series of papers by Shepard (1962a, 1962b). Prior to Shepard's work it was not believed possible to construct a dimensional representation (or, from an alternative viewpoint, to reconstruct the underlying social or psychological space) given only order relations on the distances. For example, Coombs (1964: 444) had defined the multidimensional scaling problem much more modestly, as "given order relations on the interpoint distances among a set of points, . . . construct a space *the axes of which are only recovered at the level of a rank order*" (emphasis added). And Torgerson (1958, ch. 11) considered only the case where the distances are known, measured at the interval scale level or higher, and (with one slight exception) Euclidean. But Shepard's monumental papers showed that it is possible to construct a dimensional representation whose dimensions are interval scales, from only the rank order of the interpoint distances.

This was apparently an almost unbelievable breakthrough. In fact, after writing his first paper (1962a) giving a computational procedure and its rationale, Shepard (1962b: 220) felt obliged to write the second paper "to demonstrate that the method does in fact work." The claimed ability to convert an order relation on distances into a complete dimensional representation of the points seemed "tantamount to getting something for nothing" (Shepard, 1962b: 238), and required demonstration as well as explanation. His demonstration included accurate reconstruction of known (artificial data) configurations of points using only the order relations on their interpoint distances. (The use of artificial data permitted him to have a *known* "true" configuration with which to compare the results, which is impossible when real data are used as proximities.) Perhaps even more impressive was his reanalysis of some real data on perceived differences between various colors: a factor analysis by a previous investigator had yielded five factors with no satisfactory substantive interpretation; Shepard's reanalysis gave a representation in two dimensions that made substantive sense (colors lying roughly on a circle, with red, blue, and yellow about equally spaced and the intermediate colors located properly).

One condition that makes such a procedure possible, and a necessary condition for it to work satisfactorily, is that the problem involve at least a moderately large number of points that are fairly well scattered throughout the space (the programs have problems handling certain types of configurations; for example, a space consisting of two clusters separated by a distance greater than any of the within-cluster distances). Shepard (1962b: 239) writes that perhaps one crucial condition for the procedure to work "is that the number of points be sufficiently large with respect to the number of dimensions of the configuration." As an example he cites the case of 15 points in two dimensions, where there are $15 \times 14/2 = 105$ distances involved. If the ordering of each pair of distances is known there are $105 \times 104/2 = 5460$ inequalities stating that one distance is larger than another. But a representation of 15 points in two dimensions requires only 30 coordinates to be specified. Such a contrast—5460 order restrictions versus 30 coordinates—leads to a very pleasing heuristic explanation of why the procedure works: "It is not that something is created out of nothing but, rather, that information distributed among many numbers in a dilute and inaccessible form is concentrated into a much smaller set of numbers where it can more readily be grasped and utilized" (Shepard, 1962b: 239).

Applicable Metrics

Certain of the programs (Kruskal, 1964a, 1964b; Roskam and Lingoes, 1969) permit the use of any Minkowski metric, while others are limited exclusively to the Euclidean metric, in calculating social distances from coordinates in the dimensional representation. It would appear that in some substantive problems the Euclidean metric is an implausible candidate for the function relating the components of social position (which here are not necessarily the same as dimensions of the dimensional representation) to social behavior generating the proximities. At first glance it would seem logical, in the analysis of a given set of proximities, to use the Minkowski metric we consider as most plausibly having generated them or to try various Minkowski metrics and use whichever one yields the best fit in the space of lowest dimensionality. Indeed, Gregson (1966) did try various Minkowski metrics on the same set of data; in one case he found than an exponent of $p = 6$ gave the best fit in the lowest dimensionality; in other cases he tried exponents up to $p = 10$, and found that the larger the exponent the better the fit, at least as far as he tried them.

Isosimilarity contours provide an intuitive, and perhaps the most satisfactory, means of determining the effect of the exponent, p, in the Minkowski distance function. In geometry a circle is defined as the set of all points that are the same distance (namely, the length of the radius) from a fixed point (the center); and in high school courses it is implicitly assumed that the distance in question is Euclidean distance. An isosimilarity contour is a curve that would satisfy the definition of "circle" except that the metric in question is not necessarily Euclidean distance—and isosimilarity contours do not generally look like circles when plotted.

Definition. The *isosimilarity contour* of radius R, about the center point O, in a space whose metric is M, consists of the set of all points b such that $M(O, b) = R$. (Compare Beals et al., 1968: 131.)

From this definition it follows that an isosimilarity contour in a two-dimensional space has the shape of a diamond for the city block metric, the shape of a circle for the Euclidean metric, and the shape of a square for the maximum discrepancy metric, d_∞. These are sketched in Figure A.4, for identical values of the radius, R.

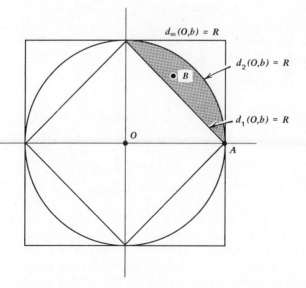

Figure A.4 Isosimilarity contours for a given radius, R, for three different Minkowski metrics. Points in the shaded region, such as B, are farther from the origin, point 0, than is point A, according to the city block metric, d_1, but are closer to the origin than is point A according to the Euclidean metric, d_2.

It should be clear why one Minkowski metric might be more compatible with a given order on the distances than another Minkowski metric: the different Minkowski metrics order distances differently. To see this consider Figure A.4, which shows the isosimilarity contours of a given radius, R, for three different Minkowski metrics. Consider any point B in the shaded region of the figure; two of the Minkowski metrics shown disagree about whether point A or point B is closer to the origin: $d_1(O, A) < d_1(O, B)$ but $d_2(O, A) > d_2(O, B)$.

The Minkowski metrics, however, also have a feature that makes their use in proximity analysis problematic: while Euclidean distances are coordinate-free (unchanged by translation or rotation of the axes) this is not true of the other Minkowski metrics. It may be shown that the Euclidean distance function is the only Minkowski metric for which the distance between each pair of points remains unchanged when the axes of the space are replaced by new axes which are rotated from the positions of the original axes.

This feature is illustrated in Figure A.5. In this figure a triangle whose sides (in Euclidean distance terms) are 1, 1, and $\sqrt{2}$ is rotated 45°. In the process of this rotation, the city block distances between its vertices, which initially are 1, 1, and 2, change to $\sqrt{2}$, $\sqrt{2}$, and $\sqrt{2}$.

The significance of rotational invariance for the social researcher is as

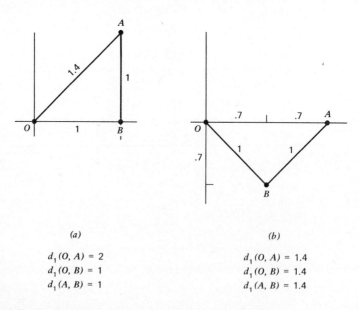

(a)

$d_1(O, A) = 2$
$d_1(O, B) = 1$
$d_1(A, B) = 1$

(b)

$d_1(O, A) = 1.4$
$d_1(O, B) = 1.4$
$d_1(A, B) = 1.4$

Figure A.5 Rotation of a rigid object changes the city block distances between its vertices. (a) A triangle with sides of Euclidean length, 1, 1, and $\sqrt{2}$, with the former two sides parallel to the axes. (b) The same triangle, but rotated 45°.

follows: The coordinate system in the output of a proximity analysis program does not necessarily have any special substantive meaning. We may want to translate or rotate the resulting dimensional representation to try to find axes to which we *can* attach substantive meaning. However, if the metric used in the dimensional representation is a Minkowski metric other than the Euclidean metric, such rotation would destroy both the absolute and relative distances between points, so that the results of a proximity analysis would be useless unless the axes it yielded turned out to be ones with substantive meanings. We conclude, then, that the Minkowski metric option available in some programs is of doubtful utility.

This, of course, says nothing about the input to the program; that is, the proximities. If we use the program with data in the form of a metric, as opposed to mere proximity measures, it can be any Minkowski (or even non-Minkowski) metric, since the form of the input proximities is quite arbitrary. For example, Blau and Duncan (1967: 67–75) used the metric $(1/2)d_1$ as input proximities and used the Euclidean metric d_2 to determine social distances from the coordinates of the resulting dimensional representation. However, if one is attempting to "recover" the underlying social space it hardly seems appropriate to require that the components of social position and the coordinates of the dimensional representation be related to social distance by two different and inconsistent functions.

The Solutions

In addition to differing on the available metrics, the various procedures also differ in what is meant by a "perfect" solution and, if none exists, which of the many possible approximations thereto should be taken. Shepard (1962a, 1962b) is especially vague about what constitutes a solution. His iterative procedure keeps shifting points in a manner designed to modify the current interpoint distances into interpoint distances having the desired rank order—by moving apart points whose interpoint distances are too low on the rank order and vice versa—but it also keeps moving points in a manner designed to stretch the large distances and shrink the small distances, in the hope (whose mathematical rationale is somewhat unclear) that this will collapse the configuration into a smaller number of dimensions. The final configuration is evaluated in terms of a monotonicity coefficient, δ, but its relation to the iterative procedure is unclear—the iterative procedure does not necessarily maximize δ.

Kruskal (1964a, 1964b) reformulated the problem as one of maximizing a somewhat different coefficient of monotonicity which he called "stress" and denoted S. It overcomes an objectionable feature of Shepard's coefficient, in that the latter depends on the numerical values of the desired distances, and not just their ranks, while "stress" depends only on their ranks. Kruskal's algorithm is explicitly designed to minimize "stress" by a gradient-type procedure; this might be explained heuristically as a matter of calculating stress of various configurations similar to the current one, and moving the configuration in the direction in which stress decreases most rapidly, repeating this procedure on the new configuration, etc.

Guttman uses a somewhat different coefficient of monotonicity, μ, based on his principle of "rank images," which is the reverse (in one sense) of Shepard's principle (Guttman, 1968: 498) and thereby overcomes the objectionable feature of the latter. Guttman's is also a gradient-type procedure, this one designed to maximize μ. Neither Guttman's nor Kruskal's monotonicity coefficient has clear superiority over the other; in fact, later programs in the Guttman-Lingoes series offer both options (Roskam and Lingoes, 1969).

Trial Dimensionality and Initial Configurations

The existing programs also differ as to the determination of trial dimensionality and initial configurations. Shepard determined both by requiring that all interpoint distances in the initial configuration be equal, which, he wrote, "insures that no bias will be introduced into the final solution" (1962a: 129). With n points this implies that the initial space has $n - 1$ dimensions, although that dimensionality is revised downward at a later stage. The points initially lie on the vertices of a regular simplex, the multidimensional analog of the equilateral triangle and regular tetrahedron. Kruskal, in contrast, used arbitrary initial configurations, largely in order to avoid the high dimensionality of Shepard's initial configurations.

The Guttman-Lingoes initial configuration and initial estimate of dimensionality (Guttman, 1968: 499–502) are obtained by a variant of the procedure for the case of Euclidean distance where the numerical values of the distances, and not just their rank orders, are known (Torgerson, 1958: 254–59). The "known" distances used are merely the rank orders to be imposed on the unknown actual distances. But these rank numbers are not ordinarily consistent as distances in a Euclidean space, so coordinates are only determined in as many dimensions as possible without running into logical inconsistencies (that is, without yielding complex numbers as coordinates). This number of dimensions is taken as a "rational" preliminary estimate of the dimensionality of the final space.

Local Optima

Kruskal (1964b: 118–19) was the one who pointed out the problem of local optima—configurations that are better than any configurations similar to themselves, but not as good as some drastically different configuration, the global optimum (compare the lowest point in a valley that is, itself, high in a mountain range). Kruskal suggests that a given set of data might be analyzed several times, from several different initial configurations. If (as is usually the case) most initial configurations lead to the same local optimum and the latter is considerably better than the few other local optima found, one could be reasonably confident he had found the global optimum. Kruskal also pointed to poor fit and lack of substantive interpretation of the configuration as possible signs that a local, rather than global, optimum had been reached. The Guttman-Lingoes discussion of local optima will be considered below.

The Guttman-Lingoes initial configuration and trial dimensionality may also be viewed (Guttman, 1968: 499–502) as the solution of a somewhat different—and considerably simpler—optimization problem than the one they intend ultimately to solve. The result gives both a trial dimensionality and an initial configuration at which to begin iterations in the more complicated optimization algorithm. This is, in their terminology, a "rational first approximation." It is the solution to a somewhat different problem, which would seem apt to be closer to the solution of the given problem than an initial configuration chosen in a completely arbitrary manner.

Guttman (1968: 473) claims to have solved the local optima problem:

A major innovation of the present approach is the notion of two-phase iterations, which assure in general that convergence take place ultimately only to the absolute minimum (or maximum) desired. This provides a solution to what has been termed "a standard difficulty of (iterative) problems" (Kruskal, 1964: 118).

The crucial part of Guttman's statement is the ambiguous expression "in general," which sometimes—notably in mathematical literature—means "in every instance," but is also used to mean "in most instances." One would presume, from the above quote, that Guttman means "in every instance," for otherwise he has *not* solved the local optimum problem. But this presumption, as we shall see, is doubtful.

In Guttman's two-phase iterations one carries out the following steps: specify a trial dimensionality. Specify an initial set of coordinates. Specify an initial set of desired distances, where the magnitudes are arbitrary since only the rank order will ultimately be taken into account. (This completes the preliminaries required before the first main iteration can begin.) Modify the coordinates iteratively by a procedure designed to minimize the discrepancies between actual and desired distances but which, however, is subject to the possibility of yielding local minima; stop after a given number of iterations or after convergence. (This completes the first phase of a single main iteration.) Replace the previous desired distances with new ones having the same rank order but different magnitudes, namely the magnitudes of the actual distances but permuted to the rank order of the previously desired distances—a process not subject to any local optima problems. (This completes the second phase of a single iteration.) Take the most recent set of coordinates and the new desired distances, and begin the next main iteration: Modify the coordinates iteratively . . . , and so on. Continue in this manner until both (1) the coordinates are modified only negligibly during the first phase of a main iteration, and (2) the desired distances are modified only negligibly during the second phase.

Guttman seems to be claiming that the two-phase process is not subject to local optima because the second phase is not. This seems plausible, but no proof is offered. Indeed, in the latter part of his paper Guttman writes of the "*relative* robustness of a two-phase over a comparable one-phase strategy with respect to the problem of avoiding local maxima," and states that the two-phase procedure "*helps* ensure convergence will not take place except to an absolute maximum," and that alternative procedures are "*more* prone to being led to undesirable stationary values" (1968: 485–86, emphasis added). Roskam (1969: 18) is more direct in discussing two-phase iterations: "Experience with this kind of algorithm does indeed show that the process may continue after a minimum is obtained and then converge to a non-minimal value." (He is trying to minimize, rather than maximize, since his coefficient, like Kruskal's, measures the degree of *departure* from monotonicity.)

Guttman (1968: 494) also remarks that the problem of local optima is "lessened, or even virtually eliminated, by starting with a good first approximation. . . ." Clearly, if one happens to choose the (or an) optimal configuration as his first approximation, any iterative procedure ought to terminate at the first iteration. What remains unclear is the set of conditions under which initial configurations suitably close to optimal will be iterated to optimal configurations rather than local optima, and conditions under which the Guttman-Lingoes rational first approximation is "suitably close to optimal" in this sense. At this point there appears to be no complete assurance that local optima are avoided.

Although he has not completely solved the local optima problem, Guttman is to be commended for his notational advances, which greatly facilitate the study of such procedures, and for an initial configuration and initial estimate of dimensionality which, though they do not appear to accomplish all we would like them to, have a rationale considerably superior to that of anything proposed previously. In particular, Guttman's formulation of the problem opens the possibility of mathematical analysis of the local optimum problem, which has previously been exclusively a matter of numerical experimentation.

The reader is referred to the original literature for further details on the various programs and distinctions between them; in particular, Gleason (1967) discusses the differences between various monotonicity coefficients and the precise adjustments used to modify a trial configuration.

This is certainly a rapidly developing field, when communication of results takes place by letter rather than formal publications (Guttman, 1967; Lingoes, 1968). At this writing a dittoed computer program abstract (Roskam and Lingoes, 1969) and a mimeographed manuscript (Roskam, 1969) cite unpublished results that apparently call for some major changes in the computational details of existing programs. However, the computational details are not our main concern; the purpose of this appendix will be fulfilled if the sociological reader understands the basic ideas of how these programs operate.

OBJECTIVES OF ITERATIVE PROCEDURES

An evaluation of where we stand must depend on our goals. Two qualitatively different types of goals have been expressed in the literature:

1. To identify the group characteristics that are important determinants of such interactions between groups as attitudes, mobility, and associational patterns. In this goal the spatial representation is viewed as merely a data reduction technique.
2. To find the quantitative laws governing these relationships. With this goal the spatial representation is intended to consist of a theory of group interactions, involving quantitative relationships between such interactions and the characteristics of the groups.

The latter is a much more ambitious goal than the former. Our achievement of the first goal would be analogous to the state of classical physics when one could only say, "the speed with which an object moves is related to how hard it is pushed." It is a long step from such a statement to a specification of the precise variables involved and the precise form of the relationship, "the force exerted on an object is directly proportional to the rate of change with respect to time of the object's speed, the proportionality constant being the mass of the object," or in symbols, $F = ma$.

Guttman (1967), in his letter to Ross, insists on confining our study to the former type of goal: "The general problem is: given nonmetric information about the data, can one find a metric representation of this which will make the study of the data easier, and uniformities more apparent than otherwise." He frowns upon the notion of attempting to "recover" the "true" social space. If our goal is merely to identify the characteristics that are important determinants of social interaction, then current methods are probably fairly satisfactory, although Beals et al. (1968: 141) have pointed out that even in data reduction the choice of a model is not a matter of indifference. The available procedures require minimization of some criterion of error, and hence "if the underlying model is inappropriate, the procedure necessarily capitalizes on noise in the data to obtain the fit . . . if the model used to perform this reduction is logically incompatible with the data generating process, it may suppress the more interesting aspects of the data and give a misleading impression" (p. 141). Despite their warning, if our goal is only the first one shown above, it is not particularly crucial whether we use an incorrect model which results in a warping of the space so that the meaningful components of social distance appear as rings, wedges, or other clusters in the space, rather than as dimensions—as long as they appear in one form or another and can be identified.

On the other hand, if we take the second type of objective listed above, current efforts are only a short step toward meeting our goal. A number of psychologists have been working in terms of such more ambitious aims. Shepard (1962b) writes of the "recovery" of an unknown spatial configuration, not of the mere data reduction problem considered by Guttman. Beals et al. (1968) and Tversky (1966) also express more ambitious goals. At various points in this chapter we have been concerned with theoretical assumptions which must be made if certain procedures are to be appropriate, thus implicitly taking the second type of goal as ours. But if that is our goal much remains to be done.

NOTES

1. For a case where $p = 2\frac{1}{2}$, see Gardner (1965).
2. Indeed, even if their ranks are not adjacent it does not necessarily constitute an "error." Consider, for example, a rank order that includes the segment

$$r(a, b) < r(u, v) < r(b, a). \tag{1}$$

The assumption that the distance function, d, is monotonically related to the proximity measure, r, implies only that

$$d(a, b) \leq d(u, v) \leq d(b, a) \tag{2}$$

or, from the symmetry of the distance function,

$$d(a, b) = d(u, v). \tag{3}$$

Equality of two or more distances may be an entirely reasonable way to interpret the data, preferable to discarding part of them as "error." In this case the proximities in inequality (1) would be accepted as admissible data.

On the other hand, if there are a large number of cases in which the corresponding proximities do not have adjacent ranks, such insistence on taking the data at face value would result in a metric space of higher dimensionality, which is difficult to interpret and otherwise quite uninformative. For example, concerning dimensionality, three points can be represented in one dimension with their interpoint distances ranked arbitrarily, as long as no tied distances are permitted. Relabel the points, if necessary, so that we require $d(A, B) < d(B, C) < d(A, C)$, and a configuration satisfying these requirements is easily found to be $A = 0$, $B = 1$, $C = 3$. Next suppose instead that we had nonsymmetric proximities with $r(A, B) < r(A, C) < r(B, A) < r(B, C) < r(C, A) < r(C, B)$; if distance is required to be monotonic with proximity we have $d(A, B) = d(A, C) = d(B, C)$. But this cannot be achieved in one dimension; it requires two dimensions.

The same argument applies to larger numbers of points with tied interpoint distances. If, among the points in a metric space, there is a subset of m points each of which is equidistant from each of the other $m - 1$ points in the subset, then an Euclidean dimensional representation of the metric space will require at least $m - 1$ dimensions. Proof: any Euclidean representation of these m points alone, temporarily ignoring the other points in the metric space, is equivalent to the set of vertices of an $m - 1$ dimensional simplex in m-space, namely the set of points $(1, 0, \ldots, 0)$, $(0, 1, 0, \ldots, 0)$, $\ldots$, $(0, \ldots, 0, 1)$. These m points require at least $m - 1$ dimensions. Inclusion of additional points can only increase the dimensionality.

This, incidentally, provides a counterexample to Guttman's (1967: 78) original formulation of his conjecture about the possibility of monotonic representation of symmetric proximities in a Euclidean space of smaller dimensionality; however, his more recent formulation (still without published proof) avoids this by permitting ties to be broken; that is, permitting equal proximities to be represented by unequal Euclidean distances (1968: 477).

Note added to galley proof: Since this was written, Lingoes (1971) has modified Guttman's conjecture in such a manner as to remove the error therefrom, and has given a proof of the modified version. For another recent contribution, see Lingoes and Roskam (1971).

3.   The proof may be obtained by writing to the senior author.

4.   This is intuitively suggestive, but less than fully satisfactory. In particular, the literature seems to contain neither a precise definition of "relative distance" nor a substantive argument to justify fully the notion that proximities are only comparable within rows, not between rows. As Coombs (1970, p. 53) has written more recently, "such an explanation for the lack of symmetry in a conditional proximity matrix needs more complete exploration, both formally and experimentally, but its reasonableness (at least to some psychologists . . .) has led to the more limited assumption that strict monotonicity of the function transforming proximity measures into distances applies only to distances from a common point . . . ." We will attempt to provide a more careful exploration of such an explanation of nonsymmetry.

5.   More precisely, the first inequality in footnote 2 above does not arise at all in the case of conditional proximities, since the first comparison would be made only if $a = u$ and the second comparison would be made only if $u = b$, and these cannot both be true for distinct a and b.

Sampling Design for 1965–66 Detroit Area Study

HOWARD SCHUMAN

INTRODUCTION

A multi-stage probability sample of dwelling units (DUs) from the Detroit metropolitan area was drawn for the 1965–66 Detroit Area Study. Within each dwelling unit having one or more eligible respondents, one person was drawn at random for interview. A total of 985 actual interviews was obtained, of which 28 have been double-weighted, yielding a final set of *1013 cases for use in analysis.* (The weighting procedure is discussed below.) These 1013 cases represent 80 percent of the eligible households sampled; a discussion of noninterviews appears below.

DESCRIPTION OF GEOGRAPHIC AREA

The area used for this study consists of that part of the Detroit Standard Metropolitan Statistical Area (SMSA) that was tracted in 1950—the same area that has been used in a number of previous Detroit Area Studies—plus some small additions that account for recent suburban population growth beyond the 1950 tracted area. This survey area consists of the city of Detroit and the densely populated suburban towns and townships on all sides. The definition results from a compromise between the time and money available and the desire to include as much of the SMSA as possible, especially those areas oriented toward the city of Detroit.

In size, the DAS area comprises less than half of the more than 2000 square miles of the three-county SMSA. But 87 percent of the occupied dwelling units and 85 percent of the population of the SMSA, as of mid-1965, are included in the DAS area:

	Detroit SMSA[1]	DAS Definition
Occupied dwelling units	1,156,200	1,003,540
Population	4,041,000	3,449,190

The major SMSA population concentration excluded under the DAS definition is in and around Pontiac.

THEORETICAL POPULATION

Only dwelling units as defined by the 1950 Census were sampled. Institutions, boarding houses, and dormitories were excluded, except insofar as they contained a dwelling unit.

Within dwelling units, an individual was considered eligible for interview only when he had all five of the following characteristics: *white; male; age 21–64* on last birthday; *born in the United States or Canada;* and a *member of the primary family* living in the dwelling unit. These restrictions resulted primarily from the content of the study, which was directly concerned with current occupational status and with ethnicity beyond the first generation. Certain important groups were excluded (for example, blacks) in order to increase the subsample sizes of other groups (especially white ethnic groups).

Where more than one eligible individual was located within a household, Kish's method for objective selection of respondents within households was used. This underweights individuals who live in dwelling units containing a large number of eligible persons, but in the present study only 7 percent of the DUs had more than one *eligible* respondent, hence for most purposes such effects will be slight.

Screening of individuals took place at the door for all characteristics except, to some extent, race. In order to reduce costs, sample addresses located in Census tracts in which blacks constituted 80 percent or more of the population in 1960 were assumed to represent only black-occupied DUs for 1966, and were ordinarily not visited by interviewers. In fact, 37 of the 179 sampled addresses located in these excluded tracts were visited on an approximately random basis; 36 of the dwelling units were occupied by blacks, one by a foreign-born white family. It seems likely that very few if any eligible respondents were missed.

SAMPLE SIZE AND SAMPLING FRACTION

A final sample size of approximately 1000 interviews was desired. This figure was set as the minimum necessary in order to include sufficiently large subsamples for analysis by ethnic group. The number of occupied DUs in the sample area at the beginning of the field period (May 1966) was estimated to be 1.01 million.

The likely coverage and response rates were estimated at 98 percent and 81 percent, respectively. A series of estimates was required to take account of the large number of ineligible DUs expected (for reasons of race, age, and other eligibility criteria mentioned above). Initial estimates of ineligible DUs proved to be too small in the light of early field returns, but fortunately it was possible to supplement the original sample. In the end, the estimate of ineligible DUs was set at 47 percent. Finally, 1 percent was allowed for eligible DUs in tracts excluded as largely black.

The figures given above lead to the following sampling fraction:

$$\frac{1,000}{1,010,000 \times 0.53 \times 0.99 \times 0.98 \times 0.81} = \frac{1}{421}$$

SELECTION OF THE SAMPLE

Addresses were selected from city directories, where they existed, and by area sampling methods elsewhere.

For the city directory sample, sample points at addresses in the following places were taken from city directories:

Detroit	Grosse Pointe Shores	Trenton
Hamtramck	Grosse Pointe twp.	River Rouge
Highland Park	Harper Woods	Wyandotte
Grosse Pointe	Dearborn	Riverview
Grosse Pointe Park	Melvindale	Ecorse
Grosse Pointe Farms	Allen Park	
Grosse Pointe Woods	Lincoln Park	

Clusters of three lines were selected systematically from the street address sections of the directories. These clusters were selected for DAS 1965 at the rate of 3/936 and most of the third lines of the clusters were used for that year's DAS. The sample addresses for the present study were taken from the unused two lines of these clusters and from the remaining third lines.

Correcting the City Directory

The city directory, dated 1964, was subject to error because of age and the possibility of inaccuracies in listing and/or preparation. The cost of an area supplement was thought to be prohibitive. In order to sample new construction and other missed DUs in the city directory listing, the following procedures were used:

1.   Additional DUs between a sample address and the next listed address were taken, except in cases 3 and 4 below. If the next listed address was on another street, the interviewers looked only up to the end of the street on which the sample address was located. If the sample address was the first listed address on a street, the interviewers looked not only for DUs between the sample address and the next listed address, but also for any DUs on that street before the sample address.

2.   If the sample address was the last listed apartment of a large apartment structure (more than four DUs), the interviewer looked for additional DUs between this apartment structure and the next listed address, but did not look for additional DUs within the same apartment structure (other than within the specific sample apartment).

3.   If the sample address was the first listed apartment of a large apartment structure (more than four DUs) the interviewer looked for unlisted apartments in the same apartment structure, but did not look for additional DUs between the sample address and the next listed address.

4.   If the sample address was neither the first nor the last listed apartment of a large apartment structure (more than four DUs), the interviewer did not look for either additional DUs within the structure (except within the specific sample apartment) or DUs between the sample address and the next listed address.

5.   Small apartment buildings (four or less DUs) were treated as multi-unit addresses.

These procedures, together with the apartment supplement explained below, to a large extent eliminate the bias that may exist in a directory sample when it is not supplemented by an area sample.

Apartment Supplement to the City Directory Sample

Sometimes entire new apartment structures for complete interview might be discovered between the sample address and the next listed address. To avoid this situation, we created and sampled from a separate stratum of large apartment structures (more than three DUs) that were not listed in the city directory.

Area Sample

Except for two towns where block statistics are available (Royal Oak and St. Clair Shores), Census Enumeration Districts were selected with probability proportional to size. The selection was carried out separately for two strata: those areas where the increase in the number of dwelling units between 1960 and 1965 had been less than 10 percent, and those areas where the increase had been 10 percent or greater. From the selected Enumeration Districts, two segments of approximately 20 DUs were listed. From each selected segment, an expectation of six DUs was included for this study. For Royal Oak and St. Clair Shores, clusters of blocks were the primary sampling units.

SPECIAL WEIGHTING

Although our original goal was to obtain approximately 1000 interviews over the course of three months, field problems led to an interviewing period that extended from late April through early November, 1966. Time pressures plus high interviewing costs made it desirable to reduce the number of cover sheets in the field after August. To accomplish this without biasing the sample, 100 active cover sheets representing addresses visited from zero to four times (but without contact as yet with any respondent) were included in the subsampling process. Fifty of these were withdrawn at random, and fifty remained in the field. The withdrawn cover sheets were paired with those that remained active, and the latter were double-weighted. Since 28 of the 50 active cover sheets resulted in completed interviews, 28 cases in the final sample are double-weighted. The remaining 22 cover sheets have also been double-weighted in calculating Refusals, Not at Homes, and other sources of noninterview.

Since only 28 records out of 1013 result from double-weighting, the complications resulting from this process are assumed to be relatively slight and not in need of special consideration for most analysis purposes. A practical problem will arise only if an analytic subgroup turns out to be heavily composed of these "56" records, in which case any peculiarities of the records are magnified. Preliminary comparisons indicate, however, that the weighted records are nearly as variable in background characteristics such as age, education, and income as is the total sample; hence, they are not likely to cluster during the analysis process.

NONINTERVIEWS

The figure of 2590 represents the number of addresses (cover sheets) with which the field staff began. This figure must be set to some extent arbitrarily; for example, it takes account of the eventual resolution of multi-DU cover sheets and it includes addresses discovered through the supplementary field procedure used to correct the city directory listing.

Of these 2590 addresses, 150 proved to be nonresidential buildings (mainly business establishments) and 33 were not located.[2] The latter have been assumed to be due both to errors in the original frame and (usually with evidence) to the recent demolition of areas within Detroit; this assumption appears reasonable in most cases, although to an unknown extent interviewer error may have resulted in noncoverage. The nonlocated addresses constitute less than 1.5 percent (33 out of 2440) of the residential DUs in the sample. We shall assume that both nonresidential and nonlocated addresses are not part of the population of occupied DUs.

Of the 2407 dwelling units located, 68 DUs, or 2.8 percent, were found to be vacant. Even increased slightly to take account of vacancies in the 80 percent and over black tracts, this vacancy rate is unexpectedly on the low side. Approximately double that rate was expected on the basis of Census estimates for North Central SMSAs in 1966 (*Current Housing Reports,* Series H-11, No. 45, August 1966). The reasons for this discrepancy are not clear.

Of the 2339 occupied DUs, 45.7 percent contained no eligible respondent. The main reasons for ineligibility are given below:

		N	Percent of Occupied DUs
1.	Located in tract having 80% or more blacks in 1960	179	7.6
2.	Located outside of 80% black tracts, but classified as black by interviewer	253	10.8
3.	White, but ineligible on basis of age place of birth, or absence of adult males	625	26.7
4.	White, but ineligible for other reasons	11	0.5
Households with eligible respondents		(1271)	(54.3)
		2339	99.9

The total estimate of 18.4 percent black households is very close to the preliminary estimate of 19 percent made on the basis of the 1964–65 DAS results.

The total number of households containing eligible respondents was 1271. The distribution of response and nonresponse DUs was as follows:

	N	Percent
Completed interviews	1013	79.7
Nonresponse		
Refusals	177	13.9
Not at home after 6 calls	70	5.5
Other	11	0.9
	1271	100.0

A response rate of 79.7 percent is similar to that obtained in several recent SRC results, but it is below the rate of 85–90 percent occasionally established in national surveys. It is also slightly below the rate of 83 percent obtained in the 1964–65 DAS. However, it is inappropriate to compare this study with most national surveys because of the severe eligibility criteria in the present case. Consideration of these criteria indicates that in almost every respect the present study was attempting to complete interviews with parts of the population that are more difficult to reach. Thus the response rates for white as against black respondents, for persons within as against outside of large cities, and for working men as against nonworking women all tend to be low. Furthermore, addresses classified as nonresponse include a substantial number of DUs (about one-third) where eligibility information could not be obtained, and therefore probably include a few cases where the DU is actually ineligible rather than a Refusal or a Not at Home. These considerations, together with an apparent general decrease in survey response rates over the past decade, suggest that the present study did about as well or possibly even better than could have been expected on the basis of past experiences.

Completed interviews, Not at Homes, and Refusals have been compared using Census information on median income and education by town or city. Taking the distribution of completed interviews as the standard, Refusals appear to be located more frequently than expected in towns with lower educational and income levels. Not at Homes do not show a consistent pattern relative to Completed interviews. Both of these findings hold regardless of whether the city of Detroit is included in the classification scheme. For this research, then, it appears that lower SES males have been slightly underrepresented in the sample, although this conclusion obviously involves several uncertain assumptions.

NOTES

1. Estimates as of July 1, 1965, by Detroit Metropolitan Area Regional Planning Commission.

2.   These and other figures given below are based on addresses actually visited. As explained above, addresses in tracts with 80 percent or more of the population black were not visited. Some of these addresses would probably have produced non-residential buildings, vacancies, and the like, but all are classified here as black DUs. Hence several figures in this section are underestimated slightly.

APPENDIX C

Detroit Area Study   Interviewer _____

Project 938   Interview No. _____

April, 1966   Time Started _____

I. A STUDY OF ATTITUDES AND RELATIONSHIPS IN THE DETROIT AREA

Q1. Now I would like to ask your views on a few public issues. First of all, consider the question of whether people from other countries should be allowed to enter the United States and work here and become citizens. What is your feeling on this? (PROBE ONCE)

_____

_____

_____

_____

Q2. Here are four different views on the number of people we should let into the United States at the present time. (HAND CARD A) Which of these comes closest to your own opinion? (READ ALTERNATIVES)

    _____(1) We should allow anyone in who wants to come, as long as they are healthy and honest.

    _____(2) We should set a definite limit, but high enough so that *large* numbers can come.

    _____(3) We should set a definite limit, low enough so that *only a small number* can come.

    _____(4) We should close off all immigration, with only a few special exceptions.

Q3. On another question, which of these four statements do you come closest to agreeing with? (HAND CARD B AND READ ALTERNATIVES)

    _____1. Labor unions in this country are doing a fine job.

    _____2. While they do make some mistakes, on the whole labor unions are doing more good than harm.

    _____3. Although we need labor unionism in this country, the way they are run now they do more harm than good.

    _____4. This country would be better off without any labor unions at all.

———▶ (*NOTE:* OBSERVE GESTURES ON QUESTIONS 4–7)

Turning to more local affairs, there are many issues that voters are asked to pass on during an election. Some of these issues are placed right on the ballot and the voter is asked to vote "yes" or "no" on them. Suppose we were having an election right now. Suppose that all these local programs are paid for out of the property tax. Which ones would you favor spending more money on?

Q4.   Do you think we should spend more money on the public schools in this city (town), even if it costs more in property taxes?

| 1. Yes | 2. No |

Q5.   Do you think we should spend more money in this county on facilities to handle juvenile delinquents, even if it costs more in property taxes?

| 1. Yes | 2. No |

Q6.   Do you think we should spend more money on public parks and zoos in this county, even if it costs more in property taxes?

| 1. Yes | 2. No |

Q7.   Do you think we should spend more on the county hospital, which is used in great part by low-income people, even if it costs more in property taxes?

| 1. Yes | 2. No |

Q8.   (RECORD GESTURES TO QUESTIONS 4–7.)

1. None or very slight	2. Primarily hand or fingers	3. One hand and arm	4. Both hands or arms

Q9.   Now I would like to turn to some questions on your activities and interests. On the average, how much time would you say you spend at your job (occupation) per week?

_____ hours per week

Q10.   *Of the remaining time,* some of course is spent sleeping, eating, and so forth. But of the seven days in the week, generally speaking, on how many do you spend at least an hour or two with friends or relatives, *not* counting those persons who live right here with you?

_____ days in a week

Q11.   And so that means you spend what free time you have on the other (FILL IN SEVEN MINUS NUMBER GIVEN TO QUESTION 11) _____ days pretty much on your own or with other persons living here? Is that right?

| 1. Yes | 2. No |

11a. (PROBE TO CLEAR UP DISCREPANCY) _____

Q12.   Here are some questions on things that concern you directly—such as friends. Some people think of themselves as having just one or two *really close* friends. Others see themselves as having a large number of people they are *really close* and *friendly* with. Which of these do you feel comes closer to yourself?

1. One or two	2. Three or four	3. Large number

(IF LARGE NUMBER)

> 12a. How many friends would you say you have of this sort?
>
> _____ No. of friends

Q13. Now would you think of the three men who are your closest friends and whom you see most often. They can be relatives or non-relatives, as you wish. I'd like to ask several questions about each, such as how long you have known them, so for convenience could you give me just their first names?

    First   _____

    Second _____

    Third   _____

Q14. Are any of the men you have named relatives of yours? (IF YES, DETER-MINE EXACT RELATIONSHIP AND ENTER IN 14a. IF *BROTHER* OR IF *BROTHER-IN-LAW ON WIFE'S SIDE,* INDICATE THERE ARE LATER QUESTIONS ABOUT BROTHERS/BROTHERS-IN-LAW, AND FOR NOW YOU WOULD LIKE NAME(S) OF ADDITIONAL FRIENDS. *ENTER FINAL THREE FRIENDS* IN 14b *IN ORDER MENTIONED* AND *ALSO ON CARD F FOR R TO HOLD.*)

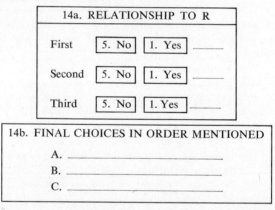

14a. RELATIONSHIP TO R		
First	5. No 1. Yes _____
Second	5. No 1. Yes _____
Third	5. No 1. Yes _____

14b. FINAL CHOICES IN ORDER MENTIONED
A. _____
B. _____
C. _____

Q15. For each of these three men, would you say he is a very close personal friend, or a good friend, or more an acquaintance? Take _____ first.

    A. 1. Very close personal   2. Good friend   3. Acquaintance

    B. 1. Very close personal   2. Good friend   3. Acquaintance

    C. 1. Very close personal   2. Good friend   3. Acquaintance

Q16. About how long have you known _____? (REPEAT FOR EACH MAN LISTED ON CARD F [Question 14b.])

A. _____ Years
B. _____ Years
C. _____ Years

Q17. Could you tell me how old _____ is? (REPEAT FOR EACH MAN, ASK R TO GUESS IF HE DOESN'T KNOW AN EXACT AGE.)

A. _____ Years
B. _____ Years
C. _____ Years

Q18. What is the main job of each man? Take _____ first. (REPEAT FOR EACH MAN. IF RETIRED, INDICATE AND OBTAIN LAST JOB. *PROBE* TO GET SPECIFIC CODABLE OCCUPATIONS, E.G., LATHE OPERATOR, BANK TELLER, GARAGE MECHANIC, *AND* FOR SELF-EMPLOYMENT.)

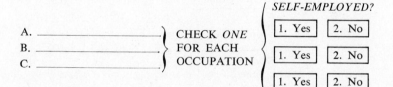

SELF-EMPLOYED?

A. _____) CHECK *ONE*   1. Yes   2. No
B. _____ } FOR EACH   1. Yes   2. No
C. _____) OCCUPATION   1. Yes   2. No

Q19. How many years of school did _____ finish? (REPEAT FOR EACH MAN)

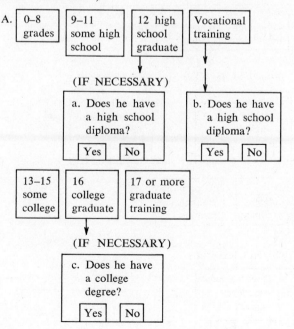

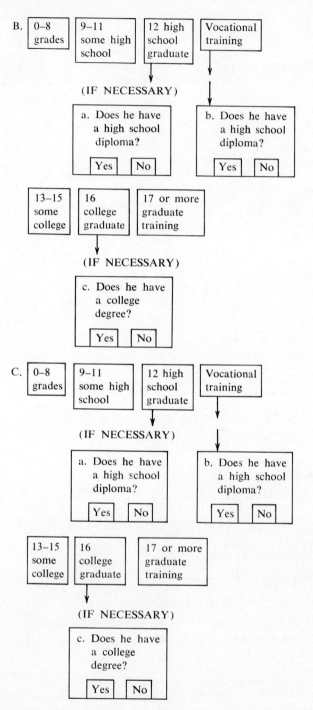

Q20. Do you know what _____'s religious preference is? (REPEAT FOR EACH OF THREE MEN. WHERE *"PROTESTANT,"* OBTAIN DENOMINATION. ENCOURAGE R TO "GUESS" IF NECESSARY: "Well, what is your guess?")

    A. _____

    B. _____

    C. _____

Q21. Do you happen to know the original nationality of _____? (REPEAT FOR EACH MAN. ENCOURAGE R TO "GUESS" IF NECESSARY. IF "AMERICAN," PROBE FOR "original nationality besides American.")

    A. _____

    B. _____

    C. _____

Q22. Is _____ generally a Republican or generally a Democrat? (REPEAT FOR EACH MAN. ENCOURAGE R TO "GUESS" IF NECESSARY.)

    A. | 1. Republican | 2. Democrat | 3. Independent |

    B. | 1. Republican | 2. Democrat | 3. Independent |

    C. | 1. Republican | 2. Democrat | 3. Independent |

FOR Q'S 20, 21, & 22: IF R RESISTS AT ALL, INDICATE REASON FOR EACH QUESTION *BUT* PERSIST.

X–20 _____

_____

_____

X–21 _____

_____

_____

X–22 _____

_____

_____

_____

Q23. Do any of the men live in this neighborhood—say, within 10 minutes of here —or do they live somewhere else in the Detroit area, or outside of the area? (IF ASKED TO CLARIFY "10 MINUTES," INDICATE THAT ANY MEANS OF TRANSPORTATION IS ACCEPTABLE. IF ASKED, THE "DETROIT AREA" INCLUDES ANY PLACE IN WAYNE, OAKLAND, OR MACOMB COUNTIES.)

    A. | 1. Neighborhood | 2. Detroit Area | 3. Outside Area |

    B. | 1. Neighborhood | 2. Detroit Area | 3. Outside Area |

    C. | 1. Neighborhood | 2. Detroit Area | 3. Outside Area |

Q24. Do you often get together with all three of your best friends at the same time?

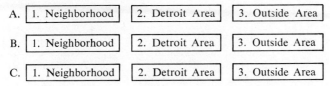

    | 1. Yes | 2. No |

(IF NO)

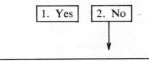

24a. Do you often get together with two of them at the same time?

    | 1. Yes | 2. No |

Q25. Of your three best friends, how many of them are good friends with one another?

| 1. All three of them | 2. Two of them | 3. None of them |

25a. CIRCLE WHICH TWO: A B C

Q26. Where do you most often meet with each of them? At one of your homes or somewhere else? Take _____ first.

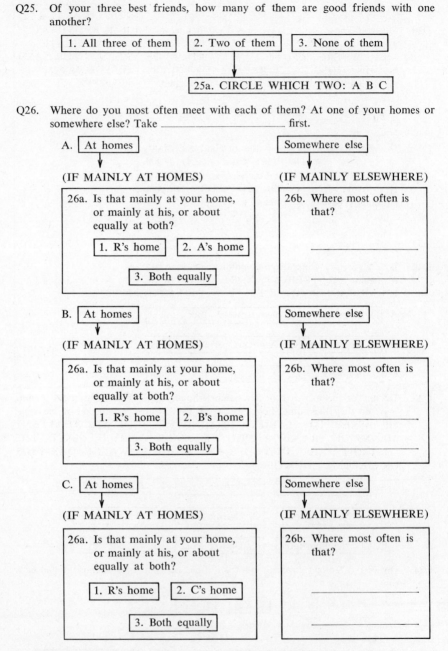

A. At homes   Somewhere else

(IF MAINLY AT HOMES)   (IF MAINLY ELSEWHERE)

26a. Is that mainly at your home, or mainly at his, or about equally at both?

| 1. R's home | 2. A's home |

3. Both equally

26b. Where most often is that?

_____

_____

B. At homes   Somewhere else

(IF MAINLY AT HOMES)   (IF MAINLY ELSEWHERE)

26a. Is that mainly at your home, or mainly at his, or about equally at both?

| 1. R's home | 2. B's home |

3. Both equally

26b. Where most often is that?

_____

_____

C. At homes   Somewhere else

(IF MAINLY AT HOMES)   (IF MAINLY ELSEWHERE)

26a. Is that mainly at your home, or mainly at his, or about equally at both?

| 1. R's home | 2. C's home |

3. Both equally

26b. Where most often is that?

_____

_____

Q27. Do you see _____ regularly where you work—that is, at least once or twice a week?

A. 1. Yes   2. No

B. 1. Yes   2. No

C. 1. Yes   2. No

Q28. All in all, how often do you usually get together with _____
(*outside of work*)? (CODE FOR EACH MAN AS FOLLOWS):

1	2	3	4	5	6
More than once a week	Once a week	Two or 3 times a month	Once a month	Several times a year	Rarely

A. _____
B. _____
C. _____

(IF R MARRIED)

Q29. When you and one or more of your best friends get together, would you say
that your wives are usually along, sometimes along, or rarely along?

1. Usually   2. Sometimes   3. Rarely   4. Never

Q30. Now I'd like to ask you several of the same questions about two of your
relatives. First, do you have any brothers?

1. Yes   2. No →(IF NO, OMIT *PART A ONLY* OF QUESTIONS
32–36)

Q30a. IF MORE THAN ONE BROTHER, ASK R TO CONSIDER
THE ONE "you feel closest to." IF R CANNOT DECIDE ON
ONE, TAKE BROTHER CLOSEST TO R IN AGE FOR
QUESTIONS 32A to 36A. NOTE HERE BASIS OF SELECTION:

1. Feels closest   2. Closest in age

Q31. Do you have any brothers-in-law on your wife's side? (IF NECESSARY
DEFINE AS: "wife's brothers" AND "wife's sisters' husbands.")

1. Yes   2. No →(IF NO, OMIT *PART B ONLY* OF QUESTIONS
Q32–36.)

(IF MORE THAN ONE BROTHER-IN-LAW, ASK R TO CONSIDER
THE ONE "you feel closest to." IF R CANNOT DECIDE ON ONE, TAKE
BROTHER-IN-LAW CLOSEST TO R IN AGE FOR 31b.)

(IF YES TO QUESTION 31)   NOT TO BE READ

Q31a. Is he your wife's brother?	Q31b. NOTE SELECTION BASIS:
1. Yes 2. No, he is wife's sister's husband	1. Feels closest
	2. Closest in age

Q32. What is your *(BROTHER'S)(BROTHER-IN-LAW'S)* main job at the present time? (IF RETIRED, INDICATE AND OBTAIN LAST JOB. BE SPECIFIC, E. G., BANK TELLER, GARAGE MECHANIC)

SELF-EMPLOYED?

A. BROTHER: _____

_____ } CHECK *ONE*
_____ } FOR EACH
B. BROTHER-IN-LAW: __ } OCCUPATION

| 1. Yes | 2. No |

| 1. Yes | 2. No |

Q33. How many years of school did your *(BROTHER)(BROTHER-IN-LAW)* finish?

A. BROTHER:

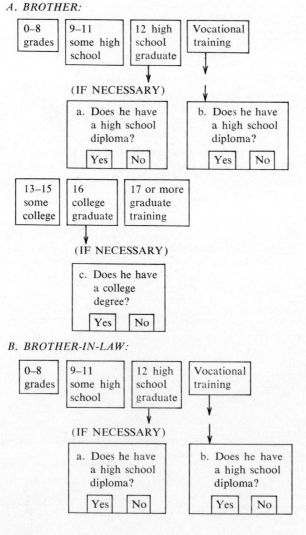

B. BROTHER-IN-LAW:

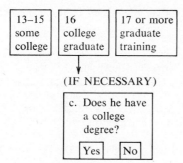

(IF NECESSARY)

c. Does he have
   a college
   degree?

| Yes | No |

Q34. Is your (BROTHER)(BROTHER-IN-LAW) generally a Republican or generally a Democrat?

A. BROTHER:

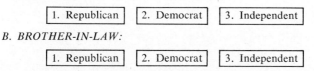

| 1. Republican | 2. Democrat | 3. Independent |

B. BROTHER-IN-LAW:

| 1. Republican | 2. Democrat | 3. Independent |

Q35. Does your (BROTHER)(BROTHER-IN-LAW) live in this neighborhood, in the area, or outside the Detroit area?

A. BROTHER:

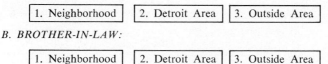

| 1. Neighborhood | 2. Detroit Area | 3. Outside Area |

B. BROTHER-IN-LAW:

| 1. Neighborhood | 2. Detroit Area | 3. Outside Area |

Q36. How often do you usually get together with your (BROTHER)(BROTHER-IN-LAW)?

A. BROTHER:

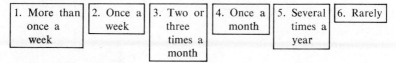

| 1. More than once a week | 2. Once a week | 3. Two or three times a month | 4. Once a month | 5. Several times a year | 6. Rarely |

B. BROTHER-IN-LAW:

| 1. More than once a week | 2. Once a week | 3. Two or three times a month | 4. Once a month | 5. Several times a year | 6. Rarely |

Q37. Now, I have two questions about neighbors. First of all, which of the following would best describe the relations you have with your several nearest neighbors? (HAND CARD C AND READ ALTERNATIVES)

_____(1) Often visit one another in each other's homes.

_____(2) Frequent casual chatting in the yard or if you happen to run into each other on the street.

_____(3) Occasional casual chatting in the yard or if you happen to run into each other on the street.

_____(4) Hardly know my neighbors.

Q38. Now let's consider a specific neighbor—the neighbor nearest to your house. (INTERVIEWER: HELP R DETERMINE MALE NEIGHBOR IN NEAREST DWELLING UNIT WITH SEPARATE *FRONT* ENTRANCE. IF NO CHOICE ON BASIS OF DISTANCE CAN BE MADE, PICK NEIGHBOR LIVING TO THE *RIGHT* OF R'S HOUSE (APARTMENT) AS YOU ENTER. IF CHOOSING THE DWELLING UNIT ON RIGHT IS *NOT* APPROPRIATE, INDICATE SITUATION AND CHOOSE AMONG EQUALLY CLOSE NEIGHBORS BY CHANCE METHOD.)

What is his main job at the present time? (BE SPECIFIC, *e.g.,* USED CAR SALESMAN, HIGH SCHOOL TEACHER. DESCRIBE *AND* CHECK)

1. Self-employed	2. Not self-employed

Q39. Now here is a list of clubs and organizations that many people belong to. Please look at this list (SHOW CARD D), and tell me which of these kinds of organizations you belong to, if any. Are there any others you're in that are not on this list? (CHECK AT *LEFT* WHERE APPROPRIATE, THEN ASK 40 and 41 FOR *EACH* ORGANIZATION R MENTIONED.)

Q40. Would you say that you are very involved or not very involved in _____? (CHECK RESPONSE IN "INVOLVEMENT" COLUMN BELOW.)

Q41 Do you usually meet any of the three friends you mentioned in meetings of _____? (CHECK *ALL* RESPONSES IN "FRIEND MEMBERSHIPS" COLUMN BELOW.)

	Q40. INVOLVE-MENT		Q41. FRIEND MEMBERSHIPS			
a.___Church-Connected Groups (but not the church itself)	1. Very	2. Not	A	B	C	None
b.___Labor Unions	1. Very	2. Not	A	B	C	None
c.___Veteran's Organizations	1. Very	2. Not	A	B	C	None
d.___Fraternal Organizations or Lodges	1. Very	2. Not	A	B	C	None
e.___Business or Civic Groups	1. Very	2. Not	A	B	C	None
f.___Parent-Teachers Associations	1. Very	2. Not	A	B	C	None
g.___Community Centers	1. Very	2. Not	A	B	C	None
h.___Organizations of People of the Same Nationality	1. Very	2. Not	A	B	C	None
i.___Sport Teams	1. Very	2. Not	A	B	C	None

j.___Country Clubs | 1. Very | 2. Not | | A | B | C | None |

k.___Youth Groups (Scout Leaders etc.) | 1. Very | 2. Not | | A | B | C | None |

l.___Professional Groups | 1. Very | 2. Not | | A | B | C | None |

m.___Political Clubs or Organizations | 1. Very | 2. Not | | A | B | C | None |

n.___Neighborhood Improvement Associations | 1. Very | 2. Not | | A | B | C | None |

o.___Charity or Welfare Organizations | 1. Very | 2. Not | | A | B | C | None |

p.___Other (Specify)_____ | 1. Very | 2. Not | | A | B | C | None |

q.___Other (Specify)_____ | 1. Very | 2. Not | | A | B | C | None |

_____NONE (IF NONE, CONTINUE WITH QUESTION 42.)

Q42.   Here is a different kind of question. Every man would like his son to be successful, but people differ in what they mean by success. What does being successful mean to you? (ONE PROBE REQUIRED)

_____

_____

_____

_____

Q43.   What is the *least* amount of schooling that you think a young man needs these days to get along well in the world?

| 0–8 grades | 9–11 some high school | 12 high school graduate | Vocational training: (Specify) |

| 13–15 some college | 16 college graduate | 17 or more graduate training |

Q44.   And what is the *least* amount of schooling that you think a girl needs these days to get along well in the world?

| 0–8 grades | 9–11 some high school | 12 high school graduate | Vocational training: (Specify) |

| 13–15 some college | 16 college graduate | 17 or more graduate training |

Q45. Suppose a boy is able to go to college. What do you think is the main thing he should get out of his education in college? (ONE PROBE REQUIRED; MORE, IF ANSWER VAGUE [*e.g.*, "good education"].)

_____

_____

_____

_____

Q46. Now I would like to turn again to your opinions on some more general issues. Would you look at this card please (HAND CARD E) and tell me which of the two statements comes closer to your own opinion? (READ ALTERNATIVES 1 AND 2, BUT NOT 3.)

____1. The most important job for the government is to make certain every person has a decent steady job and standard of living.

____2. The most important job for the government is to make certain that there are good opportunities for each person to get ahead on his own.

____3. (R BELIEVES GOVERNMENT SHOULD STAY OUT OF THIS AREA ALTOGETHER.)

(*NOTE:* OBSERVE GESTURES FOR QUESTION 47.)

Q47. (ASK ONLY ONE SET [C *OR* K] NOW. THE OTHER SET IS ASKED LATER. ASK *HERE* THE SET THAT HAS A *RED CHECK* ABOVE IT. FOR BOTH C AND K SETS, IF ASKED BY R, THE MEN ARE ASSUMED TO BE AMERICAN CITIZENS, BUT NOTHING MORE IS KNOWN ABOUT THEM.)

Fine, now these next questions are a little different.

C-SET ☐

K-SET ☐

k-0. Suppose there is a man who is a Ku Klux Klansman. How would you describe the Ku Klux Klan? (PROBE TO OBTAIN R'S DEFINITION.)

_____

_____

(ASK ALL FIVE QUESTIONS IF R CAN GIVE ANY DEFINITION, WHETHER RIGHT OR NOT.)

c-1. Suppose there is a man who admits he is a Communist. Suppose this admitted Communist wants to make a speech in your community. Should he be allowed to speak, or not?

| 1. Yes | 2. No |

k-1. Suppose this admitted Klansman wants to make a speech in your community. Should he be allowed to speak, or not?

| 1. Yes | 2. No |

c-2. Should an admitted Communist be put in jail?

| 1. Yes | 2. No | 3. Deport |

k-2. Should an admitted Klansman be put in jail?

| 1. Yes | 2. No |

c-3. Suppose he is a teacher in a high school. Should he be fired or not?

| 1. Yes | 2. No |

c-4. Suppose he is a clerk in a store. Should he be fired or not.

| 1. Yes | 2. No |

c-5. Now I would like you to think of another person. A man who has been questioned by a Congressional Committee about his suspected Communist sympathies, but who swears under oath he has never been a Communist. Suppose he is a teacher in a high school. Should he be fired, or not?

| 1. Yes | 2. No |

k-3. Suppose he is a teacher in a high school. Should he be fired or not?

| 1. Yes | 2. No |

k-4. Suppose he is a clerk in a store. Should he be fired or not?

| 1. Yes | 2. No |

k-5. Now I would like you to think of another person. A man who has been questioned by a Congressional Committee about his suspected Klan sympathies, but who swears under oath he has never been a Klansman. Suppose he is a teacher in a high school. Should he be fired or not?

| 1. Yes | 2. No |

Q48.   RECORD GESTURES FOR QUESTION 47.

| 1. None or very slight | 2. Primarily hand or fingers | 3. One hand and arm | 4. Both hands or arms |

S-1 to S-27.   Thank you. This next section goes better if you fill it out yourself. Here are some statements that some people agree with and others disagree with. Please mark each one according to whether you agree or disagree, and how strongly. (EXPLAIN BY USING FIRST ONE AS EXAMPLE, IF NECESSARY)

Respondent's living room

INTERVIEWER FILL OUT INFORMATION ON RESPONDENT'S LIVING ROOM WHILE RESPONDENT FILLS OUT S-SERIES. IF NO OPPORTUNITY TO OBSERVE LIVING ROOM OR UNABLE TO COMPLETE HH SERIES FOR SOME OTHER REASON, EXPLAIN HERE: _____

WHERE CATEGORIZATION DIFFICULT, DESCRIBE IN MARGIN FOR LATER CODING.

Check One Only for Questions HH-1 to HH-11

HH-1   *Floor:* | 1. Highly polished wood | 2. Unpolished wood |

| 3. Covered, can't tell | 4. Other _____ |

HH-2   *Carpet:* | 1. Wall-to-wall carpeting | 2. Standard size rug |

| 3. Scatter rugs | 4. Other _____ |

HH-3   *Main carpet design:* | 1. No carpet | | 2. Solid color/tweed |

| 3. Floral | | 4. Braided |

| 5. Oriental | | 6. Other _____ |

HH-4   *Walls:* | 1. Neutral or pastel paper or paint | | 2. Bright color paper or paint |

| 3. Ornate paper | | 4. Other _____ |

HH-5   *Furniture:* | 1. Modern functional | | 2. Bulky old-fashioned, stuffed |

| 3. Traditional American | | 4. Mixture, no consistent style |

| 5. Other _____ |

HH-6   *Books:* | 1. Many in shelves | | 2. A few around | | 3. None |

HH-7   *Number of complete window casements:* _____

HH-8   *Curtains and Drapes:*

| *Translucent* | *Opaque* |

| 1. Lacy, ruffled | | 4. Floral pattern | | 5. Geometric design |

| 2. Straight hanging | | 6. Light, neutral solid color |

| 3. Other _____ | | 7. Dark solid color |

| 8. Other _____ |

HH-9   *General space factor* (Density, not size):

| 1. Rather bare | | 2. Below average | | 3. Average | | 4. Above average |

| 5. Densely furnished |

HH-10 *General Neatness:*

| 1. Exceptionally orderly, nothing out of place | | 2. Average neatness and order | | 3. Things in disarray |

HH-11 *General condition of living room and furniture:*

| 1. Excellent | | 2. Above average | | 3. Average | | 4. Below average |

| 5. Poor |

FOR HH-12 CHECK EACH ITEM THAT IS PRESENT IN THE LIVING ROOM

HH-12 *Miscellaneous items:*

_____a. Fireplace

_____b. Piano

_____c. Television

_____d. Hi-Fi Set

_____e. Candle holder of any type

_____f. Religious objects

_____g. Bible

_____h. Vases

_____i. Enlarged photographs

_____j. Knick Knacks

_____k. Encyclopedia Set

_____l. Clock (type: _____)

_____m. Picture window over 4 ft. wide

_____n. Wall mirror(s)

_____o. Outdoor nature scene painting(s)

_____p. Painting(s): people as subject

_____q. Abstract painting(s)

_____r. Religious painting(s)

_____s. Still life(s) (fruit, flowers)

_____t. Cut flowers

_____u. Artificial flowers

_____v. Small potted plants on tables or sills

_____w. Large potted plants on floor

_____x. Trophies, plaques, or similar objects

_____y. Antimacassars (Doilies covering furniture)

_____z. Other notable object(s) _____

_____aa. Other notable object(s) _____

RETURN TO INTERVIEW

Q49. Now I'd like to ask you some more questions about your own interests and ideas. Would you please look at this card, (HAND CARD G AND READ ALTERNATIVES) and tell me which thing on this list you would most prefer in a job. _____ (FIRST CHOICE)

    1. High income
    2. No danger of being fired
    3. Short working hours, lots of free time
    4. Chances for improvement
    5. The work is important and gives a feeling of accomplishment

Q50. Which comes next? _____

Q51. Which is third most important? _____

Q52. Which is *least* important? _____

Q53. Some people tell us that they couldn't really be happy unless they are working at some job. But others say that they would be a lot happier if they didn't have to work and could take life easy. How do you feel about this?

| 1. Happy working | 2. Happy not working |

Q54. Why is that? _____

_____

_____

Q55. Suppose you *did* have a lot of free time. What would you most like to do with it? (ONE PROBE REQUIRED)

_____

_____

Q56. Now suppose you were starting out in life and had to choose a job (occupation) for the first time. Would you look at this list please (HAND CARD

H) and tell me whether you would be *satisfied* or *dissatisfied* about the prospect (idea) of entering each of these lines of work? (READ EACH.)

	1. Satisfied	2. Dissatisfied
a. Clerk in a store		
b. Carpenter		
c. Lawyer		
d. Bookkeeper		
e. Construction laborer		
f. Public school teacher		
g. Truck driver		
h. Garage mechanic		

Q57. Now, picture two men: one who owns his own small business, and another who works in a large office. The office worker earns a steady income and works eight hours a day. Then he can forget his work and enjoy his leisure time. The other man runs his small business for much longer hours every day and so cannot take time out to enjoy life like the office worker. The small businessman can't be certain of his income, but he does have the chance to earn more than the office worker. If you had to choose, which of these kinds of work would you prefer?

1. Office worker	2. Small businessman

Q58. Suppose the salaries were the *same* for a skilled mechanic and a clerical worker. Which would you prefer to be, assuming you had the background to do either one?

1. Mechanic	2. Clerical

Q59. Now, here's a list of several problems that might come up in a person's life. (PRESENT CARD I) Some people would ordinarily want to discuss some of these with their friends; others would ordinarily prefer not to. In each, *if this were* a problem for you, would you ordinarily discuss it with your friends, or would you ordinarily rather not? What about (a), "What kind of new car to buy?". . . . And what about (b)?. . . . (c)?. . . . (d)?. . . . (e)?. . . . (f)? (*USE LETTERS FOR (b) to (f), DO NOT READ PROBLEMS ALOUD* UNLESS R CANNOT READ. *WIFE* IS *NOT* COUNTED AS FRIEND—IF WIFE GIVEN, PROBE FOR FRIENDS.)

a.	What kind of new car to buy.	1. Discuss	2. Not discuss
b.	Who to vote for President.	1. Discuss	2. Not discuss
c.	Troubles between you and your wife.	1. Discuss	2. Not discuss
d.	Difficulties at work with your boss.	1. Discuss	2. Not discuss
e.	A serious personal medical problem.	1. Discuss	2. Not discuss

f.   Whether to change to a better but risky, new job.

Q60. Going back to some general opinion questions, in strikes and disputes between working people and employers, do you usually side with the workers or with the employers?

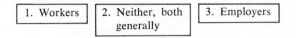

——▶ (*NOTE:* OBSERVE GESTURES FOR QUESTION 61)

Q61. These next several opinion questions are similar to some asked before, but this time they are about the (*Ku Klux Klan/Communists*). Please try to answer this set on their own merits, without regard to your earlier answers. (ASK HERE WHICHEVER SET [C OR K] *NOT* ASKED EARLIER IN QUESTION 47. FOLLOW *RED CHECK*.)

C-SET [   ]   *K-SET* [   ]

    k-0. Suppose there is a man who is a Ku Klux Klansman. How would you describe the Ku Klux Klan? (PROBE TO OBTAIN DEFINITION.)

    ————————————

    ————————————

    ————————————

    (ASK ALL FIVE QUESTIONS IF R CAN GIVE ANY DEFINITION, WHETHER RIGHT OR NOT.)

c-1. Suppose there is a man who admits he is a Communist. Suppose this admitted Communist wants to make a speech in your community. Should he be allowed to speak, or not?

| 1. Yes | 2. No |

k-1. Suppose this admitted Klansman wants to make a speech in your community. Should he be allowed to speak, or not?

| 1. Yes | 2. No |

c-2. Should an admitted Communist be put in jail?

| 1. Yes | 2. No | 3. Deport |

k-2. Should an admitted Klansman be put in jail?

| 1. Yes | 2. No |

c-3. Suppose he is a teacher in a high school. Should he be fired, or not?

| 1. Yes | 2. No |

k-3. Suppose he is a teacher in a high school. Should he be fired, or not?

| 1. Yes | 2. No |

c-4. Suppose he is a clerk in a store. Should he be fired, or not?

| 1. Yes | 2. No |

k-4. Suppose he is a clerk in a store. Should he be fired, or not?

| 1. Yes | 2. No |

c-5. Now I would like you to think of another person. A man who has been questioned by a Congressional Committee about his suspected Communist sympathies, but who swears under oath he has never been a Communist. Suppose he is a teacher in a high school. Should he be fired, or not?

| 1. Yes | 2. No |

k-5. Now I would like you to think of another person. A man who has been questioned by a Congressional Committee about his suspected Klan sympathies, but who swears under oath he has never been a Klansman. Suppose he is a teacher in a high school. Should he be fired, or not?

| 1. Yes | 2. No |

Q62.   RECORD GESTURES FOR QUESTIONS 61.

| 1. None or very slight | 2. Primarily hand or fingers | 3. One hand and arm | 4. Both hands or arms |

Q63.   Now let's turn to some local issues. If you had to choose, which would you prefer—a city run by politicians who maintained a good school system but made money for themselves by doing it, *or* a city run by honest officials who maintained a school system that wasn't quite so good?

| 1. Good schools, but dishonest | 2. Not so good schools, but honest |

Q64.   This county has been faced with many problems lately. In looking for men to help solve these problems, do you think we should get the ablest man, even if he comes from outside the county and knows nothing about them, *or* do you think we should try instead to find a good local man?

| 1. Ablest | 2. Local man |

Q65.   In this city, do you think your city councilman ought to vote to do what's best for your neighborhood or district, *or* do what's best for the city as a whole even if it doesn't really help your neighborhood or district?

| 1. Local neighborhood | 2. City as a whole |

Q66.   Here are several questions about what is sometimes called "racial imbalance." A school is said to be racially imbalanced when more than one half of the children are Negro. Would you tell me whether you agree or disagree with each of the following statements: Here is the first:

"Racial imbalance in schools hurts the education of children."

| 1. Agree | 2. Disagree |

Q67.   Here is the second:

"Children should always go to school in their own neighborhood, no matter what." Do you agree or disagree with this?

| 1. Agree | 2. Disagree |

Q68.   "Racial imbalance does exist in the public schools of the Detroit area."

| 1. Agree | 2. Disagree |

Q69. "Negro children should be bussed to white schools to bring about racial balance." Do you agree or disagree?

| 1. Agree | 2. Disagree |

Q70. See Similarity Subtest of the Wechsler Adult Intelligence Scale (Wechsler 1955:39).

→ (*NOTE:* OBSERVE GESTURES FOR QUESTIONS 71–81)

Q71. Fine. Now this final section has questions about the background of people in Michigan. Although they ask about you, keep in mind that they are to be used in a statistical form only, much like the U.S. Census.

How long have you lived in the Detroit area? (WAYNE, OAKLAND, AND MACOMB COUNTIES) _____ YEARS.

Q72. Was the place in which you mainly grew up a large city of over 50,000 population; the suburb of such a large city; a small city or town; or a farm?

| 1. City over 50,000 | 2. Suburbs of 50,000 city | 3. Small town | 4. Farm |

Q73. What state was that in? _____

Q74. About how long have you lived in this neighborhood—that is, within 10 minutes of here?

_____ YEARS

Q75. Do you own this home, are you buying it, or are you renting?

| 1. Owns | 2. Buying | 3. Renting |

Q76. There's quite a bit of talk these days about social class. If you were asked to use one of these four names for your social class, which would you say you belong in: middle class, lower class, working class, or upper class?

| 1. Middle class | 2. Lower class | 3. Working class | 4. Upper class |

(DO NOT ASK)

| 5. There are no classes |

SKIP TO Q79

Q77. Would you say you are in the average part of the _____ (*USE RESPONSE TO 76*) or in the upper part?

| 1. Average | 2. Upper |

Q78. Which kind of social club or informal social group, like a bowling team or bridge club, would you rather belong to: one whose members are all of your own social class or one whose members are persons of various classes?

| 1. Same class as own | 2. Various classes |

Q79. What do you think of the words "social class" as referring to?
(ONE PROBE REQUIRED)

_____

_____

_____

Q80. Generally speaking, do you think of yourself as a Republican or a Democrat?

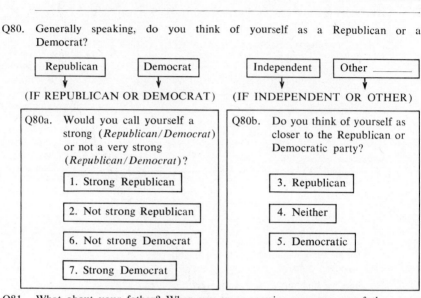

| Republican | Democrat | | Independent | Other _____ |

(IF REPUBLICAN OR DEMOCRAT)   (IF INDEPENDENT OR OTHER)

Q80a. Would you call yourself a strong (*Republican/Democrat*) or not a very strong (*Republican/Democrat*)?

1. Strong Republican

2. Not strong Republican

6. Not strong Democrat

7. Strong Democrat

Q80b. Do you think of yourself as closer to the Republican or Democratic party?

3. Republican

4. Neither

5. Democratic

Q81. What about your father? When you were growing up, was your father more a Republican or more a Democrat?

| 1. Republican | 2. Independent | 3. Democrat | 4. Other |

Q82. (RECORD GESTURES FOR QUESTIONS 71–81)

| 1. None or very slight | 2. Primarily hand or fingers | 3. One hand and arm | 4. Both hands or arms |

Q83. One of the things we are interested in is the kind of work people in Detroit do. What is your main job at the present time?

(*IF RETIRED OR UNEMPLOYED INDICATE CLEARLY, THEN USE* "last main job." IF 2 JOBS, DETERMINE WHICH IS MAIN ONE AND INDICATE.

PROBE CAREFULLY FOR SPECIFIC JOB, e.g., LATHE OPERATOR, BANK TELLER, ETC.)

_____

_____

_____

Q84. What kind of business is (was) that in? (*e.g., STEELMILL, BANK, ETC.*)

_____

_____

Q85. Do you work for yourself or for someone else?

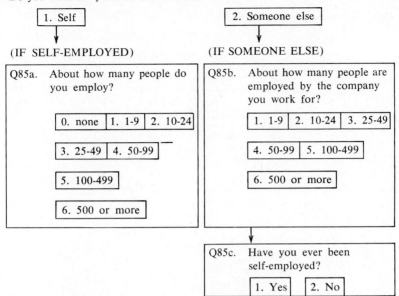

1. Self

(IF SELF-EMPLOYED)

Q85a. About how many people do you employ?

0. none	1. 1-9	2. 10-24

3. 25-49	4. 50-99

5. 100-499

6. 500 or more

2. Someone else

(IF SOMEONE ELSE)

Q85b. About how many people are employed by the company you work for?

1. 1-9	2. 10-24	3. 25-49

4. 50-99	5. 100-499

6. 500 or more

Q85c. Have you ever been self-employed?

1. Yes	2. No

Q86. What was your first full-time job after you finished school? (IF MILITARY SERVICE, ASK WHAT FIRST JOB AFTER THAT. PROBE FOR UN-CLEAR JOB.)

_____

Q87. How many years of school did you complete?

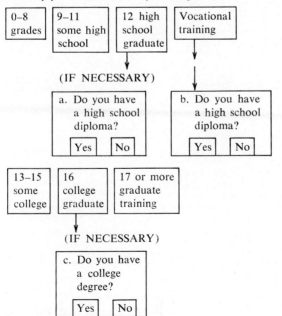

0–8 grades	9–11 some high school	12 high school graduate	Vocational training

(IF NECESSARY)

a. Do you have a high school diploma?

Yes	No

b. Do you have a high school diploma?

Yes	No

13–15 some college	16 college graduate	17 or more graduate training

(IF NECESSARY)

c. Do you have a college degree?

Yes	No

283

Q88. (*IF MARRIED*)
How many years of school did your wife complete?

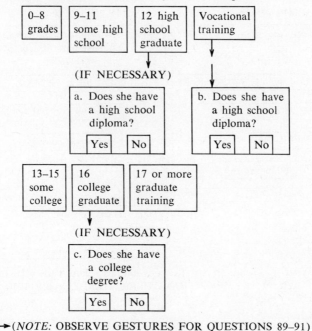

| 0–8 grades | 9–11 some high school | 12 high school graduate | Vocational training |

(IF NECESSARY)

a. Does she have a high school diploma?
Yes   No

b. Does she have a high school diploma?
Yes   No

| 13–15 some college | 16 college graduate | 17 or more graduate training |

(IF NECESSARY)

c. Does she have a college degree?
Yes   No

→(*NOTE:* OBSERVE GESTURES FOR QUESTIONS 89–91)

Q89. Do you have a religious preference? That is, are you either Protestant, Roman Catholic, Jewish or something else?

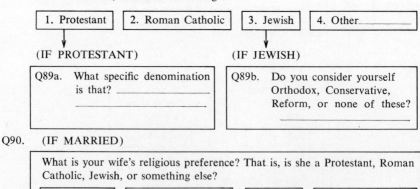

1. Protestant   2. Roman Catholic   3. Jewish   4. Other_____

(IF PROTESTANT)   (IF JEWISH)

Q89a. What specific denomination is that? _____

Q89b. Do you consider yourself Orthodox, Conservative, Reform, or none of these?

Q90. (IF MARRIED)

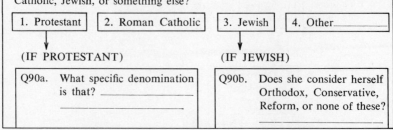

What is your wife's religious preference? That is, is she a Protestant, Roman Catholic, Jewish, or something else?

1. Protestant   2. Roman Catholic   3. Jewish   4. Other_____

(IF PROTESTANT)   (IF JEWISH)

Q90a. What specific denomination is that? _____

Q90b. Does she consider herself Orthodox, Conservative, Reform, or none of these?

Q91.   What nationality background do you think of yourself as having—that is, besides being American (Canadian)? (ACCEPT CLEAR ASSERTION OF "ONLY AMERICAN NATIONALITY" *WITHOUT* PROBE. ALWAYS RECORD EXACT ANSWER.)

_____

_____

_____

Q92.   (RECORD GESTURES FOR QUESTIONS 89–91)

1. None or very slight	2. Primarily hand or fingers	3. One hand and arm	4. Both hands or arms

Q93. to Q98.

One other thing we would like to know something about is the national and religious background of the *parents* of Michigan residents. You may not be able to answer all these questions, but please try. (HAND CARD J) Here is a "family tree." Can you tell me in what country each of these persons was born, and what his religion was, so far as you know? Also in the case of the men, their main *occupations*. Let's take them one at a time.

   a. (IF ANY OF FOLLOWING COUNTRIES ARE GIVEN—*Austria, Czechoslovakia, Hungary, Yugoslavia, or Switzerland*—ASK LANGUAGE SPOKEN BY THAT INDIVIDUAL.)
   (IF UNUSUAL COUNTRY GIVEN, *e.g.*, China, OBTAIN CIRCUMSTANCE.)
   b. (OBTAIN DENOMINATION FOR PROTESTANTS.)
   c. (PROBE OCCUPATIONS CAREFULLY.)
   (RECORD ANSWERS TO Q93–98 ON NEXT PAGE)

	a. BORN IN (and language)	b. RELIGION (and Denomination)	c. OCCUPATION (PROBE)
Q93. R's father			R's father
Q94. R's father's father			
Q95. R's father's mother			R's father's father
Q96. R's mother			
Q97. R's mother's father			R's mother's father
Q98. R's mother's mother			

Q99.   One other question about your father only. How many years of school did he finish?

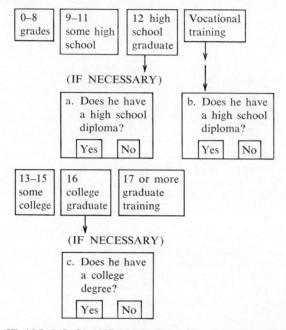

Q100. (IF ALL R'S GRANDPARENTS BORN IN USA OR CANADA)

> Do you know where your earlier ancestors lived before coming to this country (Canada)?

(IF MARRIED, WIDOWED, SEPARATED, OR DIVORCED)

Q101. Now here is a "family tree" for your wife. (HAND CARD K) Would you
to   do the same thing for her parents and grandparents, so far as you can?
Q106. In what country was each born, what was his or her religion, and in the
        case of the men their occupations? (PROBE OCCUPATION, LAN-
        GUAGE WHERE AMBIGUOUS, AND DENOMINATION FOR
        PROTESTANTS.)

	a. BORN IN (and language)	b. RELIGION (and denomination)	c. OCCUPATION (PROBE)
Q101. Wife's father			Wife's father
Q102. Wife's father's father			
Q103. Wife's father's mother			Wife's father's father
Q104. Wife's mother			
Q105. Wife's mother's father			Wife's mother's father
Q106. Wife's mother's mother			

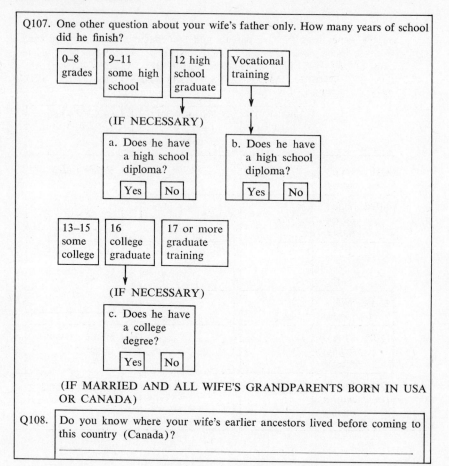

Q107. One other question about your wife's father only. How many years of school did he finish?

| 0–8 grades | 9–11 some high school | 12 high school graduate | Vocational training |

(IF NECESSARY)

a. Does he have a high school diploma?   Yes   No

b. Does he have a high school diploma?   Yes   No

| 13–15 some college | 16 college graduate | 17 or more graduate training |

(IF NECESSARY)

c. Does he have a college degree?   Yes   No

(IF MARRIED AND ALL WIFE'S GRANDPARENTS BORN IN USA OR CANADA)

Q108.   Do you know where your wife's earlier ancestors lived before coming to this country (Canada)?

Q109. *DIRECTIONS FOR CHOOSING NATIONALITIES FOR QUESTIONS Q109–Q110.*

a) Is R Jewish?   1. Yes, Jewish   2. Part Jewish   3. No, not Jewish

b) WRITE HERE *EACH* DISTINCT NATIONALITY GIVEN TO QUESTION 91 (Identify) *AND* TO QUESTIONS 93–98. (R's Parental and Grandparental Birthplace.) *DISREGARD WIFE'S SIDE OF FAMILY.*

1. _____
2. _____
3. _____
4. _____

c) ASK QUESTIONS 110–112 ABOUT *ALL* NATIONALITIES LISTED IN (b), *EXCEPT* "U.S.A." AND "CANADA." WHERE R IS *ENTIRELY* OF JEWISH ANCESTRY USE *ONLY* "JEWISH" IN PLACE OF NATIONALITIES. FOR "Part Jewish," SEE MANUAL. IF "U.S.A." OR "CANADIAN" ARE *ONLY* ENTRIES SKIP TO QUESTION 113.

Q110.   (FOR ALL NON-JEWS)

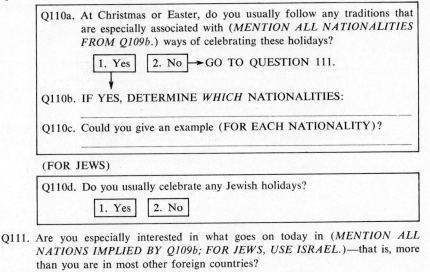

Q110a. At Christmas or Easter, do you usually follow any traditions that are especially associated with (*MENTION ALL NATIONALITIES FROM Q109b.*) ways of celebrating these holidays?

| 1. Yes | | 2. No | → GO TO QUESTION 111. |

Q110b. IF YES, DETERMINE *WHICH* NATIONALITIES: _____

Q110c. Could you give an example (FOR EACH NATIONALITY)? _____

(FOR JEWS)

Q110d. Do you usually celebrate any Jewish holidays?

| 1. Yes | | 2. No |

Q111.   Are you especially interested in what goes on today in (*MENTION ALL NATIONS IMPLIED BY Q109b; FOR JEWS, USE ISRAEL.*)—that is, more than you are in most other foreign countries?

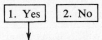

| 1. Yes | | 2. No |

(IF YES, AND MORE THAN ONE WAS ASKED)

Q111a. Which ones? _____

Q112.   Do you especially like some (*MENTION ALL NATIONALITIES IN Q109b; FOR JEWS, USE "JEWISH"*) foods—that is, more than you like most other foreign foods?

| 1. Yes | | 2. No |

(IF YES, AND MORE THAN ONE WAS ASKED)

Q112a. Which one(s)? _____

Q113.   Many people feel that—all things considered—it is better to marry someone of the same nationality background as oneself. Other people do not agree. What is your view on this?

| 1. Better if same | | 2. Not better | | 3. Other_____ |

Q114.   What about marrying someone of the same religion as oneself? Do you think this is better, or what?

| 1. Better, if same | | 2. Not better | | 3. Other_____ |

Q115. Now referring to religion again, about how often, if ever, have you attended religious services in the last year? (HAND CARD L AND READ ALTERNATIVES)

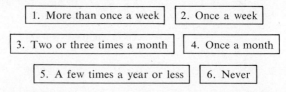

Q116. When you have decisions to make in your everyday life, do you ask yourself what God would want you to do—often, sometimes, or never?

| 1. Often | 2. Sometimes | 3. Never |

Q117. Which of these describes most accurately how often you yourself pray? (HAND CARD M AND READ ALTERNATIVES)

| 1. More than once a day | 2. Once a day | 3. Once or twice a week |

| 4. Rarely | 5. Never |

Q118. These final questions are on a different subject. What do you think is the ideal number of children for the average American family?

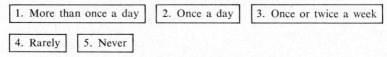

_____ NUMBER   IF "Depends," "God's Will," "Don't know," etc.

Q118a. As things are now for the average family, how many children would you say is the ideal number?
_____ NUMBER

(IF R MARRIED AND LIVING WITH WIFE. IF NOT, SKIP TO QUESTION Q124.)

Q119. We are interested in finding out how many children women in the Detroit area have had since they first married. Could you tell me in what month and year you and your wife were married?

_____ Month _____ Year

Q120. Is this your wife's first marriage?

| 1. Yes | 2. No |

(IF NO)

Q120a. In what year was she first married? _____ YEAR

Q120b. Has your wife had any children by her former marriage?

| 1. Yes | 2. No |

Q120c. How many? _____ NUMBER

Q121. How many children have you and your wife had, including those who are not living now? _____ NUMBER

Q122. What is your wife's date of birth? That is, the month and year?

_____ Month _____ Year

IF WIFE BORN *AFTER APRIL 1921,* ASK Q123a *or* Q123b. IF BEFORE 1921, SKIP TO QUESTION Q124.

(IF R AND WIFE HAVE HAD *NO* CHILDREN)

(IF R AND WIFE HAVE HAD *ONE OR MORE* CHILDREN)

Q123a. How many children do you and your wife expect to have? _____ Number

(IF DEPENDS, GOD'S WILL, FATE, ETC.)

Q123b. Many people feel as you do and accept what comes, but still they have an idea of what is likely to happen. As you think things will turn out for your family, how many children do you think you are likely to have? _____ Number

88. Can't say or won't say

Q123c. How many more children do you and your wife expect to have, in addition to those (the one) you already have? _____ Additional children

(IF DEPENDS, GOD'S WILL, FATE, ETC.)

Q123d. Many people feel as you do and accept what comes, but still they have an idea of what is likely to happen. As you think things will turn out for your family, how many more children do you think you are likely to have? _____ Additional children

88. Can't say or won't say

Q124. IF ANY LIVING CHILDREN BY PRESENT MARRIAGE, OBTAIN AGE, SEX, AND WHERE LIVING FOR EACH ONE.

SEX (CIRCLE) AGE	WHERE LIVING (CHECK *ONE* ONLY)	
1. M F ___	1. At home	2. Elsewhere
2. M F ___	1. At home	2. Elsewhere
3. M F ___	1. At home	2. Elsewhere
4. M F ___	1. At home	2. Elsewhere
5. M F ___	1. At home	2. Elsewhere
6. M F ___	1. At home	2. Elsewhere

Q125. About what was your total income last year—1965—for you and your family, including all sources such as wages, profits, interest, and so on? (HAND CARD N) Just give me the letter on the card that fits.

a. (1.) Under $3,000	e. (5.) $10,000—$14,999
b. (2.) $3,000—$4,999	f. (6.) $15,000—19,999
c. (3.) $5,000—$6,999	g. (7.) $20,000—$24,000
d. (4.) $7,000—$9,999	h. (8.) $25,000 and over

(DO NOT ASK IN ONE ADULT HOUSEHOLD)

Q125a. How much of your total family income was earned by you?
_____

Q126. Would you say your financial position is better today than it was five years ago, about the same, or less good?

1. Better   2. Same   3. Less good

IF FRIEND BOX ON COVER SHEET IS CHECKED,
CHECK BOX HERE AND ASK QUESTION Q127,
OTHERWISE GO TO QUESTION 128.

Q127. One of the things we're interested in is whether people tend to have friends that have the same interests and backgrounds as they do. With this in mind, we've asked you some questions about your three closest friends. But to get a more accurate picture we'd also like to phone one of your friends and ask him a few questions too. Here are the questions we will ask him (HAND PHONE INTERVIEW). We'd like to pick this friend by chance. Let's see, the first two friends you mentioned earlier were: (WRITE FIRST TWO NAMES OF FRIENDS IN QUESTION 14b.)

> A (Heads) _____
> B (Tails) _____

We'll let (*A. FRIEND*) be heads and (*B. FRIEND*) be tails. I'll (You) flip a coin to see which friend is the one which we'd like to get the information about. (FLIP COIN AND CIRCLE BELOW WHICH CAME UP.) The coin came up (HEADS) (TAILS). Could you give me (*THE SELECTED FRIEND'S*) last name and address? (ENTER INFORMATION BELOW). We won't mention your name, of course, and please don't tell _____ that we'll be calling.

FRIEND (CIRCLE IDENTIFYING LETTER A OR B)

	Name	Address
A or B	_____	_____

PHONE NUMBER (IF OBTAINABLE) _____

Thank you.

Q128. Would you like to hear how this survey came out? (IF YES, THEN SAY:) Let's see, I have your address on this cover sheet. Could you give me your name? Thank you.

ENTER NAME ON COVER SHEET, OR IF NOT GIVEN EXPLAIN ON COVER SHEET.

_____ TIME COMPLETED

THUMBNAIL: TO BE COMPLETED IMMEDIATELY AFTER LEAVING RESPONDENT'S HOUSE

Description of Property:

T-1. *What kind of place does R live in?* (CHECK ONE)

Single family dwelling
> 1. Single story ( )
> 2. Multiple story ( )

Trailer
> 3. Mobile ( )
> 4. Permanent Foundation ( )
> 5. Flat in Two or Three Family house ( )
> 6. Flat in Four Family house ( )
> 7. Apartment building ( )

> 7a. (How many other dwelling units in this building? _____)

T-2. *The Interview Situation*

How cooperative was R? | 1. Very cooperative throughout | 2. Average

3. Poor throughout | 4. Started poor, became good | 5. Started good, became poor

T-3. Is this interview of questionable value, generally adequate, or high quality?

1. Questionable | 2. Generally adequate | 3. High quality

(IF QUESTIONABLE)
T-3a. Why?
(CHECK EACH WHICH APPLIES TO R)
_____ Spoke English poorly
_____ Evasive, Suspicious
_____ Drunk, mentally disturbed, senile
_____ Had poor hearing or vision
_____ Confused by frequent interruptions
_____ Low intelligence

T-4. Who else was present during the interview and what effect did this have?

Only R Present

Person present	*How long*	*What effect*
_____	_____	_____
_____	_____	_____
_____	_____	_____

T-5. *Literacy of Respondent*

Q59: | 1. Read by R without difficulty

3. Some difficulty; interviewer provided some help

5. Entire question read to respondent

S-Series:

1. Read by respondent without difficulty

3. Some difficulty; some questions were read to respondent. Interviewer provided some help.

5. Entire series read to respondent

BY OBSERVATION

T-6.   *External Condition of House (CIRCLE NUMBER AT LEFT):*
1. Excellent: Expensive house, well cared for.
2. Average house: Good repair; not lavish, but *well* kept up.
3. Average house: Not good repair.
4. Poor: Ramshackle, much in need of repair.

T-7.   *How does R's house compare in general appearance with the three or four houses nearest to it? (CIRCLE NUMBER AT LEFT):*
1. Respondent's house is above average, relative to the others.
2. Respondent's house is average.
3. Respondent's house is below average relative to the others.

T-8.   *Any obvious statues or yard decorations outside house?*

  1. Yes ━━▶ *IF YES, BRIEFLY CHARACTERIZE TYPE (e.g., religious, fake animals, etc.)*

  2. No

T-9.   Was R *particularly* hospitable and friendly?

  1. Yes ━▶ *IF YES, EXPLAIN IN T-10.*

  2. No

T-10. Add here any notes that will aid in the interpretation of the interview. (USE ADDITIONAL SHEET OF PAPER IF NECESSARY)

Detroit Area Study   INT. NO. _____

Project 938   INTERVIEWER _____

II. Please indicate for each of the following sentences whether you disagree
or agree with it, and how much. Do this by checking (✓) *one* of the four
possible choices under each sentence.

S1.   I am the kind of person who plans and uses his time well.

_____   _____   _____   _____
1. Disagree strongly 2. Disagree somewhat 3. Agree somewhat 4. Agree strongly

S2.   A wife should not expect her husband to help around the house after he's home
from a hard day's work.

_____   _____   _____   _____
1. Disagree strongly 2. Disagree somewhat 3. Agree somewhat 4. Agree strongly

S3.   In this complicated world of ours, the only way we can know what's going
on is to rely on leaders or experts that can be trusted.

_____   _____   _____   _____
1. Disagree strongly 2. Disagree somewhat 3. Agree somewhat 4. Agree strongly

S4.   I think it is a sign of weakness to be concerned about what others think of me.

_____   _____   _____   _____
1. Disagree strongly 2. Disagree somewhat 3. Agree somewhat 4. Agree strongly

S5.   Most of the important decisions in the life of the family should be made by the
man of the house.

_____   _____   _____   _____
1. Disagree strongly 2. Disagree somewhat 3. Agree somewhat 4. Agree strongly

S6.   Planning only makes a person unhappy since plans hardly ever work out
anyway.

_____   _____   _____   _____
1. Disagree strongly 2. Disagree somewhat 3. Agree somewhat 4. Agree strongly

S7.   It is worth considerable effort to assure one's self of a good name with the
right kind of people.

_____   _____   _____   _____
1. Disagree strongly 2. Disagree somewhat 3. Agree somewhat 4. Agree strongly

S8.   There have always been good times and bad times, and there is nothing anybody can do that will change that. That is the way it is, and if you are smart,
you will take it as it comes and do the best you can.

_____   _____   _____   _____
1. Disagree strongly 2. Disagree somewhat 3. Agree somewhat 4. Agree strongly

S9.   To me, my work is just a way of making money.

_____   _____   _____   _____
1. Disagree strongly 2. Disagree somewhat 3. Agree somewhat 4. Agree strongly

S10. There are two kinds of people in the world, those who are for the truth, and
those who are against the truth.

_____   _____   _____   _____
1. Disagree strongly 2. Disagree somewhat 3. Agree somewhat 4. Agree strongly

S11. Nowadays with world conditions the way they are, the wise person lives for
today and lets tomorrow take care of itself.

_____   _____   _____   _____
1. Disagree strongly 2. Disagree somewhat 3. Agree somewhat 4. Agree strongly

S12. To compromise with our political opponents is dangerous because it usually leads to the betrayal of our own side.

_____ _____ _____ _____

1. Disagree strongly 2. Disagree somewhat 3. Agree somewhat 4. Agree strongly

S13. In general, husbands and wives should both share in deciding matters that are important to the family's future.

_____ _____ _____ _____

1. Disagree strongly 2. Disagree somewhat 3. Agree somewhat 4. Agree strongly

S14. The raising of one's social position is one of the more important goals in life.

_____ _____ _____ _____

1. Disagree strongly 2. Disagree somewhat 3. Agree somewhat 4. Agree strongly

> Each of the following questions has two choices.
> Choose the one ending for each statement that
> brings it _closest to describing_ you.

S15. When I am reading a magazine and come across puzzles or quizzes:
_____1. I often stop to try them
_____2. I rarely stop to try them

S16. The statement, "I become very attached to my friends":
_____1. Describes me pretty well
_____2. Does not describe me very well

S17. I like working on a problem when:
_____1. I have a fifty-fifty chance of solving it
_____2. I have a small chance of solving it

S18. When I am playing a game or participating in a sport, I am:
_____1. More concerned with having fun than winning
_____2. Very intent on winning

S19. The statement, "I make a point of keeping in close touch with the doings and interests of my friends":
_____1. Describes me pretty well
_____2. Does not describe me very well

S20. If I were a pinch hitter, I'd like to come to bat when:
_____1. My team was losing 5 to 2
_____2. The score was tied

S21. The statement, "I feel uncomfortable if I have to be by myself for any length of time":
_____1. Describes me pretty well
_____2. Does not describe me very well

S22. When I participate in a sport or game, I enjoy it:
_____1. More if a money bet is made
_____2. Less if a money bet is made

S23. Among three competitors:
_____1. I would like to be the best
_____2. I would not like to be the poorest

S24. The statement, "I enjoy working with others on a job more than working by myself":
_____1. Describes me pretty well
_____2. Does not describe me very well

S25. Do you think it's a good idea or a bad idea to buy things on the installment plan?

    _____1. A good idea

    _____2. A bad idea

S26. Which is the *more* important goal of higher education?

    _____1. To learn about new ideas and broaden one's mind

    _____2. To get the training and degree necessary for a first-rate job

S27. Once I am sure I can do a task:

    _____1. I become bored with it

    _____2. I enjoy it most

Bibliography

ABERBACH, JOEL D.
  1968   "Alienation and race." Ph.D. dissertation, Yale University.

ABRAMSON, HAROLD J.
  1969   "Ethnic diversity within Catholicism: Towards the sociology of religio-
         ethnic systems." Paper presented before the Annual Meetings of the
         Society for the Scientific Study of Religion, Boston, Mass. October 1969.

ACTON, FORMAN S.
  1966   *Analysis of Straight-Line Data.* New York: Dover.

ADAMS, BERT N.
  1967a *Kinship in an Urban Setting.* Chicago: Markham.
  1967b "Interaction theory and the social network." *Sociometry* 30: 64–78.

ADORNO, THEODOR W., ELSE FRENKEL-BRUNSWIK, DANIEL J. LEVINSON, AND R. NEVITT
       SANFORD
  1950   *The Authoritarian Personality.* New York: Harper.

ALBERT, R. S., AND T. R. BRIGANTE
  1962   "The psychology of friendship relations: Social factors." *Journal of
         Social Psychology* 56: 33–47.

ALEXANDER, C. NORMAN, JR.
  1966   "Ordinal position and sociometric status." *Sociometry* 29: 41–51.

ALEXANDER, C. NORMAN, JR., AND ERNEST Q. CAMPBELL
  1964   "Peer influence on adolescent educational aspirations and attainments."
         American Sociological Review 29: 568–75.

ALLPORT, GORDON
  1958   *The Nature of Prejudice.* Garden City, New York: Anchor Books.

ALMOND, GABRIEL, AND SIDNEY VERBA
  1965   *The Civic Culture.* Boston: Little, Brown.

ANDREWS, FRANK M.
  1963   "The revised multiple classification analysis program." Institute for
         Social Research, University of Michigan.

ANDREWS, FRANK M., JAMES MORGAN, AND JOHN SONQUIST
  1967   "Multiple classification analysis." Survey Research Center, Institute for
         Social Research, University of Michigan.

ARENDT, HANNAH
  1968   *The Origins of Totalitarianism. Part III: Totalitarianism.* New York:
         Harcourt, Brace & World.

ASCH, SOLOMON E.
  1956   "Studies of independence and conformity: A minority of one against
         a unanimous majority." *Psychological Monographs* 70, No. 9.

ATTNEAVE, FRED
1950 "Dimensions of similarity." *American Journal of Psychology* **63**: 516–66.

BABCHUK, NICHOLAS
1965 "Primary friends and kin: A study of the associations of middle class couples." *Social Forces* **43**: 483–93.

BABCHUK, NICHOLAS, AND ALAN BOOTH
1969 "Voluntary association membership: A longitudinal analysis." *American Sociological Review* **34**: 31–45.

BALES, ROBERT F.
1958 "Task roles and social roles in problem-solving groups." Pp. 437–47 in E. Maccoby, T. Newcomb, and E. Hartley (eds.), *Readings in Social Psychology*. New York: Holt, third edition.

BALTZELL, E. DIGBY
1964 *The Protestant Establishment*. New York: Random House.

BANFIELD, EDWARD
1958 *The Moral Basis of a Background Society*. Glencoe, Ill.: Free Press.

BARBER, BERNARD, AND ELINOR G. BARBER
1965 *European Social Class: Stability and Change*. New York: Macmillan.

BARNES, JOHN ARUNDEL
1954 "Class and committees in a Norwegian island parish." *Human Relations* **7**: 39–58.
1969 "Networks and political process." Pp. 51–76 in J. Clyde Mitchell (ed.), *Social Networks in Urban Situations*. Manchester, England: Manchester University Press.

BARRON, MILTON
1957 *American Minorities*. New York: Knopf.

BAUMAN, KARL E.
1968 "Status inconsistency, satisfactory social interaction and community satisfaction in an area of rapid growth." *Social Forces* **47**: 45–52.

BEALS, RICHARD, DAVID H. KRANTZ, AND AMOS TVERSKY
1968 "Foundations of munltidimensional scaling." *Psychological Review* **75**: 127–42.

BELL, DANIEL
1962 *The End of Ideology*. New York: Collier Books.

BELL, GERALD D.
1963 "Processes in the formation of adolescents' aspirations." *Social Forces* **42**: 179–86.

BELL, WENDELL, AND MARION BOAT
1957 "Urban neighborhoods and informal social relations." *American Journal of Sociology* **62**: 391–98.

BELL, WENDELL, AND MARYANNE T. FORCE
1956 "Urban neighborhood types and participation in formal associations." *American Sociological Review* **21**: 25–34.

BENDIX, REINHARD, AND SEYMOUR MARTIN LIPSET
1966 "Karl Marx's theory of social classes." Pp. 6–11 in Reinhard Bendix and Seymour Martin Lipset (eds.), *Class, Status, and Power*. Second edition. New York: Free Press.

BENOIT-SMULLYAN, EMILE
   1944   "Status, status types and status interrelationships." *American Sociological Review* 9: 151–61.

BERELSON, BERNARD, PAUL F. LAZARSFELD, AND WILLIAM N. MCPHEE
   1954   *Voting.* Chicago: University of Chicago Press.

BESHERS, JAMES M.
   1962   *Urban Social Structure.* New York: Free Press.

BESHERS, JAMES M., AND EDWARD O. LAUMANN
   1967   "Social distance: A network approach." *American Sociological Review* 32: 225–36.

BESHERS, JAMES M., EDWARD O. LAUMANN, AND BENJAMIN BRADSHAW
   1964   "Ethnic congregation-segregation, assimilation, and stratification." *Social Forces* 43: 482–89.

BETTELHEIM, BRUNO, AND MORRIS JANOWITZ
   1964   *Social Change and Prejudice.* New York: Free Press.

BLALOCK, HUBERT M., JR.
   1966a "The identification problem and theory building: The case of status inconsistency." *American Sociological Review* 31: 52–61.
   1966b "Comment: Status inconsistency and the identification problem." *Public Opinion Quarterly* 30: 130–32.
   1967a "Status inconsistency, social mobility, status integration, and structural effects." *American Sociological Review* 32: 790–801.
   1967b "Status inconsistency and interaction: Some alternative models." *American Journal of Sociology* 73: 305–15.

BLAU, PETER M.
   1956   "Social mobility and interpersonal relations." *American Sociological Review* 21: 290–95.
   1964   *Exchange and Power in Social Life.* New York: Wiley.

BLAU, PETER M., AND OTIS DUDLEY DUNCAN
   1967   *The American Occupational Structure.* New York: Wiley.

BLOOD, ROBERT, AND DONALD M. WOLFE
   1960   *Husbands and Wives.* Glencoe, Ill.: Free Press.

BLUNT, E. A. H.
   1931   *The Caste System of Northern India.* London: Humphrey Milford, Oxford University Press.

BOGARDUS, EMORY S.
   1925   "Measuring social distance." *Journal of Applied Sociology* 9: 299–308.
   1933   "A social distance scale." *Sociology and Social Research* 17: 265–71.
   1951   "Measuring changes in ethnic relations." *American Sociological Review* 16: 48–53.
   1958   "Racial distance changes in the United States during the past thirty years." *Sociology and Social Research* 43: 127–35.
   1959   *Social Distance.* Yellow Springs, Ohio: Antioch Press.

BONACICH, PHILLIP
   1967   "Associational contiguity: A critique." *American Sociological Review* 32: 813–15.

BORHEK, J. T.
   1970   "Ethnic group cohesion." *American Journal of Sociology* 76: 33–46.

BOTT, ELIZABETH
1957   *Family and Social Networks*. London: Tavistock.

BOX, STEVEN, AND JULIENNE FORD
1969   "Some questionable assumptions in the theory of status inconsistency." *Sociological Review* **17**: 187–201.

BRANDMEYER, GERARD
1965   "Status consistency and political behavior: A replication and extension of research." *Sociological Quarterly* **6**: 241–56.

BRIM, ORVILLE G., JR.
1966   "Socialization through the life cycle." In Orville G. Brim, Jr., and Stanton Wheeler (eds.), *Socialization After Childhood*. New York: Wiley.

BRODERICK, CARLFRED B.
1956   "Predicting friendship selection and maintenance in a college population." Ph.D. dissertation, Cornell University.

BUCKLEY, WALTER F.
1967   *Sociology and Modern Systems Theory*. Englewood Cliffs, N. J.: Prentice-Hall.

CAMPBELL, ERNEST Q., AND C. NORMAN ALEXANDER
1965   "Structural effects and interpersonal relationships." *American Journal of Sociology* **71**: 284–89.

CAPLOW, THEODORE
1968   *Two Against One: Coalitions in Triads*. Englewood Cliffs, N. J.: Prentice-Hall.

CENTERS, RICHARD
1949   *The Psychology of Social Classes: A Study of Class Consciousness*. Princeton, N. J.: Princeton University Press.

CHAMBLISS, J.
1965   "The selection of friends." *Social Forces* **43**: 370–80.

CHAPIN, F. STUART
1935   *Contemporary American Institutions: A Sociological Analysis*. New York: Harper.

CHAPIN, F. STUART, AND JOHN E. TSOUDEROS
1955   "Formalization observed in ten voluntary associations: Concepts and morphology." *Social Forces* **33**: 306–9.

CHINOY, ELY
1955   *Automobile Workers and the American Dream*. New York: Doubleday.

COELHO, GEORGE V.
1959   "A guide to the literature of friendship: A selectively annotated bibliography." *Psychological Newsletter* **10**: 365–94.

COHEN, YEHUDI A.
1961   "Patterns of friendship." Pp. 351–86 in *Social Structure and Personality*. New York: Holt, Rinehart and Winston.

COLEMAN, JAMES S.
1956   *Community Conflict*. Glencoe, Ill.: Free Press.

COLEMAN, JAMES S., ELIHU KATZ, AND HERBERT MENZEL
1966   *Medical Innovation: A Diffusion Study*. Indianapolis: Bobbs-Merrill.

COLEMAN, RICHARD P., AND BERNICE L. NEUGARTEN
1971   *Social Status in the City*. San Francisco: Jossey–Bass.

CONVERSE, PHILIP
1964   "The nature of belief systems in mass publics." Pp. 206–61 in David
        E. Apter (ed.), *Ideology and Discontent*. New York: Free Press.

COOMBS, CLYDE H.
1964   *A Theory of Data*. New York: Wiley.
1970   "Scaling and data theory." Chapter 3 in Clyde H. Coombs, Robyn M.
        Dawes, and Amos Tversky (eds.), *Mathematical Psychology*. Englewood
        Cliffs, N. J.: Prentice-Hall.

COSER, LEWIS
1956   *The Functions of Social Conflict*. Glencoe, Ill.: Free Press.

CROSS, DAVID VERNON
1965   "Metric properties of multidimensional stimulus control." Ph.D. dis-
        sertation, University of Michigan.

CURTIS, RICHARD F.
1963   "Differential association and the stratification of the urban community."
        Social Forces 42: 68–77.

CUTLER, STEPHEN J.
1969   "Membership in voluntary associations and the theory of mass society."
        Ph.D. dissertation, University of Michigan.

DAHL, ROBERT A.
1961   *Who Governs?* New Haven: Yale University Press.

DAVIS, ALLISON, BURLEIGH B. GARDNER, AND MARY R. GARDNER
1941   *Deep South: A Social Anthropological Study of Caste and Class*. Chicago:
        University of Chicago Press.

DAVIS, JAMES A.
1955   "Living rooms as symbols of status: A study in social judgment." Ph.D.
        dissertation, Harvard University.
1963   "Structural balance, mechanical solidarity, and interpersonal relations."
        American Journal of Sociology 68: 444–62.

DAVIS, KINGSLEY, AND WILBERT E. MOORE
1945   "Some principles of stratification." *American Sociological Review* 10:
        242–49. Reprinted in Edward O. Laumann, Paul M. Siegel, and Robert
        W. Hodge (eds.), *The Logic of Social Hierarchies*. Chicago: Markham,
        1970.

DEAN, LOIS R.
1958   "Interaction, reported and observed: The case of one local union."
        Human Organization 27: 36–44.

DEMERATH, NICHOLAS J., III
1965   *Social Class in American Protestantism*. Chicago: Rand McNally.

DEMING, WILLIAM EDWARDS
1964   *Statistical Adjustment of Data*. 1943. New York: Dover.

DOTSON, FLOYD
1951   "Patterns of voluntary association among urban working class families."
        American Sociological Review 16: 687–93.

DRIVER, HAROLD E., AND KARL SCHUESSLER
  1956   "Factor analysis of ethnographic data." *American Anthropologist* **59**: 655–63.

DUNCAN, BEVERLY, AND OTIS DUDLEY DUNCAN
  1968   "Minorities and the process of stratification." *American Sociological Review* **33**: 356–64.

DUNCAN, OTIS DUDLEY
  1961a "A socioeconomic index for all occupations." Pp. 109–31 in Albert J. Reiss, Jr. (ed.), *Occupations and Social Status*. New York: Free Press.
  1961b "Properties and characteristics of the socioeconomic index." Pp. 139–61 in Albert J. Reiss, Jr. (ed.), *Occupations and Social Status*. New York: Free Press. See also Appendix B, pp. 263–75.
  1966a "Methodological issues in the analysis of social mobility." In Neil J. Smelser and Seymour Martin Lipset (eds.), *Social Structure and Mobility in Economic Development*. Chicago: Aldine.
  1966b "Path analysis: Sociological examples." *American Journal of Sociology* **72**: 1–16.
  1968   "Socioeconomic Background and Occupational Achievement: Extensions of a Basic Model." Final Report, Project No. 5–0074 (EO–191), U. S. Department of Health, Education and Welfare, pp. 69–76.

DUNCAN, OTIS DUDLEY, AND JAY W. ARTIS
  1951   "Some problems of stratification research." *Rural Sociology* **16**: 17–29.

DUNCAN, OTIS DUDLEY, AND BEVERLY DUNCAN
  1955a "A methodological analysis of segregation indexes." *American Sociological Review* **20**: 210–17.
  1955b "Residential segregation and occupational stratification." *American Journal of Sociology* **60**: 493–503.

DUNCAN, OTIS DUDLEY, AND STANLEY LIEBERSON
  1959   "Ethnic segregation and assimilation." *American Journal of Sociology* **64**: 363–74.

DURKHEIM, EMILE
  1947   *The Division of Labor in Society*. 1893. Glencoe, Ill.: Free Press.
  1951   *Suicide*. 1897. Translated by John A. Spaulding and George Simpson. Glencoe, Ill.: Free Press.

ECKLAND, BRUCE K.
  1967   "Genetics and sociology: A reconsideration." *American Sociological Review* **32**: 173–94.

ECKSTEIN, HARRY
  1966   *Division and Cohesion in Democracy: A Study of Norway*. Princeton, N. J.: Princeton University Press.

EFRON, DAVID, AND JOHN P. FOLEY, JR.
  1947   "Gestural behavior and social setting." Pp. 33–40 in T. M. Newcomb and E. L. Hartley (eds.), *Readings in Social Psychology*. New York: Holt.

EISENSTADT, S. N.
  1954   "Reference group behavior and social integration: An exploratory study." *American Sociological Review* **19**: 175–85.

ELLIS, ROBERT A.
  1957   "Social stratification and social relations: An empirical test of the

disjunctiveness of social classes." *American Sociological Review* **22**: 570–78.

ERBE, WILLIAM
1964   "Social involvement and political activity: A replication and elaboration." *American Sociological Review* **29**: 198–215.

FARLEY, REYNOLDS, AND CARL G. TAEUBER
1968   "Population trends and residential segregation since 1960." *Science* **159**: 953–56.

FAUMAN, S. JOSEPH
1968   "Status crystallization and interracial attitudes." *Social Forces* **47**: 53–60.

FEATHERMAN, DAVID L.
1969   "The socioeconomic achievement of white married males in the United States: 1957–1967." Ph.D. dissertation, University of Michigan.
1971   "The socioeconomic achievement of white religioethnic subgroups: Social and psychological explanations." *American Sociological Review* **36**: 207–22.

FENNESSEY, JAMES
1968   "The general linear model: A new perspective on some familiar topics." *American Journal of Sociology* **74**: 1–27.

FESTINGER, LEON
1950   "Informal social communication." *Psychological Review* **57**: 271–82.
1957   A Theory of Cognitive Dissonance. Stanford, Calif.: Stanford University Press. Reprinted in William S. Sahakian (ed.), *Psychology of Learning*. Chicago: Markham, 1970.

FESTINGER, LEON, STANLEY SCHACTER, AND KURT W. BACK
1950   *Social Pressures in Informal Groups.* New York: Harper.

FROMM, ERICH
1955   *The Sane Society.* Greenwich, Conn.: Fawcett.

GALTUNG, JOHANN
1966   "Rank and social integration: A multidimensional approach." Pp. 145–98 in Joseph Berger, Morris Zelditch, Jr., and Bo Anderson (eds.), *Sociological Theories in Progress.* Volume I. Boston: Houghton Mifflin.

GANS, HERBERT J.
1962   *The Urban Villagers.* New York: Free Press.

GARDNER, MARTIN
1965   "The superellipse: A curve that lies between the ellipse and rectangle." *Scientific American* **213**: 222–32.

GAUSTAD, EDWIN SCOTT
1962   *Historical Atlas of Religion in America.* New York: Harper & Row.

GERSON, WALTER M.
1965   "Alienation in mass society: Some causes and responses." *Sociology and Social Research* **49**: 143–52.

GESCHWENDER, JAMES A.
1967   "Continuities in theories of status consistency and cognitive dissonance." *Social Forces* **46**: 160–71. Reprinted in Edward O. Laumann, Paul M. Siegel, and Robert W. Hodge (eds.), *The Logic of Social Hierarchies.* Chicago: Markham, 1970.

GLASER, DANIEL
    1958   "Dynamics of ethnic identification." *American Sociological Review* **23**: 31–40.

GLAZER, NATHAN
    1954   "Ethnic groups in America: From national cultures to ideology." In Morroe Berger et al. (eds.), *Freedom and Control in Modern Society.* Princeton, N. J.: Van Nostrand.

GLAZER, NATHAN, AND DANIEL P. MOYNIHAN
    1963   *Beyond the Melting Pot.* Cambridge, Mass.: M.I.T. Press.

GLEASON, TERRY C.
    1967   "A general model for nonmetric multidimensional scaling." Michigan Mathematical Psychology Program Technical Report Number MMPP 67–3.
    1969   "Users write-up for COMPARE." Mimeograph, Ann Arbor, Mich.: Institute for Social Research.

GLENN, NORVAL D., AND JON P. ALSTON
    1968   "Cultural distance among occupational categories." *American Sociological Review* **33**: 365–82.

GLENN, NORVAL D., AND RUTH HYLAND
    1967   "Religious preference and worldly success: Some evidence from national surveys." *American Sociological Review* **32**: 73–85.

GLOCK, CHARLES Y., AND RODNEY STARK
    1965   *Religion and Society in Tension.* Chicago: Rand McNally.

GLUCKMAN, MAX
    1955   *The Judicial Process Among the Barotse of Northern Rhodesia.* Manchester, England: Manchester University Press.
    1962   *Essays in the Ritual of Social Relations.* Manchester, England: Manchester University Press.

GOCKEL, GALEN L.
    1969   "Income and religious affiliation: A regression analysis." *American Journal of Sociology* **74**: 632–47.

GOFFMAN, ERVING
    1951   "Symbols of class status." *British Journal of Sociology* **2**: 294–304.
    1959   *The Presentation of Self in Everyday Life.* New York: Anchor Books.

GOFFMAN, IRWIN W.
    1956   "Status consistency and preference for change in power distribution." *American Sociological Review* **22**: 275–81.

GOLDBERG, DAVID, AND CLYDE H. COOMBS
    1963   "Some applications of unfolding theory to fertility analysis." In *Emerging Techniques in Population Research.* New York: Milbank Memorial Fund.

GOLDBERG, DAVID, AND GREER LITTON
    1968   "Family planning: Some observations and an interpretative scheme." *Proceedings of the Turkish Demographic Conference.*

GOLDSCHMIDT, WALTER
    1950   "Social class in America—A critical review." *American Anthropologist* **52**: 483–98.

GOLDSTEIN, SIDNEY
    1969   "Socioeconomic differentials among religious groups in the United States." *American Journal of Sociology* **74**: 612–31.

GOFFMAN, I. W.
    1957   "Status consistency and preference for change in power distributions." *American Sociological Review* **22**: 275–81.

GORDON, MILTON M.
    1958   *Social Class in American Sociology.* Durham, N. C.: Duke University Press.
    1964   *Assimilation in American Life.* New York: Oxford University Press.

GRANOVETTER, MARK S.
    1972   "The strength of weak ties," Unpublished manuscript, Department of Social Relations, Johns Hopkins University.

GREELEY, ANDREW M.
    1964   "The Protestant Ethic: Time for a moratorium." *Sociological Analysis* **24**: 20–33.
    1968   "Ethnicity as an influence on behavior." Paper delivered at the National Consultation on Ethnic Behavior sponsored by the American Jewish Committee. Fordham University, June 20.
    1971   "Political attitudes among American white ethnics." Paper read at the Annual Meeting of the American Political Science Association, September 10.

GREENBLUM, JOSEPH, AND LEONARD I. PEARLIN
    1953   "Vertical mobility and prejudice: A socio-psychological analysis." Pp. 480–91 in Reinhard Bendix and Seymour Martin Lipset (eds.), *Class, Status, and Power.* Glencoe, Ill.: Free Press.

GREER, SCOTT
    1956   "Urbanism reconsidered: A comparative study of local areas in a metropolis." *American Sociological Review* **21**: 19–25.
    1957   "Individual participation in mass society." Pp. 329–42 in Roland Young (ed.), *Approaches to the Study of Politics.* Evanston, Ill.: Northwestern University Press.

GREER, SCOTT, AND PETER ORLEANS
    1962   "The mass society and the parapolitical structure." *American Sociological Review* **27**: 634–46.

GREGSON, ROBERT A. M.
    1966   "Theoretical and empirical multidimensional scalings of taste mixture matchings." *British Journal of Mathematical and Statistical Psychology* **19**: 59–76.

GUSFIELD, JOSEPH R.
    1962   "Mass society and extremist politics." *American Sociological Review* **27**: 19–30.

GUTHREY, SCOTT B., HAROLD J. SPAETH, AND STUART THOMAS
    1968   "FASCALE, a FORTRAN IV multidimensional scaling and factor analysis program." *Behavioral Science* **13**: 426.

GUTTMAN, LOUIS
    1959   "Introduction to facet design and analysis." Pp. 130–32 in *Proceedings of the 15th International Congress of Psychology,* Brussels, Belgium.

1967   "The development of nonmetric space analysis: A letter to Professor John Ross." *Multivariate Behavioral Research* **2**: 71–82.

1968   "A general nonmetric technique for finding the smallest coordinate space for a configuration of points." *Psychometrika* **33**: 469–506.

HALD, ANDERS

1953   *Statistical Theory, with Engineering Applications.* New York: Wiley.

HALL, EDWARD

1959   *The Silent Language.* New York: Doubleday.

HANDLIN, OSCAR

1954   *The American People in the Twentieth Century.* Cambridge: Harvard University Press.

1957   *Race and Nationality in American Life.* Boston: Little, Brown.

1959   *Immigration as a Factor in American History.* Englewood Cliffs, N. J.: Prentice–Hall.

HARARY, FRANK, R. Z. NORMAN, AND DORWIN CARTWRIGHT

1965   *Structural Models: An Introduction to the Theory of Directed Graphs.* New York: Wiley.

HARDY, GODFREY H., JOHN E. LITTLEWOOD, AND GEORGE POLYA

1952   *Inequalities.* Second edition. Cambridge, England: The University Press.

HARE, A. PAUL

1962   *Handbook of Small Group Research.* New York: Free Press.

HATT, PAUL

1948   "Class and ethnic attitudes." *American Sociological Review* **13**: 36–43.

HAUG, MARIE R., AND MARVIN B. SUSSMAN

1968   "Social class measurement—II—The case of the Duncan Socioeconomic Index." Paper presented before the Annual Meetings of the American Sociological Association, Boston, Mass., August 28.

HAUSKNECHT, MURRAY

1962   *The Joiners.* New York: Bedminster.

HAYS, WILLIAM L.

1963   *Statistics for Psychologists.* New York: Holt, Rinehart and Winston.

HEIDER, FRITZ

1958   *The Psychology of Interpersonal Relations.* New York: Wiley.

HENRY, JULES

1958   "The personal community and its variant properties." *American Anthropologist* **60**: 827–31.

HERBERG, WILL

1955   *Protestant, Catholic, Jew.* Revised edition. New York: Doubleday–Anchor.

HERRIOTT, ROBERT E.

1963   "Some social determinants of educational aspirations." *Harvard Educational Review* **33**: 147–77.

HERSKOVITS, MELVILLE J.

1955   *Cultural Anthropology: An Abridged Version of Man and His Works.* New York: Knopf.

HIGHAM, JOHN

1955   *Strangers in the Land.* Rahway, N. J.: Rutgers University Press.

HILL, T. P.
   1959   "An analysis of the distribution of wages and salaries in Great Britain."
           Econometrica **27**: 355–81.

HIMMELFARB, SAMUEL, AND DAVID J. SENN
   1969   "Forming impressions of social class: Two tests of an averaging model."
           Journal of Personality and Social Psychology **12**: 38–51.

HODGE, ROBERT W.
   1966   "Occupational mobility as a probability process." *Demography* **3**: 19–34.
   1970   "Social integration, psychological well-being, and their socioeconomic
           correlates." *Sociological Inquiry* **40**: 182–206.

HODGE, ROBERT W., AND PAUL SIEGEL
   1970   "Nonvertical dimensions of social stratification." In Edward O. Laumann,
           Paul Siegel, and Robert W. Hodge (eds.), *The Logic of Social Hier-
           archies*. Chicago: Markham.
   forth- *Prestige and the Theory of Occupational Stratification*. Chicago:
   coming Markham.

HODGE, ROBERT W., AND DONALD J. TREIMAN
   1966   "Occupational mobility and attitude toward Negroes." *American Socio-
           logical Review* **31**: 93–102.

HOLDEN, DAVID E. W.
   1965   "Associations as reference groups: An approach to the problem." *Rural
           Sociology* **30**: 63–74.

HOLLINGSHEAD, AUGUST
   1950   "Cultural factors in the selection of marriage mates." *American Socio-
           logical Review* **15**: 619–27.

HOMANS, GEORGE C.
   1951   *The Human Group*. New York: Harcourt, Brace & World.
   1961   *Social Behavior: Its Elementary Forms*. New York: Harcourt, Brace &
           World.

HOULT, THOMAS FORD
   1954   "Experimental measurement of clothing as a factor in some social
           ratings of selected men." *American Sociological Review* **19**: 324–28.

HSU, FRANCIS L. K.
   1963   *Clan, Caste, and Club*. Princeton, N. J.: Van Nostrand.

HUNTER, FLOYD
   1953   *Community Power Structure*. Durham, N. C.: University of North
           Carolina Press.
   1963   "The organized community and the individual." Pp. 513–21 in Roland L.
           Warren (ed.), *Perspectives on the American Community*. Chicago:
           Rand McNally.

HYMAN, HERBERT H.
   1966   "The value system of different classes: A social psychological contribution
           to the analysis of stratification." Pp. 488–99 in Reinhard Bendix and
           Seymour Martin Lipset (eds.), *Class, Status, and Power*. New York:
           Free Press.

HYMAN, MARTIN D.
   1966   "Determining the effects of status inconsistency." *Public Opinion Quar-
           terly* **30**: 120–29.

JACKSON, ELTON F.
1962 "Status consistency and the symptoms of stress." *American Sociological Review* **27**: 469–80.

JACKSON, ELTON F., AND PETER J. BURKE
1965 "Status and symptoms of stress: Additive and interaction effects." *American Sociological Review* **30**: 556–62.

JANOWITZ, MORRIS
1952 *The Community Press in an Urban Setting.* Glencoe, Ill.: Free Press.

JENSEN, ARTHUR R.
1969 "How much can we boost I.Q. and scholastic achievement?" *Harvard Educational Review* **39**: 1–123.

JOHNSON, BARCLEY D.
1965 "Durkeim's one cause of suicide." *American Sociological Review* **30**: 875–86.

JUNKER, BUFORD H.
1955 "Room compositions and life styles: A sociological study in living rooms and other rooms in contemporary dwellings." Ph.D. dissertation, University of Chicago.

KAHL, JOSEPH A.
1960 *The American Class Structure.* New York: Rinehart and Co.

KANTROWITZ, NATHAN
1969 "Ethnic and racial segregation in the New York metropolis, 1960." *American Journal of Sociology* **74**: 685–95.

KATZ, ELIHU, AND PAUL F. LAZARSFELD
1955 *Personal Influence.* Glencoe, Ill.: Free Press.

KATZ, FRED E.
1966 "Social participation and social structure." *Social Forces* **45**: 199–210.

KATZ, F. M.
1964 "The meaning of success: Some differences in value systems of social classes." *Journal of Social Psychology* **62**: 141–48.

KELLEY, HAROLD H., AND EDMUND H. VOLKART
1952 "The resistance to change of group anchored attitudes." *American Sociological Review* **17**: 453–65.

KELLEY, JOHN L.
1955 *General Typology.* Princeton, N. J.: Van Nostrand.

KELLEY, K. DENNIS, AND WILLIAM CHAMBLISS
1966 "Status consistency and political attitudes." *American Sociological Review* **31**: 375–82.

KELMAN, HERBERT C.
1958 "Social influence and personal belief: A theoretical and experimental approach to the study of behavioral change." Unpublished manuscript.

KEMENY, JOHN G., AND J. LAURIE SNELL
1960 *Finite Markov Chains.* Princeton, N. J.: Van Nostrand.

KEMPER, THEODORE D.
1968 "Reference group, socialization, and achievement." *American Sociological Review* **33**: 31–45.

KENNEDY, RUBY JO REEVES
    1944   "Single or triple melting pot? Intermarriage trends in New Haven, 1870–1940." *American Journal of Sociology* 49: 331–39.
    1952   "Single or triple melting pot? Intermarriage in New Haven, 1870–1950." *American Journal of Sociology* 58: 56–59.

KIMBERLY, JAMES C.
    1970   "The emergence and stabilization of stratification in simple and complex social systems: Some implications of small group research." *Sociological Inquiry* 40: 73–101.

KING, MORTON B.
    1961   "Socioeconomic status and sociometric choice." *Social Forces* 39: 199–206.

KLUCKHOHN, CLYDE
    1960   *Mirror for Man.* New York: McGraw–Hill; Premier Books.

KLUCKHOHN, FLORENCE
    1950   "Dominant and substitute profiles of cultural orientations: Their significance for the analysis of social stratification." *Social Forces* 28: 376–93.

KLUCKHOHN, FLORENCE R., AND FRED L. STRODTBECK
    1961   *Variations in Value Orientation.* Evanston, Ill.: Row, Peterson.

KOHN, MELVIN L.
    1969   *Class and Conformity. A Study in Values.* Homewood, Ill.: Dorsey Press.

KOMAROVSKY, MIRRA
    1946   "The voluntary associations of urban dwellers." *American Sociological Review* 11: 686–98.

KORNHAUSER, WILLIAM
    1959   *The Politics of Mass Society.* Glencoe, Ill.: Free Press.

KROEBER, ALFRED LOUIS, AND JANE RICHARDSON
    1959   "Three centuries of women's dress fashions: A qualitative analysis." *Anthropological Records* 2, No. 2.

KRUSKAL, JOSEPH B.
    1964a   "Multidimensional scaling by optimizing goodness of fit to a nonmetric hypothesis." *Psychometrika* 29: 1–27.
    1964b   "Nonmetric multidimensional scaling: A numerical method." *Psychometrika* 29: 115–29.

LANDECKER, WERNER
    1960   "Class boundaries." *American Sociological Review* 25: 868–77.

LASSWELL, THOMAS
    1965   *Class and Stratum.* Boston: Houghton Mifflin.

LAUMANN, EDWARD O.
    1966   Prestige and Association in an Urban Community. Indianapolis: Bobbs–Merrill.
    1969a   "Friends of urban men: An assessment of accuracy in reporting their socioeconomic attributes, mutual choice, and attitude agreement." *Sociometry* 32: 54–69.

1969b "The social structure of religious and ethnoreligious groups in a metropolitan community." *American Sociological Review* 34: 182–97.

1970   *Social Stratification: Research and Theory for the 1970s.* Indianapolis:
Bobbs-Merrill.

1972   "Review of Richard P. Coleman and Bernice L. Neugarten's *Social Status
in the City,*" *American Journal of Sociology* 78: 268–71.

LAUMANN, EDWARD O., AND LOUIS GUTTMAN
1966   "The relative associational contiguity of occupations in an urban setting."
American Sociological Review 31: 169–78.

LAUMANN, EDWARD O., AND JAMES S. HOUSE
1970   "Living room styles and social attributes: The patterning of material
artifacts in a modern urban community." *Sociology and Social Research*
54: 321–42.

LAUMANN, EDWARD O., AND HOWARD SCHUMAN
1967   "Open and closed structures." Paper read at the Annual Meeting,
American Sociological Association, San Francisco, August 29.

LAUMANN, EDWARD O., PAUL M. SIEGEL, AND ROBERT W. HODGE
1970   *The Logic of Social Hierarchies.* Chicago: Markham.

LAZARSFELD, PAUL F., BERNARD BERELSON, AND HAZEL GAUDET
1948   *The People's Choice.* New York: Columbia University Press.

LAZARSFELD, PAUL F., AND ROBERT K. MERTON
1954   "Friendship as a social process." Pp. 18–66 in Morroe Berger, Theodore
Abel, and Charles H. Page (eds.), *Freedom and Control in Modern
Society.* Princeton, N. J.: Van Nostrand.

LAZERWITZ, BERNARD, AND LOUIS ROWITZ
1964   "The three-generation hypothesis." *American Journal of Sociology* 69:
529–38.

LEACH, EDMUND R.
1967   "Caste, class, and slavery: The taxonomic problem." In Anthony de
Reuck and Julie Knight (eds.), *Caste and Race: Comparative Approaches.*
London: J. and A. Churchill, Ltd. Reprinted in Edward O. Laumann,
Paul M. Siegel, and Robert W. Hodge, *The Logic of Social Hierarchies.*
Chicago: Markham, 1970.

LEBAR, FRANK M.
1964   "A household survey of economic goods on Romonum Island, Truk."
Pp. 335–50 in Ward H. Goodenough (ed.), *Explorations in Cultural
Anthropology: Essays in Honor of George P. Murdock.* New York:
McGraw–Hill.

LEE, ROBERT
1960   *The Social Sources of Church Unity.* Nashville, Tenn.: Abingdon Press.

LENSKI, GERHARD
1954   "Status crystallization: A non-vertical dimension of social status."
American Sociological Review 19: 405–13.

1956   "Social participation and status crystallization." *American Sociological
Review* 21: 458–64.

1960   *The Religious Factor.* New York: Free Press.

1964   "Comment." *Public Opinion Quarterly* 28: 326–30.

1966   *Power and Privilege: A Theory of Social Stratification.* New York: McGraw–Hill.

1967   "Status inconsistency and the vote: A four nation test." *American Sociological Review* **32**: 298–301.

1971   "The religious factor in Detroit: Revisited." *American Sociological Review* **36**: 48–50.

LESHAN, LAWRENCE L.

1952   "Time orientation and social class." *Journal of Abnormal and Social Psychology* **47**: 589–92.

LEVENS, HELENE

1968   "Organizational affiliation and powerlessness: A case study of the welfare poor." *Social Problems* **16**: 18–32.

LEWIS, OSCAR

1958   *Village Life in Northern India.* Urbana, Ill.: University of Illinois Press.

LIEBERSON, STANLEY

1963   *Ethnic Patterns in American Cities.* New York: Free Press.

LIEBOW, ELLIOT

1967   *Tally's Corner. A Study of Negro Streetcorner Men.* Boston: Little, Brown.

LINGOES, JAMES C.

1965a   "An IBM 7090 program for Guttman–Lingoes smallest space analysis—I." *Behavioral Science* **10**: 183–84.

1965b   "An IBM 7090 program for Guttman–Lingoes smallest space analysis—II." *Behavioral Science* **10**: 487.

1966a   "An IBM 7090 program for Guttman–Lingoes smallest space analysis—III." *Behavioral Science* **11**: 75–76.

1966b   "An IBM 7090 program for Guttman–Lingoes multidimensional scalogram analysis—I." *Behavioral Science* **11**: 76–78.

1966c   "An IBM 7090 program for Guttman–Lingoes smallest space analysis—RI, RII." *Behavioral Science* **11**: 322.

1966d   "New computer developments in pattern analysis and nonmetric techniques." Pp. 1–22 in *Proceedings of the 1964 IBM Symposium: Utilization of Computers in Psychological Research.* Paris: Gauthier–Villars.

1967   "Recent computational advances in nonmetric methodology for the behavioral sciences." In *Proceedings of the International Symposium on Mathematical and Computational Methods in Social Sciences.* International Computation Centre, Rome, Italy.

1968a   "The rationale of the Guttman–Lingoes series: A letter to Dr. Philip Runkel." *Multivariate Behavioral Research* **3**: 495–507.

1968b   "The multivariate analysis of qualitative data." *Multivariate Behavioral Research* **3**: 61–94.

1971   "Some boundary conditions for a monotone analysis of symmetric matrices." *Psychometrika* **36**: 195–203.

LINGOES, JAMES C., AND LOUIS GUTTMAN

1967   "Nonmetric factor analysis: A rank reducing alternative to linear factor analysis." *Multivariate Behavioral Research* **2**: 485–505.

LINGOES, JAMES C., EDWARD E. C. I. ROSKAM, AND LOUIS GUTTMAN

1969   "An empirical study of two multidimensional scaling algorithms." Unpublished manuscript, University of Michigan.

LINGOES, JAMES C., AND EDWARD E. C. I. ROSKAM
   1971   "Mathematical and empirical study of two multidimensional scaling algorithms." Michigan Mathematical Psychology Program Technical Report 71–1.

LINTON, RALPH
   1963   *The Study of Man. An Introduction.* New York: D. Appleton–Century.

LIPSET, SEYMOUR MARTIN
   1963a   *The First New Nation.* New York: Basic Books.
   1963b   *Political Man: The Social Bases of Politics.* New York: Doubleday.
   1968a   *Revolution and Counterrevolution. Change and Persistence in Social Structures.* New York: Basic Books.
   1968b   "Issues in social class analysis." Pp. 121–58 in *Revolution and Counterrevolution.* New York: Basic Books.

LIPSET, SEYMOUR MARTIN, MARTIN TROW, AND JAMES COLEMAN
   1956   *Union Democracy: The Internal Politics of the International Typographical Union.* Glencoe, Ill.: Free Press.

LITWAK, EUGENE
   1965   "Extended kin relations in an industrial democratic society." Pp. 290–323 in E. Shean and G. F. Streib (eds.), *Social Structure and the Family Generational Relations.* Englewood Cliffs, N. J.: Prentice–Hall.

LOOMIS, CHARLES, AND D. DAVIDSON, JR.
   1939   "Sociometrics and the study of new rural communities." *Sociometry* **2**: 56–76.

LOPATA, HELENA ZNANIECKI
   1964   "The function of voluntary associations in an ethnic community, 'Polonoia.'" Pp. 201–23 in Ernest Burgess and Donald J. Bogue (eds.), *Contributions to Urban Sociology.* Chicago: University of Chicago Press.

LOPREATO, JOSEPH
   1967   "Upward social mobility and political orientations." *American Sociological Review* **32**: 586–92.

LOWENTHAL, MARJORIE FISKE, AND CLAYTON HAVEN
   1968   "Interaction and adaptation: Intimacy as a critical variable." *American Sociological Review* **33**: 20–30.

LUNDBERG, GEORGE A., AND MARY STEELE
   1938   "Social attraction patterns in a village." *Sociometry* **1**: 375–419.

LUNDY, RICHARD M.
   1956   "Self perceptions and descriptions of opposite sex sociometric choices." *Sociometry* **19**: 272–77.

LYKKEN, DAVID T.
   1968   "Statistical significance in psychological research." *Psychological Bulletin* **70**: 151–59.

LUNES, RUSSELL
   1954   *The Tastemakers.* New York: Harper.

MCCALL, GEORGE J., AND J. L. SIMMONS
   1966   *Identities and Interactions.* New York: Free Press.

MCCLELLAND, DAVID C.
   1961   *The Achieving Society.* Princeton, N. J.: Van Nostrand.

MCCLELLAND, DAVID C., ALFRED L. BALDWIN, URIE BRONFENBRENNER, AND FRED L. STRODTBECK
  1958   *Talent and Society: New Perspectives in the Identification of Talent.* Princeton, N. J.: Van Nostrand.

MCCLELLAND, DAVID C., JOHN W. ATKINSON, RUSSELL A. CLARK, AND EDGAR L. LOWELL
  1953   *The Achievement Motive.* New York: Appleton–Century–Crofts.

MCCLOSKY, HERBERT
  1958   "Conservatism and personality." *American Political Science Review* **21**: 27–45.

MCCLOSKY, HERBERT, AND HAROLD E. DAHLGREN
  1959   "Primary group influence on party loyalty." *American Political Science Review* **22**: 757–76.

MCDAVID, JOHN W., AND HERBERT HARARI
  1968   *Social Psychology.* New York: Harper & Row.

MCFARLAND, DAVID D.
  1969   "Measuring the permeability of occupational structures: An information-theoretic approach." *American Journal of Sociology* **75**: 41–61.
  1970   "Intra-generational social mobility as a Markov process." *American Sociological Review* **35**: 463–76.

MCGEE, VICTOR E.
  1966   "The multidimensional analysis of 'elastic' distances." *British Journal of Mathematical and Statistical Psychology* **19**: 181–96.

MCLOUGHLIN, WILLIAM G., AND ROBERT N. BELLAH
  1968   *Religion in America.* Daedalus Library Volume 12. Boston: Houghton Mifflin.

MACCOBY, HERBERT
  1958   "The differential political activity of participants in a voluntary association." *American Sociological Review* **23**: 524–32.

MARCH, JAMES, AND HERBERT A. SIMON
  1958   *Organizations.* New York: Wiley.

MAYHEW, LEON
  1968   "Ascription in modern societies." *Sociological Inquiry* **38**: 105–20. Reprinted in Edward O. Laumann, Paul M. Siegel, and Robert W. Hodge (eds.), *The Logic of Social Hierarchies.* Chicago: Markham, 1970.

MAYNARD, THEODORE
  1960   *The Story of American Catholicism.* Two volumes. New York: Doubleday.

MAYNTZ, RENATE
  1958   *Soziale Schichtung und sozialer Wandel in einer Industriegemeinde: Eine soziologische Untersuchung der Stadt Euskirchen.* Stuttgart: Ferdinand Enke Verlag.

MEAD, SIDNEY E.
  1963   *The Lively Experiment: The Shaping of Christianity in America.* New York: Harper & Row.

MERTON, ROBERT K., AND ALICE S. KITT
  1950   "Contributions to the theory of reference group behavior." Pp. 40–105 in Robert K. Merton and Paul F. Lazarsfeld (eds.), *Continuities in*

Social Research: Studies in the Scope and Method of "The American Soldier." Glencoe, Ill.: Free Press.

MILLER, ABRAHAM H.
1968   "Ethnicity and political behavior: An investigation of partisanship and efficacy." Ph.D. dissertation, University of Michigan.

MILLER, DANIEL R., AND GUY E. SWANSON
1958   *The Changing American Parent.* New York: Wiley.
1960   *Inner Conflict and Defense.* New York: Henry Holt.

MILLS, C. WRIGHT
1956   *The Power Elite.* New York: Oxford University Press.

MINER, HORACE
1956   "Body ritual among the Nacirema." *American Anthropologist* **58**: 503–7.

MITCHELL, J. CLYDE
1969a   *Social Networks in Urban Situations. Analyses of Personal Relationships in Central African Towns.* Manchester, England: Manchester University Press.
1969b   "The concept and use of social networks." Pp. 1–50 in J. Clyde Mitchell (ed.), *Social Networks in Urban Situations.* Manchester, England: Manchester University Press.

MITCHELL, ROBERT E.
1964   "Methodological notes on a theory of status crystallization." *Public Opinion Quarterly* **28**: 315–25.

MOORE, BARRINGTON
1966   *Social Origins of Dictatorship and Democracy: Lord and Peasant in the Making of the Modern World.* Boston: Beacon.

MORENO, J. L.
1953   *Who Shall Survive? Foundations of Sociometry, Group Psychotherapy and Sociodrama.* New York: Beacon House.

MORGAN, JAMES et al.
1964   *Income and Welfare in the United States.* New York: McGraw–Hill.

MORRISON, D. E., AND R. E. HENKEL
1969   "Significance tests reconsidered." *American Sociologist* **4**: 131–40.

MORTIMER, JEYLAN
1970   "The effects of family background and the college experience on occupational value orientations and the career decision." Unpublished report to the Office of Education, University of Michigan.
1972   "Family background and college influences upon occupational value orientations and the career decision." Ph.D. dissertation, University of Michigan.

MOSTELLER, FREDERICK
1968   "Association and estimation in contingency tables." *Journal of the American Statistical Association* **63**: 1–28.

MURRAY, HENRY et al.
1962   *Explorations in Personality.* New York: Science Editions.

NADEL, S. F.
1957   *The Theory of Social Structure.* London: Cohen and West.

NAM, CHARLES B.
1959 "Nationality groups and social stratification in America." *Social Forces* **37**: 328–33.

National Opinion Research Center
1947 "Jobs and occupations: A popular evaluation." *Opinion News* **9**: 3–13.

NEAL, ARTHUR G., AND GILBERT A. ABCARIAN
1969 "Association memberships and alienation profiles: A test of the mediation hypothesis." Unpublished paper, Bowling Green State University, Bowling Green, Ohio.

NEAL, ARTHUR G., AND SOLOMON RETTIG
1967 "On the multidimensionality of alienation." *American Sociological Review* **32**: 54–64.

NEAL, ARTHUR G., AND MELVIN SEEMAN
1964 "Organizations and powerlessness: A test of the mediation hypothesis." *American Sociological Review* **29**: 216–26.

NEWCOMB, THEODORE
1961 *The Acquaintance Process*. New York: Holt, Rinehart and Winston.

NIEBUHR, H. RICHARD
1929 *The Social Sources of Denominationalism*. New York: Henry Holt.

NISBET, ROBERT A.
1953 *The Quest for Community*. New York: Oxford University Press.

OLSEN, MARVIN E.
1965 "Political assimilation, social opportunities, and political alienation." Ph.D. dissertation, University of Michigan.
1968 *The Process of Social Organization*. New York: Holt, Rinehart and Winston.

PARENTI, MICHAEL
1967 "Ethnic politics and the persistence of ethnic identifications." *American Political Science Review* **61**: 717–26.

PARK, ROBERT E.
1924 "The concept of social distance." *Journal of Applied Sociology* **8**: 339–44.

PARKMAN, MARGARET, AND JACK SAWYER
1967 "Dimensions of ethnic intermarriage in Hawaii." *American Sociological Review* **32**: 593–607.

PARSONS, TALCOTT
1951 *The Social System*. Glencoe, Ill.: Free Press.
1961 "An outline of the social system." Pp. 30–79 in Talcott Parsons, Edward Shils, Kasper D. Naegele, and Jesse R. Pitts (eds.), *Theories of Society. Volume I.* New York: Free Press.
1966 *Societies: An Evolutionary Perspective*. Englewood Cliffs, N. J.: Prentice–Hall.
1970 "Equality and inequality in modern society, or social stratification revisited." Pp. 13–72 in Edward O. Laumann (ed.), *Social Stratification: Research and Theory for the 1970's*. New York: Bobbs-Merrill.

PARSONS, TALCOTT, AND ROBERT F. BALES
1955 *Family, Socialization and Interaction Process Analysis*. Glencoe, Ill.: Free Press.

PEARLIN, LEONARD I.
1962 "Alienation from work: A study of nursing personnel." *American Sociological Review* 23: 314–26.

PELZ, DONALD C., AND FRANK M. ANDREWS
1961 "The SRC computer program for multivariate analysis: Some uses and limitations." Survey Research Center, University of Michigan.

PINARD, MAURICE
1968 "Mass society and political movements: A new formulation." *American Journal of Sociology* 73: 682–90.

POOLE, WILLARD C., JR.
1927 "Distance in sociology." *American Journal of Sociology* 33: 99–104.

PORTER, JAMES N., JR.
1967 "Consumption patterns of professors and businessmen: A pilot study of conspicuous consumption and status." *Sociological Inquiry* 37: 255–67.

PROSHANSKY, HAROLD M., AND BERNARD SEIDENBERG
1965 *Basic Studies in Social Psychology.* New York: Holt, Rinehart and Winston.

PUTNAM, ROBERT D.
1966 "Political attitudes and the local community." *American Political Science Review* 60: 640–54.

RADCLIFFE-BROWN, A. R.
1952 *Structure and Function in Primitive Society: Essays and Addresses.* London: Cohen and West.

RAMSØY, NATALIE ROGOFF
1966 "Assortative mating and the structure of cities." *American Sociological Review* 31: 773–85.

RANSFORD, H. EDWARD
1968 "Isolation, powerlessness, and violence: A study of attitudes and participation in the Watts riot." *American Journal of Sociology* 73: 581–91.

RAPHAEL, EDNA E.
1965 "Power structure and membership dispersion in unions." *American Journal of Sociology* 71: 274–83.

RAPOPORT, ANTOL
1953 "Spread of information through a population with sociostructural bias: I, assumption of transivity, II, various models with partial transivity." *Bulletin of Mathematical Biophysics* 15: 523–33, 535–43.
1963 "Mathematical models of social interaction." Pp. 493–579 in R. D. Luce, R. R. Bush, and E. Galanter (eds.), *Handbook of Mathematical Psychology.* Volume 2. New York: Wiley.

RAPOPORT, ROBERT N., AND EDWARD O. LAUMANN
1964 "The institutional effect on career achievement of the technologist: A multiple classification analysis." *Report to the National Aeronautics and Space Administration and American Academy for Arts and Sciences.*

REISS, ALBERT J., JR.
1961 *Occupations and Social Status.* New York: Free Press.

RIECKEN, HENRY W., AND GEORGE C. HOMANS
    1954   "Psychological aspects of social structure." Pp. 786–832 in G. Lindzey
           (ed.), *Handbook of Social Psychology.* Volume 2. Reading, Mass.:
           Addison-Wesley.

RIESMAN, DAVID
    1953   *The Lonely Crowd.* Garden City, New York: Doubleday-Anchor Books.

RINGER, BENJAMIN B., AND DAVID L. SILLS
    1952   "Political extremists in Iran: A secondary analysis of communications
           data." *Public Opinion Quarterly* **26**: 689–701.

ROBINSON, W. S.
    1957   "The statistical measurement of agreement." *American Sociological
           Review* **22**: 17–25.

RODMAN, HYMAN
    1965   "Technical note on two rates of mixed marriage." *American Socio-
           logical Review* **30**: 776–78.

ROGOFF, NATALIE
    1953   *Recent Trends in Occupational Mobility.* Glencoe, Ill.: Free Press.

ROKEACH, MILTON
    1960   *The Open and Closed Mind.* New York: Basic Books.
    1969   *Beliefs, Attitudes, and Values: A Theory of Organization and Change.*
           San Francisco: Jossey–Bass.

ROSE, ARNOLD M.
    1954   *Theory and Method in the Social Sciences.* Minneapolis: University
           of Minnesota Press.

ROSEN, BERNARD C.
    1956   "The achievement syndrome: A psycho–cultural dimension of social
           stratification." *American Sociological Review* **21**: 203–11.
    1959   "Race, ethnicity, and the Achievement Syndrome." *American Socio-
           logical Review* **24**: 47–60.

ROSKAM, EDWARD E. C. I.
    1968   "Metric analysis of ordinal data in psychology." Ph.D. dissertation,
           University of Nijmegen, the Netherlands.
    1969   "A comparison of principles for algorithm construction in nonmetric
           scaling." *Michigan Mathematical Psychology Program Technical Report,*
           69–2.

ROSKAM, EDWARD E. C. I., AND JAMES C. LINGOES
    1969   "MINISSA–I, a FORTRAN IV(G) program for the smallest space
           analysis of square symmetric matrices." *Behavioral Science* **14**: 204.

ROSOW, IRVING
    1957   "Issues in the concept of need complementarity." *Sociometry* **20**: 216–
           33.

ROSSI, PETER
    1955   *Why Families Move.* Glencoe, Ill.: Free Press.

ROYDEN, H. L.
    1963   *Real Analysis.* New York: Macmillan.

RUESCH, JURGEN, AND WELDON KEES
1956 *Nonverbal Communication: Notes on the Visual Perception of Human Relations.* Berkeley and Los Angeles: University of California Press.

SAENGER, GERHART H.
1953 "Social status and political behavior." Pp. 348–58 in Reinhard Bendix and Seymour Martin Lipset (eds.), *Class, Status, and Power.* Glencoe, Ill.: Free Press.

SAMUELSSON, KURT
1957 *Religion and Economic Action.* New York: Harper Torchbooks.

SAPIR, EDWARD
1931 "Fashion." *Encyclopedia of the Social Sciences.* Volume VI. New York: Macmillan.

SCHACTER, STANLEY
1959 *The Psychology of Affiliation.* Stanford, Calif.: Stanford University Press.

SCHEUCH, ERWIN K.
1965 "Die Sichtbarkeit politischer Einstellungen im Alltäglichen Verhalten." *Kölner Zeitschrift für Soziologie und Sozialpsychologie* 17: 169–214.

SCHNEIDER, ANNEROSE
1969 "Expressive Verkehrskreise. Eine empirische Untersuchung zu freundschaftlichen und verwandtschaftlichen Beziehungen." *Inauguraldissertation zur Erlangung des Doktorgrades der Wirtschafts–und Sozialwissenschaftlichen Fakultät der Universität zu Köln.*

SCHNEIDER, LOUIS, AND SVERRE LYSGAARD
1953 "The deferred gratification pattern: A preliminary study." *American Sociological Review* 18: 142–49.

SCHONEMAN, PETER H.
1966 "A generalized solution of the orthogonal Procrustes problem." *Psychometrika* 31: 1–10.

SCHUMAN, HOWARD
1971 "The religious factor in Detroit: Review, replication, and reanalysis." *American Sociological Review* 36: 30–48.

SEELEY, JOHN R., R. ALEXANDER SIM, AND ELIZABETH W. LOOSELY
1956 *Crestwood Heights: A Study of the Culture of Suburban Life.* New York: Basic Books.

SEEMAN, MELVIN
1959 "On the meaning of alienation." *American Sociological Review* 24: 483–91.
1963 "Alienation and social learning in a reformatory." *American Journal of Sociology* 69: 270–84.
1966 "Alienation, membership, and political knowledge." *Public Opinion Quarterly* 30: 354–67.
1967 "On the personal consequences of alienation in work." *American Sociological Review* 32: 273–85.

SEEMAN, MELVIN, AND JOHN W. EVANS
1962 "Alienation and learning in a hospital setting." *American Sociological Review* 27: 105–23.

SEGAL, DAVID R.
    1969   "Status inconsistency, cross–pressures and American political behavior."
            American Sociological Review **34**: 352–59.

SEGAL, DAVID R., AND DAVID KNOKE
    1968   "Social mobility, status inconsistency and partisan realignment in the
            United States." *Social Forces* **42**: 154–57.

SEGAL, DAVID R., AND MARSHALL W. MEYER
    1969   "The social context of political partisanship." Pp. 217–32 in Mattei
            Dogan and Stein Rokkan (eds.), *Quantitative Ecological Analysis in the
            Social Sciences*. Cambridge: M.I.T. Press.

SELVIN, HANAN
    1957   "A critique of tests of significance in survey research." *American
            Sociological Review* **22**: 519–27.

SELZNICK, PHILIP
    1963   "Institutional vulnerability in mass society." Pp. 13–29 in Philip Olson
            (ed.), *America as a Mass Society*. New York: Free Press.

SEWELL, WILLIAM H.
    1940   "The construction and standardization of a scale for the measurement
            of the socio–economic status of Oklahoma farm families." Stillwater,
            Okla. *Oklahoma Agricultural and Mechanical College, Agricultural
            Experiment Station, Technical Bulletin No. 9*.

SHARP, HARRY, AND ALLAN FELDT
    1959   "Some factors in a probability sample survey of a metropolitan com-
            munity (Detroit Area Study)." *American Sociological Review* **24**: 650–61.

SHEPARD, ROGER N.
    1962a   "The analysis of proximities: Multidimensional scaling with an un-
            known distance function, I." *Psychometrika* **27**: 125–39.
    1962b   "The analysis of proximities: Multidimensional scaling with an un-
            known distance function, II." *Psychometrika* **27**: 219–46.
    1966   "Metric structures in ordinal data." *Journal of Mathematical Psychology*
            3: 287–315.

SHEPARD, ROGER N., AND J. B. KRUSKAL
    1964   "Nonmetric methods for scaling and for factor analysis." *American
            Psychologist* **19**: 557–8.

SHERIF, MAZAFER
    1936   *The Psychology of Social Norms*. New York: Harper.

SHIBUTANI, TANOTSU, AND KIAN M. KWAN
    1965   *Ethnic Stratification: A Comparative Approach*. New York: Macmillan.

SHILS, EDWARD A.
    1951   "The study of the primary group." Pp. 44–69 in Daniel Lerner and
            Harold D. Lasswell (eds.), *The Policy Sciences*. Stanford, Calif.:
            Stanford University Press.

SIEGEL, PAUL M.
    1970   "Occupational prestige in the Negro subculture." Pp. 156–71 in
            Edward O. Laumann (ed.), *Social Stratification: Theory and Research
            for the 1970s*. Indianapolis: Bobbs-Merrill.

SIEGEL, PAUL M., AND ROBERT W. HODGE
    1968   "A causal approach to the study of measurement error." Pp. 28–59 in

Hubert M. Blalock, Jr., and Ann B. Blalock (eds.), *Methodology in Social Research.* New York: McGraw–Hill.

SILBERMANN, ALPHONS
1963   *Vom Wohnen der Deutschen. Eine soziologische Studie über das Wohnerlebnis.* Köln und Opladen: Westdeutscher Verlag.

SIMMEL, GEORG
1908   "The stranger." Translated from *Soziologie* in Kurt H. Wolff (ed.), 1950. *The Sociology of Georg Simmel.* New York: Free Press.
1950   *The Sociology of Georg Simmel.* Translated by Kurt H. Wolff. New York: Free Press.
1964   "The web of group affiliations." Pp. 125–95 in Kurt H. Wolff and Reinhard Bendix (eds.), *Conflict and the Web of Group Affiliations.* Translated by Reinhard Bendix. New York: Free Press.

SIMPSON, GEORGE E., AND J. MILTON YINGER
1958   *Racial and Cultural Minorities.* New York: Harper.

SLATER, MARIAM K.
1958   "My son the doctor: Some aspects of mobility among American Jews." *American Sociological Review* 34: 359–73.

SMITH, DAVID HORTON
1966a "The importance of formal voluntary organizations for society." *Sociology and Social Research* 50: 483–95.
1966b "Communication: Comparison of self–reported participation in formal voluntary organizations with ratings of participation given by organization leaders." *Rural Sociology* 31: 362–65.

SMITH, THOMAS S.
1969   "Structural crystallization, status inconsistency, and political partisanship." *American Sociological Review* 34: 907–21.

SMITH, W. ROBERTSON
1956   *The Religion of the Semites.* 1899. New York: Meridian.

SOROKIN, PITIRIM A.
1927   *Social Mobility.* Retitled *Social and Cultural Mobility* and reprinted in 1959. New York: Free Press.
1947   *Society, Culture and Personality.* New York: Harper.

SPAULDING, CHARLES B.
1966   "Relative attachment of students to groups and organizations." *Sociology and Social Research* 50: 421–35.

SROLE, LEO et al.
1962   *Mental Health in the Metropolis.* Volume I. New York: McGraw–Hill.

STARK, RODNEY, AND CHARLES Y. GLOCK
1968   *American Piety: The Nature of Religious Commitment.* Berkeley, Calif.: University of California Press.

STEPHEN, FREDERICK J., AND PHILIP J. MCCARTHY
1958   *Sampling Opinions.* New York: Wiley.

STONE, LAWRENCE
1965   *The Crisis of the Aristocracy: 1558–1641.* London: Oxford University Press.

STOUFFER, SAMUEL A.
  1940   "Intervening opportunities: A theory relating mobility and distance."
         American Sociological Review **5**: 845–67.
  1955   *Communism, Conformity, and Civil Liberties.* New York: Doubleday.

STRODTBECK, FRED
  1958   "Family interaction, values, and achievement." In David McClelland
         (ed.), *Talent and Society.* New York: Van Nostrand.

SUSSMAN, MARVIN B., AND LEE BURCHINAL
  1962   "Kin family networks: Unheralded structure in current conceptualizations
         of family functioning." *Marriage and Family Living* **24**: 231–40.

SUTTLES, GERALD D.
  1968   *The Social Order of the Slum: Ethnicity and Territory in the Inner City.*
         Chicago: University of Chicago Press.

SWANSON, GUY E.
forth-   *Rules of Descent: Studies in the Sociology of Parentage.* Ann Arbor:
coming   University of Michigan Museum of Anthropology.

SYMON, KEITH R.
  1960   *Mechanics.* Second edition. Reading, Mass.: Addison–Wesley.

TAEUBER, ALMA F., AND KARL E. TAEUBER
  1967   "Recent immigration and studies of ethnic assimilation." *Demography*
         4: 798–808.

TAFT, RONALD
  1955   "The ability to judge people." *Psychological Bulletin* **52**: 1–23.

THERNSTROM, STEPHEN
  1969   "Religion and occupational mobility in Boston, 1880–1963." *Conference
         on Applications of Quantitative Methods to Political, Social and Economic
         History,* University of Chicago, June 1970.

TILLY, CHARLES
  1961   "Occupational rank and grade of residence in a metropolis." *American
         Journal of Sociology* **68**: 323–30.

TORGERSON, WARREN S.
  1958   *Theory and Methods of Scaling.* New York: Wiley.
  1965   "Multidimensional scaling of similarity." *Psychometrika* **30**: 379–93.

TRAVERS, JEFFREY, AND STANLEY MILGRIM
  1969   "An experimental study of the Small World problem." *Sociometry* **32**:
         425–43.

TREIMAN, DONALD
  1966   "Status discrepancy and prejudice." *American Journal of Sociology* **71**:
         651–64.

TROLDAHL, VERLING C., AND FREDERIC A. POWELL
  1965   "A short form dogmatism scale for use in field studies." *Social Forces*
         44: 211–14.

TURNER, RALPH H.
  1965   *The Social Context of Ambition.* San Francisco: Chandler.

TVERSKY, AMOS
  1966   "The dimensional representation and the metric structure of similarity
         data." Unpublished manuscript, February 1966 draft.

U. S. BUREAU OF THE CENSUS
   1969   *Pocket Data Book USA 1969*. Washington, D. C.: U. S. Government
         Printing Office.

VEBLEN, THORSTEIN
   1953   *The Theory of the Leisure Class*. New York: New American Library.

VERBA, SIDNAY
   1961   *Small Groups and Political Behavior*. Princeton, N. J.: Princeton Uni-
         versity Press.

VEROFF, JOSEPH, SHEILA FELD, GERALD GURIN
   1962   "Achievement, motivation, and religious background." *American Socio-
         logical Review* **27**: 205–7.

WARNER, W. LLOYD
   1953   *American Life*. Chicago: University of Chicago Press.

WARNER, W. LLOYD, AND LEO SROLE
   1945   *The Social Systems of American Ethnic Groups*. New Haven, Conn.:
         Yale University Press.

WARREN, BRUCE L.
   1970a "Socioeconomic achievement and religion: The American case." *Socio-
         logical Inquiry* **40**: 130–55.
   1970b "The role of religion and religious group identification in the socio-
         economic achievements of Americans." Ph.D. dissertation, University
         of Michigan.

WATSON, GOODWIN B.
   1925   "The measurement of fairmindedness." *Contribution to Education*.
         No. 176, Bureau of Publications, Teachers College, Columbia University.

WEBER, MAX
   1930   *The Protestant Ethic and the Spirit of Capitalism*. New York: Scribner's.
   1958   *The Religion of India or the Sociology of Hinduism and Buddhism*.
         Translated by Hans H. Gerth and Don Martingale. Glencoe, Ill.: Free
         Press.
   1966   "Class, status, party." Pp. 21–8 in Reinhard Bendix and Seymour Martin
         Lipset (eds.), *Class, Status and Power*. Second edition. New York:
         Free Press.

WECHSLER, DAVID
   1955   *Manual for Wechsler Adult Intelligence Scale*. New York: Psychological
         Corporation.

WEISS, ROBERT S., AND EUGENE JACOBSON
   1955   "A method for the analysis of the structure of complex organizations."
         American Sociological Review **20**: 661–68.

WELLMAN, BARRY, AND MARILYN WHITAKER
   1971   "Community-network-communication: An   annotated   bibliography."
         Bibliographic Series, No. 3. Toronto: University of Toronto, Centre for
         Urban and Community Studies.

WHYTE, WILLIAM FOOTE
   1943   *Street Corner Society*. Chicago: University of Chicago Press.

WHYTE, WILLIAM H.
1956   *The Organization Man.* Garden City, N. Y.: Doubleday-Anchor Books.

WILENSKY, HAROLD L., AND CHARLES N. LEBEAUX
1965   *Industrial Society and Social Welfare.* New York: Free Press.

WILLIAMS, ROBIN M., JR.
1957   *American Society.* New York: Knopf.
1959   "Friendship and social values in a suburban community: An exploratory study." *Pacific Sociological Review* 2: 3–10.

WILSON, ALAN B.
1959   "Residential segregation of social classes and aspirations of high school boys." *American Sociological Review* 24: 836–45.

WILSON, JAMES Q., AND EDWARD C. BANFIELD
1964   "Public Regardingness as a value premise in voting behavior." *American Political Science Review* 58: 876–87.

WINCH, ROBERT F., AND D. T. CAMPBELL
1969   "Proof: No. Evidence: Yes. The significance of tests of significance." *American Sociologist* 4: 140–43.

WINSLOW, CHARLES NELSON
1937   "A study of the extent of agreement between friends' opinions and their ability to estimate the opinions of each other." *Journal of Social Psychology* 8: 433–42.

WIRTH, LOUIS
1938   "Urbanism as a way of life." *American Journal of Sociology* 44: 1–24.

WITTKE, CARL
1956   *The Irish in America.* Baton Rouge: Louisiana State University Press.

WOLFE, ALVIN S.
1970   "On structural comparisons of networks," *Canadian Review of Sociology and Anthropology* (November): 226–44.

WOLFINGER, RAYMOND E.
1965   "The development and persistence of ethnic voting." *American Political Science Review* 59: 896–908.

WOOD, ARTHUR EVANS
1955   *Hamtramck—Then and Now.* New York: Bookman.

WRIGHT, CHARLES R., AND HERBERT H. HYMAN
1958   "Voluntary association membership of American adults: Evidence from national sample surveys." *American Sociological Review* 23: 284–94.

WRONG, DENNIS H.
1959   "The functional theory of stratification: Some neglected considerations." *American Sociological Review* 24: 772–82. Reprinted in Edward O. Laumann, Paul M. Siegel, and Robert W. Hodge (eds.), *The Logic of Social Hierarchies.* Chicago: Markham, 1970.

YOUNG, FORREST W.
1968   "TORSCA-9, a FORTRAN IV program for nonmetric multidimensional scaling." *Behavioral Science* 13: 343.

YOUNG, FORREST W., AND WARREN S. TORGERSON
1967   "TORSCA, a FORTRAN IV program for Shepard–Kruskal multidimensional scaling." *Behavioral Science* 12: 498.

YOUNG, GALE, AND A. S. HOUSEHOLDER
1938   "Discussion of a set of points in terms of their mutual distances."
       Psychometrika 3: 19–22.

YOUNG, MICHAEL D., AND PETER WILLMOTT
1960   *Family and Class in a London Suburb.* London: Routledge and K. Paul.

ZALEZNIK, ABRAHAM, C. R. CHRISTENSEN, F. J. ROETHLISBERGER, WITH
GEORGE C. HOMANS
1958   *The Motivation, Productivity, and Satisfaction of Workers: A Pre-
       diction Study.* Cambridge, Mass.: Harvard University Division of Re-
       search, Graduate School of Business Administration.

ZBOROWSKI, MARK
1952   "Cultural components in responses to pain." *Journal of Social Issues* 8:
       16–30.

ZELENY, LESLIE E.
1947   "Selection of compatible flying partners." *American Journal of Sociology*
       52: 424–31.

Author Index

Abcarian, Gilbert A., 159
Aberbach, Joel D., 137
Abramson, Harold J., 169
Acton, F., 166, 174, 191
Adams, Bert N., 87, 93, 129, 137, 202
Albert, R. S., 83
Alexander, C. Norman, Jr., 27, 32
Almond, Gabriel, 136, 143
Alston, Jon P., 79, 87
Andrews, Frank M., 119
Arendt, Hannah, 134
Artis, Jay W., 32
Asch, S. E., 115

Babchuk, Nicholas, 93, 140
Bales, Robert F., 111
Banfield, Edward, 172, 186
Barber, Bernard, 210
Barber, Elinor G., 210
Barnes, J. A., 2, 6, 7
Bauman, Karl E., 162
Beals, R., 245, 252
Bell, Daniel, 137
Bell, G. D., 27
Bell, Wendell, 137, 140
Bellah, Robert N., 210
Bendix, Reinhard, 5, 81
Benoit-Smullyan, E., 161
Berelson, Bernard, 27, 84, 92, 114
Beshers, James M., 42, 45, 187, 225–226
Blalock, Hubert M., Jr., 162
Blau, Peter M., 2, 4, 10, 22, 47, 71, 73, 75,
    82, 115, 122, 189, 197–198, 247
Blunt, E. A. H., 210
Boat, Marion, 137
Bogardus, Emory S., 42, 214–216, 224,
    226–227
Bonacich, Philip, 71, 74, 238–239
Booth, Alan, 140
Borhek, J. T., 181
Bott, Elizabeth, 7, 87, 93, 112, 116, 122
Box, Steven, 162, 164
Bradshaw, Benjamin, 42
Brandmeyer, Gerard, 162
Brigante, T. R., 83
Brim, Orville G., Jr., 111, 129
Brown, Daniel, 4, 14, 23
Buckley, Walter F., 2

Burchinal, Lee, 137

Campbell, Ernest Q., 27, 32
Caplow, Theodore, 2, 84, 115
Cartwright, Dorwin, 7, 113
Chambliss, J., 162
Chapin, F. Stuart, 139
Chinoy, Ely, 80
Coelho, George V., 83
Coleman, James S., 32–33, 84, 110, 135
Converse, Philip, 40
Coombs, C. H., 221, 232, 243, 253
Coser, Lewis, 135
Curtis, Richard F., 73, 83
Cutler, Stephen J., 156–158, 203

Dahl, Robert A., 172
Dahlgren, Harold E., 27
Davidson, D., Jr., 32
Davis, James A., 114, 129–130
Davis, Kingsley, 5
Dean, Lois R., 159
Demerath, Nicholas J., III, 51–53, 58, 67
Deming, W. E., 239
Dotson, Floyd, 87, 137
Duncan, Beverly, 45, 73–74, 114, 186–187,
    196, 215
Duncan, Otis Dudley, 10, 22, 32, 42, 45,
    47, 71, 73–75, 82, 109, 114, 116,
    186–187, 193–198, 215, 225, 247
Durkheim, Emile, 106, 129

Eckland, B. K., 198
Eckstein, Harry, 135
Eisenstadt, S. N., 115, 122
Erbe, William, 136
Evans, John W., 136

Farley, Reynolds, 212
Faumann, S. Joseph, 162, 169
Featherman, David, 186, 191
Fennessey, James, 17, 120
Festinger, Leon, 2, 34, 84, 97, 129
Force, Maryanne T., 140
Ford, Julienne, 162, 164
Fromm, Erich, 134, 137

Galtung, Johann, 161

327

Gans, Herbert J., 86, 91, 93, 116, 121, 129
Gardner, Burleigh B., 252
Gaustad, Edwin Scott, 51, 58, 210
Geschwender, James A., 161
Gerson, Walter M., 136
Glazer, Nathan, 59, 162, 172
Gleason, T. C., 242–243, 251
Glenn, Norval D., 53, 79, 87
Glock, Charles Y., 27, 52–53, 57–58
Gluckman, Max, 2, 22
Gockel, Galen L., 164, 188
Goffman, I. W., 161, 169
Goldberg, David, 181, 221
Goldstein, Sidney, 164
Gordon, Milton M., 9, 45, 51, 59, 186, 188
Granovetter, Mark S., 84, 129
Greeley, Andrew M., 164, 166
Greer, Scott, 137
Gregson, R. A. M., 244
Gusfield, Joseph R., 138
Guthrey, S. B:, 243
Guttman, Louis, 4, 11, 17, 59, 74, 80, 201,
    214, 217, 220, 226, 236–239, 243,
    248–253

Hald, A., 166
Handlin, Oscar, 169, 186
Harary, Herbert, 7, 39, 43, 113
Hare, A. P., 85
Haug, Marie R., 74
Hausknecht, Murray, 97, 136, 140, 155
Haven, Clayton, 143
Hays, William L., 157
Heider, F., 34
Henry, Jules, 129
Herberg, Will, 9, 51–53, 67, 200
Herriott, Robert E., 27
Higham, John, 169, 187
Hill, T. P., 17, 119
Himmelfarb, Samuel, 160
Hodge, Robert W., 5, 10, 40, 70–71, 162,
    164, 166, 181, 225
Holden, David, E. W., 137
Homans, George C., 2, 4–5, 73
House, James S., 74, 207, 229
Hsu, Francis, L. K., 210
Hunter, Floyd, 32, 135
Hyland, Ruth, 53
Hyman, Herbert H., 87, 140
Hyman, M. D., 87, 162

Jackson, Elton F., 161
Jacobson, Eugene, 32
Janowitz, Morris, 137
Jensen, Arthur R., 198

Kantrowitz, Nathan, 164
Katz, Elihu, 27, 84
Katz, Fred E., 129
Katz, F. M., 84
Kelley, K. Dennis, 162
Kelman, H. C., 84
Kemper, Theodore D., 111
Kennedy, Ruby Jo Reeves, 51–52

Kimberly, James C., 161
King, Morton B., 73
Kitt, Alice S., 111
Knoke, David, 161, 163
Kohn, Melvin L., 10, 87
Kornhauser, William, 8, 134, 141–142, 156,
    203
Kruskal, J. B., 231, 243–244, 247–250

Lasswell, Thomas, 164, 198
Laumann, Edward O., 3–5, 10–11, 27, 29,
    39, 41–42, 45, 71, 73–74, 80, 83–84,
    87, 97, 99, 102–104, 106, 109, 114,
    134, 176, 181, 210, 214–215, 217,
    223–226, 229, 236–239
Lazarsfeld, Paul F., 27, 84
Leach, Edmund R., 210
Lebeaux, Charles N., 133
Lee, 52
Lenski, Gerhard, 11, 53, 72, 91, 161–162,
    176, 180, 186, 197, 200, 204
Levens, Helene, 136
Lewis, Oscar, 210
Lieberson, Stanley, 42, 59, 114, 169, 186
Liebow, Elliot, 121, 129
Lingoes, James C., 17, 59, 71, 241, 243–244,
    248–251
Linton, Ralph, 5, 88
Lipset, Seymour Martin, 5, 21, 51–52, 81,
    109, 136, 138, 141
Litton, G., 181
Litwak, Eugene, 86
Loomis, Charles, 32
Lopata, Helena Znaniecki, 135
Lopreato, Joseph, 175
Lowenthal, Marjorie Fiske, 143
Lundberg, George A., 32
Lundy, Richard M., 39

McCall, George J., 111
McCarthy, Philip J., 40
McClelland, David, 10, 186
McClosky, Herbert, 27
Maccoby, Herbert, 136
McDavid, John W., 39, 43
McFarland, David D., 4, 14, 23, 225, 236
McGee, V. E., 243
McLoughlin, William G., 210
March, James, 111
Marx, Karl, 1, 5, 9, 21, 81
Mayhew, Leon, 5, 86, 88–89, 108
Maynard, Theodore, 59, 211
Mead, Sidney E., 51, 58, 210
Merton, Robert K., 84, 111
Meyer, Marshall W., 137, 155
Milgrim, Stanley, 129
Miller, Abraham H., 164
Miller, Daniel R., 10
Mills, C. Wright, 137
Mitchell, J. Clyde, 2, 6–8, 21–22, 84, 129
Mitchell, Robert E., 162
Moore, Wilbert E., 5, 210
Moreno, J. L., 2

Morgan, James, 17, 119
Mortimer, Jeylan, 210
Mosteller, Fred, 71, 239–240
Moynihan, Daniel P., 59, 162, 172

Nadel, S. F., 2, 8
Nam, Charles, 186
Neal, Arthur G., 136, 141, 159
Neugarten, Bernice L., 110
Newcomb, Theodore, 5, 32, 34, 36, 41,
    84–85, 114
Niebuhr, H. Richard, 51–53, 58, 67, 210
Nisbet, Robert A., 137
Norman, R. Z., 7, 113

Olsen, Marvin E., 137, 155
Orleans, Peter, 137

Parenti, Michael, 162, 164, 166, 172
Park, Robert E., 216
Parsons, Talcott, 3–5, 22, 86, 88, 111,
    129, 130
Pearlin, Leonard I., 144
Pelz, Donald C., 119
Pinard, Maurice, 138, 144, 155
Poole, W. C., 234
Proshansky, Harold M., 115
Putnam, Robert D., 138

Radcliffe-Brown, A. R., 2
Ransford, H. Edward, 136
Raphael, Edna E., 137
Rapoport, Anatol, 109, 129
Reiss, Albert J., Jr., 10
Rettig, Solomon, 141
Riecken, Henry W., 73
Riesman, David, 135
Ringer, Benjamin B., 136
Rogoff, Natalie, 71
Rokeach, Milton, 99, 102–103, 141
Rose, Arnold M., 135, 137
Rosen, Bernard C., 186
Roskam, E. E. C. I., 243–244, 248, 250–251
Rosow, Irving, 114
Rossi, Peter, 91
Royden, H. L., 219

Samuelsson, Kurt, 210
Scheuch, Erwin K., 12, 111, 129
Schneider, Anne Rose, 5, 125
Schumann, Howard, 99, 102, 188, 197, 200,
    204
Seeman, Melvin, 136–137, 141
Segal, David R., 134, 137, 155, 161–162,
    165, 180
Seidenberg, B., 115
Selznick, Philip, 137, 154
Senn, David J., 160
Shepard, R. N., 228, 243–244, 247–248,
    252
Sherif, M., 115
Shils, Edward A., 114
Siegel, Paul M., 5, 10, 40, 70–71, 164, 166,
    181, 212

Sills, David L., 136
Simmel, Georg, 2, 84, 113, 115, 119, 203,
    214–215
Simmons, J. L., 111
Simon, Herbert A., 111
Slater, Mariam K., 186
Smith, David Horton, 135–136, 159
Sonquist, John, 119
Sorokin, Pitirim A., 160, 214, 216–217,
    226–227
Spaulding, Charles R., 143
Srole, Leo, 87
Stark, Rodney, 27, 52–53, 58
Steele, Mary, 32
Stephen, Frederick J., 40
Stone, Lawrence, 210
Stouffer, Samuel A., 102, 142, 237
Sussman, Marvin B., 74, 137
Suttles, Gerald D., 91, 121, 129
Swanson, Guy, 10

Taeuber, Alma F., 186
Taeuber, Karl E., 186, 212
Taft, Ronald, 39
Thernstrom, Stephan, 186
Torgerson, W. S., 243, 248
Travers, Jeffrey, 129
Treiman, Donald, 162
Tsouderos, John E., 139
Turkey, J. W., 166, 174, 177, 191
Turner, Ralph H., 114
Tversky, A., 222, 252

U.S. Bureau of the Census, 1

Verba, Sidney, 84, 111, 136, 143

Warner, W. Lloyd, 106, 110, 209–210
Warren, Bruce L., 6, 164, 188
Weber, Max, 1, 5, 9, 11, 21–22, 106, 180,
    186, 197, 204, 210
Wechsler, David, 130, 281
Weiss, Robert S., 32
Wellman, Barry, 2
Whitaker, Marilyn, 2
Whyte, William Foote, 121
Whyte, William H., 115
Wilensky, Harold L., 133
Willmott, Peter, 122, 129
Wilson, Alan B., 27
Wilson, James Q., 166, 172
Wirth, Louis, 111
Wolfe, Alvin W., 2
Wolfinger, Raymond E., 162, 166
Wood, Arthur Evans, 166
Wright, Charles R., 140
Wrong, Dennis H., 5

Young, F. W., 243
Young, Michael D., 122, 129

Zaleznik, Abraham, 59
Zaleny, Leslie E., 32

Subject Index

ABX model, 37; *see* Balance, ABX theory of
Acculturation, 206
Achieved characteristics, intergenerational transmission of, 189
Achieved social position, 11, 19–20
Achieved status, 74, 161–163, 166, 174–175, 180, 197, 205
  characteristics, 12
Achievement, 6, 86, 88, 96, 105
  criteria of, 6
Achievement-based hierarchies, 20
Achievement orientation, 22, 81, 87–88, 98–99, 108
Action frame of reference, adaptive system of, 22
  goal-attainment system of, 22
  integrative system of, 22
  pattern-maintenance system of, 22
Adriatic Sea, 49
Affluent societies, 144
Age, 6, 29, 31, 38–41, 86, 89, 91, 105, 119, 121–122, 142, 181, 197, 255–256, 258
Age structure, 2–3
Alienation, 133–134, 136–137, 141, 144, 159
Allen Park, 256
American Catholicism, 210–211
American Sociological Association, 27, 211
Americanization, 207
Anglo-American, 59, 64–67, 168, 173, 191–192, 195
Anglo-American Baptists, 17, 64, 89, 168, 177, 191
Anglo-American Catholics, 65
Anglo-American groups, 193, 196
Anglo-American Lutherans, 64
Anglo-American Methodists, 64, 166, 168
Anglo-American Presbyterians, 64, 168, 195
Anglo-Saxon Protestants, 42
Apathy, 134
Area sample, 257
Asceticism, 186
Ascribed social position, 19–20
Ascribed status, 161–162, 180, 204–205, 208

Ascription, 5, 86, 88, 96, 105, 160
  criteria of, 6
Ascription-based hierarchies, 20
Ascription networks, 174
Ascriptive ethnoreligious group, 205
Ascriptive groups, membership of, 6, 43, 73, 84, 89, 172, 188, 191, 196
  social structure of, 70
Ascriptive orientation, 81, 86, 88, 98, 108, 116
Ascriptive status, 161–162, 164, 174, 181, 197
  characteristics, 12, 160
  order, 22
  position, 17
  structure, 81
Ascriptive ties, 87
Ascriptively defined group, 86
Assimilation, 200, 206, 210
Association involvement, 98, 143
Associational congruence, 103
Atomization, 134
  structural, 133
Attitudes, 9, 98, 126
  common relevance of, 34, 41
  saliency of, 34
Attitude similarity, random pair model in, 35
Austria, 285
Authoritarian movements, 141
Auto workers, 40, 83
Automobile assembly line, 75
Automobile manufacturing, 80
Autonomous relations, 134

Balance, ABX diagram of, 36
  ABX theory of, 34, 36, 38, 84
Baptist, 57–58
Belief systems, definition of, 40
  in mass publics, 40
Bethnal Green, 129
Blacks, 18, 165, 198, 206, 209, 224, 255–256, 259–261
Black community, 212
Bogardus social distance scale, 42, 213–216, 224–226, 228–230, 240
Bookkeeper, 278
Boston's East End, 129

British, 49−51, 70, 187
British-American, 49
British social anthropologists, 6
Brother, 264, 269−271
Brother-in-law, 264, 269−271
Bureaucratic, 10
Bureaucratic-entrepreneurial dimension, 200, 210
Bureaucratic and entrepreneurial occupations, 9
Bureaucratic organizations, 75, 79
Business and civic groups, 149−150, 155, 158, 272
Businessmen, 197, 227

Calvinist Protestants, 197
"Calvinistic" Presbyterians, 204
Cambridge-Belmont, Mass., 74, 103, 201
Canada, 188−189, 211, 255, 286, 288
Canadians, 196, 285
Capitalism, 11, 197, 210
Career choices, 210
Carpenter, 278
Catholic, 10−11, 34, 49, 51−53, 57−59, 64−67, 71, 76, 87−89, 91−92, 97, 106−107, 121, 126, 166, 168, 173, 187−188, 197, 200, 202, 204, 207, 284
Catholic groups, 168, 172, 174, 189, 191
Catholic leadership, 211
Catholic priests, 6
Census enumeration districts, 257
Census tract, 255
Central Europe, 49
Charity or welfare groups, 150, 273
Chicago, 71, 129
Children, number of, 290
China, 217, 285
Chi-square test, 17
Christian groups, differentiation of, 58
Christian orthodoxy, 58
Christmas, 289
Church attendance, 53, 65−67, 72, 98−99, 189
   frequency of, 107, 168
Church of Christ, 57−58
Church-connected groups, 150−153, 159, 272
City block metric, 245
City councilman, 280
City directory, 256, 259
Civil liberties, 102−103, 142, 152, 155
Civil libertarianism, 169
Class, 5, 20−21, 122, 224
   status groupings of, 1, 12
   see also Economic class; Social class
Class or statusmates, 81
Class boundaries, 210
Class consciousness, 81, 99
Class groups, 208, 210
Class relations, 211
Class structure, 2, 91, 176
Class subculture, 82

Clerk in store, 230, 275, 278−279
Closed minded, 102, 107, 127
Coefficient, of alienation, 55, 59, 67, 79, 81, 217
   of monotonicity, "stress," 247
Collectivized orientations, 106
College degree, 91, 265−266, 270−271, 283−284, 286, 288
College graduate, 265−266, 273, 283−284, 286, 288
College students, 210
Common relevance, 85
Communication systems, 112
Communist, 36, 102−103, 142, 152, 156, 169, 274−275, 279−280
   tolerance of, 102, 142
Community Centers, 272
Complete monotonicity, 234
Composition, homogeneity of, 124
Conditional monotonicity, 234, 236
Conditional probabilities, 71
Conditional proximities, 232, 234, 236, 253
Congregationalists, 53, 55, 57−58; see also
   Religious groups
Congressional committee, 275, 280
Connectedness, 201
Consensual relationship, 5, 114
Conservatism, 172
Conservative, 200
   economically, 103
Construction laborer, 278
Contact situation, 93
Correlation ratio, see Eta coefficient
Country clubs, 150, 158, 273
Country of origin, 47, 99, 188
County hospital, 263
Cross-pressures, 103, 114
Crystallized class structure, 81
Crystallized status structure, 81
Cultural differentiation, 208
Cultural heritage, 208
Cultural pluralism, 180, 188
Cultural pluralism model, 9−10
"Culture of poverty," 206
Customary place of interaction, 202
Czechoslovakia, 285

Data-reduction technique, 251−252
Dearborn, 256
Deference, 161
Degree of functionality, 202
Degrees of intimacy, 202
Democratic norms, 138
Democratic Party, 17, 32, 161, 169, 172, 176, 181
Democratic party preference, 29, 31, 92, 103−104, 126, 128, 267, 271, 282
Demographic characteristics, 89, 92, 108, 113, 116, 119−120, 128
Denominations, 52
Denominational affiliations, 51, 284−285
Denver, 15
Detroit, 6, 8, 12, 18, 32, 40−41, 53, 59,

71, 82, 87, 102–103, 122, 140, 174,
    197, 201, 207, 209–210, 254, 256,
    259–260, 267, 271, 280, 282, 291
Detroit Area Study, 1, 17, 28, 197, 254,
    262
Detroit Standard Metropolitan Statistical
    Area, 18, 45, 47, 71, 254, 259
Devotionalism, 72, 98–99, 107, 189
Devotionalism scale, 53
Differentiation, 86; *see also* Structural
    differentiation
Differential status awareness, 176
Dimension, 227–228
Dimensional representation, 222, 240–241,
    243–244, 247
    computational procedure for, 243
    of metric space, definition of, 221, 253
Dimensionality, 243–244, 248, 250, 253
Discriminatory practices, 187
Distance, function, 217
Distance–generating postulate, 5, 8, 53, 85,
    201
Distances, 14, 16, 23
Division of labor, 208
Dogmatism, 102, 141, 143–146, 148–149,
    151, 153, 156–158
Dogmatism scale, 103, 141
Duncan Index of Socioeconomic Status,
    29, 74, 92; *see also* Index for Socio-
    economic Status
Duncan occupation score, 109, 150, 158
Dutch Reformed, 52
Dwelling unit, 254–255
Dyadic relation, 84, 111, 113–115, 119,
    203

Earth, curvature of, 16
Easter, 289
Eastern Europe, 49
Eastern Orthodox, 66, 72
    Communion, 51
Eastern (Slavic) Protestants, 64
Ecological segregation, 74
Economic attitudes, 9, 11, 175
Economic beliefs, 11, 103
Economic class, 1, 3, 9, 81. *See also* Class;
    Social Classes
Economic conservatives, 175
Economic ideology, 9, 175–176
Economic interests, 21
Economic issues, 169
Economic orientations, 204
Economic status, 216, 226
Economic system, 176
Ecorse, 256
Education, 40–41, 98, 102–103, 122, 124,
    145–151, 153, 156–159, 161, 163–
    164, 166, 168, 175, 180–181, 186,
    191, 204, 227, 258, 260, 274
    values of, 35
Educational achievements, 11, 21, 73, 123,
    188–189, 191
Educational attainment, 11, 29, 31, 34, 38,

40, 79, 81, 88–89, 91, 97–98, 105–
    106, 115, 119, 122, 160–161, 165,
    169, 172–173, 177, 198
Educational homogeneity, 109
Educational status, 162, 174, 189, 196
Educational structure, 2
Eligible household, 254
Employees, 75, 279
Employers, 279
Engineers, 109
England, 210
Entrepreneurial employment, 75
Episcopal, 58, 64
Equal status association, 103
Eta coefficient, 120, 123, 128, 130, 146
Ethnic affiliation, 200
Ethnic assimilation, 180
Ethnic attitudes, 28
Ethnic background, 70, 103, 112, 116, 285,
    289
Ethnic behavior, 168
Ethnic communities, 10
Ethnic differences, theory of, 169
Ethnic differentiation in America, 164
Ethnic effect, 67
Ethnic factor, 66
Ethnic groups, 19, 43, 47, 49, 54, 58–59,
    67, 70, 81, 99, 109, 113–114, 157,
    172, 176, 181, 186–187, 200, 215–
    216, 226, 256, 267, 289
    Arab, 43, 49, 51
    assimilation of, 42, 45, 71
    Czech, 45, 49, 51, 70, 196
    Dutch-Belgian, 70
    English, 31
    French, 49, 64–65, 70, 168, 173, 191
    German, 31, 49–51, 59, 64–65, 70,
        168, 173, 188, 191–192, 196
    Hungarian, 70
    Irish, 31, 49, 51, 65, 70, 168, 191, 196
    Italian, 49, 51, 65, 168, 186, 191
    linguistic differences among, 52
    Nonwhite, 154
    Polish, 49, 51, 65, 70–71, 186
    preference to marry within, 99
    principal time of arrival of, 42, 47, 86
    ranking of, 162
    Scandinavian, 70
    Scotch, 31, 49
    self-selection of, 44
    Slavic, 49, 168
    smallest space analysis of, 49
    social standing of, 47, 54, 70
    subcultural aspects of, 162, 180
    subjective interest in, 126, 188
    unidimensional rank-order of, 42
    Welsh, 31
Ethnic group membership, 86–87, 121, 162
Ethnic identification, 47, 91, 207
Ethnic identity, 12, 45, 116
Ethnic intermarriage, 52
Ethnic minorities, 186
Ethnic organizations, 272

Ethnic origin, 3, 27, 43, 59, 70, 197
  inaccuracy in report of, 31, 38
Ethnic prejudices, 42–43, 59
Ethnic-religious differences, axis of, 19
Ethnic space, 51
Ethnic status, 162
Ethnic States Index, Hodge and Siegel's,
  181
Ethnic status order, 43
Ethnicity, 161–162, 164, 202, 227, 241,
  255
Ethnoreligious community, 181
Ethnoreligious composition, 91
Ethnoreligious differences, 162
Ethnoreligious groups, 6, 9, 20, 43, 51, 67,
  73, 98, 160, 164–169, 172–173,
  175–177, 180–181, 188–189, 191,
  195, 199–200, 203–204, 206, 209–
  210
Ethnoreligious group membership, 188,
  205–206
  ascribed characteristics of, 85
Ethnoreligious group ranking, 175
Ethnoreligious groups, definition of, 59
  indexes of dissimilarity for, 59, 79
  later-generation, 11, 21
  macrostructure of, 6
  membership in, 17–18, 124, 160
  self-selection within, 81
  smallest space analysis for, 66, 87
  status ordering of, 173
  structure of, 3–4, 19, 43, 86, 108
  subcultural difference among, 11, 20–21
  third-generation, 11, 21
Ethnoreligious heterogeneity, 108
Ethnoreligious homogeneity, 88–89, 91–
  93, 96, 98–99, 103–104, 106, 108–
  109, 121, 124, 181, 202
Ethnoreligious matters, subjective interest
  in, 98
Ethnoreligious preference, 201
Ethnoreligious social structure, 9
Ethnoreligious solution, 67
Ethnoreligious status, 164, 173
Ethnoreligious status ranking, Laumann's,
  164, 181
Ethnoreligious structures, 201
Ethnoreligiously homogeneous networks,
  174; see also Homogeneity
Euclidean distance, 16, 87, 217–219, 242–
  243, 245–246, 248, 253
Euclidean metric, 244–245, 247
Euclidean space, 16, 216, 248, 253
European Catholicism, 211
Evolution, unilinear model of, 86
Extended family, 202
Extremist groups, tolerance toward, 177

Factor analysis, 244
Families, bureaucratic, 10
  entrepreneurial, 10
Family income, 47, 50, 58, 65–65, 76, 81,
  88, 91–92, 106, 149–151, 153,

  157–160, 168, 174, 189, 207, 292
Family traditionalism, 112, 181
Family tree, 285, 287
Farm laborers, 82
Farmers, 82, 197
Fatalism, 136
Father, 71, 74, 82, 126
Father-in-law, 71, 74, 82, 176
Fertility, 72
Financial position, 292
First generation, 187
Focal actor, 7
Foreign born, 18, 50, 140, 255
Foreign stock, 45, 47, 71, 187
Foreign white males, 45
France, 210
Fraternal associations and lodges, 150, 152–
  153, 158, 207, 272
French Catholics, 177
Friends, 176
  attitude agreement of, 28
  attitude similarity of, 33–34, 39
  closeness of, 34, 40, 96
  discuss marital difficulties with, 125–126
  frequency of contact with, 28, 34, 40,
    115, 123–125, 143
  level of intimacy of, 28, 123–126
  opportunity structure of, 89
  physical propinquity of, 74
  proximity of, 24
  reported closeness of, 93
  reports on occupation, 74
Friends' attributes, accuracy in reporting, 27,
  29, 38
  bias in report of, 28, 31
  correlations between, 41
Friendship, affective involvement in, 114
  average duration of, 96
  closeness of, 169, 264
  definition of, 83
  duration of, 169
  exchange in, 73
  frequency of interaction, 107, 169
  macrostructural analysis of, 7
  microstructural analysis of, 6
  mutual attraction in, 85, 96
  reciprocity in, 34, 36, 73
Friendship characteristics, accuracy of, 19
Friendship choices, 16, 45, 55, 70, 87, 164,
  209, 238
  achievement criteria of, 73
  among ethnic groups, 47, 51, 87
  by ethnicity, 45
  in group, 45
  homogeneity of, 181
  among occupations, 75, 87, 109–110
  reciprocity in, 19, 28, 32–33, 39
  self-selectivity model of, 116
  structuralist model of, 118
Friendship groups, 169
Friendship and homogeneity, 92, 105
Friendship interaction, by sex, 93
Friendship network, 19, 109, 139, 144, 153

characteristics of, 113, 124
composition of, 88
form of, 202
formal properties of, 113
homogeneity of, 85, 89, 97–98, 108, 113
size of, 107
structure of, 23
unreciprocated, 38
work-based, 93
Friendship relations, 4, 16
extensive conception of, 96–97
intensive conception of, 96
Friendship selection, achievement criteria of, 88
ascriptive criteria of, 88
occupationally based, 91
opportunity structure for, 108
Friendship set, 201
Functional differentiation, 85–86, 108
Fundamentalist Protestant denomination, 53, 57–58

Garage mechanic, 278
Gemeinschaft, 20, 96, 112, 128, 130, 202
Generations, 181
Generation of arrival, 202
Generations in the United States, 91, 99, 106, 121
Geographical mobility, 91, 115
Geometrical distance, see Physical distance
German Americans, 49, 187, 196
German Baptists, 59, 64
German Catholics, 59, 87, 196
German Lutherans, 64, 168, 177, 191, 196
German Mannerchore, 207
German Methodists, 59, 64, 172, 177
German Presbyterians, 59, 87, 166, 168, 174–175, 180–181, 191, 195, 205
German Reformed, 52
Gesellschaft, 20, 112, 128, 130, 202
Gestures, 262–263, 274, 279–282, 284–285
Global optimum, 249
God, 58
Granleigh, 129
Greensboro, North Carolina, 129
Grosse Pointe, 256
Grosse Pointe Farms, 256
Grosse Pointe Park, 256
Grosse Pointe Shores, 256
Grosse Pointe Township, 256
Grosse Pointe Woods, 256
Group boundaries, 82
Group size, 43, 45, 70
as a component of social distance, 238–240
effect of, 74–75

Hamtramck, 256
Harper Woods, 256
Herberg's tripartite religious division, 53, 58, 67
Heterogeneity, pure, 105

Highland Park, 256
High School graduates, 88, 91–92, 102–103, 107, 123, 126, 265–266, 270, 273, 283–284, 286, 288
Homogeneity, 181, 201
achievement based, 86–87, 105, 124
ascription based, 86, 105, 124
of composition, 2, 20, 84–85
measurement of, 87, 89, 92, 109
political party, 124
pure, 105, 107
types of, 106–108
Homophily, 53
Hungary, 285

Identity confusion, 129
Immigration, 187, 262
Immigration laws, 187
Income, 162, 164, 227, 258, 260, 277–278, 292
Income structure, 2
Independent party preference, 29, 31, 92, 103, 271, 282
Index for Socioeconomic Status, Duncan's two-digit, 193, 195
Index of dissimilarity, 16, 45, 47, 54, 57, 70–71, 195, 201, 219
definition of, 45
Indiana, 39
Indian caste system, 210
Industrial society, 115
Industrial structure, 4
Industry groups, 75
Influence, personal, 84, 135
Inheritance, 197–198
Initial configurations, 243, 248–250
Instrumental relationship, 85
Integration, structural, 138
Intellectual capabilities, 122–123, 130; see also Similarities subtest
Intelligence, 198; see also Similarities subtest
Interaction, density of, 2, 84
face to face, 111
sites of, 116, 123
Interaction effect, 106, 173, 165, 177, 205
"Interaction" term, 205
Interest group, 136
Interest similarity, 83
Intergenerational mobility, 174–175, 207
Intergenerational stability, 175
Interlocking network, 201–203
Interlocking nets, completely, 203
partially, 203
Interlocking network, definition of, 113, 115
Intermediate groups, 138–139, 144, 146–148, 154, 156
Interpersonal attraction, 43
Interpoint distances, 221, 242–243, 247–248, 253
Interval scale, 220–221, 243
Intervening opportunities, theory of, 237
Interview schedule, 139

Intimate relationship, 5
Intraclass correlation, 29
Iran, 136
Irish Catholics, 172, 191
Isosimilarity contour, 245–246
Israel, 289
Italian Catholics, 173
Italo-American, 86, 116, 129
Iterative procedures, 241, 247

Japan, 211
Japanese, 70
Jehovah's Witnesses, 51
Jesus, 58
Jew(ish), 10, 43, 49, 51–53, 55, 57, 59,
     64, 67, 71, 121, 165, 168, 172–175,
     180–181, 186–188, 191, 195–196,
     198, 200, 202, 205–206, 209, 284,
     289
  Conservative, 71, 284
  holiday, 289
  Orthodox, 71, 284
  Reform, 71, 284
Job, first full-time, 283
  main, 265, 270, 272, 282
Job change, 91, 99, 107, 126
Juvenile delinquents, 263

Kansas City, 110
Kin, consanguineal, 93
Kinship, 4, 86, 112, 116, 125, 129, 174
  fictive, 125
Klasse an sich, 5, 81
Klasse für sich, 5, 81
Ku Klux Klan, 102, 142, 152, 156, 169,
     274, 279–280

Labor unions, 136–137, 150–153, 155–
     156, 158–159, 262, 272
Laborers in manufacturing, 80
Later-generation Americans, 18, 121, 188–
     189, 191, 196, 206
Later-generation subsample, 191–192, 196,
     198
Latin America, 196
Lawyer, 278
Leftist ideological nonconformity, 142
Leftwing politics, 102
Liberal, 103
"Liberal" orientations, 169
Liberalism, 162
Liberalism-conservatism, economic, 103–
     104
Life cycle, 89, 106
Life Styles, see Styles of life
Linear regression analysis, 12, 116
Lincoln Park, 256
Living room décor, 207, 211, 275
Living room furnishings, 208, 229
Local optima, 248–250
London, 112, 129
Los Angeles Times, 211
Lower class, 86, 92, 106, 281

Lower middle class, 207
Lower occupational status, 28
Lutherans, 52, 58, 64, 197

Macomb County, 39, 267, 281
Macrostructural analysis, 18, 83, 108, 160,
     199, 201
Macrostructure, 19, 118
  definition of, 4
  dimensionality of, 5
  multidimensional nature of, 70
Majority American, 31
Managers, 75
Markov chains, 225–226
Marxist sociology, 21
Mass man, 134, 141
Mass media, 206, 209
Mass society, theory of, 8, 20, 133, 136–
     139, 141, 143–145, 148–149, 153–
     156. 159, 203
Maximum discrepancy metric, 245
Mean first passage time, 225–226
Means of production, 5, 81
Measurement error, 40
Mechanical solidarity, 128–129
Medical profession, 32
Mediterranean, 49
Melting-pot theory, 180–181, 188; see also
     Triple Melting Pot
Melvindale, 256
Membership, achieved criteria of, 19
  ascriptive criteria of, 19
Merit, 6
Methodist, 58
Metrics, 213, 218–224, 226–227, 229, 231,
     236, 247
  definition of, 217–218
  natural, 220–221
  properties of, 217, 222, 229, 231
  reflexive property of, 218
  symmetry property of, 218
Metric space, 217, 221–222, 253
  definition of, 221
Mexican, 70, 206
Mexico, 196
Michigan, 39, 281
Microcommunity, 96
Microstructural analysis, 19, 83, 202
Microstructural level, 160
Microstructure, definition of, 4
Middle class, 10, 87, 91, 93, 122, 281
Mileage chart, 15
Minh, Ho Chi, 211
Minkowski distance function, 245
Minkowski metrics, 219, 244, 246–247
Minorities, unpopular, 102
Minority groups, 161, 186–187
Mobility, 196, 227, 251
Modernization, 210
Monotonicity coefficient, 247–248, 251
Monotonicity condition, 226
Mormon, 51
Mortality, 72

Multidimensional analysis of data, 12, 19
Multidimensional scaling, 243
Multidimensional structures, 210
Multiple classification analysis, 17, 119, 145
Multiple correlation coefficient, 120
Multiple regression, additive assumptions of, 120
Multiple regression analysis, 119
Multi-stranded relationship, 8, 22
Multivariate analysis of data, 12
Multivariate technique, 17, 120

National Opinion Research Center, 47, 49, 54, 70–71
National origin groups, 196
Nationality-religious groups, 206
Native Americans, 196
Native born, 161, 163
Nativity, 92, 163
Need affiliation, 130
Need complementarity, 83
Negroes, 70, 166, 186, 280–281; see also Blacks
Neighbors, 176, 272
Neighbor, report on occupation, 74
Neighborhood, 112, 116, 118, 122, 124, 155, 267, 271, 280–281
Neighborhood improvement groups, 150, 159, 273
Neighborliness, 4, 137
Network, 2, 8, 86, 105, 107, 109, 112, 116, 136, 138, 160, 169, 201, 209
  approach of, 2, 6
  as anchors for attitudes, 115
  closely knit, 122, 124–126
  content of, 22, 81
  definition of, 7
  emotional involvement in, 115
  ethnoreligious composition of, 88, 91
  ethnoreligiously heterogeneous, 105, 106
  ethnoreligiously homogeneous, 88, 91, 96, 98, 106
  familial, 134
  heterogeneous, 99, 102, 107
  heterogeneous occupational, 81, 89
  higher order, 7, 133
  homogeneity of, 7, 89, 102, 105, 107–108
  homogeneous occupational, 88, 102
  informal, 138–139
  interconnectedness of, 2, 7, 20, 114
  interlocking, 20, 96, 107, 113, 115, 118, 121–124, 126, 128, 130
  kinship, 125
  linkages in, 21–22
  occupationally heterogeneous, 106
  occupationally homogeneous, 103, 106
  partially interlocking, 118
  personal, 9, 201, 209
  primary social, 18, 144
  radial, 20, 96, 107, 113–116, 118, 122, 125–128, 130
  reciprocated, 38
  secondary, 7, 133
  theory of, 8, 112
  total, 7
  types of, 116, 118, 121–122, 133
Network connectedness, 84, 92, 107, 119
Network connectivity, 203
Network formation, 20
New Haven, 52
New Migration, 172–173
Noninterview, 254
  not at home, 258, 260
  refusals, 18, 258, 260
Nonmetric techniques, 220
Northwestern European groups, 49
Nuclear family, 202–203
Nursing, 144

Oakland County, 267, 281
Occupation, 3, 27, 31, 38–41, 103, 108–109, 114, 119, 122, 124, 150, 158–159, 162, 164, 176, 186, 193, 201, 203, 224, 226–227, 263, 265, 277, 285, 287
Occupational achievements, 21, 96
Occupational categories, 4, 6, 103, 199
Occupational class, 208
Occupational code, 75, 210
Occupational community, 109, 137
Occupational differentiation, 9, 96
Occupational groups, 81, 200, 209–210, 216
  cultural distance among, 79
  differentiation among, 79
  family income of, 79
  indexes of dissimilarity for, 75
  macrostructure of, 81
  self-selection within, 75, 81
  smallest space analysis of, 7, 74, 79, 87
Occupational heterogeneity, 91, 93, 97
Occupational homogeneity, 88, 91–93, 96, 98–99, 102, 104–105, 108–109, 124
Occupational mobility, 196
  father son, 22, 122
  intergenerational, 22, 103, 122, 127
Occupational origins, 210
Occupational position, achieved, 11, 84
Occupational preferences, 9, 11, 126
Occupational prestige, 54, 74, 91–92, 109, 161, 188, 200
Occupational prestige score, 109, 189; see also Index for Socioeconomic Status
Occupation roles, 6, 197, 206
Occupational status, 34, 43, 47, 50, 88, 106, 122, 151, 160, 162–164, 168, 174, 189, 191, 193, 196, 198, 255
Occupational structure, 10, 86, 108, 201
  bureaucratic-entrepreneurial axis of, 10, 19
  dimensionality of, 22
  multidimensional nature of, 10
  prestige axis of, 19
  prestige dimension of, 10

situs differentiation of, 22
Occupational subcommunities, 75
Occupational values, 75, 200, 210
Occupations, bureaucratic, 74, 109–110,
    127
  coding of, 82
  entrepreneurial, 74, 109
  entrepreneurial-bureaucratic differences
    among, 74, 80
  homogeneity of, 87
  manual, 74, 79
  nonmanual, 74, 79
  prestige differences among, 80, 99, 103
  proximities of, 74, 79
Office worker, 80, 126, 278
Ohio, 39
Old Country, 187
Old Migration, 49, 173
Old-migration groups, 174
Ontario, 39
Open minded, 99, 102–103, 107, 127
Ordinal scale, 220
Organic solidarity, 128–129
Organization, membership in, 97, 138, 271
Orthodox, 200
Orthodox churches, 57
Osnabrük, 125

Parent-teacher associations, 150, 158, 272
Party preference, see Political party
    preference
Path analysis, 12, 116
Path diagram, 12, 116
Patrilineal origin land, interest in, 107
Pattern variables, 116, 128–130
Peasant, 186
Personality structure, 99, 116, 118, 129
Physical distance, 93, 213–217, 221–224,
    226, 228, 237
"Pietistic" Lutherans, 204
Pietism, 72
Place of work, number of employees at, 76,
    79
Planning, 9, 141, 296
Pluralistic structure, 138, 155, 204, 208
Pluralistic thesis, 138, 144
Poles, 166, 186, 191
Political associations, 152
Polish Catholics, 89, 166, 168, 191
Political attitudes, 9, 11–17, 17, 20, 28,
    32, 35, 39, 162–163, 165, 172, 175,
    180, 205
Political beliefs, 11, 103
Political clubs, 150–153, 158–159, 273
Political competence, 136, 143
Political elite, 8
Political extremists, 102–103
Political homogeneity, 92, 115
Political issues, 169
Political identification, 115
Political liberalism, 165
Political orientations, 11
Political participation, 159

Political party preference, 17, 27, 29, 34–35,
    39, 92, 124, 126, 128, 155, 173, 175–
    176, 216, 226
Political structures, 203
Political system, 176
Political values, 35
Pontiac, 255
Postgraduate education, 102
Potential class, 81
Power, 161
Powerlessness, 141, 143–146, 148–150,
    152–153, 155–159
Power structure, 2, 3, 32
Prejudice, 102
Presbyterian, 58, 173
Prestige, 10, 21, 81
Prestige axis, 19
Prestige dimension, 200
Primary environment, 12, 97, 109, 111, 116,
    129
Primary groups, 84–85, 96, 128, 130, 139,
    202
Primary social support, 97
Primary zone, 7–8, 20, 133
  interconnectedness of, 7
Primogeniture, rule of, 6
Probability sample, 254
Production, means of, 5, 81
Professional groups, 83, 109, 150, 152, 155,
    158–159, 273
Property tax, 263
Property values, 166
Protestant, 10–11, 29, 34, 40, 51–54, 57,
    59, 64, 66–67, 71, 87–89, 91–92,
    97, 106–107, 121, 126, 168, 173–
    174, 186–189, 191, 197, 200, 202,
    204, 207, 267, 284–285
Protestant-Catholic-Jew, axis of, 19
Protestant denominations, 204
Protestant Ethic, 11, 197, 204, 210
Protestant groups, 192, 204
Pxoximities, 15–16, 67, 114
Proximity measure, 47, 213–214, 229, 241,
    246–247
  concept of, 228
Public education, 206
Public parks, 263
Public schools, 263
Public school teacher, 278
Puerto Rican, 70, 206
Pythagorean Theorem, 15

Qualitative variables, 119

Race, 86, 161, 163–164, 216, 226, 255–256
Racial group, 6, 121, 234
Racial imbalance, 280
Racial minorities, 186
Radial network, 201–203
  definition of, 113
  see also Network
Rank images, 248
Reform, 200

Refusals, *see* Noninterview
Regression analysis, 191–192, 198; *see also*
    Multiple regression analysis
Relative distance, 232, 234–236, 253
Religion, 161–162, 164, 216, 226, 285,
    287, 289
Religious activities, 67
Religious affiliation, 3, 6, 43, 103, 122
Religious attitudes, 28
Religious behavior, 168
Religious beliefs, 11, 53, 57–59, 67, 73,
    124
  differences in, 10, 53
  liberal, 67
Religious belief systems, 202
Religious denomination, 204
  Congregational structure of, 58
  Episcopal structure of, 58
  preference, 27
Religious differences, social sources of, 52
Religious differentiation, 204
  tripartite model of, 53
Religious groups, 16, 19, 43, 51, 53, 55,
    58–59, 67, 71, 92, 105, 164, 216
  friendship choices among, 53
  indexes of dissimilarity for, 54
    see also Index of dissimilarity
  intermarriage choice among, 71
  relative proximities of, 53
  smallest space analysis of, 53
  social standings of, 54
  social structure of, 43
  three subcommunities of, 52
Religious intermarriage, 52
Religious involvement, 66–67
Religious outgroup selection of friends, 67
Religious preference, 31, 34, 38, 41, 43,
    51–52, 71, 88, 97, 107, 119, 121,
    187–188, 197, 267, 284
  inaccuracy in report of, 31
Religious service, 290
Religious social structure, 9
Religious subcommunities, 210
Republicans, independent, 181
Republican party, 32, 126, 160, 169, 176
Republican party preference, 29, 92, 103–
    104, 126, 128, 175, 267, 271, 282
  correlation with, educational attainment,
    32
    occupational status, 32
Residential segregation, 114, 212
Residential segregation of ethnic groups, 42
Response rate, 260
Retired, 282
Rightist ideological nonconformity, 142
River Rouge, 256
Riverview, 256
Ross, 251
Rotational invariance, 246
Roman Catholic, 192; *see also* Catholic
Royal Oak, 257–258
Russian Americans, 49, 187, 196

St. Clair Shores, 257–258
Sample, 17, 254
  biases in, 40
  completion rates of, 18, 258–260
  design of, 18, 254
  multi-stage probability, 18, 254
  selection of, 18, 256
  size of, 18, 255–256
  telephone subsample of, 28
Sample address, 257
San Francisco Bay Area, 58
Scandinavian Lutherans, 59, 87
School system, 280
School years completed, 47, 50, 76, 88, 91,
    109, 168, 172, 189, 191, 286, 288
Schooling, amount of, 265, 270, 273, 283
Second-generation Americans, 18, 106, 121,
    181, 187, 224
Second-generation members, 198
Second-generation subsample, 191
Second-order zone, 7
Secondary contact, 111
Secondary group, 128, 130, 134, 202
Secondary network, 209
Secular orientation, toward the world, 99,
    106
Self-employed, 75, 109, 283
Self-employed professionals, 75
Self-employed proprietors, 75
Self-selection ratio, 45, 71
Service workers, 79
Sex, 6, 86, 197
Sex segregation, 93, 107
Similarities subtest, 123, 281. *See also*
    Intellectual capabilities; Intelligence
Single-stranded relationship, 8, 22
Skilled workers, 109, 126, 278
Slavs, 49, 168, 191
Slavic Catholic, 196
Small businessman, 80, 126, 278
Smallest space analysis, 14, 16, 19, 53, 55,
    67, 70, 87, 199, 201, 210, 217, 227
  coefficient of alienation for, 17, 23, 49
  coordinates of, 16
  dimensions of, 15
  Euclidean space of, 14
  father-son mobility, 82
  graphic portrayal of, 16
  intuitive feel for, 14
  monotonicity condition of, 17
Smallest space solution, 5, 20, 71, 87
Smallest space techniques, 23
Sociability, 174
Sociability patterns, 162, 180
Social ambiguity, 169
Social change, 134–135, 155, 161
Social classes, 9, 21, 99, 106, 110, 128, 225,
    281–282; *see also* Economic classes
Social conflict, 135, 142
Social control, 8, 97, 111, 115, 135
Social control agents, 115
Social differentiation, 81

Social distance, 43, 47, 167, 213–216,
    218, 223–232, 234, 236–240, 244
  interaction notion of, 227–228
  quantification of, 225
  similarity notion of, 227–228
Social Distance Scale, *see* Bogardus
    Social Distance Scale
Social influence, 2, 97, 115
Social mobility, 70, 115, 122, 161
Social network, 12, 118, 155
Social participation, 11, 20, 107, 137, 162,
    164, 169, 172–173, 175, 177, 180,
    204–205, 207
Social physics, 214
Social position, 3–4, 7–9, 12, 20, 43, 161,
    199, 216, 244, 297
  achievement based, 11
  allocation to, 5
  ascription based, 11
  categories of, 4
  incumbents of, 5
Social relationships, 43, 86
  definition of, 3
  structural differentiation of, 4
Social role, 135
Social space, 214, 216–217, 237–238, 243,
    247, 251
  achieved, 11, 79
  ascribed, 11
Social structure, 9, 43, 99, 129
  achievement-based, 9
  ascription-based, 9
  definition of, 2–3, 87
  differentiation of, 82, 107, 129, 208
  formal properties of, 2
  physical analogy to, 4
Socialist, 102
Socialization, 135, 198, 207
Socioeconomic achievement, 3, 91
Socioeconomic assimilation, 59
Socioeconomic characteristics, 47, 59, 89,
    92, 116, 128
Socioeconomic composition, 53, 58, 66
  as index of prestige, 54
Socioeconomic differentiation, 200
Socioeconomic group, 88
Socioeconomic position, 5, 17
Socioeconomic status, 10, 17, 19, 40, 43,
    50, 53, 58, 65, 67, 71, 73–74, 76,
    81, 88, 92, 97–98, 102–103, 106,
    108, 113, 118, 121, 125, 137, 145,
    148, 151–152, 154, 156, 158, 160,
    175, 186, 195, 200, 203, 205–206
  axis of, 19
  two-digit Index, 74; *see also* Index for
      Socioeconomic Status
Socioeconomic success, 187
Socioemotional needs, 136
Socioeconomic choices, 73
Socioeconomic tradition, 2
Socioreligious characteristics, 59
Socioreligious differentiation, 200
Some college education, 88, 91–92, 97,
    102, 107, 265

Some high school education, 88, 99, 265
Sons of Italy, 207
South Africa, Union of, 211
Space dimensionality, 242
Spanish-American, 70
Spanish surname, persons of, 206–207
Sports groups, 149–150, 272
Standard of living, 264
Statistical interaction, 180
Status, 21, 107
  ethnic index, 164
  intergenerational transmission of, 197–
      198
Status awareness, 99
Status boundaries, 210
Status concern, 9, 169, 175–177, 180
Status crystallization, *see* Status inconsistency
Status-discrepant individuals, 169
Status display, in living room, 74
Status groups, 5–6, 9, 207–208, 210
Status honor, 5, 22
Status inconsistent individual, 160
Status inconsistency, 20, 161, 180–181
  additive effects in, 167
  effect of, 11, 162–163, 165, 167, 181,
      200, 205
  hypothesis of, 11, 205
  interaction effect in, 162, 166, 168, 172
  measure of, 176
  model of, 162
  political effects of, 162
  theory of, 163, 165, 169, 172–173, 175–
      177, 180
Status insecurity, 175
Status relations, 211
Status subculture, 82
Status systems, 176
Stratification, 200
Stratification systems, 210
Stratification tradition, 1
Structural analysis, unit of, 3
Structural change, 2
Structural differentiation, 2, 4
Structural-functional theory, 20
Structural isomorphism, 99
Structure, 2, 15
  change of, 3
  definition of, 2
  dimensional analysis of, 3
  multidimensional analysis of, 23
Structural dynamics, 201
Student, 143
Style of life, 9, 22, 75, 106–107, 110, 137,
    207–208, 211
  material, 9, 207–208
Subcultural differences, 163, 165, 188, 206,
    212
  theory of, 168, 175
Subcultural effects, 166
Subcultural patterns, 165
"Subcultures," 207
Subjective class identification, 91–92, 106
Subjective ethnic interest, 177
Suburbs, 91

Success, 273; *see also* Worldly success
Survey, underenumeration in, 40
Swedish workers, 137
Switzerland, 285
Symmetric proximity, 232; *see also*
    Proximities
Sympathetic understanding, 215, 223; *see*
    also Social distance
Sympathetic understanding scale, 216
System, 2
Systematic distortion, 31, 39

Teacher, 142, 275, 279
Technologists, 109
Telephone respondent, 40
Third generation Americans, 18, 181, 188–
    189, 191, 196, 206
Third generation subsample, 191–192, 196,
    198
Times of arrival, 186; *see also* Ethnic groups
Tolerance of ideological nonconformity,
    142–147, 149, 151–153, 156–158
Tolerance of political extremists, 149,
    151–152. *See also* Communists;
    Ku Klux Klanmen
Totalitarian movements, 134, 141
Totalitarianism, 141
Trade unionism, 81, 102
Traditionalism in family life, 11, 181
Trenton, 256
Triadic relation, 84, 119, 203
Trial configuration, 242, 251
Trial dimensionality, 217, 248–249
Triangle inequality, 218, 221, 223, 225,
    230–231
Tripartite religious division, 53, 67; *see also*
    Herberg's tripartite religious
    division
Triple melting pot, 9, 200, 203, 310
Truck driver, 278
Turkey, 166, 174, 191
Turkey test, 166, 177

Unidimensional model, 200
    of occupational structure, 200
Unidimensional structures, 3, 200, 210
Union democracy, 138
Union members, 136, 152, 156, 158
United Automobile Workers, 102
United States, 1, 12, 14, 51, 81–82, 91,
    106, 142, 161, 186, 188–189, 203–
    204, 210, 255, 262, 286, 288
U.S. Bureau of the Census, 1, 18, 82, 187,
    260, 281
University of Michigan, 17, 210
Upper class, 92, 106, 176, 281
Upper-middle class, 10, 83, 92, 122, 176,
    207
Upper working class, 92, 207
Upward mobility, 176. *See also* Inter-
    generational mobility and Occupation-
    al mobility
Urban family, 137

Urban ghettos, 172
Urban pluralism, 210
    achieved group, 208
    ascribed group, 208
    model of, 209
Urban social network, 8
Urban social structures, 2, 199, 200
Urban social systems, 1, 3
    comparative study of, 1
Urbanism, 11
Urbanization, 1, 137, 241
Utility repairmen, 79

Values, 21, 97
    family, 177
Value complementarity, 83
Value orientation, 9, 18, 19–20, 75
    family, 9
    religious, 9
Value similarity, 83
Vertical mobility, 196; *see* Intergenerational
    mobility, Occupational mobility
Veterans' organization, 150–153, 158, 272
Voluntary Associations, 8, 135–138, 143,
    145, 149–150, 152, 155–156, 169,
    174, 203
    friendship networks in, 148, 154
    involvement in, 173
    memberships in, 7, 97, 107, 133–136,
        138–143, 145–147, 151, 153–157,
        169
    number of (to which belong), 147–148,
        154, 157, 177
    oligarchic tendencies in, 139
    participation in, 20, 97, 135, 146, 148,
        152, 154, 156–157
    passive membership in, 143
    types of, 139, 149, 158

Washington, D. C., 129
Washtenaw, 39
WASP, 174, 205, 207
Watts, 136
Wayne County, 39, 267, 281
Wechsler Adult Intelligence Scale, 123, 130,
    281. *See also* Intellectual capabilities;
    Similarities subtest
Welfare recipients, 136
White, 161–162, 180, 188, 196, 198, 200,
    206, 212, 255, 260
White community, 165, 212
Windsor, 39
Women, 18
Work activities, entrepreneurial, 79
    entrepreneurial vs. bureaucratic, 81
Work attitudes, 9, 11–12
Work ethic, 197
Work hours per week, 75
Work orientations, 204
Work setting, ecology of, 75
    size of, 79
Working class, 10, 81, 83, 92–93, 103, 112,
    116, 121, 129–130, 136, 211, 224,
    281

Worldly success, 11, 73, 186, 188, 191, 200
  differences in, 11, 20
  later-generation Americans, 21
  third-generation Americans, 21
Wyandotte, 256

Youth groups, 150, 272
Youth-serving groups, 151–153
Yugoslavia, 285

Zoos, 263